SOCIOLOGY *of* DEVELOPING COUNTRIES

Education   Career

Family   Personal

CUSTOM EDITION

Taken from:
The Challenge of Third World Development, Third Edition
by Howard Handelman

1892 **STRAYER.**
U N I V E R S I T Y

PEARSON
Custom
Publishing

PEARSON
Prentice
Hall

Taken from:

The Challenge of Third World Development, Third Edition
by Howard Handelman
Copyright © 2003, 2000, 1996 by Pearson Education, Inc.
Published by Prentice-Hall, Inc.
Upper Saddle River, New Jersey 07458

This special edition published in cooperation with Pearson Custom Publishing.

Printed in the United States of America

10 9 8 7 6 5 4 3 2 1

ISBN 0-536-81419-8

BA 999266

SS

Please visit our web site at *www.pearsoncustom.com*

PEARSON CUSTOM PUBLISHING
75 Arlington Street, Suite 300, Boston, MA 02116
A Pearson Education Company

TO MICHAEL AND PHOEBE

Contents

Preface

Less than a month before this manuscript was sent off to Prentice Hall, America was traumatized by the terrorist attacks on New York and Washington, D.C. Suddenly, the country was saturated with more media coverage of Third World terrorism, Islamic fundamentalism, and civil war in the previously obscure country of Afghanistan than anyone could have imagined. But even before the events of September 11, 2001, Americans had increasingly, and often begrudgingly, been exposed to news coverage of the world's less developed nations. Afghanistan, Iraq, Rwanda, the Palestinian West Bank, Indonesia, and Mexico now occupy prominent positions on the evening news previously reserved for countries such as Russia, Japan, and Britain. Yet despite their increased importance, phenomena such as Islamic fundamentalism, ethnic warfare, and democratic transitions in developing nations remain shrouded in mystery and misunderstanding for most Americans.

For want of a better term, this book refers to the more than 150 disparate, developing nations as the *Third World* (the term is defined in Chapter 1). They include desperately poor countries such as Afghanistan and Ethiopia and rapidly developing industrial powers such as South Korea and Taiwan. Some, like Trinidad and Costa Rica, are stable democracies; others, such as Myanmar and Syria, suffer under highly repressive dictatorships. All of them, however, share at least some of the aspects of political, economic, and social underdevelopment that are analyzed in this book.

No text is capable of fully examining the political and economic systems of so many highly diverse countries. Instead, we will look for common issues, problems, and potential solutions. We start in Chapter 1 by exploring the nature of political and economic underdevelopment, and we then analyze the leading explanatory theories. The next chapter discusses what has been arguably the most important political change in world politics during the late twentieth and early twenty-first centuries—the wave of democratic change that has swept over the developing nations of Africa, Asia, Latin America, and the Middle East (as well as the former Soviet bloc of nations and southern Europe).

Because these often still-fragile transitions from authoritarian to democratic government are potentially so important, most of the chapters that follow contain discussion of how democratization is likely to influence issues such as the level of ethnic conflict, the role of women in the political system, and the proper path to economic development.

Chapters 3 to 5 on Religion and Politics, Cultural Pluralism and Ethnic Conflict, and Women and Development analyze broad social forces and gender issues that have often divided developing nations. Chapters 6 to 7 on Rural Change and Urbanization discuss the specific problems and challenges that many countries face in those two sectors of society. Next, Chapters 8 to 9 on Revolutionary Change and Soldiers and Politics consider the records of each of those regime types (e.g., revolutionary governments in China and Cuba and military regimes in Brazil and Indonesia) as alternative models of political and economic development. Finally, Chapter 10, dealing with Third World Political Economies, compares alternative paths to economic development and evaluates the relative effectiveness of each.

It is easy to despair when considering the tremendous obstacles facing most Third World nations and the failures of political leadership that so many of them have endured. Unfortunately, many of us in the First World have suffered from "compassion fatigue" or have become cynical about cooperative efforts with Third World countries. The assaults on the World Trade Center and the Pentagon in 2001 and the ensuing war with Afghanistan have reinforced many people's perception of the less developed nations (LDCs) as poor beyond redemption and saturated with fanaticism and authoritarian beliefs. Yet the recent trend toward democratization in the developing world (most notably in Latin America), the increased stability that has come to southern Africa, and the enormous economic growth that has taken place in parts of East and Southeast Asia, all provide new bases for hope. It is incumbent upon the West's next generation of citizens and leaders to renew efforts to understand the challenge of Third World development.

ACKNOWLEDGMENTS

Because of the broad geographic and conceptual scope of any book on Third World politics, I am particularly indebted to others for their kind help and advice.

First, I would like to thank St. Martin's Press for granting me permission to reproduce a portion of Chapter 1, which is incorporated from *Politics in a Changing World* by Marcus Ethridge and Howard Handelman (Copyright 1993 by St. Martin's Press). Thanks also to the many people at Prentice Hall who have worked with me through three editions of this book.

Much of the original research took place during a sabbatical leave from the University of Wisconsin-Milwaukee. I am grateful to my own university for granting me that sabbatical support and to the University of Wisconsin-Madison, whose outstanding libraries, lectures, and other scholarly activities informed me during a wonderful year there. Thanks also to the University of Wisconsin's many helpful librarians, including Beverly Phillips of the Land Tenure Center Library.

Finally, my greatest debt is to the scholars who generously agreed to read portions of the manuscript of the first edition. They include Lourdes Benería (Cornell University), Josef Gugler (University of Connecticut), Stephan Haggard (University of California-San Diego), Kathleen Staudt (University of Texas-El Paso), Mark Tessler (University of Michigan), William Thiesenhusen (University of Wisconsin-Madison), and M. Crawford Young (University of Wisconsin-Madison). Thanks also to Prentice Hall's reviewers Robert Griffiths (University of North Carolina-Greensboro), Robert W. Hunt (Illinois State University), and Jamal R. Nassar (Illinois State University); the quality of the manuscript benefitted greatly from their many insights, suggestions, and corrections. The usual caveat, of course, applies: Any remaining errors of fact or interpretation are my own responsibility.

Howard Handelman
University of Wisconsin-Milwaukee

chapter 1

Understanding Underdevelopment

To almost any observer, the problems plaguing Africa, Asia, Latin America, the Caribbean, and the Middle East today appear daunting. The most troubled countries in these regions are beset by warfare, internal violence, and massive human suffering: state-supported terrorism (until recently), war, and starvation in Afghanistan and Sudan; poverty and revolutionary conflict in Colombia and Nepal; ethnically based massacres in Rwanda and Sri Lanka; and political repression in Iraq, Togo, and Myanmar (Burma). Of course, many of those problems exist in industrialized democracies as well, though in a much milder form. For example, in recent times both Northern Ireland and the Basque region of Spain have experienced ethnic violence and terrorism. Portions of Washington, D.C. have higher infant mortality rates than Cuba or Singapore. But it is the scope and persistence of the developing world's political, economic, and social crises that ultimately draw our attention.

Understanding the nature and causes of underdevelopment is a complex task complicated by theoretical debates between scholars and a profusion of terminology. There is not even agreement on a collective name for the approximately 140 countries that constitute the developing world. At one time it was common to call these countries "underdeveloped nations." But many found this title objectionable, suggesting, as it did, that those countries' political and economic systems were backward. Because of its pejorative connotations and implied inferiority, the adjective "underdeveloped" fell into disfavor. Instead, the term "developing nations (or areas)" has often been used in its place. Though clearly more positive, this term unfortunately suffers from the opposite problem—excessive optimism.

1

At various times during the 1970s and 1980s, most African and Latin American countries suffered from political and economic decay, and today many remain trapped on a political or economic treadmill. In the late 1990s, even the previously thriving economies of East Asia were plunged into a crisis from which some have yet to fully recover. In short, for extended time periods, many of these so-called "developing countries" have shown few signs of political or economic development. Hence, the United Nations and many other international organizations favor the label "less developed countries" (or LDCs), an expression that escapes the normative flaws of its competitors.

The term *Third World countries* (or simply *the Third World*) is preferred by many social scientists and is the label most frequently employed in this book.[1] It has both the virtue and defect of being somewhat fuzzy. Simply put, Third World countries are the nations of Africa, Asia, the Middle East, Latin America, and the Caribbean that belong neither to the First World (Japan and the Western industrialized democracies, the first countries to develop advanced industrial economies and pluralist democracies),[2] nor to the Second World (the bloc of former communist nations that included the Soviet Union and Eastern Europe).

Thus, Third World is essentially a residual category. Countries fall under its banner not because of any specific quality, but simply because they are not members of either the First or Second Worlds (i.e., they are neither economically developed democracies nor former members of the Soviet bloc).[3] Like the previously discussed classifications, Third World glosses over the many political and socioeconomic differences between its members, placing all of them under one big tent. Of course, in reality they differ considerably. A few (including Singapore, Taiwan, and Kuwait)[4] are relatively affluent, while many others (such as Afghanistan, Nepal, and Somalia) are desperately poor. Some (Barbados, Costa Rica, and India, for example) are fairly stable democracies. Many others, however, suffer either from severe political instability, government repression, or a mixture of both.

Therefore, like any residual category, Third World suffers from a degree of imprecision. Its virtue, however, is that unlike "underdeveloped nations" or "developing nations," it makes no value judgment or predictions. As one author writes, paraphrasing Winston Churchill's comments on democracy, "It is the worst term we have, except for all the others."[5] With some irony, Christopher Clapham has written, "I have chosen to use the term [Third World] . . . because of its meaninglessness. Its alternatives all carry conceptual overtones which are even more misleading, in that they imply positive elements of commonality rather than a simply negative residual category."[6] Taking a less cynical position than Clapham, I argue in the next section that, despite their many differences, there are enough commonalities among Third World countries to make the category useful and usable. Of course, it may be argued that the collapse of Soviet communism has made the term Third World rather anachronistic. Since there no longer is a Second World (those nations are now called "postcommunist countries"), technically there cannot be a Third World. But like many political scientists, I continue to use the term in this book (and in the book's title) because I feel that it is conceptually useful and is still comprehensible to many readers.

In order to avoid repetitious usage of the term, throughout this book I alternate the categories Third World, less developed countries (LDCs), developing countries, and developing world, using them all interchangeably. At the same time, I disavow any negative implications or value judgments that some of these terms may carry.

THIRD WORLD COMMONALITIES: THE NATURE OF UNDERDEVELOPMENT

Despite the substantial differences between Third World nations that I have referred to, they all still share a number of common characteristics. That is, all of them suffer from some aspects of political, economic, or social underdevelopment. Although the economies of East Asia's newly industrializing countries (NICs)—South Korea, Singapore, and Taiwan—and perhaps Kuwait and Saudi Arabia are no longer underdeveloped, they share a particularly high vulnerability to global economic forces, as evidenced by East Asia's recent economic slide, and, in varying degrees, problems of political underdevelopment. On the other hand, Costa Rica and Trinidad are rather well developed politically and socially but suffer problems of economic underdevelopment. In short, while some Third World countries are less developed in all major aspects of modernization, other LDCs are far more advanced in some measures of development than in others. As we shall see, economic, social, and political underdevelopment are closely related to each other, but they are by no means perfectly correlated.

Economic Underdevelopment

Perhaps the most salient characteristic of most Third World countries is their poverty. This is manifested at the national level by some combination of low per-capita income (technically expressed as low Gross Domestic Product [GDP] per capita[7]), highly unequal income distribution, poor infrastructure (including communications and transportation), limited use of modern technology, and low consumption of energy. At the household level, economic underdevelopment connotes widespread poverty, including unemployment, substandard housing, poor health conditions, and inadequate diets.

Table 1.1 presents economic data comparing the United States with one relatively affluent developing country (Hong Kong, now a part of China but with its own economy), two middle-income Latin American countries (Mexico and Brazil), and five of the world's poorer countries (Egypt, China, India, Nigeria, and Ethiopia) drawn from the Middle East, Asia, and Africa.[8] The second column in the table, commonly referred to as *Per-Capita Income*, is, more precisely, the average dollar value of goods and services produced per person

TABLE 1.1 Measures of Economic Development

Country	Per Capita Income (Rank)	Income Distribution Poorest 40%	Richest 20%
United States	$30,600 (1)	15.7	46.4
Hong Kong	20,939 (26)	9.6	60.9
Mexico	7,719 (75)	10.8	58.2
Brazil	6,317 (81)	8.0	63.8
Egypt	3,303 (127)	23.0	39.0
China	3,291 (128)	16.1	46.6
India	1,755 (160)	19.7	46.1
Nigeria	744 (193)	12.6	55.7
Ethiopia	599 (200)	18.0	47.7

Source: World Bank, *World Development Report, 2000/2001: Attacking Poverty* (New York: Oxford University Press, 2001), pp. 274–275, 282–283. Reprinted by permission.

during the year 1999.[9] The number in parentheses after the dollar figure shows how that country's per-capita income ranks among some 206 countries in the world. Thus, the United States' current per-capita income of $30,600 places it first in the world, while Ethiopia's average income of $599 ranks it 200th internationally.

The data in Table 1.1 illustrate both the tremendous gap in living standards between most First and Third World countries and the considerable variation among Third World nations. On the one hand, it reveals that the average American earns about *four to five* times as much as a typical Mexican or Brazilian. At the same time, however, Mexicans and Brazilians earn about *nine to ten* times more than an average Nigerian. In the late 1990s, per-capita income for the entire developing world was $2,904, but there was, and still is, enormous variation among the LDCs (even more than shown in the table).[10] Singapore and a few very small countries (including Hong Kong and Kuwait) are at the top of this scale, with per-capita annual incomes of more than $20,000, equaling or exceeding European countries such as Italy and Britain. At the bottom we find a number of African nations, including Ethiopia ($599) and Sierra Leone ($414), with per-capita incomes as low as *one-fiftieth* of Hong Kong's.

Ultimately, a country's standard of living is determined not only by its per-capita income, but also by how that income is distributed. Columns 3 and 4 in Table 1.1 indicate how equitably or how poorly income is distributed in these countries. Column 3 reveals the percentage of a country's annual national income that is earned by the poorest 40 percent of the population; column 4 indicates the income share going to the wealthiest 20 percent of the population. Obviously, countries with a more equitable or even distribution of income have a comparatively larger proportion of their national income going to the poorest 40 percent of their people and a relatively lower share going to the richest 20 percent. A difference of a few percentage points between countries, such as that which separates Nigeria and Ethiopia, actually reflects a significant difference in the equity of income distribution.

Over the past 30 years, the economies of some Third World regions have performed far better than have others, further widening the gap between the LDCs. Despite a major economic setback in the late 1990s, *East Asia's* GDP per capita (that is, its economic growth above and beyond population growth) still grew at the phenomenal average annual rate of 6 percent from 1975 to 1999. That means that per-capita income more than quadrupled during that 24-year period. That region includes such stellar economic performers as China, South Korea, Taiwan, Singapore, Indonesia, Malaysia, and Thailand. No other region grew anywhere near that robustly. But *South Asia* (including India, Pakistan, and Bangladesh) enjoyed the second fastest per-capita growth rate, averaging 2.3 percent annually. *Latin America*, which grew steadily in the 1960s and 1970s, experienced a sharp downturn in the 1980s and early 1990s, thereby averaging only 0.7 percent per-capita annual growth from 1975 to 1999. Finally, *Sub-Saharan Africa*, already one of the Third World's poorest regions in the 1970s, saw GDP per capita decline at an average rate of −1 percent annually during the next 24 years as the result of poor economic management, corruption, civil war, and climatic disasters. Thus, by 1999 the average African was substantially poorer than he or she had been 25 years earlier.[11]

Despite its recent financial crisis, East Asia has emerged as the Third World's most economically advanced region. On the other hand, despite its relatively strong economic growth in the past 25 to 30 years, South Asia still includes some of the world's poorest countries (Afghanistan, Bangladesh, and India). Most Latin American nations fall in the United Nations' middle-income category, though there is a wide gap between the region's least affluent nations, including Bolivia and Honduras, and the most developed ones, such as Chile and Mexico. Finally, Sub-Saharan Africa includes most of the world's poorest countries, such as Ethiopia, Tanzania, and Sierra Leone.

Contrary to a common stereotype that suggests that "developing nations have a small class of rich people, many poor people, and few in between," most of the poorest countries in Table 1.1 (India, Ethiopia, China, and especially Egypt) have comparable or even slightly more equitable income distributions than does the United States. Others, such as Nigeria, are considerably less equitable. The more industrialized nations in the table (Brazil, Mexico, and Hong Kong) have the most concentrated income patterns, supporting earlier research that indicated that the initial transition from low to mid-level economic development actually *increases* inequality. Thus, although Brazil is far more industrialized than Egypt and has nearly twice its per-capita income (Table 1.1), the richest 20 percent of its population earns an extraordinary 63.8 percent of the nation's income, compared to only 39 percent for that group in Egypt. Indeed, World Bank data reveal that Brazil has the second most unequal income distribution in the world.

Several factors seem to influence a country's or a region's income distribution pattern. First, as we just noted, is the *level of industrialization and eco-*

nomic development. Countries moving into the middle- and upper-middle levels of development generally experience a growing gap between the middle-to-upper classes and the poor, as a new class of businesspeople and professionals emerges with far higher incomes, such as Hong Kong's super-rich bankers and financiers. But there are variations within this pattern. A second important factor is the historical *pattern of land ownership*. Regions or countries that were colonized by the Spanish or Portuguese, such as Latin America and the Philippines, saw land ownership concentrated in a relatively small number of hands (see Chapter 6). By contrast, most Asian countries have historically allowed less concentration of land ownership. Third, *government policies* on land ownership, taxation, welfare programs, and the like can either reduce or intensify income inequality. Countries with large and open educational systems, agrarian reform policies, and progressive taxation can reduce income gaps. Generally speaking, communist and former communist countries, such as Mongolia and the Slovak Republic (not shown in the table), have among the lowest levels of inequality, but they are closely trailed by some of East Asia's capitalist success stories, such as Japan, Taiwan, and South Korea (the latter two being former colonies of Japan).[12] In both cases, welfare communism or welfare capitalism produced government policies that reduced income disparities.

Consequently, depending on how these three factors play out, some Third World countries suffer from wide gaps between rich and poor, while some do not. The figures for Brazil and Mexico are relatively representative of Latin America as a whole, a region with the world's highest level of income inequality. As the data on Ethiopia and Nigeria suggest (Table 1.1), income distribution in Africa is more varied: highly concentrated in some countries (South Africa, Swaziland, and the Central African Republic) and quite equitable in others (Burundi). On the other hand, income tends to be more evenly distributed in East and South Asia, with South Asia (India, Pakistan) enjoying greater equality than the most advanced industrial nations (including the United States and Italy).[13]

Social Underdevelopment

Poverty and poor public policy adversely affect social conditions in the Third World, thereby narrowing opportunities for human development. Low levels of education and literacy rates are among the Third World's greatest challenges. Scholars and development specialists agree that the spread of education is a major component of modernization. An educated work force—from peasants who can read the instructions on insecticide containers to doctors and construction engineers—contributes to higher labor productivity. Higher educational levels also contribute to political development, though not in a linear fashion. So, for example, a major statistical evaluation of the factors contributing to democratic government throughout the world found literacy rates to be among the most important elements.[14]

Table 1.2 presents data on several important social development indicators. It compares two developed nations (Canada and the United States) with six middle-level developing countries (four from Latin America, one from East Asia, and one from the Middle East) and five poor countries (two from Asia, two from Africa, and one from the Middle East). Column 2 lists each nation's Human Development Index (HDI), a composite measurement of educational level, life expectancy, and income. More so than per-capita income or any other single indicator, HDI is considered to be an accurate measure of a nation's living standard. The highest possible HDI score a country may achieve is 1.000, and the lowest is .000. Column 2 contains both the raw HDI score and the county's rank worldwide. Thus, Canada has the world's highest HDI (.935), while India ranks 128th. The figures reveal that some Third World nations, such as South Korea, Argentina, and Kuwait, have relatively high indices; indeed, they are comparable to the less developed European nations, such as Greece and Poland. On the other hand, many South Asian and African countries, such as India, Nigeria, and Ethiopia, have extremely low scores, indicating a combination of intense poverty, low educational levels, and limited life expectancy.

Life expectancy (Column 3) and adult literacy (Column 4) are among the best individual (non-indexed) measures of mass living standards. The first statistic is greatly influenced by the availability of health care, adequate diet, and clean drinking water; the second indicates the accessibility of education. Unlike per-capita income, statistical averages for life expectancy and education are less distorted by a highly skewed distribution.[15] Note the substantial gap separating Kuwaiti and Mexican life expectancy (both close to the United States) from Nigeria and Ethiopia. Similarly, while adult literacy (Column 4) levels in Cuba,

TABLE 1.2   Indicators of Social Development

Country	Human Development Index (HDI)	Life Expectancy (years)	Adult Literacy	Real Income Rank (PPP) HDI Rank
Canada	.935 (1)	79.1	99.0%	+8
United States	.929 (3)	76.8	99.0	−1
South Korea	.854 (31)	72.6	97.5	+4
Argentina	.837 (35)	73.1	96.7	−6
Kuwait	.836 (36)	76.1	80.9	−31
Cuba	.793 (40)	75.8	96.4	+40
Mexico	.784 (55)	72.3	90.8	−3
Brazil	.747 (74)	67.0	84.5	−16
China	.706 (99)	70.1	82.8	+7
Egypt	.623 (119)	66.7	53.7	−11
India	.563 (128)	62.9	55.7	−7
Nigeria	.439 (151)	50.1	61.1	+10
Ethiopia	.309 (171)	43.4	36.3	−1

Source: United Nations Development Programme (UNDP), *Human Development Report, 2000* (New York: Oxford University Press, 2000), pp. 157–160. Reprinted by permission.

Argentina, and South Korea are close to the United States and Canada, the rates in Egypt and Ethiopia lag far behind.

Although economic development usually brings about improvement in social indicators, government social policy determines what share of the country's economic resources is invested in education, sanitation, and health care—hence, how much translates into social development. Column 5 compares a country's income rank with its rank for HDI. A high positive score, such as Cuba's, indicates that the country's social indicators are higher than its per-capita income would lead us to expect, presumably because of a strong government commitment to health, education, and economic equity. Conversely, a strongly negative score (such as Kuwait's, Brazil's, and Egypt's) indicates the government's failure to translate adequately its available economic resources into an improved quality of life. While Cuba has by far the highest score in this area, both wealthy Canada and impoverished Nigeria have positive scores as well—but not the United States. In other words, although Nigeria's HDI score is quite low (ranking 151st in the world), that score still is somewhat higher than we might expect in a country so poor. Many of the worst performers on this measure, including Kuwait (−31) and other oil-rich nations not shown in the table, owe their low scores to their failure to educate adequately their female population because of religious or other cultural barriers (see Chapter 5).

Fortunately, despite substantial economic declines in Africa and Latin America during the 1980s and early 1990s, and despite East Asia's recent economic crisis, developing countries as a whole have made considerable progress in social development during recent decades. From 1965 to 1995 alone, adult illiteracy in developing countries was cut in half, falling from nearly 60 percent to 30 percent. Improved health care and sanitation helped reduce infant mortality rates by a remarkable 60 percent. Together with other advances in public health care, these changes raised life expectancy from 53.4 years in 1960 to 64.7 years in 1990. And the United Nations Development Program (UNDP) estimates that Third World poverty has fallen faster in the past 50 years than in the previous 500. In 1965 an estimated 2 to 3 billion persons (mostly in the LDCs) lived in poverty. By the start of the twenty-first century, that figure had been reduced to 1 to 2 billion, in spite of significant increases in total Third World population.[16] These figures indicate both how much progress has been made in several critical areas and how much remains to be done.

Tables 1.3 and 1.4 reveal the remarkable strides some LDCs have made in lowering child mortality (deaths of children under the age of five) and adult illiteracy, compared to the slower rate of change in other nations. As of 1960, many African and Asian countries had very high infant mortality rates. In Angola, for example, roughly 20 percent of the babies who lived through the birth process failed to survive until the age of five (208 of 1,000 live births). In Table 1.3, seven of the nine countries listed had infant mortality rates exceeding one in ten (i.e., more than 100/1,000). By 1996, five of those countries (Senegal, China, India, Chile, and Mexico) had dropped considerably below 100/1,000. All of the countries in the list made progress, with Chile, achieving

TABLE 1.3   Reductions in Infant Mortality, 1960–1996

	Infant Mortality/1,000 Live Births		
Country	1960	1980	1996
Angola	208	153	124
Ethiopia	175	155	109
Senegal	173	91	60
China	140	42	33
India	144	116	65
Malaysia	73	30	11
Chile	107	32	12
Cuba	39	20	8
Mexico	103	51	32

Source: Chandrika Kaul and Valerie Tomaselli-Moschovitis, eds., *Statistical Handbook on Poverty in the Developing World* (Phoenix, AZ: Oryx Press, 1999), pp. 327–334. Data drawn from the World Bank.

the most impressive gains, having lowered its infant mortality rate by almost 90 percent. Cuba, which already had a low infant mortality rate in 1960, has lowered its rate to 8/1,000, about the same as the United States. In Angola and especially Ethiopia, civil wars and related famines have limited progress.

Table 1.4 lists the countries that made the most progress in reducing adult illiteracy from 1970 to 1995. South Korea and Cuba, which started the period with relatively little illiteracy (12 to 13 percent), still made dramatic strides in cutting their rates even lower. Meanwhile, Jordan and Kenya, which started with fairly high illiteracy rates in 1960 (53 and 68 percent), also made very impressive progress.

Still, as an aggregate, less developed countries continue to lag considerably behind the developed world. Third World adult literacy rates trail the industrialized nations by 33 percent, while life expectancy and calorie con-

TABLE 1.4   Greatest Improvements in Reducing Adult Illiteracy, 1970–1995

	Adult Illiteracy Rate		
Country	1970 (percent)	1995 (percent)	Percent Reduction
South Korea	12	2	83
Lebanon	31	8	75
Jordan	53	13	75
Thailand	21	6	75
Philippines	17	5	68
Kenya	68	22	68
Cuba	13	4	67

Source: United Nations Development Programme (UNDP), *Human Development Report, 1997* (New York: Oxford University Press, 1997), p. 4. Reprinted by permission.

sumption are both 20 percent below First World levels. Some 1.3 billion people (about one-third of the developing world's population) live on incomes of less than $1 per day, and 800 million of them do not get a sufficient amount to eat. While impressive progress has been made in some regions, others continue to lag, most notably Sub-Saharan Africa and South Asia. Furthermore, great gaps persist between urban centers, where, for example, 72 percent of the population has access to proper home sanitation, and rural areas, where that figure falls to 20 percent.[17] And despite overall gains in the LDCs, the absolute gap between the First and Third Worlds (and within the Third World itself) continues to widen.

Political Underdevelopment

Defining *political development* and *underdevelopment* is a more formidable task than specifying the parameters of social and economic underdevelopment. Although Marxist and market-oriented economists disagree on the proper path to development, they share a common commitment to the goals of economic growth, increased literacy, and lower infant mortality. But political analysts are more sharply divided by their ideological and cultural perspectives. Thus, Marxist and liberal-democratic political scientists differ even on such fundamental issues as the desirability of competitive elections, the role of opposition parties, and the limits of free speech.

When Western political scientists began to study the Third World seriously, they eventually recognized that evaluating political systems in very different cultural and socioeconomic settings from their own was particularly challenging. While many so-called "modernization theorists" felt that Third World governments should model themselves after Western industrialized democracies, they were also mindful of important differences between the two regions that limited that option. Recognizing that most Western European countries did not become meaningfully democratic until they were well along the path to industrial development, scholars often were reluctant to criticize the authoritarian systems that prevailed in many barely industrialized nations of the Third World. Many African social scientists added to the debate by arguing that their continent had extensive village- and tribal-based democracy that substituted for competitive elections at the national level. Others feared that in the ethnically divided countries of Africa and Asia, multiparty systems would inevitably develop along ethnic lines, contributing to national disintegration.

Conscious of such land mines, some prominent political scientists despaired of defining political development in any meaningful way.[18] Others, however, offered a set of standards that they believed were relatively free of ideological and cultural biases. Political development, they maintained, involves the creation of specialized and differentiated government institutions that effectively carry out necessary functions, such as collecting tax revenues, defending national borders, maintaining political stability, stimulating economic development, improving the quality of human life, and communicating with the citizenry. In addition, they argued, developed governments must be responsive to a broad segment of society and respect the population's fundamental freedoms and civil rights. Presumably, any government satisfying these standards would enjoy a reasonable level of *legitimacy* (i.e., citizens would recognize and accept its right to govern), leading individuals and groups to pursue their political objectives peacefully through established political institutions rather than through violent or illegal channels.

But while analysts agreed that governments should be responsive, representative, and nonrepressive, they were not all convinced that developed political systems need necessarily be democratic, at least as that term is defined in the West. That definition of democracy encompasses the following basic components: honest and competitive elections in which opposition parties have a realistic chance of winning; universal or nearly universal suffrage; widespread opportunities for political participation; free and open mass media; and government respect for human rights, including minority rights.[19] As we have seen, many political scientists initially felt that it was unrealistic and perhaps culturally biased to expect liberal democracy to flourish in developing countries. Others argued that many, if not most, developing nations were not ready for democracy. Concerned about the high levels of violence and instability in those political systems, they maintained that the LDCs' first priority had to be political stability, even if that required military rule or other forms of authoritarianism for some period of time.[20]

More recently, however, troubled by extensive government repression in the Third World, political scientists have begun insisting that democracy and some degree of social equity must be integral parts of political development.[21] Beyond its obvious moral attractions, democracy also has pragmatic appeal. For example, governments that are held accountable to their citizens by means of competitive elections are more likely to be efficient and honest (though the sorry records of democracy in countries such as Brazil and the Philippines demonstrate that there are no guarantees). Similarly, a free and independent mass media helps keep governments accountable.

The collapse of the Soviet bloc and the fall of other forms of dictatorship in the Third World since the early 1980s demonstrate that while authoritarian regimes may be stable in the short run, they are fragile in the long term. Thus, there is not necessarily a tradeoff between democracy and political stability, as many had imagined. Quite the contrary. For example, democracies are relatively immune to revolutionary insurrection and are less prone than dictatorships to other forms of mass violence. Only a relatively restricted (but growing) number of developing countries conform closely to the standards of political development listed above, including Trinidad, the Bahamas, Uruguay, and Costa Rica (all small countries). Others—such as Brazil, India, South Korea, and Taiwan—currently satisfy most of the criteria. Even a cursory review of Third World politics, however, soon reveals that most governments fall woefully short on democratic practices. At one extreme, in several countries such as Somalia and Sierra Leone, war lords divided control over the country and so undermined the capacity of the national government to function that political scientists have referred to them as "countries without a state." Most Central American regimes respond disproportionately to the demands of the affluent minority. Many Middle Eastern and North African nations are ruled by a self-perpetuating and self-serving elite, while some Sub-Saharan African governments serve the interests of the dominant ethnic groups. Political corruption, government inefficiency, and repression are endemic to much of the developing world.

In the recent past, class-based revolutionary movements have erupted in various Asian and Latin American nations, and a number of African countries have been torn apart by ethnic civil wars. Thus, until recently most Third World governments were neither democratic, nor stable, nor legitimate. In recent decades, however, democracy (and with it, government legitimacy) has advanced in much of the developing world, most notably in Latin America and East Asia (see Chapter 2). It is still uncertain, however, how enduring this positive trend will be.[22]

Some Relationships among the Components of Development

It seems logical to assume that political, economic, and social underdevelopment are interrelated. More economically advanced countries can better educate their populations and provide them with better health care. An educated citizenry, in turn, contributes to further economic growth and participates in politics more responsibly. Responsive and legitimate governments, constrained by competitive elections, are more likely to educate their people and to make responsible economic decisions. In fact, these logical intuitions are supported by empirical evidence. Wealthier LDCs tend to have greater life expectancy, higher literacy rates, and more stable and democratic governments.

But these correlations are not absolute. For example, a country's literacy and infant mortality rates depend not only on its economic resources but also on government policies in the areas of education, public health, and welfare. Thus, as we saw earlier, elitist government policies in some countries have contributed to social indicators (HDIs) that are far lower than those of other nations with comparable economic resources. This is most apparent in the petroleum-rich states (Kuwait, Brunei) but holds in countries such as Brazil and Egypt as well.[23] On the other hand, governments in Cuba, Costa Rica, Grenada, and Vietnam, with strong commitments to social welfare programs, have generated much higher life expectancy rates and educational levels than their economic resources alone would lead us to predict.

Both economic and social development also tend to correlate with political development. Wealthier, more educated countries such as Barbados, Chile, Costa Rica, and Taiwan tend to be more politically stable, more responsive, and more democratic than poor nations such as Mozambique, Haiti, and Cambodia. Indeed, Third World countries are very unlikely to become democracies unless they have attained a minimal threshold of socioeconomic development.[24] That does not imply, however, that wealthier countries are assured of becoming democratic. That economic threshold is a relatively necessary, but not sufficient, condition for democratization.

Moreover, there is not a linear relationship between economic and political development. In other words, as countries become more economically developed, often there is not a continuous movement toward greater stability, democracy, or other components of political development. In fact, Samuel Huntington has observed that while it is true that the richest countries in the world (such as Switzerland, Japan, and Canada) are politically very stable, and that the poorest countries (Afghanistan, Congo, and Haiti) are generally very unstable, countries that are still in the process of moving from economic underdevelopment to greater development often actually become more unstable as they pass through the intermediate stages of economic growth.[25] Thus, for example, some of Latin America's most economically advanced countries (Argentina, Brazil, Chile, and Uruguay) experienced internal conflict and political unrest in the 1960s and 1970s, followed by military dictatorships that toppled democracy. In 2001–2002, Argentina suffered rioting and five presidents in the space of less than a month. Huntington's explanation was that as countries modernize, the spread of urbanization, education, and mass media consumption produce an increasingly politically aware and mobilized society whose citizens make far more demands on the government. All too often, however, political institutions, particularly political parties, cannot be strengthened quickly enough to channel and respond to this rising tide of demands, and the system becomes overloaded and unstable.

Guillermo O'Donnell posited another reason for the rise of extremely repressive dictatorships in South America's most economically advanced and modern nations during the 1960s and 1970s. He suggested that as those countries reached a more advanced stage of industrial growth, they required extensive new investment that could only be secured by attracting foreign capital. That, in turn, required controlling the countries' militant labor unions and keeping down the wage levels of industrial workers. To achieve those goals, the nations' business leaders and technocrats turned to repressive military rule.[26]

In a similar vein, many analysts have noted that the Asian countries that had been enjoying the most spectacular economic growth from the 1970s to the mid-1990s—Indonesia, Malaysia, Thailand, Singapore, Taiwan, and South Korea—were all ruled by authoritarian governments during their economic takeoffs. Consequently, many observers concluded from this that an authoritarian government was necessary in the early to middle stages of industrialization in order to control labor and reduce workers' consumption levels so as to enable management to invest heavily in productive resources (see Chapter 10). Although these theories remain subject to debate, they suggest that the relationships between political, economic, and social development are complex. While the three often go hand in hand, they don't always progress at the same rate.

THE CAUSES OF UNDERDEVELOPMENT

Our initial discussion suggested that there is some debate concerning the very *definitions* of political and socioeconomic underdevelopment. Social scientists disagree even more intensely, however, over the underlying *causes* of underdevelopment and the most desirable pathways to change. How, for example, do we account for constant military intervention in Pakistani politics, for political turmoil in Kenya, or for government repression in Syria? Do these problems originate from internal factors such as authoritarian cultural values or weak political parties? Or are many of these political and economic problems caused by foreign domination from the colonial era to the age of multinational corporations and the International Monetary Fund (IMF)?

Questions on the origins of underdevelopment or the pathways to development elicit very different responses from social scientists. Frequently, their evaluations reflect their personal cultural backgrounds or ideologies. Thus, for example, theories that blame Third World political unrest or economic backwardness on local traditional cultural values generally have emanated from the United States. On the other hand, approaches such as dependency theory and world systems theory, which condemn Western exploitation as the root cause of Third World underdevelopment, are particularly popular among Latin American and African scholars. Similarly, liberal analysts are drawn to different explanations than are either conservative or Marxist.

For years, two competing paradigms have shaped scholarly analysis of Third World politics and economic change. The first, *modernization theory*, emerged in the early 1960s as American political science's mainstream interpretation of underdevelopment. The second, *dependency theory*, originated in Latin America and offered a more radical perspective on development, one more reflective of Third World scholars. In time, dependency theory came to exert tremendous influence over political research on Latin America, Africa, and other parts of the developing world.[27]

Modernization Theory and the Importance of Cultural Values

During the 1950s and 1960s, as the demise of European colonialism produced a host of newly independent nations in Africa and Asia, Western social scientists began to study Third World politics and economics. From that interest came a complex model of underdevelopment and development known as modernization theory. Its proponents included some of the most prominent figures in comparative politics: Gabriel Almond, James Coleman, Samuel Huntington, Lucian Pye, and David Apter, among others.[28] For perhaps a decade, modernization theory reigned supreme in the study of political development. Though later challenged, it has continued to influence our understanding of the Third World. While there has been some variation and disagreement among modernization theorists, they generally share a number of underlying assumptions and perspectives.

Despite the tremendous array of problems facing the LDCs, modernization theory was initially relatively optimistic about their prospects for development. After all, Western industrialized democracies had also started out as underdeveloped countries. Most Third World countries, the theory argued, could—and should—follow a path of political and economic modernization parallel to the one first traveled by the advanced Western nations. To accomplish this, the theory insisted, developing nations had to acquire modern cultural values and create modern political and economic institutions.

Transforming traditional cultures was seen as the opening step in the modernization process. Drawing on the theories of such eminent sociologists as Max Weber and Talcott Parsons, these analysts distinguished between "traditional" and "modern" values.[29] Modern men and women, they maintained, tend to judge others by universalistic standards (that is, to hire, vote for, or otherwise evaluate people based on their ability rather than family or ethnic origins); to believe in the possibility and desirability of change; to think about issues outside the sphere of one's family, neighborhood, or village; to believe that one can—and should—try to influence the political system.[30]

But how can a traditional society make the transition to modernity? How does a culture modernize its values? Education, urbanization, and the spread of mass media were identified as the central agents of change. As peasants move to cities, modernization theory argued, as more children attend schools that teach modern values, and as more citizens follow the mass media, cultural modernization will progress. Another critical component, it was suggested, was the diffusion of modern ideas from highly developed nations (especially in the West) to the developing world and from city to countryside within the LDCs. Foreign aid and institutions such as the Peace Corps could help to speed this process.

Gabriel Almond and G. Bingham Powell, depicting modernization as a rather inexorable force, contended that "the forces of technological change and cultural diffusion are driving political systems in certain directions, which seem discernible and susceptible to analysis in terms of increasing levels of development."[31] Others envisioned modernization as a process of getting developing nations to think and act "more like us" (i.e., the West). "As time goes on," Marion Levy predicted, "they and we will increasingly resemble one another . . . [The] more highly modernized societies become, the more they resemble one another."[32] Today, as the forces of modernization spread McDonald's, computer technology, Hollywood movies, and American rock music around the world, that prophecy seems increasingly accurate.

At the same time, developing nations would have to create more specialized and complex political and economic institutions to compliment those modern values. For example, whereas a tribal culture might have a council of elders that carries out legislative, executive, and judicial activities, a modern society needs separate, more specialized institutions for those tasks.

Modernizing societies need trained bureaucracies in which advancement is based on merit rather than personal connections, and decisions are made according to uniform and consistent standards. Political parties have to channel popular demands and aspirations effectively to government policy makers. Eventually, it was argued, as these cultural and institutional changes progress, a modernizing society can lay the basis for a more stable, effective, and responsive political system.

In time, however, many assumptions of early modernization theory had to be modified. To begin with, it had been too optimistic and simplistic in its initial view of change. Its proponents expected developing countries to achieve economic growth, greater equality, democracy, stability, and greater national autonomy simultaneously and smoothly. As Samuel Huntington noted, the theory erroneously assumed that "all good things go together."[33] In fact, economic growth proved to be no guarantee of democracy or other elements of political development. As we have seen, in nations such as Brazil, Mexico, South Korea, and Taiwan, industrialization and economic development originated and advanced for many years under the direction of authoritarian governments.

Analysts were particularly disturbed to find that the very process of social and economic modernization often ushered in political instability and violence.[34] For example, in some of Latin America's most economically developed nations (Argentina, Brazil, Chile, and Uruguay), industrial growth unleashed bitter class conflict, the collapse of democratic institutions, and the rise of repressive military dictatorships.[35] Elsewhere, in much of Africa, Asia, and the Middle East, the hopes once inspired by decolonization have given way to ethnic conflict, military coups, and political repression.

Thus, the process of development often turned out to be more complex and unpredictable than originally imagined. Modernization theory's initial optimism gave way to *conflict theory*. Developing nations, suggested the new perspective, would have to make hard choices between seemingly irreconcilable development goals. Concerned about the growing political turmoil in many developing nations, Samuel Huntington insisted that political stability was of paramount importance, even if maintaining it might necessitate authoritarian rule. That is to say, democracy might have to take a back seat to stability, at least temporarily. At the same time, many economists and political scientists argued that initial economic growth required wealth to be concentrated in a small number of hands so that incipient capitalists could acquire sufficient capital for investment.

More recently, the experiences of several countries in East Asia and Latin America have produced yet another new perspective. While certainly less naively optimistic than the earliest modernization theories, current analysis is also less pessimistic than conflict theory. The *reconciliation approach*, as put forth by contemporary modernization theorists, suggests that under the right circumstances developing nations can simultaneously achieve goals previously thought to be incompatible.[36] Taiwan and South Korea, for example, have shown that it is possible to achieve rapid economic development along with a highly equitable distribution of income. Trinidad-Tobago and Costa Rica have managed to achieve democracy and stability simultaneously. Consequently, current research tries to isolate factors such as state policy, historical traditions, and cultural values that may explain which factors contribute to successful development.

A different modification of modernization theory addresses its initial view of cultural change. First, the differences between traditional and modern culture, scholars now agree, are not always as stark or clear as originally thought. For example, even though the United States is a highly modern society, many Americans have retained traditional values such as judging others by the color of their skin. Second, while modern (Western) values have swept across the Third World, their appeal has not been as universal as some analysts expected. In Afghanistan, Iran, and other parts of the Muslim world, for example, many people, including some with high school or university educations, have rejected Westernization in favor of either peaceful or violent forms of Islamic fundamentalism. The September 11, 2001 attacks on New York and Washington and earlier bombings of U.S. military personnel abroad, carried out by Osama bin Laden's Al Qaeda terrorist network, are the most extreme reflections of the hatred that some Muslims feel toward Western values and lifestyles. Although extremists such as these represent only a very small fraction of the Muslim world, many other nonviolent Muslims also reject Western culture as immoral (full of pornography, extramarital sex). Finally, contrary to early modernization theory, it now appears that some traditional values not only are worth keeping, but they also contribute to political and economic development. For example, students of contemporary Japanese culture and religion have argued that traditional religious values have contributed to that nation's work ethic. Even "magic and miracles," notes one expert on East Asian religions, "are entirely compatible with the 'rationality' of industrial society."[37]

Dependency Theory

During the 1960s and 1970s, social scientists in Latin America and the United States raised more fundamental objections to modernization theory, insisting that the previously mentioned modifications to the theory failed to correct its fundamental flaws. Some, though not all, of these critics were Marxists. Under the banner of *dependency theory*, they challenged modernizationists' most fundamental assumptions.

To begin with, *dependencistas* (as dependency theorists are known) rejected the claim that Third World countries could follow the same path to development as Western nations had because the first industrialized nations changed the landscape for those that followed them. When Britain became the world's first industrial power, it faced no external economic competition. Today, however, newly industrializing countries must compete against such well-established industrial giants as the United States, Japan, and Germany. In addition, argued Brazil's Theotonio Dos Santos, Third World countries have to borrow financial capital and purchase advanced technology from the developed world, thereby making them dependent on external economic forces beyond their control and weakening their development.[38]

Indeed, whereas modernization theory views Western influence in the Third World as beneficial since it spreads modern values and institutions, dependency theorists argue that it was Western colonialism and economic imperialism that had turned Africa, Asia, and Latin America into sources of cheap food and raw materials for the colonial powers. And long after Third World nations had achieved political independence, they charge, developed countries continued to use their economic power to create an international division of labor between nations. Under that division, production and export of manufactured goods—the most profitable economic activities—were originally concentrated in the *core*, the industrialized West. Third World nations, in the *periphery*, were largely relegated to the production and export of food and raw materials and were forced to trade for industrial imports on unfavorable terms.[39]

Finally, *dependencistas* insist that this economic dependence helped determine the nature of the LDCs' political dependency. Within the periphery, Third World political, military, and economic elites, backed by the economic and military power of the core nations (especially the United States), maintained a political system that benefited the powerful few at the expense of the many. These elites reaped substantial profits from their country's relations with the West and were backed by the core's military might. Note, for example, France's frequent military intervention in French-speaking Africa to maintain friendly, but unrepresentative and corrupt, governments in its former colonies.

As one might imagine, dependency theory was enthusiastically embraced by scholars in many parts of the Third World, for it suggested that underdevelopment was not the LDC's fault, but rather the fault of foreign domination and exploitation. But even in the United States, dependency theory challenged, and often displaced, modernization theory as the major scholarly paradigm explaining the nature and causes of underdevelopment.

However, just as early modernization theory had been overly optimistic about the prospects for simultaneous economic and political development, early dependency theory proved to be excessively pessimistic about the prospects for economic or political growth. Authors such as Andre Gunder Frank had warned that Third World nations, consigned to producing nonindustrial goods and ruled by unrepresentative elites, were doomed to continued backwardness. Some *dependencistas* believed that radical revolutions were the only solution; others merely prescribed greater economic independence for developing nations; still others offered no solutions.

Yet despite the bleak prognosis of early dependency theorists, it was clear by the mid-1960s that nations such as Brazil and Mexico were undergoing substantial industrialization. In a far more sophisticated version of dependency theory, Fernando Henrique Cardoso rejected the contention that all Third World countries were condemned to underdevelopment and precluded from industrial growth.[40] Drawing heavily from the experiences of his own country (Brazil), Cardoso noted that through the active intervention of the state and the linkage of domestic firms with multinational corporations, some LDCs could industrialize and enjoy considerable economic growth. He referred to this process as *associated dependent development*.

Cardoso radically altered dependency theory by insisting that countries such as Argentina, Brazil, Colombia, and Mexico could experience industrialization and economic growth while remaining dependent on foreign banks and multinationals for loans, investment, and technology. Brazilian industrialization, he noted, had been stimulated, to a large extent, by a sharp rise in investment from multinational corporations (MNCs). But for Cardoso and his colleagues, this kind of dependent development was tainted in several important ways. It still meant that key economic decisions were being made by multinational corporations outside of the LDCs' control. Furthermore, associated dependent development was being led by companies that were heavily mechanized and, consequently, they did not hire substantial local labor. They also produced more profitable and expensive consumer goods destined for the country's middle and upper classes. Rather than reduce poverty, *dependencistas* argued, such associated dependent development had widened the income gap separating the poor from the middle and upper classes. At the same time, Peter Evans and others maintained, an alliance of the MNCs with Latin American economic, political, and military elites helped maintain the power of nonrepresentative regimes such as Brazil's military dictatorship.

Modernization and Dependency Theory Compared

The dependency approach offered useful corrections to modernization theory. Moreover, it highlighted an important influence on Third World societies that modernization theory had largely neglected: international trade, finance, and investment patterns. Indeed, many political scientists argue that the principal characteristic defining Third World countries is their peripheral economic and cultural status relative to the major core nations. Thus, even wealthy nations such as Saudi Arabia or stable democracies like Costa Rica are still considered Third World because their economic, cultural, and political values and structures are largely shaped by the developed world.[41]

Regardless of how much of dependency theory they subscribed to, subsequent analysts of underdevelopment have been forced to recognize that political and economic modernization requires more than adopting new values or changing domestic political structures. Dependency theory shifted the focus of research from exclusively internal factors to international economic and cultural relations, contributing to new fields of research, including international political economy. Dependency theorists also helped redefine the concept of economic development. Whereas early research on Third World economies focused heavily on issues of economic growth, *dependencistas* emphasized the importance of economic distribution and social justice. When rapid economic growth is accompanied by an increased concentration of wealth and income in the hands of a minority of the population, as has frequently happened, it offers little benefit to the impoverished majority, which may even be left worse off. Influenced by dependency theory and other leftist critiques, even such pillars of the establishment as the World Bank have reoriented their focus toward "growth and redistribution."[42]

Despite its contributions, however, dependency theory suffered from some serious failings. Just as early modernization theorists overemphasized the *internal* causes of underdevelopment, *dependencistas* erroneously attributed virtually all of the Third World's problems to *external* economic factors. Furthermore, periphery nations (LDCs) were often portrayed as helpless pawns with no way out of their poverty. Indeed, what is striking about much of the dependency literature are its economic determinism and neglect of independent social or political influences. Its proponents frequently dismissed Third World governments as agents of the local economic elite who colluded with Western- or Japanese-based MNCs. Consequently, there is a disturbing sameness to some of the dependency-based studies of politics in particular nations. The details of Mexican, Colombian, or Peruvian politics may differ, but they all allegedly follow the same broad pattern. Cardoso refined the theory by insisting that developing nations had options within the limits of dependency. Depending on the relationships between a nation's social classes as well as government policies (both internal factors), various types of associated dependent development were possible. Combining Cardoso's ideas with elements of modernization theory, Argentinean political scientist Guillermo O'Donnell offered a powerful explanation for the problems of industrialization and the rise of authoritarian military governments in the more developed nations of South America.[43]

However, East Asia's "economic miracle" from the 1960s through the 1990s—most notably in South Korea, Taiwan, Hong Kong, and Singapore—confounded dependency theory. These countries had tied themselves very closely to the developed world through trade, credit, investments, and technology transfers. Contrary to what even the more sophisticated dependency scholars had predicted, however, they achieved spectacular economic growth coupled with comparatively equitable economic distribution. Countries like Singapore and Taiwan now have standards of living approaching or even matching those of First World nations (Singapore's per-capita income, for example, exceeds Britain's and Italy's). Some *dependencistas* may object that East Asia's recent economic woes validate dependency theory, since that financial crisis originated from massive external debt and was exacerbated when foreign capital fled the region, sending Asian stock markets and currencies on a downward spiral. Still, most scholars see this as a temporary setback or perhaps a signal that the Asian growth model needs some modification. But the current East Asian crisis is unlikely to revive dependency theory to its former stature. Even Fernando Henrique Cardoso—once dependency theory's most brilliant exponent in his role as a university scholar—now enthusiastically seeks foreign investment, trade, and technology for Brazil in his current role as that nation's president.

Contemporary Perspectives

Today, few analysts accept either modernization or dependency theory in their entirety, particularly not in their original formulations. Subsequent theories and approaches, such as *bureaucratic authoritarianism* (which tried to explain the rise of military dictatorships in some of the Third World's most economically developed nations) or *neoliberal economics* (which offered a set of conservative prescriptions for the LDCs), have generally avoided global explanations of development and underdevelopment and focused instead on more specific issues. Indeed, most contemporary scholars reject the very idea of a single theory of development.[44] For one thing, it is now apparent that the Third World is too diverse and the processes of political and socioeconomic development too complex to be explained by a single theory of change.

This does not mean, however, that the insights offered by dependency and modernization theories have not been useful. Our current understanding of development draws on the strengths of both approaches, while recognizing the limitations of each. But today, most political scientists limit themselves to more manageable and specific issues, such as the function of political parties, the role of government in the economy, or the prerequisites for consolidated democracy.

The chapters that follow turn from general development theory to important issues facing less developed countries today. Chapter 2 discusses what is surely the most important development in world politics during the past half century: the spread and legitimization of democratic government. The causes and effects of democratization will be an underlying theme of this text, and most of the succeeding chapters will include some discussion of the effects of democratic change. Chapters 3 through 7 discuss some of the broad social forces that impact on contemporary politics in the developing world: the political impact of religion; the nature of ethnic politics and ethnic conflict; the role of women in Third World economic and political development; agrarian reform and rural change; and the political implications of rapid urbanization. Chapters 8 and 9 explore two types of political regimes—revolutionary and military—often found in the Third World and examine each one's approach to the problems of development and the reasons for each one's rise and fall. Finally, Chapter 10 examines economic development strategies currently being employed in much of the Third World.

DISCUSSION QUESTIONS

1. To what extent is democracy an integral part of political development? Why were political scientists initially reluctant to include democracy in their definitions of political development?
2. To what degree do social and economic development contribute to or undermine political development?
3. What do you believe are the most important differences between modernization theory and dependency theory?
4. How have both early modernization theory and early dependency theory been modified? Why were those modifications needed?
5. What is the difference between economic and social underdevelopment?

NOTES

1. For a discussion of the strengths and many weaknesses of the term, see Allen H. Merriam, "What Does 'Third World' Mean?" in *The Third World: States of Mind and Being*, ed. Jim Norwine and Alfonso Gonzalez (Boston: Unwin Hyman, 1988), pp. 15–22.

2. The term *pluralist democracy* indicates that the political system not only supports contested elections and civil liberties (formal democracy) but also allows a large number of independent interest associations (business groups, labor unions, farmer's associations, women's groups, environmental organizations, and the like) to operate politically or otherwise, free of government controls. For more on different aspects of democracy, see chap. 10.

3. Scholars have disagreed on whether to include non-European communist nations such as China, Cuba, and Vietnam in the Third World. I include them in this category because they resemble other developing nations on many dimensions.

4. Taiwan and especially Singapore were less damaged by East Asia's economic depression in the late 1990s than were countries such as Indonesia, Malaysia, and South Korea.

5. Merriam, "What Does 'Third World' Mean?" p. 20.

6. Christopher Clapham, *Third World Politics: An Introduction* (Madison: University of Wisconsin Press, 1985), p. 2.

7. Gross Domestic Product (GDP) is a measure similar to Gross National Product (GNP), the indicator often used in the United States, but excludes "net factor income from abroad." Economists and international agencies such as the U.N. use GDP more often than GNP for comparing the living standards of different countries.

8. Some countries' GNP or GDP rankings vary considerably depending on what statistical method is applied to the data. There may also be considerable variation *within* particular nations. Thus, China's coastal region is quite developed, comparing well with South Korea or Mexico. Its interior, however, is generally quite impoverished, more analogous to rural India or Bangladesh.

9. While most non-specialists speak of a country's "per-capita *income*" (the average income per person), economists and the sources of these data call the figures in Column 2 "Real Gross National Product (GNP) per capita converted to Parity Purchasing Power (PPP)." That is to say, it is a measure of average economic *production* per person (in a given year), which is then statistically controlled to remove the influences of inflation and varying price structures in different countries.

10. Unless otherwise indicated, all data in this section come from the same sources as Tables 1.1 and 1.2.

11. Data from United Nations Development Programme, *Human Development Report, 2001* (New York: Oxford University Press, 2001), p. 10, fig. 1. By contrast, the world's

most developed economies (the OECD economies) grew at an annual per-capita rate of 2.0 percent during that period, faster than Latin America but slower than South or East Asia.

12. Robert Wade, *Governing the Market* (Princeton, NJ: Princeton University Press, 1990).

13. United Nations Development Programme, *Human Development Report, 2001*, p. 18.

14. Axel Hadenius, *Democracy and Development* (London: Cambridge University Press, 1992).

15. A simple example illustrates the problem with income averages. If one person in a generally poor village makes a million dollars a year, he or she will totally distort the town average, producing a figure that in no way reflects how the average villager really lives. But the same kind of distortions do not take place with social indicators such as life expectancy, infant mortality, and literacy.

16. All data in this paragraph come from United Nations Development Programme (UNDP), *Human Development Report, 1997* (New York: Oxford University Press, 1997), pp. 24–26.

17. Ibid.

18. Samuel P. Huntington, "The Goals of Development," in *Understanding Political Development*, ed. Myron Weiner and Samuel P. Huntington (Boston: Little, Brown, 1987), p. 3.

19. Hadenius, *Democracy and Development*; Robert A. Dahl, *Democracy and Its Critics* (New Haven, CT: Yale University Press, 1989); Scott Mainwaring, "Transitions to Democracy and Democratic Consolidation," in *Issues in Democratic Consolidation: The New South American Democracies in Comparative Perspective*, ed. Scott Mainwaring, Guillermo O'Donnell, and Samuel Valenzuela (Notre Dame, IN: University of Notre Dame Press, 1992); Samuel P. Huntington, *The Third Wave: Democratization in the Late Twentieth Century* (Norman: University of Oklahoma Press, 1991).

20. Samuel P. Huntington, *Political Order in Changing Societies* (New Haven, CT: Yale University Press, 1968).

21. Guillermo O'Donnell and Philippe Schmitter, *Transitions from Authoritarian Rule: Tentative Conclusions about Uncertain Democracies* (Baltimore, MD: Johns Hopkins University Press, 1986); Abraham Lowenthal, ed., *Exporting Democracy* (Baltimore, MD: Johns Hopkins University Press, 1991); Dahl, *Democracy and Its Critics*.

22. Huntington, *The Third Wave*.

23. Eighty-six members of the United Nations have been ranked on both economic resources (per-capita GNPs) and socioeconomic indicators of living standards (HDIs). If we subtract each country's HDI rank from its GNP rank, a positive score indicates the country is performing better on social indicators than its economic ranking would predict, while a negative score suggests the opposite.

24. Huntington, *The Third Wave*; Mitchell A. Seligson, "Democratization in Latin America: The Current Cycle," in *Authoritarians and Democrats: Regime Transition in Latin America*, ed. James M. Malloy and Mitchell A. Seligson (Pittsburgh, PA: University of Pittsburgh Press, 1987); Hadenius, *Democracy and Development*.

25. Huntington, *Political Order*.

26. Guillermo O'Donnell, *Modernization and Bureaucratic-Authoritarianism: Studies in South American Politics* (Berkeley: University of California Press, 1973).

27. For a useful summary of major theories of development, see Alvin Y. So, *Social Change and Development* (Newbury Park, CA: Sage Publications, 1990); for ongoing contributions in these areas, see Weiner and Huntington, *Understanding Political Development*; Vicky Randall and Robin Theobald, *Political Change and Underdevelopment* (London: Macmillan, 1985).

28. The modernization literature is extensive. The most important works include Huntington, *Political Order*, widely considered the best work in this area; Gabriel Almond and James Coleman, eds., *The Politics of Developing Areas* (Princeton, NJ:

Princeton University Press, 1960); Lucian Pye and Sidney Verba, *Political Culture and Political Development* (Princeton, NJ: Princeton University Press, 1965); and Cyril E. Black, ed., *Comparative Modernization: A Reader* (New York: Free Press, 1976). These works, as well as those mentioned below regarding dependency theory, are recommended for advanced undergraduates.

29. Max Weber, *The Protestant Ethic and the Spirit of Capitalism* (New York: Scribner, 1958); Talcott Parsons, *The Social System* (Glencoe, IL: Free Press, 1951).

30. For examples of such arguments, see Parsons, *Social System*; Gabriel Almond and Sidney Verba, *The Civic Culture* (Princeton, NJ: Princeton University Press, 1963); Pye and Verba, *Political Culture*; Alex Inkeles and David Horton Smith, *Becoming Modern: Individual Change in Six Developing Countries* (Cambridge, MA: Harvard University Press, 1974); Daniel Lerner, *The Passing of Traditional Society* (Glencoe, IL: Free Press, 1958); David McClelland, *The Achieving Society* (Princeton, NJ: Van Nostrand, 1961).

31. Gabriel A. Almond and G. Bingham Powell, *Comparative Politics: A Developmental Approach* (Boston: Little, Brown, 1966), p. 301.

32. Marion Levy, Jr., "Social Patterns (Structures) and Problems of Modernization," in *Readings on Social Change*, ed. Wilbert Moore and Robert Cooke (Upper Saddle River, NJ: Prentice Hall, 1967), p. 207.

33. Huntington, "The Goals of Development."

34. Huntington, *Political Order in Changing Societies*.

35. See Juan Linz and Alfred Stepan, eds., *The Breakdown of Democratic Regimes: Latin America* (Baltimore, MD: Johns Hopkins University Press, 1978); David Collier, ed., *The New Authoritarianism in Latin America* (Princeton, NJ: Princeton University Press, 1979).

36. Huntington, "The Goals of Development."

37. Winston Davis, "Religion and Development: Weber and the East Asian Experience," in Weiner and Huntington, eds., *Understanding Political Development*, p. 258; see also So, *Social Change and Development*, chap. 4.

38. Theotonio Dos Santos, "The Structure of Dependence," *American Economic Review* (May 1970).

39. Werner Baer, "The Economics of Prebisch and ECLA," in *Latin America: Problems in Economic Development*, ed. C. T. Nisbet (New York: Free Press, 1969). Major early dependency studies include Andre Gunder Frank, *Capitalism and Underdevelopment in Latin America* (New York: Monthly Review Press, 1967); and Paul Baran, *The Political Economy of Growth* (New York: Monthly Review Press, 1957).

40. The most influential work on this sophisticated version of dependency theory is Fernando Henrique Cardoso and Enzo Faletto, *Dependency and Development in Latin America* (Berkeley: University of California Press, 1979). A more readable work on the same topic is Peter Evans, *Dependent Development: The Alliance of Multinational, State and Local Capital* (Princeton, NJ: Princeton University Press, 1979).

41. Clapham, *Third World Politics*, p. 3.

42. Hollis Chenery et al., *Redistribution with Growth* (London: Oxford University Press with the World Bank and the University of Sussex, 1974).

43. O'Donnell, *Modernization and Bureaucratic-Authoritarianism*.

44. See, for example, two recent works that dismiss the search for a single paradigm of development: James Manor, ed., *Rethinking Third World Politics* (New York: Longman, 1991), especially the introduction by Manor and the chapter by Geoffrey Hawthorn; Paul Cammack, David Pool, and William Tordoff, *Third World Politics*, 2d ed. (Baltimore, MD: Johns Hopkins University Press, 1993).

chapter 2

Democratic Change and the Change to Democracy

The years 2000 and 2001 were particularly hard for former dictators and quasi-dictators. The former president of Yugoslavia, Slobodan Milosevic, arrested months earlier by Serbian[1] authorities, was put on trial at the United Nations International War Crimes Tribunal in the Hague (Netherlands). The father of Serbia's genocidal war against Bosnia and its attacks on the Serbian province of Kosovo, Milosovic became the only head of government since World War II to face charges of human rights violations before an international court. August Pinochet, Chile's military dictator for 16 years (1973–1989), fought charges of human rights violations in Chilean courts after returning from a humiliating extended house arrest in England. Indonesia's long-term dictator, General Suharto, also faced possible arrest after having been forced from office. Like Pinochet, this once all-powerful leader now hid behind the humiliating court plea that he was too old and mentally incompetent to stand trial. Alberto Fujimori, who had subverted Peruvian democracy after having been fairly elected to that country's presidency, took refuge in Japan (the home of his parents) rather than face anticipated arrest charges in Peru. In Argentina, Carlos Menem, who like Fujimori had been democratically elected initially but then used his presidential powers to weaken democracy, was indicted for illegal arms sales and held for a time under house arrest.

These events capped nearly three decades of transitions from authoritarian to democratic government throughout the world. Beginning with a 1974 military revolt that brought down Portugal's fascist dictatorship, authoritarian regimes throughout the world, and especially throughout the Third World, began to fall with the advent of spreading democratic movements. The collapse of Soviet and Eastern European communism was the democratic wave's most dramatic manifestation. But in the developing nations, equally dramatic events inspired our attention. In early 1990, Nelson Mandela, the world's most renowned political prisoner, left his cell in Pollsmoor prison and was transported triumphantly to South Africa's capital, Pretoria, ending 27 years of incarceration. There, he and other freed Black leaders of his recently legalized political party, the African National Congress, eventually negotiated an end to White minority rule. President Mandela's triumph accelerated Africa's "second independence"—a wave of political liberalization (easing of repression) that has sometimes culminated in electoral democracy.[2]

In Asia, Corazon (Cory) Aquino succeeded her assassinated husband as leader of Filipino "people's power"—mass peaceful demonstrations for democracy staged by students, shopkeepers, professionals, businesspeople, and even nuns. Backed by the Catholic clergy, her supporters took to the streets day after day, peacefully challenging government troops. Ultimately, when then dictator Marcos tried to deny Ms. Aquino her apparent victory in a hastily called "snap presidential election" (1986), the commander of the armed forces, General Fidel Ramos, along with Defense Minister Juan Ponce Enrile, joined the opposition, forcing Marcos to step down. Soon after, student-led demonstrations against South Korea's military regime (inspired, in part, by events in the Philippines) accelerated that country's transition to democracy. More recently (1998), "people's power" demonstrations in Indonesia toppled the 30-year dictatorship of President Suharto. Of course, not all Asian pro-democracy movements have been successful. In China, massive student demonstrations were crushed by army tanks in Tiananmen Square, while Myanmar's military squashed democratic protests by killing thousands of Burmese citizens. But these setbacks notwithstanding, much of Asia has made significant progress toward democracy in the past two decades.

The most sweeping democratic changes, however, took place in Latin America (1978–1990), affecting almost every country in the region. Whereas all but a handful of countries (Colombia, Costa Rica, and Venezuela) had some type of authoritarian or semi-authoritarian government in the mid-1970s, 20 years later only Cuba, Mexico, and Haiti had failed to establish electoral democracy. Since that time, Mexico also has made the transition to democracy while Venezuela has regressed, as did Peru for most of the 1990s. Unlike Asia and Africa, Latin America's democratization generally lacked charismatic heroes in the mold of Mandela, Aquino, or Burmese opposition leader and Nobel Peace Prize winner Daw Aung San Suu Kyi. Nor was it typically precipitated by mass demonstrations. Instead, democratic transitions often followed extended negotiations between the outgoing authoritarian government and its opponents, with change coming in stages.

Yet Latin America enjoyed two important advantages over Africa and Asia. To begin with, prior to its wave of military takeovers in the 1960s and 1970s, the region had enjoyed the developing world's strongest democratic tradition, most notably in Chile, Costa Rica, Uruguay, and Venezuela. Furthermore,

Latin American nations were among the first LDCs to achieve the levels of literacy and economic development that are usually needed for stable democratic government. Not surprisingly, then, the region's current transition or return to democracy has been more sweeping and more successful than elsewhere in the Third World, ultimately affecting virtually every country in the hemisphere except Cuba.

In all, since the 1970s the upsurge of political freedom in the developing world, coupled with the collapse of Soviet and Eastern European communism, has produced history's greatest advance ever toward democracy. If these changes can be maintained, they promise to influence virtually every aspect of Third World politics discussed in this book.[3]

DEMOCRACY DEFINED

Discussions of democratic transformations have frequently been complicated by disagreements over the precise meaning of democracy. Currently, most political scientists define democracy procedurally. That is, democracy is explained in terms of essential procedures governing the election and behavior of government officials. The least demanding, minimalist definition focuses almost exclusively on elections. It simply defines democracy as a political system that holds relatively fair, contested elections on a regular basis.[4] We will call countries that meet that minimal standard *electoral democracies.* Although this bare-bones definition seems reasonable (after all, most Americans define democracy in terms of free elections), it allows a number of rather questionable governments to be included in the "democratic club." For example, the current governments in Colombia, Turkey, and Sri Lanka meet this standard, yet they massively violate human rights while battling armed insurgencies.[5] In all of those countries, government troops routinely massacre villagers and torture prisoners. Guatemala and Thailand also meet the standards of electoral democracy, yet their armed forces regularly intervene in politics, often overriding decisions made by elected officials.

As the norm of open elections has become more universally accepted in recent decades, the number of electoral democracies worldwide has more than doubled. But many of these governments still manipulate the mass media and violate their citizens' civil liberties. In this chapter I use the term *semidemocracies* to refer to those *electoral democracies* whose governments repress civil liberties and otherwise breach the principles of a free society. Their elections may be relatively free, but their societies are not. Semidemocracies currently include Guatemala, Malaysia, and Singapore.

A more stringent definition of democracy, the one used here, demands more than just fair elections. Instead, it defines *full democracy* (sometimes called "liberal democracy") as a political system in which most of the country's leading government officials are elected[6]; there is nearly universal suffrage[7]; elections are largely free of fraud and outside manipulation; opposition-party candidates have a real chance of being elected to important national offices; and minority rights as well as general civil liberties are respected, including free speech and a free press. All of these conditions help guarantee that democratic governments are accountable to their citizens in a way that authoritarian regimes are not.[8] Thus, full democracies require not only freely contested elections but also respect for civil liberties, support for pluralism in civil society,[9] respect for the rule of law, accountability of elected officials, and civilian control over the armed forces. This definition suggests that competitive elections have limited value if unelected individuals or groups who are not accountable to the public (such as the heads of the armed forces, organized crime bosses, business elites, or foreign powers) control elected officials from behind the scenes. And free elections don't establish true democracy if elected officials arbitrarily arrest opposition leaders or violate their citizens' civil liberties.

Finally, some scholars offer an even higher standard for democracy. They argue that *any* purely procedural definition of democracy, no matter how exacting, is incomplete. Instead, they insist, real democracy requires not only fair elections and proper government *procedures* (as just outlined) but also fair and just government *policy outcomes* ("substantive democracy"). For example, true substantive democracy requires that citizens have equal access to public schooling and health care regardless of their social class or ethnicity. Consequently, they argue, any procedural democracy—such as India, El Salvador, or Bangladesh— that tolerates gross economic inequalities, ethnic prejudices, or other major social injustices is not truly democratic.

These critics make an important point. Procedural democracy alone does not guarantee a just society; it is merely a step in the right direction. But it is a more important step than they acknowledge. Because governments in procedural democracies are accountable to the people, they are less vulnerable to revolution and other forms of civil unrest. They are also extremely unlikely to make war against other democracies (indeed, war between two democracies is essentially unknown). Prodded by a free press and public opinion, they are more responsive to domestic crises such as famines (consequently, there has never been an extended famine in any procedural democracy), and the many previously cited exceptions notwithstanding, democracies are generally more respectful of civil liberties.[10]

Mindful of the fact that democratic societies never correct all social injustices (the United States, for example, has long tolerated racial discrimination and poverty), I define democracy strictly procedurally. Issues of substantive democracy (eradicating poverty, racism, sexism, and the like) are obviously important, but they are a separate matter.

DEMOCRATIC TRANSITION AND CONSOLIDATION

In the discussion that follows, the term *democratic transition* (or "transition to democracy") means the process of moving from an authoritarian regime to a democratic one. The transition period begins when an authoritarian government shows the first significant signs of collapsing or of negotiating an exit from power. It ends when the first freely elected government takes office. Thus, for example, in South Africa the democratic transition began in 1990 when the White minority government of President Frederik de Klerk decided to free Nelson Mandela and open negotiations with the African National Congress Party. It concluded four years later when Mandela was inaugurated as the nation's freely elected president. Even after a transition is complete, however, new democracies often remain fragile, with the distinct possibility that they will falter.

Only when democratic institutions, practices, and values have become deeply entrenched in society can we say that a country has experienced *democratic consolidation*. Consolidation is a process through which democratic norms (democratic "rules of the game") become accepted by all powerful groups in society—including labor, business, rural landlords, the church, and the military—and no important political actor contemplates a return to dictatorship. Or as Juan Linz and Alfred Stepan put it, democracy is consolidated when it becomes "the only game in town," even in the face of severe economic or political adversity.[11] Consolidation may begin when the democratic transition ends, and it is only complete when democracy is securely entrenched.

Unfortunately, however, not all transitions to democracy are subsequently consolidated. Many countries revert to dictatorship or remain mired in political disorder. For example, between 1958 and 1975, 22 countries that had democratized during the postwar era (1943–1962) slipped back to authoritarianism. Similarly, some of the most recently installed democracies have already collapsed, while democratic values and practices in other countries—such as Russia, Guatemala, Mali, and Mozambique—are anything but secure. It is worth noting, for example, that Russia's parliament has been dominated for years by antidemocratic parties (especially the Communists and Liberal Democrats), and that presidents Boris Yeltsin and Vladimir Putin have frequently violated the Russian constitution and democratic norms either in dealing with parliament or in pursuing the war against Chechyn rebels.

On the other hand, in successfully consolidated (or reconsolidated) democracies such as South Korea, Chile, and Uruguay, democratic values predominate. Even previously antidemocratic political parties and groups (such as Chile's Communist Party and Uruguay's former Tupamaru guerrillas) accept democracy as "the only game in town," and the once-dominant armed forces now seemingly accept civilian control. That does not mean that consolidated democracies can *never* collapse. "Never" is a long time, and in the past, seemingly consolidated Third World democracies such as the Philippines, Chile, and Uruguay were toppled by authoritarian forces. But, at the least, consolidated democracies are secure for the foreseeable future. And they will continue to endure unless some deep societal divide emerges to tear them apart.

AUTHORITARIAN BEGINNINGS

With the disintegration of Soviet bloc communism and the expansion of democracy in the developing world, a growing worldwide consensus emerged in support of democracy as the best form of government. But that has not always been so. In the decades after World War II, as a legion of African, Asian, and Middle Eastern countries achieved independence, many Third World leaders and foreign observers believed that these emerging nations were not ready for democratic government, and perhaps that democracy was not even desirable at that stage of their socioeconomic development. To be sure, a number of newly independent countries, particularly former British colonies in Africa, Asia, and the Caribbean, established parliamentary government and other democratic political institutions modeled after their former colonial masters, just as Latin American countries more than a century earlier had patterned their political institutions after those of the United States. But only in a small number of cases (including India, Lebanon, Jamaica, and other small island nations in the Caribbean) did democracy take hold.

Since that time, Middle Eastern nations have been ruled by monarchs (Saudi Arabia, Kuwait, Morocco, and Jordan), all-powerful single parties (Egypt, Sudan), or personalistic military and civil-military dictators (Iraq, Syria). In Sub-Saharan Africa, single-party systems were established in many new nations (including Tanzania, Senegal, Guinea), often to be followed by military dictatorships (Nigeria, Liberia) or absolute, one-man rule (Uganda, Central African Republic). Democracy fared somewhat better in Asia but was frequently cut short by the military (Thailand, South Korea, Myanmar). Corrupt and inept postwar governments in China, Vietnam, Cambodia, and Laos were overthrown and replaced by communist revolutionary regimes. Latin America, benefiting from more than a century of self-rule and from greater socioeconomic development, had the most success in nurturing democracy. Indeed, during the 1950s relatively democratic governments were pervasive in that region. But political intervention by the armed forces persisted, and in the 1960s and early 1970s a new wave of military takeovers swept the region. It was not until the 1980s that democracy once again became the norm.

JUSTIFYING AUTHORITARIAN RULE

In the midst of democracy's current worldwide advance, it seems hard to believe that not long ago, freely elected governments and flourishing civil societies were often seen as unattainable or even undesirable in many LDCs. Modernization theorists frequently claimed the newly emerging states of Africa and Asia were not sufficiently developed, economically or socially, to sustain political democracy.[12] And dependency theorists declared that democracy was unlikely to emerge in the LDCs because powerful industrialized nations were allied with local political and economic elites to bolster unrepresentative governments.

Some scholars worried that levels of mass political participation were outstripping many governments' capacities to accommodate society's political demands. Unless Third World political institutions could be strengthened, they warned, political unrest threatened to derail economic and political development.[13] Given the dangers of social disorder, some analysts and Third World leaders used this argument to justify authoritarian rule as a necessary stopgap. Only with more advanced socioeconomic modernization, it seemed, could LDCs produce citizens capable of effective political participation. Increased education and literacy were seen as necessary to expand society's political knowledge and develop effective political participation. We now know that countries are unlikely to establish stable, democratic government unless they have risen above the bottom ranks of poverty (as expressed by GNP per capita) and have reached a literacy rate of at least 50 percent.[14] In addition to raising literacy, modernization also enlarges the size of the middle class and the organized (unionized) working class, both of whom are essential for a more stable and inclusive democracy.[15]

But an obvious chicken-and-egg quandary presented itself. If socioeconomic modernization is necessary to establish democracy, how can a democratic government be the agent of modernization? Some answered that it couldn't; only a strong and stable authoritarian government—such as General Augusto Pinochet's dictatorship in Chile or South Korea's various military governments—could jump-start modernization. Only later, when the country was "ready," should dictatorships give way to democracy.[16] Other scholars noted yet another obstacle to democratic government in the developing world. They argued that many LDCs, held back by authoritarian traditional values, lacked a democratic political culture and that democracy would have to be preceded by modernization of social values.[17]

Not long ago, many Third World leaders insisted that not only would it be difficult to establish democracy in their countries, but that it was not even desirable at that stage of their development. In Africa, many first-generation, postcolonial leaders created single-party systems, banning or restricting opposition political parties. They often argued that ethnic tensions in their country made competitive elections too risky because they would prompt different political parties to represent contending tribes or clans, further polarizing the country (see Chapter 4). Other leaders of emerging nations were influenced by Marxist-Leninist ideology, more popular at that time than now. They maintained that poverty, tribalism, and dependency at home were so severe that an all-powerful state linked to a "vanguard party" (one that knows what is in the best interests of the people) was needed to lead the country forward. Later, as many of these governments failed miserably, military dictators took their place, claiming that civilian rulers were too corrupt or too weak to govern effectively. In the Middle East, similar justifications were used for one-party or military rule. More recently, Islamic fundamentalist governments in Iran, Sudan, and Afghanistan have prohibited political opposition groups whom they regard as infidels.

While many Latin American nations had democratic or semidemocratic governments in the 1950s and early 1960s, during the two decades that followed, a series of military coups installed repressive governments in most of the region. These new authoritarian leaders often justified their rule by pointing to perceived leftist threats and the need to reinvigorate the economy. Meanwhile, in East Asian nations such as South Korea, Taiwan, and Singapore, authoritarian rulers clung to power long after their countries had surpassed the thresholds of economic and social modernization normally associated with democratic transitions. They insisted that their dictatorships were necessary to ward off external threats (from China or North Korea) and claimed that their own society's Confucian culture was not receptive to political opposition groups, which they regarded as disruptive to social harmony.

According to one expert count, in the mid-1970s only 39 of the world's nations were functioning democracies. Virtually all of them were industrialized, economically prosperous countries in North America, Europe, and Australia-New Zealand. Meanwhile, democracy seemed to be in retreat in the Third World, as countries such as Argentina, Chile, Nigeria, and the Philippines succumbed to dictatorships. Thus, Larry Diamond notes:

> Indeed, the mid-to-late 1970s seemed a low-water mark for democracy . . . and the empirical trends were reified by intellectual fashions dismissing democracy as an artifice, a cultural construct of the West, or a "luxury" that poor states could not afford.[18]

THE THIRD WAVE AND ITS EFFECT ON THE THIRD WORLD

Since that time, however, developing countries have been a part of the world's most sweeping transition from authoritarianism to democracy or semidemocracy. Writing shortly before the fall of the Soviet Union, Samuel Huntington counted 29 countries throughout the world that had democratized in the previous 15 years alone (1974–1989). Of these, 20 were LDCs.[19] While some of the countries on that list had questionable democratic credentials (Romania, Peru, and Pakistan, for example) and others slid back to authoritarian rule, there can be no denying that the worldwide trend toward democracy since the mid-1970s has been palpable.

Huntington noted that the current surge of democratic expansion is, in fact, the third such wave that the modern world has experienced since the early 1800s. In each case, democratic political forces and intellectual trends in key countries had a contagious impact on other nations. However, the first two waves were followed by periods of backsliding in which some countries reverted to authoritarian rule. As we have noted, that process has already begun in some third-wave nations.[20] The first democratic wave (1828–1926), by far the longest, began under the influence of the American and French Revolutions (as well as the Industrial Revolution) and ended not long after World War I. Change was largely confined to Europe and to former British colonies with populations of primarily European descent (the United States, Canada, New Zealand, and Australia). The second, much shorter wave (1943–1962) was precipitated by the struggle against fascism during World War II and the subsequent collapse of European colonialism in Africa and Asia. In this period, democracy was introduced to a number of LDCs, but in most cases the new governments at best only met the standards of electoral democracy (competitive elections).

It is the recent third wave (1974–) that most draws our attention here because of its pervasive and seemingly lasting reverberations in the Third World. Of course, third-wave transitions were most dramatic in the former Soviet Union and its Eastern European communist allies. Pictures of young Germans chopping at the Berlin Wall and of Boris Yeltsin facing down a military coup in Russia were among the most powerful political images of the late twentieth century. But in developing nations as diverse as South Africa, Mali, the Philippines, South Korea, Argentina, and Chile, years of authoritarian or semi-authoritarian rule were ending as well.

This wave of democratization continued into the start of the new century, with some notable setbacks in countries such as Pakistan and Sudan. According to Larry Diamond, between 1988 and 1994 the number of electoral democracies in Africa rose from only 3 to 18.[21] Using a less stringent definition, Michael Bratton and Nicolas van de Walle calculate that 5 of 47 Sub-Saharan states were electoral democracies in 1988 (with leaders chosen in "free and fair" elections) and that the number rose to 21 by 1994.[22] Since that time, student demonstrators in Indonesia, the world's fourth most populous nation, toppled Asia's most enduring military dictator and opened the way to the country's first democratic elections since independence. At the close of the twentieth century, Nigeria, Africa's most populous nation, also restored democracy. And at the start of the current century, Vicente Fox was elected president of Mexico, ending the 71-year reign of the PRI, the world's longest-ruling political party.

As of 1974, only 27.5 percent of the world's countries allowed free and fair national elections. By 1996, however, that proportion had risen to 63 percent.[23] Four years later, Freedom House, probably the most cited source of worldwide statistics on democracy, rated 85 of the world's countries as free, 60 as partly free (based on a measure of competitive elections and civil liberties), and only 47 as not free—a vast improvement over the situation two or three decades earlier.[24]

INTERNATIONAL CAUSES AND CONSEQUENCES OF THE THIRD WAVE

Obviously, worldwide political changes of this magnitude are inspired and influenced by broad currents that transcend national boundaries. A number of factors contributed to the most recent democratic revolutions. For one thing, the economic crisis that devastated so many Third World countries in the 1980s revealed that authoritarian governments are no more effective and no less corrupt (and are often less efficient and more corrupt) than the elected governments that they had earlier so contemptuously swept aside. Furthermore, because dictatorships lack the legitimacy that free elections bestow on democratic governments, their support depends much more heavily on satisfactory job performance. So when authoritarian governments in countries such as Argentina, Nigeria, and Peru dragged their country into war or economic decay, their support rapidly eroded. In Africa, the gross mismanagement and corruption of both military and single-party regimes caused their countries' economies to implode, as the continent's per-capita GNP declined by some 2 percent annually in the 1980s. In Latin America, military rulers performed well economically in Chile, and for a period of time in Brazil, but fared poorly elsewhere. In time, almost all of the region's authoritarian regimes were undermined by the 1980s' debt crisis.

By contrast, many East Asian dictatorships (most notably in South Korea, Taiwan, Indonesia, and Singapore) enjoyed spectacular economic success until the continent's 1997 financial crisis. Ironically, however, rather than generate wider support for those governments, rapid economic growth and modernization often generated a burgeoning middle class possessed of democratic aspirations and the political skills to pursue them. As in Africa and Latin America, this growing number of informed citizens were often incensed by the lack of opportunities for meaningful political participation, the scope of government repression, and the extent of state corruption.

Throughout the world, no sooner had democratic upheavals occurred in one nation than they then spread quickly to neighboring countries. In Eastern Europe, Poland's Solidarity movement inspired democratic efforts in Hungary, East Germany, and what was then Czechoslovakia. They, in turn, prompted antigovernment protests in Bulgaria, Albania, and Romania. Students in South Korea watched evening news stories covering anti-government demonstrations in the Philippines and took the lessons of "people's power" to heart.

As the democratic tidal wave swept forward, some authoritarian leaders began to get the message. Generals in Ecuador and Paraguay watched neighboring military dictatorships fall and decided to abdicate while the going was still good. After more than 40 years of political domination by the mainland Chinese minority and authoritarian rule by the Guomindang Party, Taiwan's government opened up the political system to authentic electoral competition and political freedom. In Africa, a number of single-party states liberalized their political systems, allowing more freedom and greater political space for opposition groups, while a smaller number established authentic electoral democracy.

As we noted earlier, the demise of Soviet and Eastern European communism exposed more clearly the deficiencies of Marxism-Leninism. As communism was discredited, even among many of its once-fervent adherents, democracy assumed greater worldwide legitimacy. The end of the Cold War also permitted the United States to be more consistent in its defense of democracy. That is to say, the United States now had no reason to coddle friendly Third World dictators whose support it had previously cultivated in the struggle against Soviet communism. For example, the United States had supported corrupt and repressive dictators in Zaire, Somalia, the Philippines, Nicaragua, and Iran because they were considered necessary allies in the Cold War. With the collapse of the Soviet Union, there no longer was reason to stand by such rulers.

To be sure, the United States and Western Europe had already begun more actively championing Third World democratic reform in the years preceding the fall of the Soviet Union. The Reagan administration, for example, reversed its initial support for Chile's military dictatorship and allowed the reform-minded U.S. ambassador there to work closely with the democratic opposition. But the end of the Cold War allowed Washington to pursue its democratic agenda more aggressively. In the Caribbean—where the United States was once known for supporting such notorious dictators as Fulgencio Batista (Cuba), Rafael Trujillo (Dominican Republic), and "Papa Doc" Duvalier (Haiti)—President Bill Clinton threatened U.S. military intervention in Haiti unless its generals allowed the country's ousted elected president, Jean Bertrand Aristide, to return to office.[25]

THE PREREQUISITES OF DEMOCRACY IN INDIVIDUAL COUNTRIES

Although the international trends just discussed served as catalysts, providing developing countries with incentives and opportunities to democratize, they cannot explain important differences in how Third World nations reacted to such forces. At the start of the twenty-first century (twenty-five years after the start of the third wave), some LDCs—such as Togo, Vietnam, and Iraq—remain mired in dictatorship, with little or no opening in the political system to date. Others—such as El Salvador, Mozambique, and Thailand—are in some stage of democratic transition. And, finally, some fortunate countries (including Chile, Costa Rica, Botswana, Mauritius, South Korea, and Taiwan) seem to have consolidated their democracies.[26]

What accounts for these differences? What determines whether a specific country embarks on the road toward democracy, whether it completes that voyage successfully, and whether it eventually consolidates democratic values, practices, and institutions? For example, how do we know if democracy eventually will take root and survive in Brazil or Russia? Why is it that democratization has advanced further in Latin America than in Africa or the Middle East?

As with most fundamental questions about politics, there are no simple answers. Scholars have debated these issues for decades and have identified a number of historical, structural, and cultural variables that help account for democracy's presence in, say, India and Uruguay, and its absence in countries such as Syria and Laos. But these analysts still disagree about the relative importance of specific variables and about the minimum levels a country must attain in order to achieve democracy. In the discussion that follows, I examine a number of factors that have been widely identified as prerequisites for democracy.

Social and Economic Modernization

Some 40 years ago, Seymour Martin Lipset observed that democracy was far more prevalent in industrialized countries such as the United States and Sweden than in poorer nations—a finding congruent with modernization theory (Chapter 1).[27] Subsequent research by a wide range of political scientists has supported that claim. The reasoning behind this relationship was that

> industrialization leads to increases in wealth, education, communication and equality; these developments are associated with a more moderate lower and upper class and a larger middle class, which is by nature moderate; and this in turn increases the probability of stable democratic forms of politics.[28]

Over the years, statistical analysis has identified more precisely the particular aspects of modernization that promote democracy. Philips Cutright determined that when other factors are held constant, there is a strong correlation between the extent of a country's mass communications and its degree of democracy, stronger even than the correlation between economic development and democracy.[29] A free and active mass media and opportunities for citizens to exchange ideas, he reasoned, promote a free society. More recently, Axel Hadenius, examining the influence of dozens of independent variables, found that democracy correlates most strongly with higher levels of literacy and education.[30] An educated population, it appears, is more likely to follow politics and to participate. It is also more capable of defending its own interests. One hopeful sign for the future of democracy in the Third World is the substantial growth of literacy in recent decades. For example, from 1965 to 1995, adult illiteracy in developing countries fell by one half, with Third World literacy levels reaching nearly 70 percent.[31] As we have noted, countries whose populations are over half literate are far more likely to sustain democracy than those that fall below that mark. Similarly, Mitchell Seligson has found an income threshold for sustaining democracy. Although that dollar amount has varied over the years (because of inflation and changing exchange rates), the point at which democracy became likely at the start of this century was a per-capita GNP of roughly $2,000.[32]

That does not mean that countries inevitably become more democratic as their economies develop. In fact, there is evidence that middle-income countries are frequently *less* stable and more prone to dictatorship.[33] For example, in the 1960s and 1970s, although South America's most industrialized countries (Argentina, Brazil, Chile, Uruguay) were ranked as upper-middle-income nations by the World Bank, their democratic governments were toppled by military dictatorships. These exceptions are quite important, but the long-term global evidence still shows a correlation between economic development and democracy. In recent decades, for example, East Asia's rapid economic growth, higher literacy, and expanding middle classes promoted democratic transitions in South Korea, Thailand, and Taiwan. In Latin America, where levels of modernization are relatively high by Third World standards, democracy has been growing since the close of the 1970s. Conversely, Africa, which is home to most of the world's poorest nations, has had far less democratic success.

Class Structure

Some scholars maintain that it is not economic growth per se that induces democracy but rather the way in which that growth affects a country's social structure. Specifically, they reason, economic development supports stable democracy only if it induces appropriate changes in the country's class structure.

Since the time of Aristotle, political theorists have linked democracy and political stability to the presence of a large and vibrant middle class. The middle class, they suggest, tends to be politically moderate and serves as a bridge between the upper and lower classes. Its members also have the political and organizational skills necessary to create political parties and other important democratic institutions. So, in those countries where economic growth fails to create a politically independent and influential middle class, modernization does not necessarily buttress democracy and may even weaken it. In fact, the independence and power of the emerging middle class have varied greatly in different regions of the world that industrialized in disparate historical eras. For example, industrialization and urbanization produced a larger, more powerful, and more independent middle class in Northern Europe than it did one century later in Latin America, where wealth and income were far more concentrated and the middle class correspondingly weaker and more dependent. Predictably, democracy did not take hold as readily in Latin America as it had in Northern Europe.

Barrington Moore, Jr., in his widely acclaimed study of economic and political change, *The Social Origins of Dictatorship and Democracy*, identified three discrete paths to modernization, each shaped by the relative power of the state (the national government apparatus) and the strength of significant social classes. In one path, typified by nineteenth- and early-twentieth-century Germany, modernization was led by a strong state allied with powerful and antidemocratic agricultural land owners and a bourgeoisie (business class) that was dependent on the state. In Germany and subsequently in Third World countries with a similar political configuration, that combination ultimately resulted in the rise of fascism (or other ultra-rightist, authoritarian regimes). A second path to modernization, found in countries such as China, featured a highly centralized state, a repressive land-owning class, a weak bourgeoisie, and a large and eventually rebellious peasantry. The end result of that alignment was a communist revolution fought by the peasantry.

Finally, Moore's third path, identified most closely with Britain, was distinguished by an internally divided state and a strong bourgeoisie that was at odds with the rural land-owning elite. Only this final alignment of forces, distinguished by the urban business class's (the bourgeoisie's) powerful and independent political role, has led to liberal democracy. "No [strong and independent] bourgeoisie," Moore noted, "no democracy."[34] Similarly, in developing nations today, a vibrant middle class, including an influential bourgeoisie, is a necessary ingredient for establishing and consolidating democracy. It should come as no surprise, then, that in countries as diverse as Chile, the Philippines, and South Korea, middle-class citizens, including university students (often the children of the bourgeoisie), have been on the front lines in recent struggles for democracy. During the 1992 pro-democracy street demonstrations that brought down Thailand's military government, student leaders could be seen using their cell phones to coordinate their protests—a far cry from Southeast Asia's peasant revolutions decades earlier.

Very poor countries, such as Afghanistan, Haiti, Kenya, or Nepal, whose middle classes are small and dependent on the state or on rural landlords, are far less likely to attain or maintain democracy. But it is also important to remember that even though a strong middle class and bourgeoisie are *necessary* for democracy, those groups are not *always* democratically oriented. For example, in pre-Nazi (Weimar) Germany and in Argentina and Chile during the 1970s, as the middle class felt threatened by social unrest from below, it threw its support to fascist or other right-wing extremist dictatorships.

More recently, Rueschemeyer, Huber Stephens, and Stephens have focused attention on the importance of organized labor in building democracy. They argue that while the bourgeoisie and the middle class generally fostered democracy in Western Europe, Latin America, and the Caribbean, those groups usually favored a restricted form of democracy that enhanced their own political strength (vis-à-vis the upper class and the state) but also limited the political influence of the lower class. Consequently, countries have only achieved comprehensive democracy when, in addition to a large bourgeoisie, they also had a politically potent working class organized into strong labor unions that pushed for broader political representation and increased social justice.[35]

In summary, democracy tends to flourish best where economic modernization produces a politically influential and independent bourgeoisie/middle class and where labor unions effectively defend the interests of the working class. When any of those classes are small, weak, or politically dependent on authoritarian elements in society such as large rural land owners, democratic development is less likely.

Political Culture

In the final analysis, however, neither a country's level of socioeconomic development nor its class structure can fully explain successful or failed democratization. For example, during the early decades of the twentieth century, Argentina was one of the most affluent nations on earth (far wealthier than Italy or Japan), with substantial middle and working classes. Yet rather than develop into a liberal democracy, by the 1930s that country had embarked on a half century of recurring coups and military dictatorships. More recently, Singapore, South Korea, and Taiwan retained authoritarian governments for many years after those countries had attained considerable socioeconomic development.[36] And, Middle Eastern petroleum states such as Kuwait and Saudi Arabia have made little progress toward democracy despite their considerable economic wealth. On the other hand, India has sustained democracy for most of its 50 years of independence despite its extensive poverty and low literacy rate.

Along with its level of economic development and its class structure, a nation's democratic potential is also influenced by its *political culture*—that is, its cultural norms and values relating to politics. A country's constitution may require contested elections, a free press, and the separation of powers, but unless the people, especially elites and political activists, value these objectives, constitutional protections are unlikely to hold up. Some of the most important values needed to sustain democracy include the conviction that voting and other forms of individual political participation are important and potentially productive; tolerance of dissenting political opinions and beliefs, even when those views are very unpopular; accepting the outcome of fair elections as definitive, regardless of who wins; viewing politics as a process that requires compromise; and commitment to democracy as the best form of government, regardless of how well or poorly a particular democratic administration performs.

The recent wave of successful and failed democratic transitions has renewed interest in how a country's political culture affects its potential for consolidating democracy. Survey research allows us to measure more precisely the nature of a nation's political beliefs. For example, surveys conducted after the collapse of the Soviet Union revealed that Russia had yet to develop a broadly based democratic political culture. Only one in eight Russians expressed confidence in President Boris Yeltsin's postcommunist government. A substantial minority, distressed by Russia's economic decline, yearned for the security and stability of the communist era, and many respondents cared little for protecting civil liberties and minority rights. For example, almost one in three favored the death penalty for homosexuals and for prostitutes. A smaller, but still significant, number actually supported the execution of physically disabled people.[37] Ordinary Russians have also been highly intolerant of ethnic minorities such as central Asians in their midst. And the country's political elite has manifested little spirit of compromise. One cause for optimism, however, is that younger Russians are more likely to endorse democratic values than older citizens are. To date, in spite of such authoritarian sentiment, Russian democracy has survived the test of severe economic hardship. But it remains on shaky ground. For example, in the 1999 parliamentary election, two antidemocratic parties, the Communists and Liberal Democrats (contrary to its name, the latter party is racist and neofascist) won almost one-third of the seats.

Robert Dahl, a renowned democratic theorist, observes that all political systems eventually confront a serious crisis (such as U.S. racial unrest in the 1960s, Russia's economic crises, tribal violence in Nigeria, or the terrorist attacks on Washington and New York in 2001). At those times, political leaders in unconsolidated democracies are often tempted to seek authoritarian solutions such as limiting civil liberties or imposing martial law. But if a broad segment of the population, including political elites, shares democratic values—that is, if a democratic political culture has begun to take root in society—democracy can survive the crisis intact. Dahl stresses two particularly important democratic values: first, the armed forces and police must willingly submit to the control of democratically elected civilian authorities; second, government and society must tolerate and legally protect dissident political beliefs.

The first value (civilian control of the military) is taken for granted in industrialized democracies, but not in countries such as Argentina, Guatemala, Nigeria, and Thailand, where the armed forces have long exercised veto power over the policy decisions of elected officials. Even in a relatively consolidated democracy such as contemporary Chile, the military still insists on substantial autonomy. Dahl's second cultural standard (tolerance of dissent) also presents a challenge to many developing countries where even freely elected governments sometimes silence critics and muzzle opposition leaders. The crucial question, then, says Dahl, is: "How can robust democratic cultures be created in countries where they previously have been largely absent?"[38] He responds that there is no easy answer; developing a democratic culture is a gradual process in which socioeconomic modernization and political development need to mutually reinforce each other.

Sometimes external actors may promote or even impose a democratic political culture on another country, as U.S. occupation forces did in Japan after World War II. Many African and Asian countries were first introduced to modern politics by the colonial powers that controlled them. Statistical analysis of developing countries reveals that one of the variables most closely associated with democratic government is having once been a British colony.[39] Of course, not all former British colonies are democracies; in fact, most of those in Africa are not. But, in general, countries that experienced British colonial rule were far more likely to maintain democracy after independence than were those nations previously colonized by France, Belgium, Netherlands, Spain, or Portugal. This pattern suggests that Britain more successfully inculcated its colonies with democratic values than did other European powers.

It seems obvious that a country's political culture influences its political system in some manner. For example, communities with high levels of mutual tolerance and whose citizens actively follow politics are more hospitable to democracy than are less tolerant or less knowledgeable societies. But how fixed in a nation's psyche are such values? Is there something inherently more democratic or more authoritarian about Norwegian, French, or Chinese cultures? Are some religions, such as Christianity, more conducive to democracy than, say, Hinduism? Here we find scholars disagreeing strongly. Cultural stereotypes are inherently controversial and are sometimes prejudiced. But is it not possible that careful and objective analysis might show that countries with certain religions or cultural traditions are more likely to support democratic values, while others are more prone to authoritarianism? In fact, we do find that predominantly

Christian nations, particularly Protestant ones, are more likely to be democratic than are countries with other dominant religions, even when other possible causal factors (such as economic development or literacy) are held constant. "Protestantism is said to foster individual responsibility and is . . . thereby also more skeptical and less fundamentalist in character."[40]

More recently, observers have noted democracy's poor track record in Islamic countries, especially in the Middle East. Some maintain that Islamic beliefs do not readily support democratic institutions because they fail to separate religion and politics (i.e., church and state). Similarly, when impressive economic growth and increased educational levels during the 1970s and early 1980s failed to bring democracy, at least initially, to China, Singapore, South Korea, and Taiwan, some experts concluded that cultural constraints must be overriding the positive influences of economic modernization. They argued that Confucian culture promotes rigidly hierarchical societies and encourages excessive obedience to authority, both of which are antithetical to democracy.[41]

Not surprisingly, cultural explanations such as these are highly controversial. They are very difficult to prove and often smack of prejudice and ethnocentrism. Thus, Catholics naturally feel uneasy with theories that contrast the traditional strength of democracy in the United States, Canada, and the English-speaking Caribbean with Latin America's authoritarian tradition and suggest that Catholic values are inherently more authoritarian than Protestant norms.[42] Similarly, most Muslims and Confucianists reject theories that depict their religions as authoritarian. But do the facts support these hypotheses, however unpleasant some people may find them?

Although Protestant nations are more likely to be democratic than are countries with other religions, and democracy certainly has not fared well in most Islamic nations, it is difficult to ascertain how much these disparities reflect different religious values rather than myriad other historical, economic, and cultural factors that are not easily controlled for. We know that some Islamic cultures *have* sustained democracy. Malaysia, for example, is among Asia's most stable democracies (or, at least, semidemocracies). Indonesia, the world's largest Muslim country, has recently democratized. And in democracies with multiple religions, Muslims are no less democratic than their fellow citizens who follow other religions. For example, the Muslims of India and of Trinidad-Tobago are apparently as committed to democratic values as are their Hindu and Christian counterparts, just as American Catholics are as democratically inclined as American Protestants are. And Bosnia's Muslim population clearly has shown more respect for basic civil liberties and democratic institutions than have their Serbian Christian adversaries.

Even if it could be established that certain religions tend to predispose a population toward democracy or authoritarianism, there is so much variation within particular world religions (for example, Unitarian and Southern Baptist versions of Christianity, or Shi'ia, Sunni, and Sufi branches of Islam), each with a distinct political culture, that it sheds little light to depict Protestant, Muslim, or Buddhist cultures as uniform.

Finally, and most important, religions and national cultures are capable of change and do not permanently mire a country or region in a particular political culture. During World War II, it was widely believed that the Japanese and German political cultures were inherently warlike and authoritarian. Today these countries are highly consolidated democracies whose citizens are more likely to support disarmament or pacifism than Americans are. Not long ago, many analysts felt that Confucian values blocked democratic transitions in East Asia, yet Confucianism has not impeded South Korea's and Taiwan's democratization. The fact that Catholic societies were less hospitable to democracy in the past does not mean that their political values remain the same. Indeed, from Portugal and Spain to Chile, Brazil, and Uruguay, democracy has recently taken root in Catholic nations that not long ago were depicted as culturally authoritarian. Moreover, in recent decades the Church hierarchy itself has been a pivotal voice for democratic change in Catholic countries such as Poland, the Philippines, Chile, and Brazil.

In short, political cultures appear to be far more malleable than previously recognized. And, as Larry Diamond notes, often "democratic culture is as much the product as the cause of effectively functioning democracy."[43] Just as a democratic political culture helps to consolidate democracy, sustained democratic behavior helps society cement democratic values. So, while it may be difficult for some countries to develop a democratic political culture initially, the longer they continue democratic practices, the better are their chances of absorbing democratic values. Indeed, if countries can sustain democracy for two decades, they are unlikely to ever see it fail. Thus, Robert Dahl's examination of 52 countries in which democracy had collapsed identified only two (Chile and Uruguay) that had enjoyed democracy for more than 20 years prior to that collapse.[44] And even those two exceptions have since more successfully reinstituted democracy than have countries such as Bolivia and Peru, which lack comparable democratic traditions. The Czech Republic has enjoyed a similar advantage over its Eastern European neighbors.

CONCLUSION: DEMOCRATIC CONSOLIDATION

What makes democracy endure? Now that a substantial number of developing countries have become democratic, which ones have the qualities to maintain and consolidate democracy? To answer that question, Adam Przeworski and his associates analyzed statistics covering a 40-year period (1950–1990) from 135 different countries.[45] Democracy, they found, is most fragile in poor countries (with per-capita incomes of less than $1,000) and becomes more stable as national income rises. "Above $6,000 [per-capita income], democracies are impregnable and can be expected to live forever; no democratic system has ever fallen in a country where per-capita income exceeds $6,055 (Argentina's level in 1976)."[46] Several factors explain why richer democracies are more likely to endure. For one thing, they have a crucial foundation for democratic government—higher educational levels. For another, class conflicts over the distribution of economic rewards are less intense in more affluent societies.

Przeworski and colleagues found that other economic indicators are also important. Contrary to the beliefs of many political scientists, the faster a nation's economy grows, the more likely it is to sustain democracy. Conversely, democracies suffering economic decline, high inflation rates, or other forms of economic crisis (such as the Russian ruble's collapse in 1998 or Argentina's financial crisis in 2002) are the most likely to become derailed from democratic consolidation. Finally, they found that, surprisingly, international conditions exert a more powerful influence on a country's chances for democratic survival than domestic economic factors do. Specifically, the more prevalent and fashionable democratic government becomes worldwide, the more likely any particular Third World country is to sustain democracy, regardless of its per-capita income, literacy level, or economic growth rate. In other words, as many scholars have suspected, democracy is contagious.

Other analysts have noted that developing and maintaining effective political institutions—representative and responsible political parties, a broad array of interest groups, a representative and influential legislature, a strong but controlled executive branch, an honest and independent judicial system—are absolutely critical for stable and effective democracy. Too often Third World judicial systems are insufficiently independent from the executive branch, have inadequate legal training, and are excessively corrupt. Consolidating democracies need to strengthen the judiciary so that it can stand up to a power-hungry president or prime minister and so that its decisions are respected by the citizens.

Similarly, the legislative branch in many new democracies is too dependent on an overly powerful executive. Even democratically elected leaders often appropriate excessive power upon taking office, assuming that the voters had, in effect, delegated absolute authority to them to govern the country. For example, although elected democratically, presidents Carlos Menem (Argentina) and Alberto Fujimori (Peru) ran roughshod over their nation's congress and court system upon assuming office. For that and other reasons, Juan Linz has found that democracy is more likely to collapse in presidential systems than in countries with parliamentary forms of government.[47]

Finally, emerging democracies need to address serious social and economic injustices that threaten democratic consolidation. Without improved social conditions, democratic governments may be unable to continue commanding the support of the country's poor. In Latin America, where income inequality is high by world standards, the gap between "haves" and "have nots" has generally widened since the region's recent transition to democracy, with the notable exception of Uruguay and possibly Chile. Similarly, the gap between rich and poor has widened greatly in the newly democratizing countries of Eastern Europe and the former Soviet Union. In those countries, much of the deterioration has been caused by an economic transition from communism to a very corrupt form of "crony capitalism." Seeing corrupt and powerful new business tycoons use their government ties to accumulate vast wealth, some 30 percent of Russians apparently yearn for the greater economic security and equality of the old communist regime, no matter how repressive that political system was and no matter how shoddy the quality of consumer goods.

From the Philippines to Pakistan, from Colombia to Peru, the urban and rural poor suffer from highly unequal land and income distribution, pervasive poverty and crime, deficient public health systems, and corrupt and repressive local police. Until such injustices are addressed, democracy will remain incomplete and precarious.

DISCUSSION QUESTIONS

1. Discuss the differences between electoral democracy, liberal democracy, and substantive democracy. Which definition seems most useful to you?
2. What is the "third wave" of democracy, and what accounts for its emergence?
3. Which social classes have historically been most supportive of democracy, and which have been most antagonistic? What kind of class structure is most likely to support democratic consolidation?
4. What is the evidence that some religions are more supportive of democracy than are others? What are the strengths and weaknesses of the argument that there is a link between a country's religion and its potential for democracy?
5. What is the relationship between social and economic development, on the one hand, and political democracy, on the other?
6. What arguments would suggest that the third wave of democratization is coming to an end in the Third World, and what might suggest that more developing nations will become democratic?

NOTES

1. Serbia is a part of the Yugoslav federation, which once included the republics of Croatia, Slovenia, and Bosnia, among others. When those states left Yugoslavia the country was reduced to two republics. In 2002 those two agreed to change the name of the country from Yugoslavia to the Federation of Serbia and Montenegro.

2. Richard Joseph, "Africa: The Rebirth of Political Freedom," in *The Global Resurgence of Democracy*, ed. Larry Diamond and Marc F. Plattner (Baltimore, MD: Johns Hopkins University Press, 1993), pp. 307–320. In retrospect, Joseph's chapter was overly optimistic about Africa's progress toward democracy.

3. By definition, consolidation of democracy reduces military rule. It also lowers the likelihood of revolutionary movements. Greater democracy also should eventually contribute to better conditions for women, the urban poor, and peasants, though those effects are not necessarily apparent immediately.

4. For example, Samuel P. Huntington, *The Third Wave: Democratization in the Late Twentieth Century* (Norman: University of Oklahoma Press, 1991).

5. Colombia is one of Latin America's more enduring electoral democracies, but its government is perhaps the region's worst human rights violator. See *New York Times* (April 26, 1994). Sri Lanka's civil war seems to be nearing an end.

6. Of course, in all democracies some major officials are appointed, such as the justices of the U.S. Supreme Court and members of the U.S. national cabinet. But these people are appointed by a popularly elected official (the president) and are subject to confirmation by the Congress.

7. If this standard is rigorously applied, the United States could not be considered a full democracy prior to the 1960s because large numbers of southern Blacks were barred from voting. In the nineteenth and early twentieth centuries, women could not vote.

8. There has been a long, ongoing debate over what conditions, and how many of those conditions, a country must meet in order to be called a democracy. The definition offered here represents the current consensus and is drawn from the following sources: Philippe C. Schmitter and Terry Lynn Karl, "What Democracy Is . . . and Is Not," *Journal of Democracy* 2, no. 2 (Summer 1991), pp. 75–88; Scott Mainwaring, "Transitions to Democracy and Democratic Consolidation," in *Issues in Democratic Consolidation: The New South American Democracies in Comparative Perspective*, ed. Scott Mainwaring, Guillermo O'Donnell, and Samuel Valenzuela (Notre Dame, IN: University of Notre Dame Press, 1992), pp. 297–298; Robert A. Dahl, *Polyarchy: Participation and Opposition* (New Haven, CT: Yale University Press, 1971); Robert A. Dahl, *Democracy and Its Critics* (New Haven, CT: Yale University Press, 1989); Huntington, *The Third Wave*.

9. Civil society is essentially the array of societal organizations—churches, unions, business groups, farmers' organizations, women's groups, and the like—that influence the political system but operate *independently* of government control. Typically, authoritarian governments attempt to weaken civil society trying to place these groups under government command. So rebuilding and strengthening civil society becomes an essential task for establishing and consolidating democratic government.

10. Huntington, *The Third Wave*, pp. 28–30.

11. Juan Linz and Alfred Stepan, "Toward Consolidated Democracies," in *Consolidating the Third Wave Democracies*, ed. Larry Diamond, Marc F. Plattner, Yun-han Chu, and Hung-mao Tien (Baltimore, MD: Johns Hopkins University Press, 1997), p. 15.

12. Seymour Martin Lipset, *Political Man: The Social Basis of Politics*, expanded and updated ed. (Baltimore, MD: Johns Hopkins University Press, 1980). For a review of such research see Dietrich Rueschemeyer, Evelyne Huber Stephens, and John D. Stephens, *Capitalist Development and Democracy* (Chicago: University of Chicago Press, 1992), chap. 2.

13. Samuel P. Huntington, *Political Order in Changing Societies* (New Haven, CT: Yale University Press, 1968).

14. Mitchell A. Seligson, "Democratization in Latin America: The Current Cycle" in *Authoritarians and Democrats: Regime Transition in Latin America*, ed. James M. Malloy and Mitchell A. Seligson (Pittsburgh, PA: University of Pittsburgh Press, 1987), pp. 7–9.

15. It is generally agreed that the emergence of the middle class and business class (bourgeoisie) in Western Europe was associated with the growth of modern democracy. See, for example, Barrington Moore, Jr., *The Social Origins of Dictatorship and Democracy* (Boston: Beacon Press, 1966). More recently, political scientists such as Rueschemeyer, Huber Stephens, and Stephens, *Capitalist Development*, have emphasized the contributions of organized labor.

16. Of course, even defenders of authoritarian governments had to concede that most dictatorships are not efficient modernizers. Far from it. The developing world has had more than its share of corrupt dictators (Mobutu in Zaire, Somoza in Nicaragua, Marcos in the Philippines) who have stolen millions, run their country's economy into the ground, and wrecked the nation's infrastructure and educational system. What these scholars did claim, however, was that *efficient* dictatorships such as Taiwan or Singapore offered the best hope for modernization. Communists, of course, saw revolutionary dic-

tatorships such as Cuba or China as necessary for greater social equality, improved literacy, better health care systems, and related indicators of modernization.

17. For example, Glen Caudill Dealy, *The Latin Americans, Spirit and Ethos* (Boulder, CO: Westview Press, 1992). The ground-breaking study of political culture was Gabriel A. Almond and Sidney Verba, *The Civic Culture: Political Attitudes and Democracy in Five Nations* (Boston: Little, Brown and Company, 1965), which examined political culture in the United States, Britain, Germany, Italy, and Mexico.

18. Larry Diamond, "Introduction: In Search of Consolidation," in *Consolidating the Third Wave Democracies*, p. xv. The earlier figure as well as most other tallies of democracies found in this chapter come from surveys published annually by Freedom House in their report *Freedom in the World*. While Diamond suggests there were 39 democracies, Samuel Huntington counted only 30 at that time. Huntington's lower total partially reflects the fact that he did not consider countries with a population under 1 million.

19. Huntington, *The Third Wave*, p. 271. That figure includes Turkey, which I have characterized as a less developed country.

20. Huntington, *The Third Wave*.

21. Larry Diamond, *Prospects for Democratic Development in Africa* (Stanford, CA: Hoover Institution Press, 1997), Appendix; Adrian Karatnycky, "The 1999 Freedom House Survey: A Century of Progress," *Journal of Democracy* 11 (January 2000): 187–200.

22. Michael Bratton and Nicolas van de Walle, *Democratic Experiments in Africa: Regime Transitions in Comparative Perspective* (New York: Cambridge University Press, 1997), p. 120.

23. Diamond, *Consolidating the Third Wave Democracies*, p. xvi.

24. Aili Piano and Arch Puddington, "Gains Offset Losses: The 2000 Freedom House Survey," *Journal of Democracy* 12 (January 2001): 87–92.

25. For a broader discussion on international influences favoring democratization, see Laurence Whitehead, ed., *The International Dimensions of Democratization: Europe and the Americas* (New York: Oxford University Press, 1996); Abraham F. Lowenthal, ed., *Exporting Democracy: The United States and Latin America* (Baltimore, MD: Johns Hopkins University Press, 1991).

26. Determining whether democracy has been consolidated (i.e., has become "the only game in town") in any particular country is a judgment call over which experts may disagree. Only the test of time ultimately reveals whether a democratic government endures.

27. Seymour Martin Lipset, *Political Man*, 1st ed. (Garden City, NY: Anchor Books, 1960).

28. Rueschemeyer, Huber Stephens, and Stephens, *Capitalist Development and Democracy*, p. 14.

29. Philips Cutright, "National Political Development: Measurement and Analysis," *American Sociological Review* 28 (April 1963).

30. Axel Hadenius, *Democracy and Development* (New York: Cambridge University Press, 1992).

31. United Nations Development Programme, *Human Development Report, 1997* (New York: Oxford University Press, 1997), pp. 24–26.

32. Seligson, "Democratization in Latin America: The Current Cycle."

33. Huntington, *Political Order in Changing Societies*. On the rise of repressive authoritarian regimes in Latin America's most industrialized nations, see Guillermo O'Donnell, *Modernization and Bureaucratic Authoritarianism* (Berkeley, CA: Institute of International Studies, 1973).

34. Barrington Moore, *The Social Origins*, p. 418.

35. Rueschemeyer, Huber Stephens, and Stephens, *Capitalist Development and Democracy*.

36. South Korea and Taiwan have subsequently democratized, but Singapore still has not.

37. Stephen White, "Russia's Experiment with Democracy," *Current History* 91 (October 1992): 313.

38. Robert Dahl, "Development and Democratic Culture," in *Consolidating the Third Wave Democracies*, p. 34.

39. Kenneth A. Bollen and Robert Jackman, "Economic and Non-economic Determinants of Political Democracy in the 1960s," in *Research in Political Sociology*, ed. R. G. Braungart (Greenwich, CT: Jai Press, 1985).

40. Hadenius, *Democracy and Development*, pp. 118–119.

41. Samuel P. Huntington, "Will More Countries Be Democratic?" *Political Science Quarterly* 99 (1984): 193–218; Huntington, *The Clash of Civilizations and the Remaking of World Order* (New York: Simon & Schuster, 1996).

42. For an argument along those lines, see Dealy, *The Latin Americans*.

43. Larry Diamond, "Three Paradoxes of Democracy," in *The Global Resurgence of Democracy*, p. 104.

44. Robert A. Dahl, "The Newer Democracies: From the Time of Triumph to the Time of Troubles," in ed. Daniel N. Nelson, *After Authoritarianism: Democracy or Disorder?* (Westport, CT: Greenwood Press, 1995), p. 7.

45. Adam Przeworski et al., "What Makes Democracies Endure?" in *Consolidating Third Wave Democracies*, ed. Larry Diamond et al., pp. 295–311.

46. Ibid., p. 297. All dollar figures are in constant dollars, meaning that they are adjusted for inflation so that a per-capita income of $1,000 in 1960 and 1990 is actually equivalent.

47. Juan Linz and Arturo Valenzuela, eds., *The Failure of Presidential Democracy* (Baltimore, MD: Johns Hopkins University Press, 1994).

chapter 3

Religion and Politics

The rise of urban civilization and the collapse of traditional religion are the two main hallmarks of our civilization and are closely related. . . . What is secularization? . . . It is the loosening of the world from religion. . . . The gods of traditional religions live on . . . but they play no role whatever in the public life of the secular metropolis. . . .[1]

This death knell for traditional religion was sounded in the 1960s, not by an opponent of religion, but by one of America's preeminent Protestant theologians, Harvey Cox. He was not predicting the demise of religion per se, but rather of its traditional form, including its historic role in politics and other forms of public life. Cox's influential book *The Secular City* coincided with the observations and predictions of social scientists at that time. And while religion obviously remained a pervasive force in the Third World, secularization of society seemed inevitable there as well.

In Latin America the Catholic church no longer exercised nearly as much control over education as it once did. Following independence, the government of India tried to ameliorate the injustices of the caste system, a cornerstone of Hindu religious practice. And in the Middle East, modernizing regimes in Egypt, Iraq, and Syria created more secular political systems. Accordingly, one leading authority, Donald Eugene Smith, observed, "Political development includes, as one of its basic processes, the secularization of politics, the progressive exclusion of religion from the political system."[2]

Generally speaking, early modernization theorists viewed religion as an impediment to political and economic development, while dependency theorists deemed it so unimportant as to warrant only an occasional footnote in their writings (see Chapter 1). Since the time Cox and Smith chronicled its decline, however, religion has been an unexpectedly resilient political force, withstanding the onslaughts of modernization, and even, at times, being stimulated by it. As David Little observed, "Modernization was supposed to mean the gradual decline and eventual disappearance of religion from public life, but, as we know, that hasn't happened. . . . Religion is very much alive as a part of politics."[3] In fact, since the 1970s much of the Third World, and the developed world too, for that matter, has experienced a religious resurgence intensifying the role of religion in the political arena.[4] In the Middle East, "ironically, the technological tools of modernization have often served to reinforce traditional belief and practice as religious leaders who initially opposed modernization now use radio, television, audio- and videotapes to preach and disseminate. . . ."[5]

Nowhere is that more apparent than in the Middle East and parts of Asia, where a renewal of Islamic fundamentalism (or *Islamism*, the term preferred by many analysts) has had a dramatic political impact on Afghanistan, Iran, Lebanon, Algeria, Egypt, and Pakistan. The seizure of American hostages in Iran and Lebanon, the assassination of Egyptian President Anwar Sadat, the bombings of a U.S. military housing installation in Saudi Arabia and of two U.S. embassies in East Africa, and, especially, the attacks on the World Trade Center and the Pentagon have all focused Western attention on "religion and politics." In fact, with the collapse of Soviet communism and the end of the Cold War, many politicians and journalists labeled radical (militant) Islamic fundamentalism as the greatest threat to Western security. Even before the 1991 Gulf War, a Gallup Poll survey revealed that 37 percent of British respondents expected a war in the 1990s between Muslims and Christians.[6] The war in Afghanistan and Al Qaeda have revived such sentiments. While these perceptions are often based on prejudice and misunderstanding, the discussion of Islamic and Hindu fundamentalism later in this chapter indicates some valid reason for concern.

THE MEETING OF CHURCH AND STATE

Many of our preconceptions about religion and politics are based on serious misunderstandings, both of our own government and of political systems elsewhere. Americans generally accept a constitutional separation between church and state as natural. Such formal barriers, however, do not exist in many industrial democracies or LDCs. Moreover, even in the United States, religious organizations and beliefs continue to influence political behavior. Black Baptist churches, for example, have always been in the forefront of the American civil rights movement. Recently, conflicts over issues such as school prayer and abortion have led one expert to observe that "far from rendering religion largely irrelevant to politics . . . the structure of [American] government . . . may actually encourage a high degree of interaction."[7] Most Western European nations, though more secular than the United States in most aspects of everyday life, have not built walls between religion and politics. In Britain, for example, the Anglican church (or Church of England) is the official state religion. The Catholic church was closely linked to the Italian Christian Democratic Party, once that nation's leading party.[8]

Religion is more firmly embedded in most Third World cultures, and its impact on politics is correspondingly more pronounced than is ours. Indeed, religion is so central to traditional values that we often identify national or regional cultures by the predominant religion: Buddhist culture in Thailand, Confucian culture in China and Korea, Hindu culture in much of India and Nepal, and Islamic culture in North Africa and the Middle East.[9]

The blending of religion and politics is most apparent in theocratic states such as Iran where, since that nation's 1979 Islamic revolution, public policy has been shaped by the Shi'ite clergy. But it is also significant in Islamic fundamentalist states like Sudan, and more moderate Muslim nations such as Pakistan and Saudi Arabia. Afghanistan's Taliban government was a religious movement that made politics totally subservient to religion. In Brazil and Nicaragua, the theology of liberation, espoused by progressive members of the Catholic church, motivated priests and nuns to organize the poor against economic and political injustices. And in India, the Bharatiya Janata Party (BJP), currently the country's largest political party and head of its governing coalition, carries the torch of Hindu fundamentalism.

GREAT RELIGIONS OF THE THIRD WORLD

Four of the world's "great religions" are predominant in the Third World. *Catholicism*, the only major religion to have penetrated extensively into both the industrial democracies and the developing world, is preeminent throughout the Philippines and Latin America, while also representing important portions of the population in countries such as Lebanon and parts of Sub-Saharan Africa. *Hinduism* is confined primarily to India, along with neighboring Nepal and parts of Sri Lanka. *Buddhism* is a major factor in East Asia and Southeast Asia, along with parts of South Asia. Finally, *Islam*, the world's second largest religion, predominates across a broad span of Asia, the Middle East, and Africa, stretching from Indonesia in the east through Pakistan and Bangladesh in the Indian subcontinent, the former Soviet republics of Central Asia, the Middle East, and North Africa. It also represents about half the population of Malaysia and Nigeria, as well as substantial minorities in countries as far flung as the Philippines, Tanzania, and Trinidad.[10]

To be sure, not everyone in the developing world subscribes to one of these major religions. Protestantism is the leading religion in the English-speaking islands of the Caribbean and represents important minorities in a number of other LDCs. Confucianism still influences Chinese society, even after its revolution. Christian Orthodox minorities are significant in Lebanon and Egypt, and a large portion of Black Africa's population believes in local traditional religions (animism). The impact of these religions on politics, however, is more limited. Consequently, this chapter limits its analysis to the four global religions described earlier, with particular emphasis on Islam and Catholicism.

None of the Third World's major religions is monolithic, though the Catholic church, with its doctrine of papal infallibility and its hierarchical structure, comes closest. Buddhism has two major schools, each basing its doctrines on different ancient texts. Theravada ("Way of Elders") Buddhism, practiced in Myanmar (Burma), Sri Lanka (Ceylon), Thailand, Laos, and Cambodia, is believed to be closer to the original teachings of the Buddha. Mahayana ("Great Vehicle") Buddhism emerged in China, Japan, Korea, Vietnam, and Tibet.[11]

Perhaps the most import division within Islam is between its Sunni and Shi'ite branches, although Sufism is also of some importance. The split between them, dating to the period following the death of the Prophet Muhammad, centered on the issues of "who should succeed him and the nature of the successor's role" spiritually and politically.[12] Ninety percent of the Muslim population is Sunni, while Shi'ism, which has drawn great attention in the West because of its periodic nationalistic and militant manifestations, accounts for only about 8 percent. Shi'ism is the dominant faith only in Iran, where it is centered. But it also represents 50 to 60 percent of Iraq's population, a plurality in Lebanon, and significant minorities in Afghanistan, Pakistan, Syria, Kuwait, and other Gulf states. In countries having both significant Sunni and Shi'ite populations, there are commonly sharp political and cultural tensions between the two.[13]

Even religions that have no formal divisions experience important political differences. Latin American Catholics span the ideological spectrum from right-wing followers of *opus dei* to radical adherents of liberation theology. In the name of God and anticommunism, some Latin American Catholics have supported fascist movements, rightist death squads, and repressive military regimes. Conversely, in the name of God and social justice, other Catholic priests and nuns have supported the Sandinista revolution in Nicaragua, fought with Marxist guerrillas in Colombia, and politically organized the poor in the slums of Brazil and Peru.

RELIGION, MODERNITY, AND SECULARIZATION

We have already observed that modernization does not necessarily produce a decline in religious observance, at least not in the short run. What about the other side of the relationship? That is, what is the impact of religion on modernity? Here again, early theorists felt they were incompatible. "It is widely, and correctly, assumed," said Donald Smith, "that religion is in general an obstacle to modernization."[14] In the realm of politics, this interpretation suggested that the intrusion of religious institutions into government impedes the development of a modern state. Others associated traditional Catholic, Islamic, and Hindu beliefs with authoritarian values.

Subsequently, political scientists have developed a more nuanced understanding. Religious institutions may inhibit development in some respects, while encouraging it in others. For example, all of the great religions have legitimized the state's authority at some point in history. As nations modernize their political systems, religious authorities or groups may oppose important aspects of change (Hindu and Islamic fundamentalists, for example), or they may offer explicit or tacit support (Islamic leaders in Indonesia and Catholic clergy in Chile). No longer facilely dismissing religion's possible contribution to development, many scholars have now credited Confucianism with facilitating East Asia's rapid modernization in recent decades.[15] Specifically, they have noted that religion's work ethic and spirit of cooperation.

Depending on their theology and structure, individual religions may either bolster or impede government development initiatives. Different religions emphasize distinctive values; thus, states wishing to create welfare programs based on communal responsibility (i.e., programs tied to ethnic communities) often receive strong support from Islamic leaders or the Catholic church. At the same time, modernizing political leaders who emphasize individual rights and responsibilities find those values warmly received by Buddhist monks. Ultimately, then, organized religions can strengthen the modern nation-state by bestowing legitimacy and by disseminating the government's political message. Should religious leaders oppose the state, however, they can often delegitimize the political system.[16]

The argument that political modernization requires secularization has two components, one empirical and the other normative. The *empirical* component notes that as Western societies modernized (i.e., became more literate, urban, institutionally organized, and industrial), their political systems invariably became more secular. In effect, there has been a specialization of functions. Increasingly, the state has controlled politics, while the church has overseen religion, and each has refrained from interfering in the other one's realm. Political scientists anticipated that as the Third World modernized, it would experience the same division of responsibilities. The related *normative* assumption holds that secularization is not only a common trend, but it is also *desirable* since it increases religious freedom, reduces the likelihood of state persecution of religious minorities, and permits the state to make more rational decisions free of religious bias.

We have already indicated the weakness of the first assumption. To be sure, modernization has induced political secularization in many developing countries, such as Turkey and Argentina. But elsewhere it has not altered church-state relations; indeed, it has precipitated a religious backlash when pursued too rapidly. Saudi Arabia, India, and Iran illustrate three possible governmental approaches to managing the forces of modernization. In the most cautious approach, the Saudi royal family has introduced far-reaching socioeconomic changes but has carefully controlled the style of modernization in order to preserve a very traditionalist Islamic culture and maintain the close links between Islam and the state. India represents an intermediate case, where the modernization of politics and constitutional secularization were generally accepted (at least until recently). Religious factors in India do affect government in some respects; thus, Hindus and Muslims are governed by distinct legal norms in areas such as family law. And while the prime minister's post has always been held by a Hindu (the religious majority), the largely ceremonial presidency has been reserved for a Muslim. Iran represents the most marked example of religious backlash against modernization and a relinking of church and state. As we shall see, the Shah (emperor) imposed rapid Western-style socioeconomic development (including "unveiling" women), which destabilized society and helped precipitate radical Islamic revivalism.

At an individual level, many people in Africa, Asia, and the Middle East have defied the notion that more educated and professionally trained citizens will be less religiously orthodox. For example, Hindu and Islamic fundamentalist activists in India, Afghanistan, and Egypt are frequently educated professionals, not poor uneducated peasants.[17] Most of the terrorists who attacked the Pentagon and World Trade Center in 2001 were relatively well-educated and middle class. Nor are traditional religious values and modern technology necessarily incompatible. In Iran, opponents of the Shah undermined his authority by distributing audiotapes of Ayatollah Ruhollah Khomeini's political message throughout the country. Once in power, the theocratic government made extensive use of television and other modern technologies to maintain its influence.

Normative evaluations of the church-state relationship need to be more complex than early development theory had assumed. Clearly, some religious influences contradict accepted norms of modernity, as when they induce political leaders to violate the rights of religious minorities (or majorities). Iran's Islamic government, for example, has persecuted members of the Baha'i faith.[18] In Guatemala, the government of General Efraín Rios Montt, a right-wing Evangelical, converted Catholic peasants to Protestantism at virtual gunpoint. Similarly, religiously inspired restrictions on racial minorities or women (such as the Taliban's prohibitions against Afghan girls and women working or attending school) are clearly antithetical to modernization.

Can one infer from such cases, however, that there need always be a strict wall between politics and religion or between clerics and politicians? The same people who lamented the political activities of Catholic priests in Nicaragua and Brazil, the protest marches by Buddhist monks in Sri Lanka, or the fundamentalist government in Afghanistan, may have cheered political involvement by the Reverend Martin Luther King, Jr., or the Reverend Jerry Falwell in the United States.

Ultimately, most people's normative evaluations of religion's role in politics are influenced by whether that religious activity furthers the goals and policies they believe in. Perhaps this is as it should be. The recent histories of Iran and Tibet illustrate this point well. Iran has been a theocracy (a religiously driven political system) since its 1979 revolution, just as Tibet had been prior to its absorption by China in the 1950s. Each has had a political system "in which the political structures are clearly subordinate to the ecclesiastical establishment."[19] Yet the world has judged them quite differently.

Under the leadership of the Ayatollah Khomeini and the Islamic mullahs (clerics) who succeeded him, Iran has become an international outcast because of its repression of civil liberties, persecution of religious minorities, interference in the affairs of neighboring countries, and support for international terrorism. Until the late 1950s, Tibetan politics was also dominated by clerics.[20] Viewed as divine by his people, the Dalai Lama had been the country's secular and spiritual leader. Buddhist monks held key posts in the government bureaucracy. Because of Tibetan Buddhism's record of pacifism and tolerance, however, theocratic rule aroused no foreign indignation. Indeed, the world was appalled when China occupied Tibet and secularized the state. Since that time the Dalai Lama's long struggle to free his people has won him worldwide admiration and the Nobel Peace Prize. All of this suggests that the issue of separation of church and state may be less important than the way in which "the church" uses its political influence when it holds power.

STRUCTURAL AND THEOLOGICAL BASES OF CHURCH-STATE RELATIONS

The extent to which religions influence political attitudes and behavior and the degree of political involvement by organized religions vary considerably from place to place. Just as the separation of church and state in Western Europe has historically been more clearly defined in predominantly Protestant nations (for example, Denmark and Britain) than in Catholic ones (Italy and Spain), the political impact of the Third World's four major religions also differs. Two factors are particularly relevant: the particular religion's theological view on the relationship between temporal and spiritual matters, and the degree of hierarchical structure within the religion. The second factor refers to how well organized and centrally controlled a religion is.

Donald Smith distinguishes two different types of religio-political systems: the organic and the church. In the first case, the *organic* system, the clergy is insufficiently organized to challenge the country's political leaders who are, consequently, less restricted by religious institutions. Examples of organic systems include the Hindu and most Sunni Islamic cultures. *Church* religio-political systems, on the other hand, have a well-organized ecclesiastical structure that exercises considerable authority over politics. Such churches include Catholicism, Shi'ite Islam, and sometimes Buddhism (in countries such as Tibet and Burma). All have more formalized relations between church and state, with greater potential for religious challenges to the political order or political domination of the church than in organic systems. In some church systems, the state dominates the religious order; in others, the church dominates; and yet in others, there is an equal partnership.[21]

Islam

From its inception in seventh-century Arabia, Islam was a "religio-political movement in which religion was integral to state and society."[22] Perhaps more than any other great religion, traditional Islam usually recognized no borderline between religion and politics. On the one hand, the Islamic faith and its clergy legitimized the state. At the same time, however, the political leadership recognized the supremacy of Islamic law, called the *Shariah* (path of God). Thus, prior to the intrusion of colonialism, Muslims assumed that they lived in an Islamic state. Since religious Muslims believe that God wants them to live in a community governed in accordance with the Quran (divinely revealed law, much of it temporal), the very concept of separating church and state is alien to their culture. This does not mean that traditional Islamic culture and theology were inhospitable to other religions. Perhaps because it accepted Jewish and Christian scriptures and drew from both of those religions since its inception, Islam was often highly tolerant of other faiths. During the Middle Ages, for example, the large Jewish community in Muslim-controlled Spain enjoyed perhaps their greatest period of freedom and influence anywhere in Europe.[23] But even then, ultimate political authority remained Muslim.

The bond between Islam and politics remains strong in most Muslim societies today, though there is considerable variation. John Esposito distinguishes three types of Islamic regimes: the secular state, the Islamic state, and the Muslim state.[24] Turkey is perhaps the most noted *secular state* in the Islamic world. Starting in the 1920s, Mustafa Kemal Ataturk (the father of modern Turkey) ousted the sultan of the Ottoman Empire, abolished the basis of the sultan's religious authority, emancipated women, closed seminaries, and westernized Turkish society in many ways. Today, Turkey is not fully secularized because its constitution still endorses belief in God, but the political system offers Islam no special status and, in fact, prohibits certain traditional Islamic practices.[25]

During the 1980s and 1990s, however, an Islamic political party, the Refah (Welfare) Party steadily gained strength, particularly among residents of Turkey's urban slums, who had migrated from the countryside to large cities and had found modern, secular culture difficult, corrupt, and oppressive. As its name indicates, the Welfare Party gained considerable support among the poor by offering them social services that the government had failed to provide. In the 1995 parliamentary elections, Refah won the largest number of seats, setting off a frantic effort by Turkey's other major parties to exclude it from power. When those parties were unable to put together a stable governing coalition, Refah formed the new government. Despite its sometimes radical and inflammatory rhetoric, the Welfare Party's policies in office were relatively moderate when compared to those of many other Islamic parties in the region. Still, its program of religious reforms—including a proposed amendment eliminating the constitutional ban on religious dress so as to allow female students to cover their hair with scarves at school—was unacceptable to the powerful Turkish military, which views itself as the guardian of the country's secular tradition. In 1998, the military forced parliament to remove the Welfare Party from office and dissolve it as a legal political party.[26]

At the other end of the spectrum, *Islamic states* base their governing philosophies on the Quran and other Islamic law. Taliban Afghanistan, Iran, and Saudi Arabia are among the best-known examples, but Sudan, Pakistan, and Libya also fall in this category. These regimes can be quite distinct from each other. Whereas Iran subscribes to Shi'ite Islam, the other countries are all primarily Sunni. Afghanistan (until the recent war), Libya, Iran, and Sudan have pursued militantly anti-Western foreign policies and have supported terrorism, while Saudi Arabia is quite conservative and closely allied to the West. The new, post-Taliban government in Afghanistan is likely to be Islamic, moderate, and somewhat tied to the West. Thus, the term *Islamic state* (like the concept of fundamentalism) must be used carefully to avoid creating artificial categories that hide more than they reveal.

Finally, *Muslim states*, such as Egypt and Morocco, occupy an intermediate position on church-state relations and the role of religion. Unlike secular states, they identify Islam as the official religion and require the head of state to be Muslim. However, the impact of religion on politics is far more limited than in Islamic states. For example, unlike Taliban Afghanistan and Iran, political leaders are not clerics, and some are even non-Muslims. In Iraq and Egypt, Christians have served as foreign ministers or deputy foreign ministers (most notably, Egypt's Boutros Boutros-Ghali, who later served as secretary general of the United Nations), and many of the founders of Syria's ruling Baath party were Christians. Christians also occupy high posts in the Palestinian Authority.

Catholicism

More than any other major religion, Catholicism has a well-defined and hierarchical ecclesiastical structure that enables it to have a great impact on the political order. At the Church's apex is the Pope, whose authority is unchallenged and whose pronouncements on matters of faith and morals are believed to be infallible. Consequently, papal declarations can carry considerable political weight. For example, many of the twentieth-century, Catholic-based reform movements in Latin America can be traced to Pope Leo XII's 1891 encyclical, *Rerum Novarum*, which included an indictment of early capitalism's exploitation of the working class. Within each country, the Church hierarchy is headed by bishops, who often have tremendous political influence in Latin America and in Catholic countries such as the Philippines.

Like Islam in the Middle East, Catholicism used to be the state religion in most Latin American countries. For example, in Colombia as recently as 1953, government treaties with the Vatican gave the Church special authority in areas such as education.[27] Over the years, however, most Latin American nations either ceased having an official state religion or have rendered the link unimportant. Still, Church doctrine has generally supported the established political regime and helped legitimize it. "The ruling powers," said one encyclical, "are invested with a sacredness more than human. . . . Obedience is not the servitude of man to man, but submission to the will of God."[28]

That does not mean, however, that the Church has always supported the government. Over the years, there have been periodic clashes between the two, most notably when the state challenged Church authority in areas such as education. In the Philippines, Church support of Corazón Aquino's political reform movement helped topple the dictatorship of Ferdinand Marcos. Similarly, Catholic authorities opposed conservative military dictatorships in Brazil and Chile during the 1970s and 1980s. Church relationships with Marxist regimes in Cuba and Nicaragua were often tense, though relations with Castro's government have improved substantially since the Pope's visit to Cuba.[29] And in El Salvador, Archbishop Romero spoke out forcefully against the regime's severe human-rights violations in the 1980s. Shortly after one of his most powerful pronouncements, Romero was assassinated by the military. In other countries, however, the local hierarchy has been far more cautious about criticizing the government.

Hinduism and Buddhism

Asia's organic religions, Hinduism and Buddhism, generally have been less directly involved in politics than have Catholicism and Islam. (India's powerful BJP, a Hindu party, is not a part of the Hindu religious order.) Of course, Hinduism's cultural and philosophical values, most notably the caste system, have affected Indian and Nepalese politics profoundly. For example, the king of Nepal is worshiped as the incarnation of the god Vishnu.[30] But the religion is so diverse, composed of local religious groups, cults, and sects loosely tied together by a common set of beliefs, that there is no centralized political influence. Moreover, although there are gurus, holy men, temple priests, and even a priestly caste (Brahmans, though most of them no longer choose to be priests), there is no ecclesiastical organization.

Buddhism grew out of the Hindu religion in the sixth century B.C., emerging from the teachings of a Nepalese prince, Siddartha Gautama, who later came to be known as the Buddha (Enlightened One). Though greatly influenced by Hinduism, Buddhism rejects one of its basic tenets, the caste system. Indeed, as Buddhism spread through Asia, one of its great appeals was its egalitarian outlook. Today, many of India's untouchables continue to leave Hinduism for Buddhism, a religion far more hospitable to them.[31] Buddhism differs from Hinduism in having an organized ecclesiastical organization, namely the *sangha* (the monastic orders). In some countries, such as Myanmar, each sangha has its own leader, providing a hierarchical structure. Still, when compared to the Roman Catholic church or the mullahs of Shi'ite Islam, Buddhism's religious structure is less centralized and, thus, less able to impact the political system.

To be sure, Buddhist and Hindu groups sometimes have strongly influenced their nation's politics. During the early 1960s, Burma was declared a Buddhist state, though that was terminated after a few years. Protests led by Buddhist monks during that decade also helped topple three successive South Vietnamese leaders in a short period of time.[32] Monks have led major protests against government human-rights violations in Tibet, Myanmar, and Thailand as well. The modern liberator of India, Mahatma Gandhi, drew upon reformist Hindu theology when demanding greater equality for untouchables and the lower castes. Conversely, the Bharatiya Janata Party (BJP), currently heading the Indian government, and other contemporary fundamentalist Hindu groups support the traditional caste system.

In addition to having less hierarchically organized ecclesiastical orders, Eastern religions are less theologically oriented toward political involvement than are Catholicism and Islam. Their otherworldly philosophy places less emphasis on such temporal matters as politics; hence, the remainder of this chapter focuses more heavily on the political impact of Islam and Catholicism in the Third World.

RELIGIOUS FUNDAMENTALISM: ISLAM AND HINDUISM

No manifestation of religious influence on Third World politics has attracted more attention or inspired more fear and loathing than Islamic fundamentalism. Highly influential Washington columnists such as *U.S. News and World Report*'s Morton Zuckerman and the *New Republic*'s Charles Krauthammer have warned of "religious Stalinism" and a fanatical international movement orchestrated from Iran.[33] Nor are such concerns limited to Westerners. They are frequently expressed by the leaders of moderate Muslim nations who find themselves under siege from militant fundamentalists. Thus, for example, Tunisia's president, Zine Abidine Ben Ali, cautioned about a "fundamentalist international" financed by Iran and Sudan.[34]

The horrific September 11, 2001 plane highjackings and attacks on the World Trade Center and the Pentagon confirmed the world's worst nightmares about Islamic fundamentalist terrorism. However, most experts on Islam maintain that it is unfair to blame a major world religion that has hundreds of millions of adherents for the actions of a small minority. President George W. Bush and other leading U.S. government officials went out of their way to make that very point in the days after the attack. Some people have noted that blaming the Islamic religion for Osama bin Laden's actions would suggest that we should hold Christianity responsible for violent actions taken in the name of that religion. Recall that David Koresh and the Branch Davidians in Waco, Texas, claimed to be acting in the name of Christianity, as did "pro-life" extremists who bombed abortion clinics, killing workers inside, or assassinated doctors.

Others scholars further argue that not all Islamic fundamentalists support violence. Indeed, many of them reject the very term "fundamentalism" to describe current militant revivals. The word, they charge, may falsely imply the existence of a unified threat to the West and, in the case of Islam, it lumps together groups and regimes that have little in common, such as conservative Saudi Arabia and radical Libya. Instead, these analysts prefer such terms as "revivalism" or "militancy" or "Islamist movements" rather than Islamic fundamentalism.[35] Still, a number of leading authorities accept and even use the label "fundamentalism" in their writings.[36] Fred Halliday notes that "there are some problems with applying the term fundamentalist to Muslim movements, but with the necessary caveats it can legitimately be so used."[37] In this chapter I use "fundamentalism" because of its common usage in contemporary political discourse. On occasion, however, I employ the term "revivalism" interchangeably (referring to the desire to revive the true faith) or use "Islamism" to refer to Islamic fundamentalism.

Semantic questions aside, experts such as John Esposito and Fred Halliday warn that whatever labels they use, Western writers too often distort and exaggerate the nature of the "Islamic threat."[38] Many of these writers also seem unaware of a long tradition of liberal theology within Islam that has advocated religious tolerance, progress for women, and democratic values.[39]

> At the very core of this supposed challenge or conflict lie confusions: the mere fact of peoples being "Islamic" . . . [has been confused] with that of their adhering to beliefs and policies that are . . . "Islamist" or "fundamentalist." It has been assumed . . . that most Muslims seek to impose a political program supposedly derived from their religion. The fact that most Muslims are not supporters of Islamist movements is obscured.[40]

Clearly, the recent upsurge in Islamist terrorism in Israel, the United States, and elsewhere (including the September 11 attacks on the World Trade Center and the Pentagon) indicate that though it is wrong, as Esposito and Halliday insist, to speak of an "Islamic threat," it is reasonable to speak of an "Islamic *fundamentalist* threat." Hopefully, this chapter's discussion of Islamic (as well as Hindu) fundamentalism conveys that distinction. When I discuss Islamic and Hindu revivalism at some length, two caveats should be kept in mind: most Muslims and Hindus are not fundamentalists, and not all fundamentalists are repressive at home or violent abroad.

Defining and Explaining Fundamentalism

> Fundamentalism is the . . . effort to define the fundamentals of a religious system and adhere to them. One of the cardinal tenets of Islamic fundamentalism is to protect the purity of Islamic precepts from the adulteration of speculative exercises. Related to [Islamic] fundamentalism is . . . revival or resurgence, a renewed interest in Islam. Behind all this is a drive to purify Islam in order to release all its vital force.[41]

The precise meaning of fundamentalism varies somewhat from religion to religion.[42] But revivalists do share certain points of view across religions. To begin with, they all wish to preserve their religion's traditional worldview and resist the efforts of religious liberals to reform it. They also desire to revive the role of religion in private and public life, including politics, lifestyle, and dress.

In the developing world, fundamentalism usually appeals particularly to people who are disgusted by the inequalities and injustices in their country's political-economic system. This disgust reflects popular revulsion against local political and economic elites, against pervasive corruption and repression. In Lebanon the radical Hizbullah grew out of Shi'ite resentment against the economically powerful Christian community, as well as anger against Israel and the West. In India, the BJP attracts much of its support from voters (including some non-Hindus) embittered by government corruption. And in Algeria, Egypt, and the Sudan, militant fundamentalists expanded their support as a result of the government repression directed against them.[43] Ironically, then, many Muslims and Hindus are attracted to radical fundamentalism for the same reasons that drew Latin Americans to Marxist movements.

Radical fundamentalists also tend to be nationalist or chauvinistic, rejecting "outside" influences they feel challenge or pollute their culture and their true faith. Western culture is perceived as particularly deleterious, with its immodest dress, films, and music that allegedly promote promiscuous sex, drugs, and the like. But Western values are rejected for another reason. For years government leaders such as the Shah of Iran and Egypt's President Anwar Sadat promoted Western-style modernization as the route to national development. After decades of failed development in the Middle East, North Africa, and other parts of the Third World, however, many of those regions' citizens feel that they were deceived and must look elsewhere for answers to their problems.

Fundamentalists: Radical and Conservative

Finally, a distinction must be made between radical and conservative fundamentalists. Radicals, inspired by a "sacred rage," feel that they are conducting a holy war against forces that threaten to corrupt their fundamental religious values.[44] As a Hizbullah manifesto declared, "We have risen to liberate our country, to drive the imperialists and the invaders out of it and to take our fate in our own hands."[45] Holy war was first waged by Islamic mujahadeen in Afghanistan against the country's Soviet occupiers as well as the Afghan Marxist government, which Soviet troops defended.[46] Iran's Ayatollah Khomeini declared a *jihad* (holy war) against both the United States ("the great Satan") and Soviet communism. Elsewhere, the battle has been waged against internal enemies as well. Having been denied an almost certain electoral victory in 1992 (the military canceled the elections after the first round), Algeria's fundamentalist Islamic Salvation Front (FIS) attacked the nation's armed forces, police, and secular politicians, as well as foreigners.[47] More violent militants, most notably the Armed Islamic Group (GIA), also launched massive terrorist attacks on civilians, often mixing banditry with supposed religious warfare. From 1992 through early 2001, more than 100,000 people were killed either by armed Islamic groups or by the Algerian military and its allied civilian militias, which reacted with equal savagery. In India, Hindu fundamentalists have periodically directed their rage against the country's Muslim minority. (For a more detailed discussion of the massive communal violence between Hindus and Muslims in the post-independence period, see Chapter 4.) Because these are perceived to be holy wars against a grave threat, religious radicals feel justified in attacking their Muslim neighbors in India, or killing 3,000 people in New York City, or pronouncing a *fatwah* (religious edict) sentencing author Salman Rushdie to death for having written *The Satanic Verses*.

Such radical militancy contrasts with the views and behavior of conservative fundamentalists, including Hasidic Jews and Saudi Arabian princes, who do not envision themselves in such a battle. They too wish to shield their flocks from unwanted outside influences, but they do not view adherents of other religions or nonfundamentalist members of their own faith as enemies.[48]

In recent years, radical Islamic fundamentalists have become a major political force in Middle Eastern and North African countries such as Algeria, Lebanon, and Sudan. Afghanistan's Taliban government was perhaps the world's most rigidly fundamentalist, prohibiting girls and women, for example, from attending school or being employed and banning television, sports, and dancing. They also sheltered Osama bin Laden and his Al Qaeda terrorist group. Until that group's attack on the World Trade Center and the Pentagon, however, nowhere had radical Islamic fundamentalism had a greater international impact than in Iran. Moreover, more than Afghanistan and well before the emergence of bin Laden, the Iranian revolution had been a beacon for other revivalist movements throughout the Muslim world.

"Sacred Rage": Radical Fundamentalism and the Iranian Revolution

The origins of the Iranian revolution can be traced to the early decades of the twentieth century, with the Muslim clergy's ongoing resistance to secular modernization imposed by the royal family.[49] Military, political, and economic intervention by a series of foreign powers—Czarist Russia, Britain, and finally, the United States—turned the country into "a virtual protectorate" and made the ruling Shahs (emperors) appear to be tools of the great powers.[50] Indeed, the last Shah, Mohammad Reza Pahlavi, was placed on the throne in 1941 by a joint Soviet-British invasion and restored to power by the CIA in 1953 after he had been briefly ousted. Not surprisingly, resentment against foreign domination was later to become an important component of the Islamic revolution.

During the 1920s and 1930s, Shah Reza Khan antagonized the Muslim mullahs (religious clergy) with a series of reforms.[51] Seeking to reinvigorate the country's ancient (pre-Islamic) Persian traditions, he needlessly slighted Islamic cultural practices of Arabic origin, a practice that his son continued.[52] At the same time, influenced both by the West and the secularization of Turkey, he prohibited the veiling of women, opened all public places to women, required Western dress for both sexes, limited the mullahs' economic resources, and established state control over schools, courts, and taxes that previously had been controlled by the clergy. This secularization of society and its accompanying diminution of Islamic power inspired the quiet opposition of a popular young mullah, Ruhollah Khomeini.

In the decades after he assumed the royal throne in 1941, Shah Mohammad Reza Pahlavi accelerated his father's policies, funneling the country's massive oil wealth into one of the Third World's most ambitious modernization programs. In 1963, prodded by the United States, he launched a "White Revolution" involving land reform, expanded literacy, voting rights for women, and other socioeconomic reforms. In the United States, the Shah was hailed as a progressive modernizer. Thus, when President Jimmy Carter visited Iran in 1977 (only two years before the Islamic revolution), he praised the monarch for establishing "an island of stability in one of the more troubled areas of the world." "This is a great tribute to you, Your Majesty," added Carter, "and to . . . the respect, admiration and love which your people give to you."[53]

To be sure, the land reform had benefited some three million peasants, education had expanded greatly, and oil wealth had doubled the size of the middle class.[54] By 1976, Iran had the highest GNP per capita in the developing world. At the same time, however, the gap between rich and poor had widened, and the government was widely resented for its corruption and repression. Indeed, the Shah's secret police (SAVAK) had a well-deserved international reputation for torture and brutality. At the same time, the Islamic clergy opposed some of the government's progressive changes, like land reform, which cost the religious community substantial revenue. Even Iranians who had become more affluent frequently felt psychologically wounded by the pace of Westernization. The Shah was widely viewed as a tool of American neocolonialism. The mullahs, supported by other religious Muslims, objected to the erosion of their political influence, the progressive secularization of society, and the decline of traditional values. Together with urban merchants, middle-class nationalists, and students, they resented the tremendous political influence of the American government and Western petroleum companies. Indeed, resentment against the West, especially against the United States and Israel, is a central theme of Islamism. Like Afghanistan's Taliban government and supporters of bin Laden's Al Qaeda movement, the Iranian mullahs despised globalization, the spread of Western political and economic influence, and, perhaps most of all, Western cultural values.

In the early 1960s, as tensions between the government and the clergy intensified, Ruhollah Khomeini became one of the Shah's most acerbic critics. When he was briefly imprisoned in 1964, riots broke out in a number of cities, culminating in the massacre of up to 10,000 demonstrators by the Shah's army.[55] Khomeini was sent into exile for nearly 15 years. The effect was to turn him into a martyr in a culture that especially admires martyrdom, thereby greatly enhancing his influence over the masses. By 1978 a substantial segment of Iran's urban population was involved in strikes and demonstrations against the regime. Brutal government crackdowns only intensified popular opposition.

Finally, in January 1979, the Shah went into exile amid growing mass unrest. Khomeini returned home to a frenzied welcome shortly thereafter. By then he had achieved the rank of Grand Ayatollah, the most exalted level of religious interpreters in the Shi'ite clergy.[56]

Like many new revolutionary regimes, Iran's turned increasingly radical in its early stage.[57] Over the years, three interrelated developments set the tone for the Islamic revolution. First was the merger of the country's religious and political leadership. In a national referendum held soon after Khomeini's triumphal return, 98 percent of all voters allegedly favored the establishment of an Islamic republic. The new regime, declared the Ayatollah, was "the government of God."[58] Nonclerical figures have continued to hold a significant number of government posts since that time; in 1988, 73 percent of the members of parliament were not Muslim clerics.[59] But even today, ultimate power still resides in the hands of the Revolutionary Council (a body of hardline Islamist clerics), which can, and often does, overrule both the parliament and the president.

The second important development has been the revival of traditional Islamic observances. Women must be veiled in public and are strongly encouraged to wear the *chador*, the shapeless shroud that conceals all parts of the body. Highly intrusive Revolutionary Guards penetrated all aspects of Iranian life, policing possible violations of Islamic behavior (as defined by the mullahs). Together with neighborhood vigilante committees, they arrested and occasionally executed suspected enemies of the Islamic order, though these unpopular intrusions have diminished in recent years. In the Shi'ite tradition of martyrdom, thousands of young volunteers died in the holy war against Iraq. Assuring their families that it is a privilege to die for the faith, the Ayatollah Khomeini proclaimed, "We should sacrifice all our loved ones for the sake of Islam. If we are killed, we have performed our duty."[60]

Finally, Iran's radical revivalism embraced an aggressive foreign policy. That encompassed support for kindred radical groups abroad, such as Lebanon's Hizbullah, and a burning hostility toward foreign powers that are perceived as enemies of Iran's brand of Islam. Prior to the revolution, Khomeini had declared, "America is worse than Britain! Britain is worse than America! The Soviet Union is worse than both of them! They are all worse and more unclean than each other!"[61] Once in power, he and his successors reserved their most bitter attacks for the United States and Israel. It is every Muslim's duty, Khomeini declared, "to prepare himself for battle against Israel."[62]

Iran's hostility toward the outside world was best illustrated by two events. On November 4, 1979, revolutionary students seized the U.S. embassy in Tehran, taking diplomats and embassy staff hostage in an extraordinary breach of diplomatic protocol.[63] While the Iranian regime claimed that the students had acted independently, no one doubted that the government was capable of releasing the hostages any time it chose. It was not until 444 days later that the last of the 52 hostages was released. In the West, the incident created widespread animosity toward Iran and, unfortunately, toward Islam in general.

For the Iranian people, however, a second manifestation of their country's radical foreign policy—a prolonged war against Iraq (1980–1988)—was far more tragic. The war had multiple origins, most of them unrelated to religion. The most proximate cause was a long-standing border dispute. Also at play was Iran's support for Iraq's repressed Shi'ite population, as well as each government's desire to lead the Gulf region. Once the conflict began, however, "both sides . . . portrayed the war as a noble crusade: Iraq as a historic defense of Arab sovereignty . . . against the marauding Persians; Iran as a holy war against the [Iraqi] infidels."[64] When Saddam Hussein's troops attacked Iran, in what he erroneously thought would be a quick victory, Khomeini declared a *jihad* against the infidel invading army. Before the war finally ground to a halt in 1988 with no victor, it had inflicted grave damage on the Iranian economy and cost the country several hundred thousand lives. Even then, Khomeini, who had vowed to pursue the battle until Saddam Hussein was toppled, only reluctantly agreed to the truce, which he called "more deadly than taking poison."[65]

Since Khomeini's death at the end of the 1980s, the Islamic revolution has moderated somewhat. The Revolutionary Guard has relaxed its grip on daily life; in the secrecy of their homes, middle-class Iranians dance to Western music at social gatherings and women shed their veils; and the country has retreated from its aggressive foreign policy.[66] In recent years, the Iranian people have twice elected a reformist president, Mohammad Khatemi, bent on moderating the revolution and increasing individual liberties. Reformers now also have a clear majority in parliament. As I noted, until now both the president and parliament have been stymied by the hardline Revolutionary Council and the military. But many observers feel it is just a matter of time before an increasingly assertive population forces the Islamist *mullahs* to accept moderating reforms.

It is interesting to note that the Iranian national leadership—including both hardliners and tentative reformers—had long been strongly opposed to the Taliban government in neighboring Afghanistan and had given arms and support to guerrillas trying to overthrow that government. Although the reasons for this hostility are complex and are tied, in part, to Taliban persecution of Shi'ite Muslims in Afghanistan, it clearly demonstrates that there is no united front, even among militant Islamic fundamentalists. While Iran's official brand of Islam once struck Westerners as extreme, it was nowhere near as extreme as the Taliban's later interpretation.

Radical Hindu Fundamentalism

Compared to its Muslim counterpart, Hindu fundamentalism has received scant attention in the West. This is probably because Hinduism is largely confined to one country (India); its leading political voice—the Bharatiya Janata Party (BJP)—has only emerged from political obscurity to national leadership in the past 15 years or so; and the party has not pursued an expansionist or anti-Western foreign policy.[67] The BJP itself is divided into factions. Hardliners take a militant stance and often use inflammatory language against the nation's Muslim minority. Indeed, leaders of India's center and left opposition parties, and many of India's 120 million Muslims, blame that faction for the destruction of a major Muslim mosque in 1992 and for anti-Muslim riots that killed 3,000 people in 1995. On the other hand, BJP moderates and pragmatists who currently head the national government recognize that the party has nowhere near a parliamentary majority and must cooperate with secular parties and act responsibly if it is to govern.These leaders preach a form of Hindu nationalism that stresses broad Indian cultural themes and even opens its arms to Muslims, a small portion of whom vote for the BJP.

But the roots of Hindu revivalism lie in India's communal politics, that is, the tensions between the Hindu majority (more than 80 percent of the country), the Muslim minority (12 percent of the population), and the smaller Sikh population (about 2 percent) (see Chapter 4). During the 1980s, militant Hinduism grew rapidly, partly as a response to the surge of Islamic revivalism in Pakistan and the Middle East. Indeed, Muslim, Sikh, and Hindu fundamentalists all feed on their common hostility toward each other. The rise of fundamentalism of all kinds was indirectly encouraged by politicians from the ruling Congress Party, most notably Prime Minister Indira Gandhi, who played the dangerous game of using communal politics for their own advantage. Another factor that has troubled many Hindus and increased their militancy is the conversion of large numbers of untouchables to Buddhism or Islam. In the eyes of many middle- and higher-caste Hindus, these conversions threaten the caste system, a linchpin of Hinduism. The BJP and other Hindu nationalist groups also gained considerable support among voters disgusted with corruption within the secular parties, such as the powerful Congress Party. BJP strength is rooted in northern India's Hindi-speaking heartland but extends throughout the country, particularly within the urban middle class.

Because Hinduism is a less well-organized religion than Islam and lacks a formal church structure, its fundamentalist beliefs are less clearly spelled out as well. Nationalism is certainly an important element, specifically the demand that India cease giving legal support to multiculturalism and, instead, define itself as a Hindu nation. Sometimes fundamentalist spokespersons endorse traditional religious practices shunned or prohibited by modern Indian society. For example, some party leaders have defended *sati*, the brutal traditional Hindu practice in which a widow throws herself on her husband's funeral pyre and dies in flames. However, the BJP has several female members of parliament and a number of active women's organizations.

In the absence of an organized Hindu church or clergy, revivalist leadership has been divided between various interest groups and parties, not all of which share the same positions. Furthermore, some groups (including the BJP itself) have changed their positions sharply over time. Two of the most militant groups, the Vishwa Hindu Parishad (VHP) and Shiv Sena, have openly encouraged attacks on Muslim mosques and neighborhoods, most notably in the Hindu strongholds of Uttar Pradesh, Madhya Pradesh, and Bihar states. The political consequences of Hindu-Muslim conflicts can be significant. For example, in 1990 Prime Minister V. P. Singh's government fell when he sent troops to prevent a Hindu mob from tearing down a famed Muslim mosque. The mosque, built on the site where the Hindu god Ram is believed to have been born, is bitterly resented by Hindu militants. Bloody communal riots regarding the site in 1989, 1992, and 2002 left thousands dead.

The majority of India's Hindus rejected the fundamentalist position for many years. The BJP and its predecessor party, the Bharatiya Jana Sang (BJS), were shunned by the country's secular parties and excluded from national and state coalition governments. Since the mid-1980s, however, the party's electoral support has soared as voters have become increasingly disenchanted with the mainstream secular parties, particularly the once-dominant Congress Party. A 1992 BJP rally in New Delhi calling for limits on Islamic rights attracted one million demonstrators. In its platform, the BJP called for Indian production of nuclear weapons (India has since tested such weapons), limits on foreign investment, greater economic self-sufficiency, and reduced imports. Party leaders also opposed birth control programs and expressed the belief that it is not necessary for peasants and other poor Indians to be literate.[68] After moderating its rhetoric, however, the BJP emerged as the largest party in parliament following the 1996 national elections and headed the new government coalition. Faced with the need to maintain the support of their secular coalition partners, the party's pragmatic leadership has generally avoided anti-Muslim positions or other forms of extremism. A BJP-dominated parliamentary coalition has ruled much of the time since, consolidating its power in the 1999 national elections.

THE PROGRESSIVE CATHOLIC CHURCH

At roughly the same time that many Muslims and Hindus were turning in a reactionary direction, important sectors of Latin America's Catholic church were embarking on a progressive path. From the time of Spanish colonialism through the first half of the twentieth century, the Church had supported the political and economic status quo, thereby legitimizing Latin America's elite-based governments. In a region marked by a high concentration of income and wealth, the Church was often a major land owner. Alienated by the anticlerical sentiments of European and Latin American liberals, it usually allied with conservative political factions.

In the decades after World War II, however, that pattern began to change dramatically among important portions of the clergy, particularly at the parish level. The process of change accelerated greatly in the 1960s, when Pope John XXIII moved the "Church universal" in a far more liberal direction, placing greater emphasis on social concerns. "The Second Vatican Council [convened by Pope John between 1962 and 1965] moved international Catholicism from a generally conservative and even authoritarian position to one that supported democracy, human rights and social justice."[69] Catholics were encouraged to address social issues and to enter into a political dialogue with liberals and even leftists.

In 1968, the Latin American Bishops Conference (CELAM) met in Medellín, Colombia, to apply the lessons of Vatican II to their own region. Boldly challenging the status quo, their ideas reflected the influences of the reformist and radical theologians who represented the "progressive church."[70] The themes of dependency and liberation of Latin America's oppressed poor echoed through many of CELAM's pronouncements. The clergy, said the bishops, must heed the "deafening cry . . . from the throats of millions asking their pastors for a liberation that reaches them from nowhere else." To do so, the Church must "effectively give preference to the poorest and the most needy sectors." In short, an institution historically allied with the region's power elite was now to be the Church of the poor.[71]

The Medellín conference must be understood in the broader context of political change that was shaking Latin America at the time. In 1959, the triumph of Cuba's revolutionaries spotlighted the poverty and oppression afflicting so much of Latin America. The far-reaching educational, health, and land reforms being carried out in Cuba impressed and radicalized many Catholics. In Colombia, Father Camilo Torres had left the priesthood to join a guerrilla movement three years before the conference. He was soon killed by counterinsurgency forces, thereby becoming a hero to leftists throughout Latin America.[72] Elsewhere in Latin America, few priests or nuns became involved in an armed struggle. Many, however, organized and politicized the poor and accepted important elements of Marxist political and economic analysis.

Though always a minority within the Church, leftist clergy had an important influence in Central America during the 1970s and 1980s, most notably in Nicaragua, El Salvador, and Guatemala.[73] Many Nicaraguan priests and nuns actively supported the Sandinista revolution in the 1970s. When the Sandinistas came to power, Father Miguel D'Escoto was named foreign minister, Jesuit priest Xabier Gorostiaga was appointed head of national planning, Father Ernesto Cardenal served as minister of culture, and his brother, Father Fernando Cardenal, became director of the national adult literacy campaign and was subsequently named minister of education. No government in Latin America has had nearly the number of priests in its cabinet as did Nicaragua's Marxist revolutionary government.

For most of Latin America, however, the 1960s and 1970s were not years of revolution. Instead, much of the region was governed by right-wing military dictatorships. Reacting to a perceived radical threat, repressive military regimes replaced civilian democracies in Brazil, Argentina, Chile, and Uruguay. At the same time, armed-forces rule continued in much of Central America and the central Andes, where democratic traditions had never been strong. Ironically, right-wing repression spurred the growth of the progressive Church more than the Cuban or Nicaraguan revolutions did.

Not surprisingly, radical clergy and laity were outspoken in their criticism of the military regimes and, consequently, suffered severe reprisals. Dozens of priests and nuns were murdered and many more persecuted in Brazil, El Salvador, and Guatemala. In El Salvador, for example, a far-right death squad called the White Warriors distributed handbills reading, "Be a Patriot, Kill a Priest."[74] But such repression only brought more moderate Catholic figures into the opposition. "When committed Catholics were imprisoned, tortured, and even killed, bishops in a significant number of cases then denounced the state, setting off a spiral of greater repression against the Church, followed by new Church denunciations of authoritarianism."[75]

In Chile, Brazil, El Salvador, and Peru, the Church became a leading critic of government human-rights violations.[76] The most celebrated example was El Salvador's Archbishop Oscar Romero, the nation's highest-ranking cleric, who, ironically, had begun his tenure as a conservative.[77] Increasingly appalled by his government's massive human-rights violations, he gradually moved to the left. In 1980, Romero wrote President Carter asking him to terminate U.S. military aid to the ruling junta until human-rights violations had ended. Subsequently, he broadcast a sermon calling on Salvadorian soldiers to disobey orders to kill innocent civilians. "No soldier is obliged to obey an order against God's law," he declared. "In the name of God and in the name of this suffering people . . . I implore you, I beg you, I order you—stop the repression."[78] The following day Archbishop Romero was murdered by a right-wing hit squad as he said a Requiem Mass.

Like Romero, Latin America's progressive clergy are far more likely to be reformers than radicals. At times their political rhetoric and analysis may find some common ground with the Left. Thus, they share the Marxists' indignation over the plight of the poor, and many of them identify dependency and U.S. domination as root causes of Latin American underdevelopment. But they reject revolutionary violence and the Leninist state as solutions. Reform, not revolution, was also the proscription of CELAM's bishops when they suggested progressive Catholic theology as an alternative to both capitalism and Marxism.

A number of the bishops' pronouncements at Medellín originated with a radical Peruvian priest, Gustavo Gutiérrez, the father of liberation theology. In the succeeding decades, writings by Gutiérrez and other liberation theologians greatly influenced the progressive Church in Latin America and other parts of the world. Liberation theology calls on Catholic laity and clergy to become politically active and to direct that activity toward the emancipation of the poor. Drawing on Marxist analysis, Gutiérrez accepts the notion of class struggle, but his form of struggle is nonviolent. The poor, liberation theologians argue, should organize themselves into Christian (or Ecclesial) Base Communities (CEBs) where they can raise their social and political consciousness. In that way, they can recognize the need to transform society through their own mobilization.[79] Starting in the early 1960s, CEBs spread through much of Latin America, most notably to Brazil, Chile, Peru, and Central America. While the number of communities and even their precise definition are subject to debate, a CEB is essentially "any group that meets on a regular basis to deepen its members' knowledge of the gospel, stimulate reflection and action on community needs, . . . and evangelize."[80] In part, the Church created CEBs as a response to the serious shortage of priests in Latin America, particularly among the poor.

Typically composed of 10 to 40 people, Ecclesial Base Communities are primarily found in poor urban neighborhoods and, to a lesser degree, in rural villages (though there are also some middle-class CEBs). Guesses as to how many exist in Latin America vary widely, but one estimate placed the number at their peak in the 1980s at perhaps 200,000, with a total membership of several million people. Perhaps 40 percent of all communities were in Brazil, home of the world's largest Catholic population.[81] The majority of CEB members are probably not politically active and join for strictly religious purposes.[82] Still, many communities were the foundations for popular protests against oppression, most notably in Central America but also in Brazil, Chile, and Peru.[83] In other cases, CEBs helped raise political awareness and sharpen political skills among the poor.

Since the early 1980s, the influence of Latin America's progressive Church has diminished considerably.[84] One cause, ironically, has been the transition from military dictatorships to democracy in much of the region. Absent massive human-rights violations and open assaults on the poor, the clergy has had less motivation to enter the political arena. Furthermore, without a common foe, moderate and radical priests no longer have a common cause. Finally, many political activists who had used the Church as a protective "umbrella" during the military dictatorships (it was, after all, respectable to be an active Catholic) are now able to participate in politics through other, newly legal political organizations.[85]

Since the 1980s, the Vatican, under the pontificate of John Paul II, has been unsympathetic to any type of political activism among priests and nuns, particularly when related to the CEBs and liberation theology. "Rome has called liberation theologians such as Leonardo Boff and Gustavo Gutiérrez to account, if not to recant. . . ."[86] As progressive bishops and archbishops such as Brazil's Don Helder Camara have died or retired, they have been replaced by more conservative clerics.[87] Though liberation theology and the progressive Church have lost much of their momentum, they have still made an important contribution to the political mobilization of Latin America's poor.

RELIGION AND POLITICS IN THE DEVELOPING WORLD: LOOKING TO THE FUTURE

The hold of religion on the human heart and its consequent impact on the political process have been frequently misunderstood by Western scholars. As we have seen, the initial error of both modernization and dependency theorists was to underestimate its significance. Several factors account for the unanticipated resurgence of fundamentalism and other forms of religiously based politics in recent decades. In many countries, rapid modernization has left people psychologically adrift, searching for their cultural identity. The breakdown of traditional village life and long-accepted customs often creates a void not filled by the material rewards of modern life. In the Middle East, the indignities of colonialism and then neocolonialism, resentment against Israel and the West, and a feeling of failed development have all contributed to that region's religious revival.[88] In Latin America, the progressive Church offered a shield against political repression and a voice for the poor. As different as they are, Islamic revivalism and the progressive Catholic church both received much of their impetus from government repression and corruption. In short, the resurgence of Third World religion was, in part, a reaction to the deficiencies of social and economic modernization and the corruption and incompetence of the new political-economic order.

Contemporary analysts also risk miscalculating the impact of religion on Third World politics by overstating its importance. To begin with, the political weight of the movements that have attracted the most attention—Islamic and Hindu radical fundamentalism and progressive Catholicism—must be put into perspective. Influential as they have been, they are not representative of the religions from which they have sprung. This point requires particular emphasis in relation to Islam, since a militant minority has left many Westerners with an extremely negative image of the entire Muslim religion. Islam is seen as backward and intolerant when, in fact, like all religions, it encompasses a range of outlooks, some very progressive.[89] For example, the media may suggest that Muslim women are all repressed and confined, yet there are many Islamic feminists and professional women in countries such as Egypt, Lebanon, and Malaysia. It is worth remembering that four Muslim nations—Bangladesh, Indonesia, Pakistan, and Turkey—have had female prime ministers or presidents in recent years, something the United States has yet to accomplish. Similarly, contrary to stereotype, some Muslim countries, including fundamentalist Saudi Arabia, are on very good terms with the West. Finally, in at least some cases, such as Turkey and India, when fundamentalist parties finally led national governments, their behavior in office was moderated by their need to attract coalition partners in parliament and to appeal to a wider range of voters in future elections.

When considering the broader scope of the current religious revival, again, its importance should be recognized but not exaggerated. History reveals that "religious resurgence is a cyclical phenomenon."[90] Some analysts feel that the contemporary religious surges in Islamic and Catholic activism reached their peaks in the late 1970s. Thus, Jeff Haynes argues, "There is no reason to doubt that the current wave of religion-oriented political ideas and movements will in time give way . . . to [a] partial resurrection of secular ideologies."[91] For the foreseeable future, however, religion will continue to be an important force in the politics of many developing nations. Nowhere is this more dramatically evidenced than in fundamentalist terrorist groups such as Al Qaeda.

CONCLUSION: RELIGION AND DEMOCRACY

Two important questions come to mind when discussing the relationship between religion and democracy. First, does liberal democracy require the separation of church and a secular political system? Second, are the cultural values of some religions more supportive than others of democracy?

In his classic work, *Democracy in America*, the French author Alexis de Tocqueville suggested that a linchpin of democracy in the United States was the separation of church and state.

> I learned with surprise that [the clergy] filled no public appointments . . . [and] I found that most of its members seemed to retire from their own accord from the exercise of power, and that they made it the pride of their profession to abstain from politics. . . . They saw that they must renounce their religious influence if they were to strive for political power. . . .[92]

Today, many analysts still believe that maintaining the pluralist values and the tolerance that underlie democracy requires limiting the influence of religion on politics. But other contemporary analysts reject the notion that democracy requires a strict separation of church and state. In their recent publication, *Religion and Democracy*, David Marquand and Ronald Nettler insist:

> Even in the absence of a . . . bargain keeping church and state apart, religion and democracy can coexist. Communities of faith do not necessarily imperil the foundations of pluralist democracy by seeking to pursue essentially religious agendas through political action.[93]

But, they add, there is a restriction that is necessary if this intermingling of religious political action and democracy is to work. "A degree of mutual tolerance, or at least of mutual self-restraint, is indispensable. Religious groups have to accept the right of other religious groups—and . . . the right of the non-religious—to abide by their own values."[94] Often that tolerance is present, but in many fundamentalist religions—Islamic or otherwise—it frequently is not.

Our second question—whether certain religious cultures are more supportive than others of democratic values—has been the subject of intense debate. Various empirical studies have shown that Protestant countries are significantly more likely to be democratic than are Catholic or Muslim nations.[95] By contrast, Islamic nations have had a rather poor track record for maintaining democracy, leading some analysts to conclude that Islam and a number of other religions (including Catholicism) have authoritarian underpinnings. For example, in the mid-1990s, Turkish sociologist Serif Mardin suggested that the values of democracy may be tied to broader Western cultural values, values the Islamic world does not accept.[96]

The problem with such arguments is that, while they may have an element of truth, they fail to take into account differences within religions or important value changes over time. Not all religious Catholics or priests, for example, have the same political values. Militant Islamic fundamentalist cultures such as Afghanistan's or Sudan's are indeed unacceptable environments for democracy. Yet many scholars feel that Islamic values can be quite compatible with democracy in a more moderate Muslim setting such as Indonesia.[97] Consider, for example, Abdurrahman Wahid, Indonesia's first democratically elected president (in 1999). Wahid is a Muslim cleric who supported the values of tolerance so essential to democracy. He spoke out against grass-roots violence directed against Indonesia's Christian minority and insisted that Christians were equal to Muslims in the eyes of God. In a rather dramatic departure from most Islamic heads of state, he publically and enthusiastically supported Zionism and made one of his first state visits as president to Israel.[98] Similarly, while it is true that historically the Catholic church has been associated with authoritarian political forces in Europe and Latin America, since the 1970s it also has been in the forefront of the fight against right- and left-wing dictatorships in those regions.

Like most institution and value systems, religions change over time. Once it was widely understood that Protestant countries were more hospitable to both economic growth and democracy, while Catholic and Confucian nations were less so. Today both parts of that argument are far less tenable. Confucian East Asia and Catholic Southern Europe both enjoyed rapid economic growth in the second half of the twentieth century, faster growth than in many Protestant countries. And more recently, as democracy has spread to a variety of Catholic and Confucian nations (including Spain, Portugal, Poland, Brazil, Mexico, Taiwan, and South Korea), the suggested linkage between religions and democratic norms has become more questionable. That doesn't mean that some religions are not more tolerant or less authoritarian than others. Rather, it does mean that we need to avoid sweeping generalizations and consider differences *within* religions and changes over time.

DISCUSSION QUESTIONS

1. Discuss the various types of relationships that exist between church and state in Islamic societies.
2. What factors caused the growth of the progressive Church in Latin America, and what is distinct about its followers' beliefs? Why has the progressive Church lost much of its influence in recent years?
3. Discuss why the Buddhist and Hindu religions have usually been less actively involved in national politics than Islam or Catholicism. How has that changed in India in recent years?
4. What factors have led to the resurgence of Islamic fundamentalism (or revivalism) in Afghanistan, Iran, and other parts of the Muslim world? Why do you think so many people in that part of the world (albeit a minority) admire Osama bin Laden?

NOTES

1. Harvey Cox, *The Secular City* (New York: Macmillan, 1966), p.1.

2. Donald Eugene Smith, ed., *Religion and Modernization* (New Haven, CT: Yale University Press, 1974), p. 4.

3. Quoted in Timothy D. Sisk, *Islam and Democracy* (Washington, DC: United States Institute of Peace, 1992), p. 3.

4. Emile Sahliyeh, ed., *Religious Resurgence and Politics in the Contemporary World* (Albany, NY: SUNY Press), pp. 1–16.

5. John L. Esposito, *Islam and Politics*, 4th ed. (Syracuse, NY: Syracuse University Press, 1998), p. 311.

6. Jeff Haynes, *Religion in Third World Politics* (Boulder, CO: Lynne Rienner Publishers, 1994), p. 3.

7. Kenneth D. Wald, "Social Change and Political Response: The Silent Religious Cleavage in North America," in *Politics and Religion in the Modern World*, ed. George Moyser (New York: Routledge and Kegan Paul, 1991), p. 240.

8. The Christian Democratic Party was the dominant party in Italian politics for decades but was devastated in the early 1990s by scandal. It has since changed its name to the Italian Popular Party.

9. One of the most influential and controversial books using the framework of clashing, religiously based cultures is Samuel P. Huntington, *The Clash of Civilizations and the Remaking of World Order* (New York: Simon & Schuster, 1996); see also Bernard Lewis, "The Roots of Muslim Rage," *Atlantic Monthly* 226, no. 3 (September 1990). Leonard Binder, a leading specialist on the Middle East, is critical of such terminology, arguing, for example, that Islam is only one part of Middle Eastern culture; see *Islamic Liberalism* (Chicago: University of Chicago Press, 1988), pp. 80–81.

10. For data on the size and percentage of the Islamic populations in the nations of the world, see John L. Esposito, ed., *Islam in Asia* (New York: Oxford University Press, 1987), pp. 262–263. While the absolute size of Muslim populations has obviously changed since Esposito's book was published, his data are still relevant for comparative measurements.

11. Donald Eugene Smith, *Religion and Political Development* (Boston: Little, Brown, 1970), p. 40.

12. Latif Abul-Husn, *The Lebanese Conflict: Looking Inward* (Boulder, CO: Lynne Rienner Publishers, 1998), p. 35; see also Robin Wright, *Sacred Rage: The Crusade of Modern Islam* (London: Andre Deutsch, 1986), p. 63; William Montgomery Watt, *Islamic Fundamentalism and Modernity* (London: Routledge and Kegan Paul, 1988), pp. 125–131; Dilip Hiro, *Holy Wars: The Rise of Islamic Fundamentalism* (New York: Routledge and Kegan Paul, 1989), pp. 5–26.

13. Akbar S. Ahmed, *Discovering Islam* (New York: Routledge and Kegan Paul, 1988), pp. 55–61; Saleem Qureshi, "The Politics of the Shia Minority in Pakistan," in *Religious and Ethnic Minority Politics in South Asia*, ed. Dhirendra Vajpey and Yogendra K. Malik (New Delhi, India: Monhar, 1989), p. 109.

14. Smith, *Religion and Political Development*, p. xi.

15. For a discussion of the strengths and weaknesses of such arguments, see Winston Davis, "Religion and Development: Weber and the East Asian Experience," in *Understanding Political Development*, ed. Myron Weiner and Samuel Huntington (Boston: Little, Brown, 1987), pp. 221–280.

16. Terrance G. Carroll, "Secularization and States of Modernity," *World Politics* 36, no. 3 (April 1984): 362–382.

17. John L. Esposito, *Islamic Revivalism* (Washington, DC: American Institute of Islamic Affairs, American University, 1985), pp. 5–6; Eden Naby, "The Changing Role of Islam as a Unifying Force in Afghanistan," in *The State, Religion, and Ethnic Politics*, ed. Ali Banuazizi and Myron Weiner (Syracuse, NY: Syracuse University Press, 1986), p. 137; Yogendra K. Malik and V. B. Singh, *Hindu Nationalism in India* (Boulder, CO: Westview Press, 1994), pp. 53 and 206.

18. John L. Esposito, *Islam and Politics*, 2d ed. (Syracuse, NY: Syracuse University Press, 1987), p. 231.

19. Smith, *Religion and Political Development*, p. 70.

20. H. E. Richardson, *Tibet and Its History* (London: Oxford University Press, 1962).

21. Smith, *Religion and Political Development*, pp. 57–84.

22. Esposito, *Islam and Politics*, 2d ed., p. 1.

23. Contemporary hostilities between Jews and Muslims in the Middle East, as well as Islamic fundamentalist hostility toward the West, are relatively recent phenomena that are not rooted in Islam's core beliefs.

24. John L. Esposito, *The Islamic Threat: Myth or Reality?* (New York: Oxford University Press, 1992), pp. 78–79.

25. Anthony H. Johns, "Indonesia: Islam and Cultural Pluralism," in *Islam in Asia*, p. 203.

26. In 2001 the Welfare Party tried to reorganize under a new name.

27. Donald Eugene Smith, *Religion, Politics and Social Change in the Third World* (New York: Free Press, 1971), pp. 12–22.

28. Smith, *Religion and Political Development*, p. 54.

29. At the same time, however, many parish priests and nuns supported the revolution in Nicaragua, and several priests served in the first Sandinista cabinet.

30. Ibid., pp. 57, 34–39; Haynes, *Religion in Third World Politics*, p. 146.

31. Janet A. Contursi, "Militant Hindus and Buddhist Dalits: Hegemony and Resistance in an Indian Slum," *American Ethnologist* 16, no. 3 (August 1989): 441–457.

32. Donald Eugene Smith, "The Limits of Religious Resurgence," in *Religious Resurgence and Politics*, pp. 36–39.

33. Morton Zuckerman, "Beware of Religious Stalinists," *U.S. News and World Report*, March 22, 1993, p. 80; Charles Krauthammer, "Iran: Orchestrator of Disorder," *Washington Post*, January 1, 1993, p. A19. Both articles are also cited in the 1993 preface to the paperback edition of Esposito, *The Islamic Threat*.

34. Esposito, *The Islamic Threat*, p. vii.

35. Contursi, "Militant Hindus"; Esposito, *The Islamic Threat*, pp. 7–24; Shireen T. Hunter, ed., *The Politics of Islamic Revivalism* (Bloomington: Indiana University Press, 1988); Esposito, *Islamic Revivalism*; Sisk, *Islam and Democracy*, pp. 2–7, 73, fn. 1, 2.

36. Among the many examples are Watt, *Islamic Fundamentalism and Modernity* and Hiro, *Holy Wars*.

37. Fred Halliday, *Islam and the Myth of Confrontation: Religion and Politics in the Middle East* (London: I. B. Tauris Publishers, 1996), p. 233, fn. 1.

38. Esposito, *The Islamic Threat*; Akbar S. Ahmed, *Discovering Islam* (New York: Routledge and Kegan Paul, 1988); Esposito, *Political Islam: Revolution, Radicalism or Reform* (Boulder, CO: Lynne Rienner Publishers, 1997); Halliday, *Islam and the Myth of Confrontation*.

39. Charles Kurzman, ed., *Liberal Islam: A Source Book* (New York: Oxford University Press, 1998).

40. Halliday, *Islam and the Myth*, p. 107.

41. Hiro, *Holy Wars*, pp. 1–2.

42. Watt, *Islamic Fundamentalism and Modernity*, p. 2.

43. Peter Woodward, "Sudan: Islamic Radicals in Power," in *Political Islam* (Bolder, CO: Lynne Rienner Publishers, 1997) ed. John Esposito.

44. Wright, *Sacred Rage*.

45. Robin Wright, "Lebanon," in *The Politics of Islamic Revivalism*, p. 66.

46. Naby, "The Changing Role of Islam," pp. 124–154; Paul Overby, *Holy Blood: An Inside View of the Afghan War* (Westport, CT: Praeger, 1993).

47. For a discussion of the origins of the FIS and the nature of Algeria's violence since 1992, see Claire Spencer, "The Roots and Future of Islamism in Algeria," in *Islamic Fundamentalism*, ed. Abdel Salam Sidahmed and Anoushiravan Ehteshami (Boulder, CO: Westview Press, 1996), pp. 93–109; also Esposito, *Islam and Politics*, 4th ed., pp. 302–307.

48. To be sure, some Israeli "ultra-orthodox" Jews are radical fundamentalists who have carried out violent attacks against Muslims and secular Jews. The most notorious examples were the attack by an ultra-orthodox Jewish gunman against worshipers in a Hebron mosque and the assassination of Israeli Prime Minister Izhak Rabin by a Jewish fundamentalist who objected to Rabin's efforts to achieve peace with the Palestinian Liberation Organization (PLO). But they are exceptional.

49. Useful sources on the background of the revolution include Robin Wright, *In the Name of God: The Khomeini Decade* (New York: Simon & Schuster, 1989); Hiro, *Holy Wars*, chap. 6.

50. Hiro, *Holy Wars*, p. 151.

51. Ibid., pp. 151–153.

52. Shireen T. Hunter, *Iran after Khomeini* (New York: Praeger, 1992), pp. 11–12. Hunter argues that the shahs foolishly made their people choose between their Persian and their Islamic heritage. Faced with that option, they chose the latter.

53. Ibid., p. 57.

54. Cheryl Bernard and Zalmay Khalilzad, *The Government of God: Iran's Islamic Republic* (New York: Columbia University Press, 1984), pp. 12–13.

55. Hiro, *Holy Wars*, p. 160.

56. M. M. Salehi, *Insurgency through Culture and Religion: The Islamic Revolution of Iran* (New York: Praeger, 1988), p. 54.

57. The classic study of the natural cycle of revolutions is Crane Brinton, *The Anatomy of Revolution* (New York: Vintage, 1965).

58. Wright, *In the Name of God*, p. 65.

59. A few parliamentary seats were even reserved for religious minorities, including Jews, Christians, and Zoroastrians (though not the persecuted Baha'i minority); Wright, *In the Name of God*, pp. 180–181.

60. Ibid., p. 87.

61. Quoted in Bernard and Khalilzad, *The Government of God*, pp. 151–152.

62. Ibid., p. 154. Ironically, it emerged during the so-called "Irangate" Senate hearings that Iran had purchased arms from the United States by way of Israel in a deal arranged by Oliver North.

63. Wright's *In the Name of God* offers one of the better accounts, but there are many others.

64. Gary Sick, "Trial by Error: Reflections on the Iran-Iraq War," in *Iran's Revolution*, ed. R. K. Ramazani (Bloomington: Indiana University Press, 1990), p. 105.

65. Ibid., p. 104.

66. Wright, *In the Name of God*, p. 191; Hunter, *Iran after Khomeini*, pp. 32–41. Hunter gives a more cautious view of the move toward moderation.

67. This section draws heavily on Gail Omvelt, "Hinduism, Social Inequality and the State," in *Religion and Political Conflict in South Asia*, ed. Douglas Allen (Westport, CT: Greenwood Press, 1992), pp. 17–36. See also Ian Talbot, "Politics and Religion in Contemporary India," in *Politics and Religion in the Modern World*, pp. 135–161; and Malik and Singh, *Hindu Nationalism in India*.

68. *New York Times*, February 26, 1993.

69. Paul Sigmund, *Liberation Theology at the Crossroads* (New York: Oxford University Press, 1990), p. 19; David Lehmann, *Democracy and Development in Latin America* (Cambridge, England: Polity Press, 1990), pp. 108–110.

70. Scott Mainwaring and Alexander Wilde, eds., *The Progressive Church in Latin America* (Notre Dame, IN: University of Notre Dame Press, 1989).

71. Sigmund, *Liberation Theology at the Crossroads*, pp. 29–30.

72. Father Camilo Torres, *Revolutionary Writings* (New York: Harper & Row, 1962).

73. Philip Berryman, *Stillborn Hope: Religion, Politics and Revolution in Central America* (Maryknoll, NY: Orbis Books, 1991); Margaret E. Crahan, "Religion and Politics in Revolutionary Nicaragua," in *The Progressive Church*.

74. Jennifer Pearce, "Politics and Religion in Central America: A Case Study of El Salvador," in *Politics and Religion*, p. 234.

75. Mainwaring and Wilde, *Progressive Church*, p. 13.

76. Scott Mainwaring, *The Catholic Church and Politics in Brazil* (Stanford, CA: Stanford University Press, 1986); Brian H. Smith, *The Church and Politics in Chile* (Princeton, NJ: Princeton University Press, 1982).

77. Philip Berryman, "El Salvador: From Evangelization to Insurrection," in *Religion and Political Conflict in Latin America*, ed. Daniel H. Levine (Chapel Hill: University of North Carolina Press, 1986), pp. 58–78.

78. Ibid., p. 114.

79. Sigmund, *Liberation Theology at the Crossroads*, pp. 28–39.

80. W. E. Hewitt, *Base Christian Communities and Social Change in Brazil* (Lincoln: University of Nebraska Press, 1991), p. 6.

81. Hewitt, *Base Christian Communities*; Thomas C. Bruneau, "Brazil: The Catholic Church and Basic Christian Communities," in *Religion and Political Conflict in Latin America*, pp. 106–123.

82. John Burdick, "The Progressive Catholic Church in Latin America," *Latin American Research Review* 24, no. 1 (1994): 184–198; Hewitt, *Base Christian Communities*.

83. Daniel H. Levine and Scott Mainwaring, "Religion and Popular Protest in Latin America," in *Power and Popular Protest: Latin American Social Movements*, ed. Susan Eckstein (Berkeley: University of California Press, 1988).

84. Burdick, "The Progressive Catholic Church."

85. Thomas C. Bruneau, "The Role and Response of the Catholic Church in the Redemocratization of Brazil," in *The Politics of Religion and Social Change*, ed. Anson Shupe and Jeffrey K. Hadden (New York: Paragon House, 1986), pp. 95–98.

86. Mainwaring and Wilde, *Progressive Church*, p. 30.

87. Lehmann, *Democracy and Development*, pp. 144–145.

88. Mark Tessler and Jamal Sanad, "Women and Religion in Modern Islamic Society: The Case of Kuwait," in *Religious Resurgence*, p. 209.

89. For a collection of writings by progressive Islamic scholars and political figures, see Kurzman, ed., *Liberal Islam*.

90. Smith, "The Limits of Religious Resurgence," p. 34.

91. Haynes, *Religion in Third World Politics*, p. 155.

92. Alexis de Tocqueville, *Democracy in America,* ed. Alan Ryan (London: Everyman's Library, 1994), pp. 309–312.

93. David Marquand and Ronald L. Nettler, "Forward," in *Religion and Democracy,* ed. David Marquand and Ronald L. Nettler (Oxford, England: Blackwell Publishers, 2000), pp. 2–3.

94. Ibid., p. 3.

95. Axel Hadenius, *Democracy and Development* (New York: Cambridge University Press, 1992).

96. Serif Mardin, "Civil Society and Islam," in *Civil Society: Theory, History, Comparison,* ed. John A. Hall (Cambridge, England: Polity Press, 1995); For a similar perspective, see Chris Hann, "Introduction: Political Society and Civil Anthropology" in *Civil Society: Challenging Western Models,* ed. Chris Hann and Elizabeth Dunn (London: Routledge, 1996), pp. 1–26.

97. Robert W. Hefner, *Civil Islam: Muslims and Democratization in Indonesia* (Princeton, NJ: Princeton University Press, 2000).

98. In 2001, parliament removed Wahid from office based on his incompetence as president and possible corruption. I am not arguing that Wahid was a perfect democrat. When faced with impeachment, he acted questionably on a number of occasions. Nor am I suggesting that all Indonesian Muslim leaders were as tolerant as he was. I am merely noting that Wahid, despite his obvious faults as president, represented a brand of Islam that is quite compatible with democracy. Despite the enormous economic and ethnic problems facing Indonesia's new government, democracy stands a good chance of surviving.

chapter 4

The Politics of Cultural Pluralism and Ethnic Conflict

The conflicts of the future are more likely to be between people rather than states over issues related to culture, ethnicity or religion.[1]

From 1915 to 1916, in the midst of World War I, the new governing regime in Turkey massacred some 1.5 million Armenians who had been living within that country's borders.[2] Some 30 years later, as Britain relinquished power over India, it divided that "jewel in the [imperial] crown," into two nations, largely Hindu India and Muslim Pakistan. The religious communities in each country then turned on each other savagely, with a resulting death toll of perhaps one million. More recently, Hutu villagers in the African nation of Rwanda massacred some half-million of their Tutsi countrymen, while in the former country of Yugoslavia, Serbian militias initiated "ethnic cleansing" of their Muslim and Croat neighbors, killing and raping untold thousands more. During the twentieth century, violent confrontations, civil wars, and genocidal activity were frequently motivated by religious conflict (India, Northern Ireland, Lebanon), tribal animosities (Nigeria, Rwanda), racial hatred (South Africa), and other forms of ethnic animosities. Continuing ethnic tensions in Macedonia, Kashmir (India), and the Congo in the early years of the twenty-first century seem to confirm Mahabun ul Haq's prediction in the quotation above, that wars between "peoples"—ethnic, religious, and cultural groups—will continue to far outnumber wars between nation-states.

To be sure, many political analysts since the time of Karl Marx (1818–1883) have insisted on the primacy of *class* as the basis for political conflict in both industrialized and developing nations. But significant as class conflict has been, no cleavage has more sharply, and oftentimes violently, divided nations in modern times than has ethnicity. "Cultural pluralism [i.e., ethnic diversity]," argues Crawford Young, "is a quintessentially modern phenomenon." It has been closely linked to the growth of the middle class and the emergence of politicians who articulated nationalist or other ethnic aspirations while mobilizing workers and peasants behind that ideal.[3]

Of course, ethnic minorities have been victimized by violence for hundreds of years. One needs only look to the nineteenth-century frontier wars between White settlers and Native Americans in the United States and Chile to identify just two examples. And contrary to common perception, the level of ethnic protests and rebellions within states has actually diminished somewhat since the start of the 1990s, after rising steadily for the previous 50 years.[4] Alarmist warnings notwithstanding, the world has not been crumbling into a maze of small ethnically based states.[5] Still, as we begin a new century, the level of ethnically based *internal* conflict is still far higher than in the decades prior to the 1990s, in marked contrast to the dramatic decline in wars *between* nations during that period. Indeed, over the past 50 years, the most frequent arenas for violent conflict have not been wars between sovereign states, but rather internal strife tied to cultural, tribal, religious, or other ethnic animosities.[6] Any listing of the world's most brutal wars in the past few decades would include ethnically based internal confrontations in Bosnia, Kosovo (Serbia), Rwanda, Congo, Ethiopia, Sudan, Lebanon, and Indonesia (East Timor).[7] At least 15 to 20 million people have died in ethnic violence since World War II.[8] Most recently, the collapse of Soviet and Eastern European communism has released a torrent of pent-up ethnic hatreds in Azerbaijan, Armenia, Georgia, Chechnya, the former Yugoslavia, and other parts of Central and Eastern Europe. Particularly since the end of the Cold War, the world's attention has focused increasingly on ethnic clashes.

Warfare between Serbs, Croats, Bosnian Muslims, and Kosovars in the former Yugoslavia, separatist movements among French-speaking Québécois, racially based riots in Los Angeles, Basque terrorism in Spain, and Protestant-Catholic clashes in Northern Ireland all clearly demonstrate that interethnic friction and violence can erupt in Western democracies as well as in former communist countries. But ethnic conflict has been particularly widespread and cruel in Africa, Asia, and other parts of the Third World—in part because countries in those regions tend to have more ethnically diverse populations, and in part because their political systems are generally less capable of peacefully resolving tensions. A recent study determined that there are some 275 "minorities at risk" throughout the world (ethnic groups facing actual or potential repression), with a total population of slightly more than one billion (about one-sixth of the world's populations) scattered in 116 countries. Approximately 85 percent of those at risk live in the LDCs. While Asia has the highest *absolute* population of ethnic minorities, Sub-Saharan Africa has the highest *proportion* of its population at risk (some 36 percent), followed by North Africa and the Middle East (26 percent).[9]

This chapter focuses on the most protracted and extreme conflicts between ethnic groups in the developing world. In doing so, it runs the risk of presenting readers with the mistaken notion that all LDCs are aflame with violent ethnic clashes. In actuality, interethnic warfare is most pronounced in the Indian subcontinent, the Middle East, Southeast Asia, and portions of Africa; it is less common in Latin America and the Far East. Many developing countries—Argentina, Uruguay, and Nepal, for example—either lack substantial ethnic minorities, thereby eliminating the possibility of internal conflict, or have arrived at relatively stable, if not always just, relations between ethnicities—Bolivia, Ghana, and Thailand. Thus, while this chapter focuses on the most unstable cases in order to illustrate the obstacles that ethnic conflicts often present to political and economic development, it should not give the reader the false impression that *all* LDCs are riddled with ethnic conflict.

DEFINING ETHNICITY

Although it is difficult to define ethnicity precisely, certain common qualities set ethnic groups apart. Most analysts agree that ethnic identity is a *social construction*—a way that certain groups have come to view themselves as distinct from others over time. Each ethnicity "share[s] a distinctive and enduring collective identity based on a belief in a common descent and on shared experiences and cultural traits."[10] While usually having a basis in fact, these identities and histories are often partly created, or at least embellished, by entrepreneurial politicians—intellectuals or journalists who gain some advantage by "playing the ethnic card." The real or imagined common history, traditions, and values not only unite the group's members but distinguish them from other cultures with whom they come in contact, and at times they encourage group conflict.[11] Thus, J. E. Brown's cynical definition of a "nation" can be applied to many other ethnic identities: "A group of people united by a common error about their ancestry and a common dislike of their neighbors."[12] In times of great change and uncertainty (including national independence or subsequent rapid economic modernization), ethnic intellectuals and politicians are likely to create historical myths that give their ethnic group a sense of security in the face of perceived challenges from other groups. In the words of Vesna Pesic, a Serbian intellectual and peace activist, ethnic conflict is caused by the "fear of the future, lived through the past."[13]

Pakistanis in Uganda, Chinese in Malaysia, Kurds in Iraq, Hmong in Laos, or highland Indians in Ecuador may each join together in political organizations, business groups, social clubs, and mutual-benefit societies. This does not necessarily mean that these ethnic groups are socially homogeneous or politically united. In fact, they are often divided by factors such as class, ideology, or religion. For example, Sri Lanka's Tamil minority is divided between those who have lived in the country for centuries and those brought from India in the nineteenth century to work the coffee and tea plantations. These subgroups are, in turn, split by caste. Indian Muslims and Nigerian Ibos are divided by class. And African Americans may be Protestant, Catholic, Muslim, or even Jewish. Still, the factors that bind an ethnic group together are more powerful than those that separate it. Ibo peasants generally identify more closely with businesspeople from their own tribe than they do with fellow peasants from the Hausa or Yoruba tribes. Cynthia Enloe has noted, "Of all the groups that men [or women] attach themselves to, ethnic groups seem the most encompassing and enduring."[14]

Sometimes ethnic classifications were artificially imposed initially by outsiders. In the Belgian Congo, for example, White colonial administrators, missionaries, explorers, and anthropologists erroneously lumped together people of the upper Congo region into a nonexistent tribe (or ethnicity) called the Bangala. After a number of decades, the "myth of the Bangala" took on a life of its own, as migrants from the upper Congo settling in the city of Kenshasa joined together politically under the ethnic banner that had been externally imposed on them.[15] Similarly, the classification of "Colored" once used to denote racially mixed South Africans was an artificial construct established by the White regime. And while Ecuadorians, Nicaraguans, Cubans, and Mexicans generally feel little in common with each other when they live in their home countries, they become a new ethnic group called "Latinos" or "Hispanics" when they immigrate to the United States and are viewed as a homogeneous mass by their "Anglo" neighbors. Once individuals begin to accept the group label imposed on them, however, even those externally created ethnic classifications become politically relevant.[16]

Ethnic groups may have their own social clubs, soccer teams, schools, or cemeteries. For the insecure Peruvian Indian recently arrived in Lima from her rural village, or the Hausa seeking a job in Lagos, ethnically based social clubs are often invaluable for finding employment, housing, and friendships in an otherwise cold and inhospitable city. In the threatening environment associated with modernization and social change, "fear, anxiety and insecurity at the individual level can be reduced within the womb of the ethnic collectivity."[17] At the same time, however, ethnic consciousness usually creates barriers between groups. Interreligious or interracial marriages, for example, may be frowned upon. In countries such as Canada, Malaysia, and Trinidad, ethnic divisions are managed relatively amicably and peacefully. More frequently, however, they are not. In multi-ethnic countries such as the United States, India, Liberia, and the Congo, common consciousness and culture bind together certain religious, caste, tribal, or racial groups while creating barriers to other ethnicities.

ETHNIC AND STATE BOUNDARIES

If the world were composed of relatively homogenous nations such as Uruguay, South Korea, or Denmark, ethnically based wars might continue between states, but there would be no internal strife based on communal antagonisms.[18] In other words, the underlying cause of most internal ethnic conflict is that boundaries for *nations* (distinct cultural-linguistic groups such as Serbs,

Russians, or Kurds) and other ethnicities so often fail to coincide with boundaries for *states* (self-governing countries).[19] If large numbers of Albanians had not lived in Kosovo and Macedonia, there would not have been such carnage in those regions in the past decade. The absence of an independent state to house the Kurdish nation has spurred ongoing conflict in Iraq, Iran, and Turkey. Sikh militants in the Indian state of Punjab have demanded the creation of an independent state. In all of these cases, ethno-national and political boundaries do not correspond. When minority (or, on occasion, majority) groups feel they have been denied their fair share of political and economic power, they will turn to protest and confrontation.

A look at the world's population map, particularly for the less developed countries, reveals how many independent nation-states include multiple ethnic groups that are frequently uncomfortable with each other or even hostile. One study of 132 countries throughout the world revealed that only 12 of them (9 percent) are ethnically homogeneous (populated by a single ethnic group), with another 25 (19 percent) overwhelmingly populated by a single ethnic group. The remaining 72 percent of the world's nations, then, have substantial minority group populations. In fact, in 39 countries (30 percent of the total), no single ethnic group accounts for half of the state's population.[20] This pattern is most striking in Sub-Saharan Africa, where virtually every country is composed of several ethnic (tribal) groups.[21] For example, it is estimated that Nigeria, the most populous Black African state, has more than 200 linguistic groups.[22]

Africans often attribute their continent's legacy of tribal conflict to the European colonizers who divided the region into administrative units little connected with ethnic identities. In some areas, antagonistic groups were thrown together in a single colonial unit, while elsewhere individual tribes were split between two future countries. In Africa, Asia, and the Middle East, colonial powers often exacerbated ethnic tensions by favoring some groups over others, using "divide and conquer" strategies to control the local population. Yet colonialism must be seen as but one of many factors contributing to ethnic discord. Given the enormous number of tribal groups in Africa, even if the European powers had shown greater ethnic sensibility, some combination of multi-ethnic nations inevitably would have developed. The only alternative would have been the creation of hundreds of small states that would not have been economically viable.

Ironically, the breakdown of European colonialism in the Third World has also led to some singularly unhappy ethnic marriages. In Southeast Asia, when the Portuguese withdrew from the colony of East Timor in 1975, neighboring Indonesia annexed it against the local population's will. In its efforts to crush the indigenous organized opposition, the Indonesian military caused some 150,000 deaths (about 25 percent of the area's population), either directly through military action or, more commonly, indirectly through policies leading to mass starvation and disease. After the local population was finally allowed to vote for independence in 1999, Timorese militias tied to the Indonesian military slaughtered thousands more. Elsewhere, following years of Italian colonial rule and a brief British occupation, the East African colony of Eritrea was forcibly merged with Ethiopia in the 1940s. The Eritrean people (who were generally more westernized and modernized than the Ethiopians) were barely consulted and subsequently began a long struggle for independence.[23] The result was three decades of civil war that resulted in the deaths of hundreds of thousands. Ultimately, the Ethiopian army fell to rebel forces from the provinces of Eritrea and Tigray.[24] The associated collapse of the Ethiopian revolutionary government allowed both provinces to achieve independence, though bloody warfare resumed between Ethiopia and Eritrea in the late 1990s.

TYPES OF ETHNIC-CULTURAL DIVISIONS

In order to better grasp the variety of ethnic tensions that currently pervade much of the developing world, I will first classify all ethnicities into a set of somewhat overlapping categories: nationality, tribe, race, and religion.[25]

Nationality

In ethnic analysis the term *nation* takes on a specialized meaning distinct from its more common usage designating a sovereign country (as in the United *Nations*). It refers, instead, to a population with its own language, cultural traditions, historical aspirations, and, often, its own geographical home. Frequently, nationhood is associated with the belief that "the interests and values of this nation take priority over all other interests and values."[26] As opposed to other types of ethnicity, nationalities often claim sovereignty over a specific geographic area. But, as we have seen, these proposed *national* boundaries often do not coincide with those of sovereign states. For example, Russia, India, Spain, and Sri Lanka are all *sovereign states* (independent countries) that encompass several distinct *nationalities* (cultural identities). In each case, members of at least one of those nationalities—Chechyns (Russia), Muslim Kashmiris (India), Basques (Spain), and Tamils (Sri Lanka)—are currently fighting for independence. On the other hand, the Chinese are a nationality that, through migration, has spilled over to several East Asian states and to other parts of the world. The Kurds also reside in several countries, including Iraq, Turkey, and Iran. Unlike the Chinese, however, they are a nation without a state of their own.

    As with many types of ethnicity, the political significance of national identity is grounded in highly subjective factors. That is to say, nationality becomes politically important only when members believe themselves to have a common history and destiny that both unites them and *distinguishes them from other ethnicities* in their country. Perhaps the most important factor is the extent to which a group maintains a distinct spoken language. Because French Canadians, Turkish Kurds, and Malaysian Chinese have maintained their "mother tongues," their national identities remain politically salient. Chicano nationalists in Texas, California, and New Mexico have sought to protect Mexican-American rights and cultural integrity. Some have run for local government office under the banner of *la raza unida* ("the united race") but have no interest in separating from the United States. Chinese speakers in Southeast Asia have maintained their own cultural and political organizations while feeling strong emotional, and sometimes financial, ties to China. In countries such as Indonesia and Vietnam, the Chinese have periodically been persecuted and attacked by their non-Chinese neighbors. Quebec's government, currently headed by the separatist Parti Québécois, supports independence for the province. On the other hand, whenever migrants to countries such as the United States or Australia fully assimilate into the national language and culture, gradually dropping their original language, their previous national identity diminishes in significance.

The appeal of militant ethnic nationalism may vary over time as a result of changing political and economic conditions. Despite its distinct language and culture, Spain's Basque population began to assimilate into Spanish society in the nineteenth century. However, during the 1970s two factors caused an upsurge in militant Basque nationalism aimed at self-rule (marked by terrorist bombings and assassinations). The first was the democratization of Spain's political system following the death of long-time dictator Francisco Franco, which raised Basque hopes for greater autonomy and allowed nationalist parties to campaign openly. The other was an economic downturn in the region's industrial economy.[27]

In their most limited manifestations, nationalist movements may simply seek to preserve their group's cultural identity and promote their collective economic and political interests. For example, Lebanese in Brazil, Irish in Liverpool, or East Indians in Guyana and Trinidad have not entertained visions of self-governance. On the other hand, nationalist aspirations become far more volatile when they seek to create an independent ethnic state. Such separatist movements are most likely to arise when an ethnic minority is concentrated in a particular area of the country and represents a majority of the population in that region. Those conditions exist in Sri Lanka (formerly Ceylon), off the coast of India, where the Tamil-speaking population is most heavily concentrated in the country's northern and eastern provinces, particularly the Jaffna region in the far north.[28] Even before the intrusion of Dutch, Portugese, and British colonizers, the Tamils kept themselves apart from other ethnicities inhabiting Ceylon. The British conquest and colonization of the entire island (from 1815 onwards) produced a nationalist reaction linked to Buddhist chauvinism within the Sinhalese majority and provoked friction between them and the Tamil minority.

Since independence in 1948, political power has been concentrated in the hands of the Sinhalese (about three-fourths of the country's population). As in most domestic controversies between nationalities, language issues intensified the conflict. In 1956, Sinhalese replaced English as the country's official language, giving the Sinhalese population a significant advantage in securing government jobs. As one Tamil political leader put it, "Not until 1956 did we really believe that we were second-class citizens. Until then all we were engaged in were preventive measures, which we thought would hold."[29] From that point forward, however, the battle for Tamil self-rule intensified. When Tamil was given legal status in 1978, many Sinhalese, particularly those aspiring to government jobs, felt victimized. Religious differences between the largely Hindu Tamils and the predominantly Buddhist Sinhalese augment their language and cultural divisions.

As early as 1949, Tamil leaders (representing some 18 percent of the country's population) demanded a federal system that would grant Tamil areas substantial autonomy.[30] Sinhalese nationalists, in turn, tried to impose their language on the entire nation. Even though they were far more numerous than the Tamils, the Sinhalese population suffered from a "minority complex," feeling threatened by the 50 million Tamils living nearby in the Indian mainland. In 1958, Sinhalese mobs attacked Tamils in various parts of the country, and in 1964, the Sri Lankan government signed an agreement with India calling for the eventual return to India of 525,000 Tamils whose families had once migrated from India.[31] Faced with such threats, from the 1950s through the late 1980s Tamil nationalism became increasingly strident and violent. Early calls for separatism or autonomy (a degree of self-rule within the Sri Lankan state) were superseded by demands for full secession and the creation of a sovereign Tamil state. By the early 1980s, the most powerful force in the country's predominantly Tamil areas was the Liberation Tigers of Tamil Eelam[32] (better known as the Tamil Tigers, or LTTE), a secessionist force engaged in guerrilla warfare and terrorism.

In 1987, following a major national government offensive against the LTTE, India (with its own Tamil minority) intervened militarily in Sri Lanka. The resulting Indo-Lanka Peace Accord called for a multi-ethnic, multilingual Sri Lankan state with greater regional autonomy for Tamil areas. Though signed by the Indian and Sri Lankan governments and supported by most Tamils, the accord was rejected by many Sinhalese, particularly the ultra-nationalist National Liberation Front (JVP). From 1987 to 1989, the JVP launched their own campaign of strikes, boycotts, and terrorism, resulting in thousands of deaths. A brutal government campaign eventually crushed the JVP, but the war against the Tamil Tigers continued. While many Tamils welcomed the Indo-Lanka accord, the Tigers viewed it as inadequate. Instead, they expanded their bloody guerrilla war, first against the 60,000–man Indian army of occupation, and then, after the withdrawal of Indian troops in 1990, against the Sri Lankan government and moderate Tamils.

The LTTE alledgedly raises more than $60 million annually by smuggling illegal immigrants and drugs into Europe and the United States and receives millions more in donations from Tamil supporters living abroad. It is believed to be responsible for the 1993 assassination of Sri Lankan president Ranasinghe Premadasa and the June 2000 bombing that killed a cabinet member and 22 others. Human rights groups have condemned the Tigers for using young girls to conduct suicide bombings because they are more likely to get past police and army check points with bombs strapped to their bodies. As of mid-2000, an estimated 62,000 people in a relatively small nation had been killed in the civil war. However, a 2002 truce shows some sign of holding and restoring peace.

Tribe

The very use of the term *tribe*, especially as applied to African cultures, is fairly controversial. Many anthropologists and political scientists find it arbitrary and unhelpful. They note that cultural anthropologists who first worked in Africa, parts of South Asia, and Australia-New Zealand frequently assumed that the social characteristics of the small groups of people they were studying could automatically be extended to larger units they called a *tribe*.[33] (In this regard, I wrote previously about the upper Congo's "myth of the Bangala.") Critics also point out that the term is sometimes used to describe groups in Africa as large as Nigeria's 15 million Yorubas, a population that elsewhere in the world would be called a *nationality*. Hence, many scholars prefer the term *ethnicity* to *tribe*. This section, however, still refers to tribal groups for the simple reason that the term is familiar to most readers and has long been used by many scholars of ethnic politics and by numerous political leaders in Africa and Asia. For example, in describing the problems of his own country, former Ugandan president Milton Obote lamented "the pull of the tribal force."[34] In this chapter I use *tribe* to describe *sub*national groups, particularly in Africa, that share a collective identity and language and believe themselves to hold a common lineage. In India, Vietnam, Burma, and other parts of Asia, tribe refers to nonliterate hill peoples, such as the Laotian Hmong, living very traditional lifestyles in relative isolation from modern society. The term has also been used, of course, in regard to North American Indians as well as the lowland (Amazonian) Indians of South America. In none of these regions do we use the term pejoratively.

Intertribal conflict has frequently sparked violence in Sub-Saharan Africa, affecting more than half the countries on that continent at one time or another. Nigeria, Ethiopia, Rwanda, Burundi, Uganda, Sudan, and Congo (Zaire), among others, have been torn apart by civil wars that were largely, or at least partially, ethnically based. In Liberia, Angola, and Mozambique, civil conflicts initially fought over other issues were aggravated by overlapping ethnic divisions. From the time of its independence, Nigeria experienced antagonism between the Muslims in the North and the peoples of the South and East. With 50 percent of the country's population, the Hausa-Fulani and other northern tribes were a dominant political force, resented by southerners such as the Ibo, who considered them backward.[35] Northerners, in turn, feared the influence of the more modern and commercially successful Ibo people who prevailed in the East. Each of the three major ethnic groups (Hausa-Fulani, Ibo, and Yoruba) prevailed in one region of the country, casting a shadow over smaller tribes in their area. Each major tribe, in turn, feared being dominated by the other.[36]

Two military coups in 1966 intensified friction between officers of differing ethnic backgrounds and sparked violence against the many Ibos who had migrated to the North. In fear of their lives, more than a million Ibos (perhaps as many as two million) fled to their homeland. In May 1967, Colonel Chukwuemeka Ojukwa, an Ibo military leader, declared that Eastern Nigeria was withdrawing from the country to become the independent nation of Biafra. Backed by the Organization of African Unity (OAU), the Nigerian national government was determined not to let Biafra secede.[37] Despite its initial military success, Biafra eventually suffered from the antipathy that many smaller eastern tribes felt toward the Ibos. A number of those tribes sided with the federal army. Ultimately, the armed forces surrounded Biafra and tightened their grip. Many thousand Ibos starved to death in a pattern of war and famine that subsequently became tragically familiar in other parts of Africa. When Biafra finally did surrender in early 1970, however, the Nigerian military government was impressively disciplined and refrained from acts of vengeance. Since that time, the Ibos have been successfully reintegrated into Nigerian society, but intertribal tensions and periodic religious violence persist.[38]

Unfortunately, the Nigerian conflict was merely one of the earliest African civil wars that transpired over the years between antagonistic tribal and cultural groups. One of the most tragic was the long and bitter fight by the Eritrean and Tigrayan minorities to secede from Ethiopia. Elsewhere, Burundi's ruling Tutsi minority crushed a series of uprisings by the majority Hutus (some 85 percent of the population) over the last three decades, massacring perhaps 100,000 people in 1972 alone.[39] In 1993, when a Tutsi soldier assassinated Melchior Ndadaye, a Hutu who was the country's first elected president, new intertribal bloodshed erupted. One year later, in the neighboring country of Rwanda, the Hutu president's death in a plane crash set off an orgy of violence. A government-directed massacre led by Hutu extremists was directed at the minority Tutsis and, to a lesser extent, moderate Hutus. Within weeks, approximately 500,000 Tutsi were beaten or hacked to death by local Hutu militia and villagers.[40] Eventually, a disciplined Tutsi revolutionary army, supported by neighboring Uganda, gained control of the country and jailed thousands of Hutus. Hundreds of thousands more fled to nearby Congo, where many of them were massacred or starved to death by the anti-Hutu regime of then-president Laurent Kabila.

In other conflicts, such as the Angolan and Mozambican civil wars (which had both ideological and ethnic bases), external intervention intensified the war and added to the carnage. Cold War superpowers often armed opposing sides or interceded through surrogates. For example, acting in consort with the Soviet Union, Cuba provided military assistance to the leftist national governments of Ethiopia, Angola, and Mozambique. The United States armed UNITA, the Angolan rebel force, while the South African military supported Mozambique's bloody RENAMO guerrillas. Belgium and France armed the Rwandan regime prior to its genocidal attacks on its Tutsi population. In each of those countries, hundreds of thousands perished from warfare or starvation.

While the end of the Cold War has reduced external intervention in Africa's tribal conflicts, the recent brutal wars in Liberia and Sierra Leone demonstrate that the so-called "New World Order" will continue to include African interethnic violence for the foreseeable future. During the late 1990s, Rwanda, Uganda, Zimbabwe, and Angola all intervened in the ethnically related civil war in the Congo. Several million people probably died there, either directly from the warfare or, more commonly, from resulting famines. In other cases, corrupt dictators launched campaigns against tribal minorities in order to curry favor among powerful ethnic groups and thereby deflect protest against their own government. Thus, in recent years Kenyan president Daniel Arap Moi brutalized the Kikuyu, and Congolese president Laurent Kabila massacred the Hutu minority in his country for precisely that purpose.

Race

Race is normally the most visible ethnic division within society. That is to say, while it may be difficult to pinpoint a person's religion or tribe from his or her appearance, physical differences between Blacks, Whites, and East Asians are usually rather apparent. In some instances, however, even racial distinctions are more subtle and elusive. The Aymara-speaking woman in La Paz, Bolivia, who wears a bowler hat and a distinctive native skirt, is obviously an Indian yet her Spanish-speaking son, wearing a suit and teaching at a nearby high school, is considered a Mestizo (a person of mixed Indian and White heritage). African Americans or South African "Coloreds" of mixed racial origin are sometimes physically indistinguishable from Whites. Unlike other ethnic divisions, racial divisions are not necessarily linked to language or cultural differences.

We have noted that cultural identity involves a common set of values and customs and a shared sense of history and destiny. Of course, people of the same race living in a particular country may not experience that sense of community. Serbs, Croats, Bosnian Muslims, and Albanian Kosovars in the former Yugoslavia are all Whites; Lebanese Shi'ites and Christians are both Arabs; and Ethiopia's Amharic majority as well as the Eritreans and Tigrayans who seceded from the country are all Blacks. Yet despite their common racial backgrounds, these groups most assuredly do not share a common cultural bond. Since there were no other races in each country, race could not be an ethnic marker. Only when people live in *multiracial* settings do individual racial groups define themselves and set themselves apart from "others" on the basis of race. Indeed, "there was no common sense of being 'African', 'European,' or [American] 'Indian,'" notes Crawford Young, "prior to the creation of multiracial communities by the population movements of the imperial age."[41] Slavery and other manifestations of Western imperialism in the Third World produced a wide range of negative racial stereotypes about Asians, Africans, and (North and South) American Indians. The subsequent migration of Asians to the plantations of East Africa and the Caribbean created further racial cleavages.

South Africa presented the most notorious and intractable example of racially based political conflict. From its colonization by the British until its 1994 transition to majority rule, the country was ruled by a White minority constituting only 15 percent of the population as of the 1990s. In the years following World War II, political power shifted from English-speaking Whites to the more conservative Afrikaners, descendants of Dutch and French Protestant settlers.[42] Meanwhile, Blacks (constituting about 70 percent of the nation's population) were denied fundamental legal and economic rights, including the right to vote or hold political office.

Until renounced by President F. W. de Klerk's administration (the last White minority government), the legal centerpiece of South African racial policy was *apartheid* (separateness). That system rigidly segregated employment, public facilities, and housing, envisioning a day when most Blacks lived in eight allegedly self-ruling "homelands." In fact, these homelands, consisting of desolate rural regions, could not possibly support the country's Black population. Moreover, since important sectors of the South African economy, most notably its mines, are dependent on Black labor, the geographical segregation envisioned by apartheid was implausible even from the perspective of the White business community. But the millions of Blacks who still lived outside the homelands were denied the right to own land or to enjoy fundamental civil liberties.

Apartheid was based on a fourfold racial classification that defied international ethical standards and often fell victim to its own logical contradictions. *Blacks* were the largest group and were subjected to the greatest level of legal discrimination. *Coloreds* (constituting less than 10 percent of the country's population) and *Asians* (about 3 percent) had greater legal rights than Blacks but still ranked considerably below Whites. Finally, *Whites*, of course, maintained virtually all political and economic power. Although the Constitutional Act of 1983 established a three-house Parliament—representing Whites, Coloreds, and Asians, but not the Black majority—the powers of the Colored and Asian houses were minimal.

By the 1980s, however, cracks began to develop in South Africa's segregation policies, as many middle-class Coloreds and Asians moved into "Whites only" neighborhoods by subletting from Whites. Hoping to isolate Colored professionals and businesspeople from the Black population, the government often turned a blind eye to such violations, while simultaneously brutally repressing Black civil rights demonstrations in the townships.

At the same time, South Africa came under intense domestic and international pressure to end apartheid and White domination. The country had become an international pariah, subject to diplomatic and cultural isolation, including a United Nations boycott restricting trade, travel, and investment. South African athletes could not compete in the Olympics or other international sporting events. Though slow to take effect, economic sanctions, particularly restrictions on investment, eventually began to limit the country's economic growth. Growing protest and unrest in the Black townships, coupled with international isolation and a worldwide trend toward democracy, compounded the pressures for change.[43] Finally, a growing number of powerful voices within the White economic, legal, and intellectual elites (including Afrikaners) were pressuring the government for racial reform.

By the start of the 1990s, then, the de Klerk government, recognizing that apartheid was no longer viable, began to rescind a variety of segregation laws. It also legalized the African National Congress (ANC), the leading Black opposition group, along with two more radical organizations after decades of banishment. The Congress's legendary leader, Nelson Mandela, perhaps the world's most renowned political prisoner, was released from jail together with hundreds of other political prisoners. These changes, coupled with the ANC's suspension of their armed struggle, opened the door to a new constitution enfranchising the Black majority and ending White minority rule.

In December 1991, the Convention for a Democratic South Africa (CODESA) brought together the government, the ANC, the Zulu-based Inkatha Freedom Party, and 16 smaller groups for discussion of the new political order. Public opinion among Whites was mixed but generally supportive of the process. Thus, Nelson Mandela expressed amazement at the hundreds of Whites who lined the road to cheer him when he was released from prison. In a 1992 national referendum called by de Klerk, nearly 70 percent of all White voters endorsed negotiations with the ANC and other Black groups. The following year the government and the ANC agreed to the election of a constitutional assembly that would create a new political system with equal rights for all South Africans. Universal suffrage ensured a Black majority in the assembly, but Whites were guaranteed special minority protection until 1999. In May 1994 the ANC parliamentary majority elected Nelson Mandela president of the new South Africa.

Nearly a decade later, the road to multiracial democracy remains difficult. Blacks have discovered that while majority rule has engendered greater social justice and human dignity, it has not particularly improved living standards. The governments of President Mandela and his successor, Thabo Mbeki, have pursued moderate economic policies to reassure the White business community. Over time, however, if Black living conditions do not improve and if there is not a substantial redistribution of economic resources, the ANC's Black constituency may demand more radical policies. The country's soaring crime rate, a reflection of widespread poverty and pervasive inequality, could also turn into wider political violence.

Finally, ethnically based violence among Blacks could also resurface. Prior to the 1994 transition, conflict within the Black community took a terrible toll, often pitting the more radical ANC, primarily backed by members of the Xhosa tribe, against the conservative Zulu-dominated Inkatha party. Some of that violence, it has subsequently been revealed, was fomented by the security forces of the outgoing White government. By including Inkatha in his government, Mandela somewhat quieted that conflict. Until now, the Mandela and Mbeki administrations have impressively contained earlier ethnic animosities, but enduring tensions lie just beneath the surface, both between Blacks and Whites and amongst Blacks.

Religion

Because it involves deeply felt values, religion has frequently been the source of bitter communal strife. In Chapter 3, we examined the influence of religious *beliefs* on political attitudes and behavior, particularly those of fundamentalists and others favoring close links between church and state. We saw that people's religious orientation shapes their views of their political rights and obligations, the nature of their constitution and legal system, and other fundamental political issues. In some countries with multiple religions, the state must create inheritance and family laws that are acceptable to religious communities with dissimilar views on these issues. In Israel, for example, different codes of family law apply to Jews, Muslims, and Christians. The same is true in India for Hindus, Muslims, and Sikhs.[44]

In this chapter, we look at a related but distinct aspect of religion, namely the degree to which coreligionists identify strongly with each other and seek to dominate or exclude other religious groups. In other words, we are concerned here, not with the constitutional and legal ramifications of religion (considered in Chapter 3) but with the relations and disagreements *between* religious groups (defined here as ethnic communities) living in the same country. The likelihood of conflict between these religious groups is influenced by at least two important factors: first, the extent to which one community feels dominated by another; and, second, the degree to which any religion in a given country believes that it is the one true faith and that alternate theologies are unacceptable. Thus, Catholics and Protestants coexist rather harmoniously in the United States and Germany because neither of these conditions applies. On the other hand, in Northern Ireland, where Catholics resent the Protestants' political and economic power, and Protestants fear that Catholics are taking over, even the widely hailed peace accord has not fully ended more than three decades of conflict.

In 1992, Hindu fundamentalists destroyed a sixteenth-century Muslim mosque in the north Indian town of Ayodhya. Like many such clashes, the incident grew out of centuries-old beliefs and hostilities.[45] The Ayodhya mosque had been built by the Mogul emperor Babur on the spot where many Hindus believe their god Ram had been born some 5,000 years earlier. To the Bharatiya Janata Party (BJP), the leading Hindu political party, and to the militant World Hindu Council, the mosque was a symbol of Islamic foreign domination during the hundreds of years of Mogul rule prior to the British colonial era. Indeed, only two years before the attack, Indian Prime Minister Vishwanath Pratap Singh's National Front government had been forced to resign because of its refusal to raze the mosque and replace it with a Hindu temple. Within days of the assault, rioting in northern and central India left about 2,000 dead.

Ironically, some of the worst Hindu-Muslim bloodshed took place in Bombay, India's financial and cultural center and one of the country's most modern and least sectarian cities. An extremist Hindu group, Shiv Sena, with some 30,000 armed members in that city, was responsible for much of the violence. Since that time, not only have city authorities failed to prosecute Shiv Sena's leader, but he has been protected by the Bombay police. In neighboring Islamic countries, Pakistani crowds attacked Hindu temples while Bangladeshis assaulted Hindu-owned shops and burned Air India offices.

To be sure, India and Pakistan were born of communal violence, and neither has been free of it since. Although both countries had been part of a single British colony, when negotiations for independence advanced in the late 1940s, the Muslim League insisted on the creation of a separate Muslim state. Using language that classically defines an ethnic group, League leader Mohammed Ali Jinnah declared: "We are a nation with our own distinctive culture and civilization, language and literature . . . customs . . . history and tradition."[46] In 1946, as independence approached, political conflict between the Muslim League and the leading voice of Indian independence, the Congress Party (a nonreligious party led largely by secular Hindus) touched off Hindu-Muslim communal violence that left thousands dead. Finally, the British reluctantly divided their most important colony into two countries: India, with roughly 300 million Hindus and 40 million Muslims, and Pakistan, with approximately 60 million Muslims and 20 million Hindus. No sooner had independence been declared (August 15, 1947), when horrendous religious massacres began in both countries. Whole villages were destroyed, 12 million refugees of both faiths fled across the border, more than 75,000 women were abducted and raped, and up to one million people were killed in one of the twentieth century's worst ethnic conflagrations.[47] Two decades later, Pakistan split in two as language and cultural differences divided the Muslim population. With support from India, the country's Bengali-speaking eastern region broke away from the primarily Urdu-speaking West to form the country of Bangladesh. Today, Muslim separatists in the Indian state of Kashmir are waging guerrilla warfare aimed at either Kashmiri independence or unification with Pakistan. In 2001 Muslim fundamentalists attacked the Indian parliament, once again bringing India and Pakistan (both nuclear powers) to the brink of war.

Other religious conflicts also continue to extract a heavy toll from India's political system. In the economically dynamic state of Punjab (where members of the Sikh religion constitute 55 to 60 percent of the population), Sikh militants demand the creation of their own nation, called Khalistan.[48] Ironically, it is believed that former Indian prime minister Indira Gandhi bears some responsibility for the spread of Sikh extremism. Allegedly, her government secretly financed and encouraged the most militant Sikh organization, the outlawed Dal Khalsa, thereby hoping that its violent behavior would discredit the more limited cause of Sikh autonomy favored by moderate Sikh parties.[49] If so, the tactic proved to be a serious miscalculation. Sikh terrorism, including random murders of Hindu civilians, and police-military brutality against Sikhs created an ever-rising cycle of violence. In 1984, government troops attacked the holy Golden Temple of Amristar where the militant Sikh leader Sant Jarnail Singh Bhindranwale and many of his followers were holed up. In a three-day battle on the temple grounds, more than 1,000 people, including Bhindranwale, were killed. Thousands of Sikh troops in the Indian armed forces then mutinied, some of them battling loyal army units. Finally, on October 31, months after the attack on the Golden Temple, two Sikh members of Prime Minister Gandhi's personal bodyguard assassinated her, as she became the victim of her own earlier strategy. Lashing out after the assassination, roaming Hindu mobs killed thousands of innocent Sikh civilians. Despite attempts at reconciliation by Indira's successor, her son Rajiv Gandhi, government repression and Sikh terrorism continued unabated. By the mid-1990s, following some 20,000 deaths on both sides, the Indian military seemed to have contained the separatist movement, but the Punjab could easily erupt again at any time.

During the 1970s and 1980s, Lebanon was also a battlefield for warring religious factions. Among the 17 religious communities that shared political power after independence, the most important were Maronite Catholics, Shi'ite Muslims, Sunni Muslims, and Druse (a Muslim sect).[50] Ironically, despite such religious heterogeneity, for the next 30 years the country was considered "the Switzerland of the Middle East"—a bastion of peace and economic prosperity in the midst of a troubled region. During that time the dominant Maronite and Sunni communities coexisted under the terms of a political power-sharing arrangement dating back to the 1920s (during limited home rule) and reinforced by a national pact two decades later (1943) as the country neared independence.

But power-sharing and the peace it had brought broke down in the 1970s as the Muslim population, particularly the Shi'ite community, perceived that the terms of the old agreement no longer reflected the population sizes of the various religious groups. Muslims, with between 55 and 70 percent of the population (depending on which side's estimate one believed), had long been allocated only 50 percent of the nation's bureaucratic and political posts. Religious, economic, and political differences also caused conflict between Shi'ite and Sunni Muslims. Shi'ites had less political power and a lower standard of living than the Sunnis, and their illiteracy rate was three times higher than the Christians. Moreover, although the Shi'ites were the country's largest religious community, they were allocated less than 20 percent of the seats in the parliament. At the same time, Lebanon's two most important political offices—president and prime minister—were reserved, respectively, for a Maronite Christian and a Sunni.[51]

Tensions were further exacerbated by external interventions. The influx of many Palestinian refugees (mostly fleeing Jordan), including armed PLO militia, radicalized the country's political debate. Many impoverished Shi'ites were drawn to the Palestinians' revolutionary rhetoric. On the other hand, Christian leaders became concerned that PLO attacks against Israel were provoking retaliatory Israeli raids into Lebanon. Soon, Israel allied itself with Christian militias who feared both Shi'ite militias and the Palestinian guerrilla fighters and were determined to maintain their community's privileged economic and political position. Syria, wishing to expand its power in the Middle East and create a buffer between its territory and Israel, occupied much of Lebanon and manipulated various factions.[52] By 1975 Lebanon's national government had become a hollow shell as power shifted to a range of communal warlords, each defending his own turf and using his militias for both political and criminal purposes. Confrontations between the army and civilian protestors, along with clashes between Palestinian guerrillas and Christian militias, engulfed Lebanon in a civil war that lasted more than 15 years and took more than 150,000 lives. The country's religious conflict had elements of a class struggle as well, pitting the more prosperous Christian community against Shi'ites, who saw themselves as the oppressed poor. Foreign forces in the form of Palestinian national aspirations, Israeli occupation of parts of southern Lebanon, and Syrian military domination of much of the rest of the country all added to the bloodshed. Over time, alliances sometimes shifted, with Shi'ites and Syrians, for example, supporting the Palestinians at some points and fighting them at others. Finally, as key Lebanese cities lay in ruins and Palestinian, Israeli, and Syrian forces threatened to destroy the nation's sovereignty, the Arab League (representing the Arab countries of North Africa and the Middle East) helped negotiate a treaty between the warring Lebanese factions. The Taif Accord, signed in late 1989 in Saudi Arabia, raised the percentage of Muslim government officials relative to the Christians and established the basis for a "national pact" between the warring factions[53] While the peace has held for over a decade and Lebanon has rebuilt much of its shattered economy and infrastructure, external interventions by the Palestinian Liberation Organization (PLO), the Syrians, or the Israelis could destabilize the country once again.

INDEPENDENCE, MODERNIZATION, AND ETHNIC CONFLICT

Scholars and other analysts once assumed that improved education and communications in the Third World would break down ethnic conflicts. Because of their own history as a "melting pot" for so many immigrant groups, Americans in particular have supposed that socioeconomic modernization enhances ethnic integration and harmony.[54] Yet in Africa and Asia, political development (in the form of national independence) and socioeconomic modernization have quite frequently politicized and intensified ethnic antagonisms. Indeed, Crawford Young notes that "cultural pluralism [and ethnic strife] as a political phenomenon" was not significant in traditional societies but, rather, emerged "from such social processes as urbanization, the revolution in communications and spread of modern education."[55] Early modernization theorists, who were quite optimistic regarding the positive effects of literacy, urbanization, and modern values, clearly underestimated the extent to which these factors might mobilize differing ethnic groups and set them against each other. Dependency theorists, on the other hand, provided a rather superficial analysis of ethnic issues, tending to blame conflicts on colonialism or neocolonialism (economic domination of the developing world by developed capitalist nations even after the LDCs had achieved independence).

During the era of European colonialism, ethnic divisions in Africa and Asia were kept somewhat in check by independence movements, which sought a common front against the Europeans. "The transcendent obligation of resistance to the colonizer . . . largely obscure[d] the vitality of ethnicity as a basis of social solidarity."[56] After independence, however, previously submerged ethnic rivalries frequently rose to the surface.[57] In the new political order, religious, racial, tribal, and nationality groups compete with each other for such state resources as roads, schools, medical clinics, irrigation projects, and civil service jobs. Subsequently, rural-to-urban migration brought many ethnic groups into close proximity for the first time. At the same time, urbanization, rising educational levels, and the spread of mass communications politicized previously unmobilized sectors of the population. Because so many of them identify primarily with their own caste, religion, nationality, or tribe, their newly acquired political awareness often brings them into conflict with others. Furthermore, the spread of higher education, rather than generating greater harmony, often produces a class of ethnically chauvinistic intellectuals who became the ideologists of ethnic hostilities. For all of these reasons, then, ethnic conflict has remained a potent and often growing phenomenon in the developing world.

LEVELS OF INTERETHNIC CONFLICT

Although most countries are ethnically heterogenous, there are wide variations in how the various ethnicities relate to each other. In some cases, different races or religions interact fairly amicably; in others, deep resentments inspire the most horrifying barbarities. Having examined the various *categories* of ethnic communities, we will now consider the *nature* and *intensity* of relations *between* them. To gauge these relationships, we may employ such measures as the frequency of interethnic friendships and marriages, the presence or absence of political parties, trade unions and other civic organizations that represent specific ethnic groups, and the correlation between ethnic affiliation and social class. In any particular country, relations between ethnic communities may range from relative harmony (Brazil) to systematic violence (the former Yugoslavia).

Relative Harmony

Modernization, as we have seen, often intensifies ethnic antagonisms in the short run, but it usually ameliorates them in the long term. Consequently, affluent democracies are more likely than LDCs to boast of amicable ethnic relations. In Switzerland, for example, German-, French-, and Italian-speaking citizens have lived together peacefully for centuries. That record is particularly impressive because linguistic barriers within a country are generally the most difficult ethnic divisions to overcome.[58] The United States and Canada also enjoy relative ethnic harmony, having successfully assimilated a large assortment of immigrant groups. In North Dakota or Saskatchewan, for example, few are concerned when a person of Ukrainian-Orthodox or German-Catholic origin marries a Lutheran of Norwegian ancestry. Despite considerable progress in recent decades, race relations in the United States constitute the one glaring exception to the pattern of ethnic harmony.

Instances of *relative ethnic harmony* in developing countries are less plentiful. However, in Brazil and the island nations of the Caribbean, relations between Blacks and Whites are generally more harmonious than in the United States. Interracial dating and marriages, for example, are quite common, particularly among lower-income groups. Still, that harmony is relative, since even those countries have maintained a clear social hierarchy between races. While there are many middle-class Black Dominicans, Brazilians, and Panamanians, most Blacks remain mired in the lower class, and virtually none of them make it to the highest ranks of the political and economic order.

In short, even the countries classified as harmonious are only categorized that way relative to other, more conflict-ridden societies. Glaring examples of ethnic antagonisms and discrimination persist. In Cuba, for example, despite a long history of interracial marriage and more recent government efforts to promote equality, Blacks have yet to attain their share of political leadership positions. Racial slurs remain common in personal conversations.[59] And Canada, in many ways a more successful melting pot than the United States, has not resolved the vexing problem of French separatism in Quebec. But such tensions are the exception, and conflict is rarely or never violent, except in cases such as the African-American urban riots of the 1960s and more recently in Los Angeles.

Uneasy Balance

In developing nations such as Trinidad-Tobago and Malaysia, divisions between the principal ethnic groups are somewhat sharper than in the previous category of relative harmony. While still generally peaceful, interethnic relations are at times strained; for example in Malaysia, the Muslim Malay majority has largely controlled the political system, including parliament and the government bureaucracy, while the Chinese minority has dominated the private sector. Race riots in 1969 led the Malaysian government to introduce a "New Economic Policy" designed, in part, to redistribute more of the country's wealth to the Malays. Fearful of Chinese domination, the Malays have also benefited from a system of ethnic preferences in education and the civil service.[60] Today the two communities continue to maintain a social distance, and some analysts see signs of slowly growing communal antagonisms. Still, despite the stress created by the economic crisis at the end of the 1990s, ethnic relations have remained peaceful.

The Caribbean nation of Trinidad-Tobago offers another interesting example of uneasy balance. During the second half of the nineteenth century, British colonial authorities encouraged the migration of indentured plantation workers from India who joined the Black majority and the small White elite. Contrary to the usual Caribbean practice of extensive racial mixing, there was little interracial marriage or childbearing between Blacks and East Indians.[61] Although there was little overt hostility, each group developed negative stereotypes about the other.[62] Following Trinidadian independence in 1962, ethnic frictions increased as Blacks and Indians began to compete for state resources. Most of the important political, civil service, military, and police positions since that time have been held by Blacks, who predominate in the country's urban middle class and working class. The upper ranks of the business community continue to be filled by the small White minority. For many years the East Indian population generally belonged to one of two groups: middle- and upper-middle-class urban businesspeople (especially merchants) with considerable collective economic power; and a large, impoverished rural population of farm workers and small farmers.

Trinidadian politics does not feature the same overt ethnic appeals that characterize many LDCs, but most of its political parties and unions largely represent one race. For 24 years (1962 to 1986) the national government was headed by the People's National Movement (PNM), a political party primarily headed and supported by Blacks. During that time the opposition was led by various Indian-dominated parties, including the Democratic Labour Party (DLP) and the United Labour Front (ULF). Major labor unions tended to be either primarily Black or largely East Indian.[63] Only in 1986 did the newly formed National Alliance for Reconstruction (NAR) finally dislodge the PNM from power by forging an electoral alliance between Indian voters and the Black middle- and upper-middle classes.[64] While Black and Indian political and labor leaders have cooperated periodically over the years in efforts such as this, the two communities continue to maintain their social, political, and economic distance. In the 1990s, a radical Black Power movement managed to briefly capture the parliament building, but violent behavior of this sort is an aberration.

Enforced Hierarchy (Ethnic Dominance)

As we have seen, one important factor permitting ethnic balance in countries such as Malaysia and Trinidad-Tobago has been the division of political and economic power between the different ethnicities. In *enforced hierarchies*, however, both forms of power are concentrated in the hands of the ruling ethnic group. South African apartheid represented the most blatant example of such a relationship. Through the 1980s, Whites dominated both the private sector and the state, including the courts, police, and armed forces. Blacks were denied the most basic rights of citizenship. Until the dismemberment of apartheid legislation, the legal system even restricted or prohibited interracial marriage, sexual relations, and housing.

Latin American nations with large Indian populations—including Guatemala, Bolivia, Ecuador, and Peru—have a less overt, but still significant, form of hierarchy. Historically, being an Indian in those countries was virtually synonymous with being a poor peasant at the bottom of the social and political ladder. Even today, despite important recent gains in Indian rights, virtually all positions of political and economic influence are still held by Whites and Mestizos. At the same time, however, racial classifications in Latin America are more culturally and less biologically defined than in the United States, thereby allowing for some upward mobility. In other words, if a young Indian villager moves to the city, adopts Western dress, and speaks Spanish, he or she is con-sidered a Mestizo. And in the rural highlands of Ecuador and Peru, many peas-ant communities that spoke Quechua a generation ago have switched to Spanish in a process of *mestizaje* (becoming Mestizo). Consequently, over the years the percentage of the population viewed as Mestizos (a more prestigious category than Indian) has increased, while the proportion speaking indigenous (Indian) languages has diminished. Although defining race culturally has cre-ated a somewhat more open society, unfortunately it also meant that Indians could only enjoy upward mobility by abandoning their own culture. Since the 1980s, however, Indians in these countries have begun to assert their cultural rights and political influence. In Bolivia, the head of an Indian-based political party was elected vice president of the country. In Ecuador, a national Indian federation seized Congress and joined the military in a coup that ousted the president and briefly installed a three-person ruling junta that included the president of the Indian federation.[65] In Mexico, the Zapatista rebels of rural Chiapas, who had staged an uprising in behalf of Indian rights, received a remarkable amount of national support from Mexicans of all ethnicities and social classes.

In all of these cases of enforced hierarchy, racial and class distinctions are closely intertwined. Those higher up the social ladder tend to be lighter skinned; those at the lower ranks of society are generally darker. One study of more than 80 members of the Ecuadorian industrial and commercial elite revealed only a single business leader who admitted having any amount of Indian ancestry, though some others likely had some small proportion.[66] And in Brazil, being Black is largely synonymous with being poor. Indeed, people of color who rise to the middle or upper-middle class frequently are no longer considered Black by their peers. But while upward mobility through the class-race hierarchy is possible, it remains difficult. Racial prejudice shapes social relationships and creates subtle, or not so subtle, barriers to equality.

Unlike South African apartheid, Latin America's racial hierarchy is infor-mal and not written into the legal system. And unlike South Africa, it hasn't been enforced by a repressive police and military apparatus. But during nearly 40 years of revolutionary upheaval and intense government repression, the Guatemalan armed forces considered rural Indian communities to be breeding grounds for leftist guerrillas. Consequently, successive military regimes massa-cred tens of thousands of Indian peasants in a policy bordering on genocide.

Fortunately, since the 1990s a peace treaty with the guerrillas has curtailed such violence.[67] Indian villagers in Peru also suffered greatly from the military's recent war against the Maoist Shining Path and from the revolutionaries' brutal tactics. While Shining Path organizers focused on class struggle rather than racial divisions, much of their support came from Indian peasants resentful of the White-Mestizo power structure.[68] And since the mid-1990s, Mexico's Zapatista rebels have explicitly demanded rights for the country's indigenous population during their armed, but relatively nonviolent, confrontation with the government.

Systematic Violence

In the worst case scenario, deep ethnic resentments have sometimes burst into open violence or even civil war. As we have seen, in a number of Third World countries as well as in some European nations, *systematic violence* has resulted in thousands or hundreds of thousands of deaths and huge numbers of displaced refugees, rape victims, and the like. This category includes Bosnia, Chechnya, Lebanon, India, Bangladesh, Ethiopia, Nigeria, Rwanda, and Sudan, among others. Often, just as with enforced hierarchies, violence develops when ethnic divisions are reinforced by class antagonisms. In Northern Ireland, for example, Catholics have resented the Ulster Protestants' dominance over the region's economic and political structures. The 1998 Good Friday peace settlement, even if it can be kept on track, changed the political relationship but not the economic imbalance. Antipathy between Lebanon's Christian and Muslim communities was fueled by the former's economic superiority. Similarly, in Nigeria many Islamic northerners have taken exception to the economic success of the Christian Ibos. Ethnic bloodshed may follow when a shift in political power from one ethnicity to another provokes retribution against the former ruling group. Thus, when General Idi Amin seized power in Uganda, he ordered the slaughter of Langi and Acholi soldiers who were identified with the regime of ousted President Milton Obote. Following the overthrow of the communist government in 1992 in Afghanistan, the country began to disintegrate as Tajiks, Hazars, and Uzbeks challenged the long-standing political dominance of the Pashtun (Pathan) population.

OUTCOMES AND RESOLUTIONS

When ethnic antagonisms arise from competition for government resources, from resentments over the division of political power or economic resources, or from an ethnic community's demands for greater autonomy, a number of results are possible. While some outcomes are entirely peaceful, many others spawn intense violence. And while some resolutions are successful, others do not endure. Potential solutions are always constrained by the broader political culture and by the intensity of ethnic cleavages. Inevitably, potential outcomes and the options available to political leaders are limited, both by historical ethnic animosities and past patterns of cooperation. Within these constraints, however, the ethnic and government leaders' political creativity and statecraft can contribute to successful solutions. Political elites may seek reasonable, negotiated solutions, or they may choose to play on ethnic tensions for their own advantage. For example, the surprisingly peaceful final dismantling of South Africa's White minority rule was made possible by the leadership and spirit of compromise demonstrated by ANC leader Nelson Mandela and national president F. W. de Klerk.

All too often, however, self-serving, chauvinistic political leaders make a bad situation worse. For example, although Bosnian Serbs and Muslims had enjoyed relatively amicable relationships for many years, extremist leaders such as former Serb president Slobodan Milosevic aroused ethnic hatred and promoted atrocities in order to build their own political power base. In the end, Milosevic (tried before an international tribunal for crimes against humanity) brought both Bosnia and his own country to ruin. Similarly, the appalling 1994 massacres in Rwanda were substantially directed from above. Government officials induced Hutu villagers to attack their Tutsi neighbors with whom they had been living peacefully and whom they had often married over the years.

When elites are willing to resolve intense ethnic conflicts through negotiations, they arrive at several types of resolutions. In the next section, we examine those possible outcomes and also look at several options that have been attempted when negotiations failed. Although the alternatives presented here are not exhaustive, they cover a wide range of Third World experiences.

Power Sharing: Federalism and Consociationalism

Power-sharing arrangements are designed to create stability by constitutionally dividing political power among major ethnic groups. These settlements generally follow protracted negotiations and constitutional debate. If power sharing is introduced into the constitution at the time of independence, it may head off ethnic conflict before it gets started. Unfortunately, however, such arrangements often break down.

Federalism, the primary form of power sharing, is "a system of government [that] emanates from the desire of people to form a union without necessarily losing their various identities."[69] It may involve the creation of autonomous or semi-autonomous regions, each of which is governed by a particular ethnicity.[70] For example, prior to its collapse, Yugoslavia consisted of six autonomous republics governed by individual nationalities, including Serbs, Croats, and Slovenes. The constitution mandated power sharing between the various republics at the national level. That compromise began to unravel in the 1970s, however, following the death of Marshal Joseph Broz Tito, the country's long-term strong man. It collapsed completely in the early 1990s when the Communist Party lost its grip on several republics. The Soviet Union represented another federalist effort that lasted for nearly 70 years but also disintegrated with the demise of Communist Party rule. It should be noted, however, that, unlike Yugoslavia, Soviet federalism was largely a fraud, since Moscow exercised firm control over the ethnically based republics, and Russians (constituting slightly over half the Soviet population) dominated the union entirely.

Industrial democracies have had greater success with ethnically based federalism. Each of Switzerland's 22 cantons is dominated by one of the country's three major language groups, and German, French, and Italian cantons coexist rather harmoniously. Canada's federalism, though not based on ethnic divisions, has allowed the primarily French-speaking province of Quebec a substantial amount of autonomy on language and other cultural matters. Although the country's constitutional arrangement has not satisfied Québécois nationalists, it has accommodated many of their demands and, at least until now, has induced the province's voters to reject independence. Whether such harmony can be maintained in the future remains to be seen, particularly because the French-nationalist party, which has governed Quebec since 1994, continues to advocate independence. On two occasions Québécois voters rejected that option in provincial referenda. But the margin of difference narrowed the second time, and a third plebiscite could yield a different result.

In the developing world, power sharing has had a spotty record at best. After independence, Nigeria sought to accommodate its ethnic divisions through federalism. As previously noted, the country's northern region was dominated by the Hausa-Fulani, the east by the Ibos, and the west, to a lesser extent, by the Yoruba. Although the Biafran war took a terrible toll, a new federal solution has subsequently taken hold. On the other hand, Pakistani federalism failed to overcome the antipathy between the country's more powerful western region (populated largely by Urdu speakers) and the Bengali-speaking east. In 1971, relations between the two regions broke down completely, resulting in the massacre of some 500,000 Bengalis by western Pakistani troops.[71] When India went to war with Pakistan, the eastern region was able to secede and form the new nation of Bangladesh. Federalist arrangements also failed to prevent the breakup of Ethiopia because they were not adequately supported by the central government.[72]

Consociationalism offers another potential solution to ethnic conflict. Like federalism, however, it has had limited success. Consociational democracy in plural (multi-ethnic) societies entails a careful division of political power designed to protect the rights of all participants.[73] It involves the following components:

1. The leaders of all important ethnic groups form a ruling coalition at the national level.
2. Each group's leader has veto power over government policy, or at least over policies that affect his or her constituents.

3. Government funds and public positions, such as the civil service, are divided between ethnicities on a roughly proportional basis.
4. Each ethnic group is afforded a high degree of autonomy over its own affairs and over the region it populates.[74]

Thus, consociational democracy consciously rejects pure majority rule. Instead, it seeks to create a framework for stability and peace by guaranteeing minorities a share of political power—even, if need be, veto power—to protect them against the majority. Not surprisingly, negotiators for South Africa's outgoing White government insisted on consociational features in the country's new constitution that would provide protective guarantees for the White minority under the new Black-led regime. The irony of those demands could hardly be lost on South African Blacks, who had enjoyed no such protection under White rule.

Consociational democracy has been tried in several developing nations, including Cyprus (where it failed) and Malaysia (where it has generally succeeded). Perhaps the most widely known effort has been in Lebanon. From independence in 1943 until civil war erupted in 1975, Lebanon's government positions and political authority were divided proportionally between the nation's many Muslim and Christian communities. As we saw, the system ultimately broke down, in part because formulas for the proportional division of government posts were not adjusted to reflect the higher rate of population growth among Shi'ites and other Muslims over the years. After 15 years of fighting that left that once-admired Middle Eastern country shattered, Lebanon's civil war came to an end in 1990. The settlement restored consociational rule with a division of government positions that more accurately reflected the increased size of the country's Islamic population.

Arend Lijphart argues that the very success of consociational systems in reducing ethnic conflict often causes them to wither away. For example, after World War II, the Netherlands, Austria, Belgium, and Switzerland all crafted consociational democracies to manage internal ethnic divisions. Since the late 1950s, however, each of them moved away from these arrangements as ethnic divisions diminished in all but Belgium, largely as the result of consociationalism. Such success requires a high level of elite consensus across ethnic lines. Indeed, a degree of mutual trust and cooperation between the leaders of contending ethnic groups is the key to effective consociational arrangements. Trust is not easy to establish, however, and becomes ever more problematic when interethnic hostilities erupt in bloodshed.

Lijphart notes that power-sharing arrangements are most likely to succeed under two circumstances: first, when no single ethnic group constitutes a majority of the country's population; and, second, when the socioeconomic gap between the ethnic groups is not large.[75] But there are no certain formulas for success or, for that matter, for failure. Malaysia meets neither of these two standards (its Malay population constitutes a majority, and its Chinese minority is far more affluent), yet it has succeeded reasonably well with power sharing. Other countries with more auspicious circumstances have failed.

Secession

When power sharing or other forms of compromise fail, disgruntled ethnic minorities may attempt to withdraw from the country in order to form their own nation or join their ethnic brothers and sisters in a neighboring state. As one author put it, "Secession, like divorce, is an ultimate act of alienation."[76] It offers a potential way out of the "failed marriage" of ethnic groups within a nation-state. Unfortunately, however, like many divorces, secessionist movements almost always provoke bitterness and hostility.[77]

Ralph Premdas indicates that these movements have several characteristics:

1. An ethnic group—defined by factors such as language, religion, culture, or race—claims the right of self-determination. That is to say, secession involves not just greater autonomy from the central government, but rather full independence. It should be noted, however, that disenchanted ethnic groups often begin by seeking only autonomy, but subsequently, when their modest objectives are denied, they escalate their position to demand full independence.
2. The ethnic community has a defined territorial base that it claims as its homeland.
3. There is virtually always some organized struggle.[78]

Given the large number of ethnically divided LDCs, we should not be surprised to find many secessionist movements. Central governments faced with breakaway efforts virtually always seek to repress them because they are unwilling to part with some of their country's territory or resources, just as U.S. President Abraham Lincoln was unwilling to part with the Confederate states. This chapter previously examined secessionist movements by Tamils in Sri Lanka, Ibos in Nigeria, Eritreans in Ethiopia, and Sikhs in northern India. To that list we might add Blacks in southern Sudan, Karens in Myanmar, Moros in the Philippines, Muslims in Kashmir (India), and many others.

Following the Gulf War, the world briefly focused its attention on Saddam Hussein's persecution of Iraq's Kurdish population. But the Kurdish secessionist movement preceded Saddam's government and transcended Iraq's borders. Separatist efforts date to the collapse of the Ottoman Empire at the close of World War I. Residing in a largely mountainous region that they call Kurdistan, more than 20 million Kurds live in neighboring regions of Turkey, Iraq, and Iran, with smaller communities in Syria and parts of the former Soviet Union.[79] Over the years, the Kurds have been subjected to severe repression in all of the Middle Eastern countries in which they reside, and today they still have little prospect of attaining the independent Kurdistan that so many of them desire.

While secession is the solution desired by many nationality groups that have been repressed or that feel aggrieved, rarely have secessionists been able to break away, though there have been several successful secessions in Eastern Europe since the fall of communism there. The breakaway from Bangladesh of Bengali-dominated East Pakistan is one of the few "successful" secessions in the Third World, though achieved at a great cost in human lives. As we have noted, however, it required military intervention by India. Eritrea also achieved independence from Ethiopia in 1993 after decades of struggle. More often than not, however, the most that secessionist movements can hope to achieve is greater autonomy and greater government recognition of their group's rights.

Noting the spread of secessionist conflicts in the 1970s and 1980s and the disintegration of the Soviet Union, Yugoslavia, and Czechoslovakia following the collapse of communism, many analysts have predicted that Eastern Europe and many LDCs will experience the disintegration of an ever-growing number of nation-states. Some voiced alarm about this prospect. For example, a widely cited book by former U.S. senator and scholar Patrick Moynahan predicted that the number of independent states in the world would increase from about 200 to some 300 by the middle of the twenty-first century.[80] Contrary to that expectation, however, the number of secessionist wars has actually declined significantly since the start of the 1990s. From 1991 to 1999, 16 such wars were settled and 11 others were limited by cease fires or continuing negotiations. Particularly in Africa, successful peace negotiations in one country have seemingly encouraged parallel efforts in other nations. Thus, as the new century began, only 18 secessionist wars remained worldwide, fewer than at any time since 1970.[81]

Outside Intervention

"If the Bosnian Muslims had been needle-nosed dolphins," Edward Luttwak asked, "would the world have allowed the Croats and Serbs to slaughter them by the tens of thousands?"[82] His blunt words raise important ethical and pragmatic questions about the world's obligations and limitations in such situations. Historical research has shown that the United States and Western Europe sidestepped many opportunities to save Jews from the Nazi holocaust, feeling that voters at home wouldn't want to get involved. More recently, the world community has stood by and allowed, or even indirectly abetted, ethnic bloodbaths in Bosnia, Indonesia, Rwanda, the Congo, and Sudan, despite immediate and graphic evidence (often in the mass media) documenting the carnage. Indeed, Belgium and France had armed and trained the Rwandan (Hutu-dominated) military right up to the time of the 1994 mass slaughter, despite being warned by experts that it was likely that those weapons would be turned on Tutsi civilians. Furthermore, scholars and journalists have uncovered official documents that confirm that the U.S. government ignored reports of the Hutu slaughter that were being sent daily from the American embassy in Rwanda.[83] Rather than promote international intervention to save the Tutsis, the United States supported the withdrawal of the small United Nations contingent already in the country. Although the rapid rate of mass murder there—about 500,000 to 800,000 people killed in three weeks—exceeded even the Nazi holocaust, the U.S. State Department refused to call the events "genocide" for fear that the international antigenocide treaty passed after World War II might obligate the United States and other Western powers to intervene. What motivated such a seemingly callous position? One year earlier, the American public had been horrified when 18 U.S. Rangers had been killed while participating in a U.N. peacekeeping operation in Somalia, and television news had shown a mob dragging several of the bodies through the streets. When Rwandan events began to unfold, policy makers in Washington assumed that U.S. public opinion, still shaken by the images from Somalia, would preclude any new American intervention. Even a decade later, the "Somali Effect" made Washington policy makers reluctant to come to the defense of Bosnia's Muslims.

Outside intervention raises important questions of national sovereignty unless the affected government is the one who invited that intervention, as when Sri Lanka invited Indian troops. Normally, however, such invitations are unlikely to happen since it is usually the government itself that has perpetrated, encouraged, or at least condoned any widespread ethnic violence. In the majority of cases, external interference raises a number of difficult questions: At what point, if any, do other nations or international organizations (such as the United Nations, NATO, or the Organization of African Unity) have the right to violate a country's sovereignty in order to save innocent lives? For example, should the United Nations or the West have intervened militarily in Bosnia at a much earlier point, with or without the permission of the Yugoslav government, in order to stop so-called "ethnic cleansing"? If so, should the U.N. have had similar authority to send troops into Birmingham, Alabama, or rural Mississippi during the 1960s to protect the lives of civil rights workers and other Blacks then being terrorized by the Ku Klux Klan and the local police? Who is to decide whether outside intervention is legitimate or not? Under what circumstances does outside intervention (including military intervention) prevent ethnic persecution and impose a durable solution, and when will such efforts be futile, or will any success be short-lived? Will countries such as the United States, Sweden, India, and Nigeria be willing to commit their soldiers and economic resources on a sustained basis to support future peacekeeping operations? How many casualties among their own personnel are peacekeeping nations prepared to accept?[84] Ultimately, governments contemplating a humanitarian intervention will have to weigh their own national interests against any commitments to sustain human rights abroad.

Most nations, including the major Western powers, are reluctant to risk their soldiers' lives for humanitarian purposes. As we have just noted, after losing a relatively small number of peacekeepers in Somalia, Washington refused to intervene in Rwanda, was very slow in responding to atrocities in Bosnia, and offered no more than logistical support to NATO peacekeepers in Macedonia. The international community sent only a very small force to maintain peace in Afghanistan after the 2001 war there despite the great potential for ethnic conflict. For the most part, peacekeeping forces are sent only to enforce or monitor a settlement that the warring factions have already negotiated (as in Bosnia and, if it holds up, in Macedonia), but not to impose peace or stem ethnic violence at an early stage. At other times, when world opinion has forced the host government to accept external intervention, as with U.N. intervention in East Timor, troops are sent in *after* the worst outrages have already happened.

To be sure, some seemingly intractable ethnic conflicts have had resolutions imposed on them by outside forces. The intervening power is often a neighboring state that either has ties to one of the warring ethnic groups or has a strategic interest in the country it invades. For example, India interceded on behalf of the Bengalis in East Pakistan. Without that intervention, the nation of Bangladesh could not have been born. The Turkish invasion of Cyprus imposed an ethnic settlement by partitioning the island between its Greek and Turkish communities. And in Central Europe, extensive NATO bombing of Serbia in 1999 forced that government to cease persecution of its Albanian minority in the province of Kosovo and allow in foreign troops. But the Western powers intervened only after their earlier embarrassing refusal to take action in Bosnia left so many people dead. Even in Kosovo, the West only undertook bombing missions (not ground action), which posed minimal risk to NATO pilots (primarily American).

In many cases, however, externally imposed solutions are not desirable, nor do they last. Following the Gulf War, U.S. air power created a "no fly zone" in northern Iraq, affording that country's Kurds a certain degree of autonomy. But it is not clear whether this solution will be viable over the long run. Indeed, the Kurds have bitter memories of past American assistance. During the early 1970s, the United States had secretly channeled aid to the Iraqi Kurds in order to support a rebellion that would destabilize or topple that country's government. But Kurdish interests were secondary to the U.S. policy objective of supporting the government of Iraqi's enemy and U.S. ally, Reza Shah of Iran. Consequently, in 1975, when Iran temporarily resolved its differences with Iraq and broke off its relations with the Iraqi Kurds, the United States withdrew its aid for the Kurdish rebellion in response to the Shah's request. As a result, thousands of Iraqi Kurdish families were driven from their homes or killed.[85] Other external interventions have also produced unhappy results. In recent years, several central African nations, including Uganda and Rwanda, have supported tribal armies in neighboring countries to advance their own geopolitical interests.

As we have seen, India's attempt to settle the Tamil-Sinhalese conflict in Sri Lanka actually triggered greater bloodshed. After the invasion, the Tamil separatists first turned their guns on the Indian army and then assassinated Indian prime minister Rajiv Gandhi. Years later, the civil war in Sri Lanka has yet to be settled. Foreign intervention did bring ethnic violence to a halt in the former Yugoslavia (Bosnia and Kosovo), but it is far from certain that this peace will last once external forces are removed.

Thus, Glynne Evans notes:

> A half-hearted [outside] military response [to ethnic conflict] without any underlying political action is a poor option. . . . Conflicts with a high degree of ethnic mobilization last for generations rather than years, and are intense in their impact . . . as neighbors turn on neighbors. An intervention for humanitarian purposes in such cases becomes a major military commitment, and one of long duration.[86]

Events in Bosnia, Rwanda, and the Congo suggest that this is a commitment that outside powers are rarely prepared to make. The world's leading superpower, the United States, has been among the most reluctant to risk its soldiers in such situations.

Settlement through Exhaustion

Ultimately, many ethnic conflicts are resolved less through statecraft, constitutional arrangements, or external intervention than through the exhaustion of the warring parties. Although the Arab League helped negotiate an end to Lebanon's lengthy civil war, it was the weariness of the Lebanese, after the virtual destruction of Beirut, that permitted a settlement. While the Ugandan government continues to clash periodically with the Acholi and Langi tribes, conflict has been kept in check as no Ugandans want to return to the ethnically based bloodshed of the Amin and Obote governments. And in Mozambique and Angola, exhaustion helped drive the warring factions toward U.N.-brokered peace treaties that halted (at least temporarily) their long and bitter civil wars.

Toward a Peaceful Resolution of Conflict

If developing nations are to avoid the horrors of civil war, secession, and foreign intervention, they must arrive at legal, political, and social solutions that can constrain ethnic tensions. A conference of U.S. foreign assistance officials and scholars in 1991 proposed the following measures:

- Writing a new constitution [that] offers the possibility of creating new institutional arrangements, such as federalism, for power-sharing between . . . ethnic groups.
- Establishing protection for ethnic minority rights, not only through constitutional and legal guarantees but also through civic education. . . .
- Creating electoral systems with incentives for cooperation and accommodation among groups.[87]

While these recommended objectives are obviously desirable, the devil is in the implementation.

CONCLUSION: ETHNIC PLURALISM AND DEMOCRACY

As modernization theory would have us believe, in the long term socioeconomic development is likely to reduce ethnic antagonisms by increasing education, creating a more homogenous society, and creating more economic resources and government assistance for all ethnic groups. Highly developed countries like Belgium or Canada are less likely than are LDCs to experience violent ethnic conflicts. However, during the second half of the twentieth century, the major forces of change in the Third World—urbanization, education, increased literacy, and greater media exposure—often seemed to fan the flames of ethnic conflict in the earlier stages of modernization. Dependency theorists, on the other hand, point to divide-and-rule tactics by colonial powers and the intensification of economic inequalities between ethnic groups during the spread of world capitalism as evidence of how the industrialized core has exploited the less developed countries of the periphery and exacerbated ethnic tensions. But foreign intervention fails to explain many ethnic conflicts and can hardly be the root cause of all the ethnic violence in Africa and Asia.

Crafting peaceful solutions for multicultural societies will remain one of the greatest challenges facing Third World leaders in this century. The number and intensity of ethnic conflicts peaked during the late 1980s and early 1990s and have decreased somewhat since that time. While Africa remained home to some of the world's most brutal conflicts during the last ten to fifteen years (Sierra Leone, Sudan, Congo), it also enjoyed the most progress of late in bringing ethno-warfare to a halt. Realizing that their countries and the powers of the state were being destroyed by ethnic hostilities and decades of economic decay, many of Africa's political leaders (government and rebel) have become more accommodating. Worldwide, few new ethnic conflicts have broken out of late, though some, like the war between the Russian army and Chechyn rebels, have flared up again after periods of cease fire or abortive truces. Thus, almost all of the ethnic wars still being waged in the early years of the twenty-first century are unresolved conflicts dating back to the mid-1990s or earlier.

During the 1970s and 1980s, increased ethnic violence in much of the developing world and in the former communist states of Eastern Europe coincided chronologically with the spread of democratic government in those areas. This raises two questions about the relationship between democracy and ethnic politics: First, are multi-ethnic countries any more or any less likely to maintain democracy than are culturally homogenous societies? Second, does the growth of citizen participation and the creation of democratic government intensify or diminish conflict between ethnic communities?

The first question is answered relatively easily. Democracy is clearly harder, though far from impossible, to maintain in multi-ethnic countries. Even where such countries have established a democratic government, ethnic hostilities may tear it apart. We have seen how Lebanon's political system, long admired as one of the most democratic in the Middle East, was devastated by civil war. Looking more generally at democracy's failure to take root in most of Africa and Asia during the 1960s and 1970s, Alvin Rabushka and Kenneth Shepsle concluded that ethnic antagonisms were an important obstacle. Democracy, they concluded, "is simply not viable in an environment of intense ethnic preference."[88] By this statement they refer to societies in which favored ethnic groups receive special privileges while others suffer discrimination.

An examination of both economically developed nations and LDCs reveals that, worldwide, democracy has fared best in countries that have been relatively ethnically homogeneous (such as Finland, Denmark, and Japan) or in countries of "new settlement" (including the United States, Canada, and Australia) populated primarily by immigrants who have created a new common culture.[89] In Africa and Asia, where many countries labor under strong ethnic divisions, the growth of democracy and mass political participation may unleash communal hostilities, often egged on by cynical politicians who make use of these tensions to secure votes among a particular group.

Ethnic pluralism poses a particular obstacle to democracy in poorer countries where each group must contend for limited government resources (schools, roads, civil service jobs, and the like) in a "politics of scarcity." But although democracy is more difficult to achieve in plural societies, it is not impossible. Despite its history of religiously based violence, India, one of the world's most ethnically diverse countries, has maintained democratic government for most of its half-century of independence. Trinidad-Tobago, a country divided by religion and race, has been among the Third World's most democratic countries.

To be sure, the initial transition to democracy frequently intensifies existing ethnic animosities. Newly formed political parties often base their support in competing ethnic communities. Opportunistic politicians, even those opposed to violence, are tempted to use ethnic appeals as a means of gaining public support. As public resources (such as roads, schools, clinics, and irrigation projects) are distributed through more open legislative decisions, ethnically based interest groups and political parties will likely fight for their fair share. In the long run, however, the only way ethnicities can resolve their differences is through open discussion and bargaining in a relatively democratic political arena. While dictatorships in Yugoslavia and the Soviet Union were able to repress ethnic conflicts for many years, ultimately they actually intensified these grievances by denying their existence, silencing them, and failing to deal with them. After the fall of communism, long-repressed antagonisms in Croatia, Bosnia, Kosovo, and Chechnya burst to the surface, producing civil war or lesser forms of violence. Worse yet, dictators such as Laurent Kabila (Congo), Suharto (Indonesia), and Saddam Hussein (Iraq) presided over ethnic massacres that would have been unthinkable in a democracy monitored by public opinion and a free press.

Conversely, democratic politicians are open to interest group pressure from ethnic minorities and, hence, are more likely to settle disputes peacefully before they degenerate into violence. Indeed, a recent exhaustive study of "minorities at risk" throughout the world revealed that democratic regimes are more likely than dictatorships to negotiate peaceful settlements of ethnic warfare. And during the 1990s, political discrimination and, to a lesser degree, economic discrimination against ethnic minorities declined more frequently in democracies than under authoritarian governments.[90] In short, to accommodate ethnic pluralism and resolve tensions, what is needed is democratic, mature, and enlightened political leadership, a spirit of compromise, and the implementation of politically negotiated solutions such as federalism and consociational democracy.

DISCUSSION QUESTIONS

1. What do we mean by *ethnicity* and what are some of the most important types of ethnic identification?
2. Discuss the effect that modernization has had on ethnic identification and ethnic conflict.
3. What are some factors that may cause interethnic relations to become violent?
4. How might outside intervention reduce or increase ethnic tension? Cite some specific successful examples of such intervention and some failures.
5. Discuss how a country's transition to democracy might increase ethnic tensions in some cases and decrease it in others?

NOTES

1. Mahabun ul Haq, Special United Nations Development Program adviser quoted in Jack David Eller, *From Culture to Ethnicity to Conflict* (Ann Arbor, MI: University of Michigan Press, 1999), p. 1.

2. Eric Hobsbawm, *The Age of Extremes* (New York: Vintage Books, 1996), p. 50.

3. Crawford Young, *The Politics of Cultural Pluralism* (Madison: University of Wisconsin Press, 1976), pp. 23–26. The quotation appears on p. 23.

4. Ted Robert Gurr, "Preface" and "Long War, Short Peace: The Rise and Decline of Ethnopolitical Conflict at the End of the Cold War," in *Peoples versus States: Minorities at Risk in the New Century*, ed. T. Gurr (Washington, DC: United States Institute of Peace Press, 2000), pp. xiii and 27–56; David Carment and Frank Harvey, *Using Force to Prevent Ethnic Violence* (Westport, CT: Praeger, 2001), p. 5.

5. For a hard-hitting attack on such gloom and doom prophecies, see Yahya Sadowski, *The Myth of Global Chaos* (Washington, DC: The Brookings Institution, 1998), esp. chap. 10.

6. Analysis of the years 1958 to 1966, for example, shows that of 164 conflicts with significant violence, only 15 involved clashes between two or more states. Most involved ethnic conflict within countries. See Abdul A. Said and Luiz R. Simmons, "The Ethnic Factor in World Politics," in *Ethnicity in an International Context*, ed. Said and Simmons (New Brunswick, NJ: Transaction Books, 1976), p. 16.

7. During this period, only two or three international conflicts—the Iran-Iraq War, the Soviet war in Afghanistan, and perhaps the Gulf War—had comparable death tolls. Ironically, the last two were followed by internal ethnic violence. Of course, some brutal civil wars, such as those in El Salvador and Nicaragua, have not been ethnically related.

8. One study estimated some 10 million deaths as of the early 1970s. Harold Isaacs, *Idols of the Tribe: Group Identity and Political Change* (New York: Harper & Row, 1975), p. 3. Millions more have died since that time in the former Yugoslavia, Chechnya, Sudan, Mozambique, Angola, Congo, Rwanda, Burundi, Ethiopia, India, Iraq, Guatemala, Afghanistan, and elsewhere.

9. Gurr, *Peoples versus States*, pp. 10–11.

10. Ibid., p. 5.

11. Donald Rothchild and Victor A. Olorunsola, "Managing Competing State and Ethnic Claims," in *State versus Ethnic Claims: African Policy Dilemmas*, ed. Rothchild and Olorunsola (Boulder, CO: Westview Press, 1983), p. 20.

12. Quoted in Francine Friedman, *The Bosnian Muslims: Denial of a Nation* (Boulder, CO: Westview Press, 1996), p. 1.

13. Quoted in David A. Lake and Donald Rothchild, "Spreading Fear: The Genesis of Transnational Ethnic Conflict," in *The International Spread of Ethnic Conflict*, ed. Lake and Rothchild (Princeton, NJ: Princeton University Press, 1998), p. 7.

14. Cynthia Enloe, *Ethnic Conflict and Political Development* (Boston: Little, Brown, 1973), p. 15.

15. Charles W. Anderson, Fred R. von der Mehden, and Crawford Young, *Issues of Political Development*, 2d ed. (Upper Saddle River, NJ: Prentice Hall, 1974), pp. 31–33; Crawford Young, *Politics in the Congo* (Princeton, NJ: Princeton University Press, 1965), chap. 11.

16. Donald Horowitz, *A Democratic South Africa? Constitutional Engineering in a Divided Society* (Berkeley: University of California Press, 1991), pp. 44–48.

17. Young, *Cultural Pluralism*, p. 20.

18. "Communal" conflicts or relations refer to conflicts or relations between ethnic communities of any kind.

19. Uri Ra'anan, "Nation and State: Order Out of Chaos," in *State and Nation in Multiethnic Societies*, ed. Ra'anan et al. (Manchester, England, and New York: Manchester University Press, 1991), pp. 4–7.

20. Said and Simmons, *Ethnicity in an International Context*, p. 10. With the spread of migration across state borders, even countries like Norway and Sweden (each having experienced an upsurge of Third World and Eastern European immigrants) are no longer fully homogeneous.

21. Scholars specializing in African culture and politics generally reject the use of the term *tribe* to describe the region's various cultural-linguistic groups; they prefer the term *ethnicity*. *Tribe* is used here because it is a term more familiar to readers and one still used in much of the ethnic literature. It also avoids confusion with the more broadly used meaning of the word *ethnicity*. More will be said of this later in the chapter.

22. Omo Omoruyi, "State Creation and Ethnicity in a Federal (Plural) System: Nigeria's Search for Parity," in *Ethnicity, Politics, and Development*, ed. Dennis L. Thompson and Dov Ronen (Boulder, CO: Lynne Rienner Publishers, 1986), p. 120. Since social scientists do not always agree on what constitutes a distinct ethnic group, other calculations would be far different.

23. Crawford Young, "Comparative Claims to Political Sovereignty: Biafra, Katanga, Eritrea," in *State versus Ethnic Claims*, pp. 211–219.

24. On Ethiopia and the secessionist wars, see Christopher Clapham, *Transformation and Continuity in Revolutionary Ethiopia* (Cambridge, England: Cambridge University Press, 1988), and J. Markakis, *National and Class Conflict in the Horn of Africa* (Cambridge, England: Cambridge University Press, 1987). Subsequent events have superseded the material in both books.

25. Scholars such as Crawford Young maintain that "caste, race and religion belong to a larger genus . . . called cultural pluralism." I will not discuss caste as an ethnic category because it exists only in India and a handful of other countries.

26. John Breuilly, *Nationalism and the State* (Manchester, England: Manchester University Press, 1982), p. 3.

27. David Brown, *Contemporary Nationalism: Civic, Ethnocultural and Multicultural Politics* (London and New York: Routledge, 2000), pp. 70–88.

28. For a helpful recent analysis of Tamil-Sinhalese conflict in Sri Lanka, see A. Jeyaratnam Wilson, *Sri Lankan Tamil Nationalism* (Vancouver: University of British Columbia Press, 2000).

29. Appapillai Amirdhalingam, quoted in Eller, *From Culture to Ethnicity to Conflict*, p. 123.

30. S. W. R. de A. Samarasinghe, "The Dynamics of Separatism: The Case of Sri Lanka," and K. M. de Silva, "Separatism in Sri Lanka: The Traditional Homelands'of the Tamils," in *Secessionist Movements in Comparative Perspective,* ed. Ralph R. Premdas, S. W. R. de A. Samarasinghe, and Alan B. Anderson (London: Pinter Publishers, 1990), pp. 32–67; also, K. M. de Silva, *Managing Ethnic Tensions in Multi-Ethnic Societies: Sri Lanka 1880–1985* (Lanham, MD: University Press of America, 1986).

31. Eller, *From Culture to Ethnicity to Conflict*, pp. 130–132.

32. *Eelam* is the Tamil word for Sri Lanka.

33. Aidan Southall, "The Illusion of Tribe," in *The Passing of Tribal Man in Africa, Journal of African and Asian Studies* 5 (special issue), nos. 1–2 (January–April 1970): 28–50. Cited by Young, *Politics of Cultural Pluralism*, p. 19.

34. Milton Obote, *Proposals for New Methods of Election of Representatives of the People to Parliament* (Kampala, Uganda: Milton Obote Foundation, 1970), p. 6. Quoted in Donald Rothchild, "Hegemonial Exchange: An Alternative Model for Managing Conflict in Middle Africa," in *Ethnicity, Politics and Development*, p. 77. The term *tribe* is used by various scholars in that volume as well as in Enloe, *Ethnic Conflict*.

35. Dov Ronen, *The Quest for Self Determination* (New Haven, CT: Yale University Press, 1976), pp. 79–86.

36. Young, "Comparative Claims to Political Sovereignty," pp. 204–211; Enloe, *Ethnic Conflict*, pp. 89–92.

37. Frederick Forsyth, *The Biafran Story* (Baltimore, MD: Penguin Books, 1969).

38. See Toyin Falola, *Violence in Nigeria: The Crisis of Religious Politics and Secular Ideology* (Rochester, NY: University of Rochester Press, 1998), pp. 193–226.

39. Basil Davidson, *The Black Man's Burden* (New York: Times Books, 1992), p. 250.

40. Gérard Prunier, *The Rwanda Crisis, 1959–1994* (London: Hurst & Company, 1995).

41. Anderson, von der Mehden, and Young, *Issues of Political Development*, p. 21.

42. Horowitz, *A Democratic South Africa*, p. 47.

43. Khehla Shubane, "South Africa: A New Government in the Making?" *Current History* 91 (May 1992): 202–207; Pauline H. Baker, "South Africa on the Move," *Current History* 89 (May 1990): 197–200, 232–233.

44. Jacob T. Levey, *The Multiculturalism of Fear* (Oxford and New York: Oxford University Press, 2000), p. 179.

45. *New York Times*, December 8, 1992, p. 1.

46. Cited in T. Walker Wallbank, *A Short History of India and Pakistan* (New York: Mentor, 1958), p. 196.

47. Bernard E. Brown, "The Government of India," in *Introduction to Comparative Government*, 2d ed., ed. Michael Curtis et al. (New York: HarperCollins, 1990), pp. 479–480; Robert L. Hardgrave, Jr., *India: Government and Politics in a Developing Nation*, 3d ed. (New York: Harcourt Brace Jovanovitch, 1980), pp. 40–42. Hardgrave offers an estimate of half a million dead. For personal accounts of the violence that followed partition, especially the recollections of women, see Urvashi Butalia, *The Other Side of Silence: Voices from the Partition of India* (Durham, NC: The Duke University Press, 2000).

48. Originating in the fifteenth century, the Sikh religion is related to both the Hindu religion and Islam.

49. Mohammed Ayoob, "Dateline India: The Deepening Crisis," *Foreign Policy* 85 (Winter 1991–1992): 173; Surendra Chopra, "Ethnic Identity in a Plural Society: A Case Study of System Breakdown in the Punjab," in *Ethnicity, Politics, and Development*, pp. 196–197.

50. Latif Abul-Husn, *The Lebanese Conflict: Looking Inward* (Boulder, CO: Lynne Rienner Publishers, 1998), pp. 29–44.

51. Elizabeth Picard, "Political Identities and Communal Identities: Shifting Mobilization Among the Lebanese Shi'a Through Ten Years of War, 1975–1985," in *Ethnicity, Politics, and Development*, pp. 159–175. In the absence of dependable census information, estimates of Lebanon's religious composition varied widely.

52. Ronald D. McLaurin, "Lebanon: Into or Out of Oblivion?" *Current History* 91 (January 1992): 29–30.

53. Latif Abul-Husn, *The Lebanese Conflict;* Carole H. Dagher, *Bringing Down the Walls: Lebanon's Postwar Challenge* (New York: St. Martin's Press, 2000).

54. Of course, the American image as a successful melting pot has often been exaggerated. For example, substantial racial tensions continue to divide society. In recent decades, many Hispanic immigrants have found it difficult to integrate into the mainstream of American life, and various forms of prejudice abound against African Americans, Asian Americans, Hispanics, and other minority groups.

55. Young, *Cultural Pluralism*, p. 65.

56. Anderson, von der Mehden, and Young, *Issues*, p. 29.

57. A similar process is currently taking place in Eastern Europe, where the collapse of the Soviet multinational empire and the removal of repressive political systems have unleashed ethnic conflict in Bosnia, the former Soviet Union, and elsewhere.

58. Karl W. Deutsch, *Nationalism and Social Communication* (Boston: MIT Press and John Wiley and Sons, 1953).

59. The Cuban government has been much more explicit in its campaigns against sexism than it has against racism. It tends to insist that pre-Revolutionary racial divisions were merely surrogates for class divisions. Consequently, the government erroneously maintains that the social and economic gains the Revolution brought to the lower classes have, by themselves, ended racism.

60. Gordon Means, "Ethnic Preference Policies in Malaysia," in *Ethnic Preference and Public Policy in Developing States*, ed. Neil Nevitte and Charles H. Kennedy (Boulder, CO: Lynne Rienner Publishers, 1986), pp. 95–115; Young, *Cultural Pluralism*, pp. 121–124.

61. The designation *East Indian* is used in Trinidad, Guyana, and other Caribbean nations to distinguish them from indigenous American Indians in the hemisphere.

62. Bridget Brereton, "The Foundations of Prejudice: Indians and Africans in 19th Century Trinidad," *Caribbean Issues* 1, no. 1 (1974): 15–28; John Gaffar LaGuerre, "Race Relations in Trinidad and Tobago," in *Trinidad and Tobago: The Independence Experience, 1962–1987*, ed. Selwyn Ryan (St. Augustine, Trinidad: University of the West Indies, 1988), p. 195.

63. Selwyn D. Ryan, *Race and Nationalism in Trinidad and Tobago* (Toronto: University of Toronto Press, 1972).

64. Kevin Yelvington, "Trinidad and Tobago, 1988–89," in *Latin American and Caribbean Contemporary Record*, ed. James Malloy and Eduardo Gamarra (New York: Holmes and Meier, 1991).

65. In recent years, for the first time some government bureaucrats in Bolivia, Ecuador, and Peru can be seen wearing indigenous dress and speaking Aymara or Quechua, though much of their work is still conducted in Spanish.

66. Howard Handelman, "The Origins of the Ecuadorian Bourgeoisie: A Generational Transformation," paper presented at the XVII International Congress of the Latin American Studies Association, Los Angeles, 1992.

67. Susanne Jonas, *The Battle for Guatemala* (Boulder, CO: Westview Press, 1991).

68. D. Scott Palmer, *The Shining Path of Peru* (New York: St. Martin's Press, 1992).

69. J. Isawa Elaigwu and Victor A. Olorunsola, "Federalism and the Politics of Compromise," in *State versus Ethnic Claims*, p. 282.

70. Enloe, *Ethnic Conflict,* pp. 89–134.

71. Ibid., p. 111.

72. Young, "Comparative Claims to Political Sovereignty."

73. Consociationalism can exist between conflicting groups other than ethnicities, but we confine our discussion of it to that area.

74. Arend Lijphart, *Democracy in Plural Societies* (New Haven, CT: Yale University Press, 1977), pp. 25–40.

75. Arend Lijphart, "The Power-Sharing Approach," in *Conflict and Peacemaking in Multiethnic Societies,* ed. Joseph V. Montville (Lexington, MA: Lexington Books, 1990), p. 497.

76. Ralph R. Premdas, "Secessionist Movements in Comparative Perspective," in *Secessionist Movements,* p. 12.

77. The only amicable secession that comes to mind took place in Central Europe where, not long after the collapse of Czechoslovakia's communist regime, the Czech Republic acceded to the Slovakian demand that the country be split in two.

78. Ibid., pp. 14–16.

79. Kurdish leaders have claimed that their people number 35 million, but this is considered an exaggeration. On the other hand, national governments cite figures that are too low. Laura Donnandieu Aguado, "The National Liberation Movement of the Kurds in the Middle East," in *Secessionist Movements;* Nader Entessar, *Kurdish Ethnonationalism* (Boulder, CO: Lynne Rienner Publishers, 1992), pp. 1–10.

80. Daniel Patrick Moynihan, *Pandemonium: Ethnicity in International Politics* (Oxford and New York: Oxford University Press, 1993).

81. Gurr, *People versus States,* p. 276.

82. Edward Luttwak, "If Bosnians Were Dolphins . . . ," *Commentary* 96 (October 1993), p. 27.

83. Samantha Power, "Bystander to Genocide," *The Atlantic Monthly* 288, no. 2 (September 2001); see also the *Frontline* documentary on PBS entitled "The Triumph of Evil": <www.pbs.org/wgbh/pages/shows/evil>.

84. Carment and Harvey, *Using Force to Prevent Ethnic Violence.*

85. Entessar, *Kurdish Ethnonationalism,* pp. 119–127. The Pike Commission of the U.S. House of Representatives revealed details of U.S. involvement with the abortive Kurdish revolt.

86. Glynne Evans, *Responding to Crises in the African Great Lakes* (New York: Oxford University Press, Adelphia Paper 33, 1997), p. 75.

87. Project on Democratization, *Democratization and Ethnic Conflict* (Washington, DC: National Academy Press, 1992), p. 16.

88. From *Politics in Plural Societies.* Quoted in Larry Diamond and Marc F. Plattner, ed., *Nationalism, Ethnic Conflict, and Democracy* (Baltimore, MD: Johns Hopkins University Press, 1994), p. xix.

89. Francis Fukuyama, "Comments on Nationalism and Democracy," in *Nationalism, Ethnic Conflict and Democracy,* pp. 23–28.

90. Gurr, *People versus States,* pp. 152–163, 169, 204.

chapter 5

Women and Development

A Chinese saying observes that "Women Hold Up Half the Sky." Yet for many years, scholars, Third World governments, and Western development agencies appeared strangely oblivious to women's role in the modernization process. Early studies of political and economic change in the LDCs usually said little or nothing about women's issues. In the past two to three decades, however, two factors have contributed to a new understanding of women in developing nations: the emergence of feminist or gender-related social science research, and the growing recognition by policy planners that women play a distinct and important role in national development.

Gender-related economic and political analysis is instructive in the same way that analysis of ethnic groups or social classes is. To begin with, Third World women are often relegated to particular occupations. In most LDCs they work primarily in agriculture or the semi-legal, underground urban economy known as the "informal sector" (discussed below).[1] Those who work in industry are disproportionately employed in labor-intensive and lower-wage industries such as apparel and electronics in the Far East and Southeast Asia and assembly plants in Mexico and the Caribbean. Like their counterparts in industrialized nations, professional women are over-represented in nurturing professions such as nursing and teaching. Divisions between "women's work" and "men's work" have obvious economic and political implications, with women's jobs invariably earning lower wages or salaries and wielding less power. At the same time, women are also very underrepresented in the political arena. Not only do they hold far fewer government posts than men do, but their share also diminishes for positions of greater political power.

Although evidence of gender inequality and exploitation exists in most societies, the problem is most severe in many parts of the developing world. In its most horrifying form, the litany of injustices includes forced and painful female circumcision in Islamic areas of Africa; the virtual enslavement and frequent rape of women working in Pakistan's brick-making industry; the sale of child brides for dowries in India; wife beatings in Zambia and the Andes; the murders of some 5,000 women annually in India committed by husbands who were dissatisfied with the size of their dowries[2]; the Brazilian judicial system that rarely convicts men who kill their wives; and economic conditions that force large numbers of Third World women into prostitution. Less chilling, but no less significant, examples of gender inequality include divorce laws that greatly favor husbands; barriers to women seeking commercial credit for small businesses; the "double day" that working women typically face (coming home after a day's work and having to do most of the housework and child care); and restricted opportunities for women in government, the professions, and better-paid, blue-collar jobs.

But the study of women in the developing world is by no means confined to issues of inequality and victimization. After years of neglect, many international agencies and government planners have begun to recognize women's special status and needs in development projects. Nor have women necessarily been passive subjects who are "acted upon." Their political activity has ranged from the quiet subversion common to many oppressed groups to more vigorous assertion of their political, economic, and social rights. A growing body of scholarly literature now focuses on women's *empowerment*. Throughout Latin America, for example, women have played a decisive role in the independent, grass-roots political organizations known as "new social movements (NSMs)" that have burst upon the scene since the 1970s. Focusing on gender issues, human rights, poverty, and a range of other concerns, NSMs have provided an important alternative to mainstream political organizations such as parties and unions.[3] Elsewhere, revolutionary movements in countries such as El Salvador, Nicaragua, and China have opened up opportunities for female activism and leadership that had not existed previously. And in nations as diverse as India, the Philippines, Panama, and Nicaragua, women have headed the national government. All of these aspects of women's economic and political activity deserve our attention.

THE POLITICAL AND SOCIOECONOMIC STATUS OF THIRD WORLD WOMEN

One of the notable problems in the developing world is that women receive far fewer educational opportunities and have lower literacy rates than do men. In the most extreme, and obviously atypical, case, Afghanistan's Taliban government banned all girls and women from going to school.[4] Since education and literacy consistently have been shown to substantially influence income, health practices, and political participation, the gender gap in education obviously impacts important aspects of political and economic life. It has been demonstrated, for example, that as women's average educational levels rise in LDCs, birth rates and family size tend to decline.

Table 5.1 presents the relative literacy rate of adult men and women (all people 15 years of age or older) and that of young men and women (ages 15 to 24 only) in major regions of the Third World. It is important to keep in mind that *the percentages in Table 5.1 do not represent the actual percentage of men or women who are literate.* Rather, they reflect a *comparison* between female and male literacy rates within each region. The lower the score in this table, the greater the *gender gap*. Thus, a country or region could have a high literacy rate for both men *and* women but have a greater gender gap than an area in which both men and women have low, but similar, rates of literacy. For example, if in some imaginary region males have a literacy rate of 90 percent and women have a rate of 60 percent, the *comparative* figure for that region would be 67 percent (i.e., the women's literacy is two-thirds, or 67 percent, as high as men's). On the other hand, if both men and women in another region were far less educated, with each gender only 30 percent literate, that region would have a comparative score of 100 percent, since there is no gender gap at all (i.e., male and female literacy levels are equally low).

If we examine the figures in Table 5.1, we find that South Asia (including India, Pakistan, and Bangladesh) and the Arab world have the greatest gender gaps in literacy. Thus, for example, in South Asia young women are only 78 percent as likely as young men to read and write. Among all adults, the gap in that region is even larger, with the literacy rate among women only about two-thirds as high (65 percent) as men's. On the other hand, Latin America and the Caribbean (including English-speaking islands such as Jamaica) have totally eliminated the gender gap in literacy, with young

TABLE 5.1   Women's Literacy Rates Compared to Men's

Region	Women's Literacy as a Percentage of Men's (15 years and older)	Young Women's Literacy as a Percentage of Men's (15–24 years old only)
Latin America and the Caribbean	98%	101%
East Asia	86	98
South Asia	65	78
Sub-Saharan Africa	77	89
Arab Nations*	67	84

*Arab nations include countries from the Middle East and North Africa.

Source: United Nations Development Programme, *Human Development Report, 2001* (New York: Oxford University Press, 2001), p. 221. Reprinted by permission.

women actually enjoying a slightly higher literacy rate than their male counterparts. East Asia ranks next best, with Sub-Saharan Africa in the middle. One encouraging finding is that the gender gap for all regions is substantially smaller among young adults (aged 15 to 24) than it is among adults generally. This clearly suggests a trend toward reducing the literacy gap between the genders; of course, in Latin America and the Caribbean the gap has already been eliminated.

Table 5.2 turns from educational opportunities (as indicated by literacy) to measures of women's influence in society. Column 2 presents the Gender Empowerment Measure (GEM) for each of the countries listed, a composite *index* that indicates the degree to which woman hold important positions in politics and the private sector. The highest GEM possible (that is, the highest level of female political and economic empowerment) is 1.0, and the lowest possible is 0. Next to each country's GEM in Column 2 (in parentheses) is that country's GEM rank compared to other nations. Thus, with a GEM of .836, Norway had the highest GEM score in the world, while the United States ranked tenth. Egypt's score of .425 placed it 64th among countries that have data on GEMs. It should be added that GEM scores are not available for most of the world's poorest nations, including all of Africa.

As modernization theory predicts, the more developed nations in Table 5.2—Norway, the United States, Japan, and perhaps Singapore—have the highest GEMs. Japan's score, however, is unimpressive for one of the world's most developed and modern nations. Singapore, Malaysia, and Mexico rank fairly closely behind Japan in terms of their international GEM rankings. As expected, most of the countries on the list had GEM rankings that were fairly similar to their rankings on the Human Development Index (HDI, see Chapter 1). In other words, the higher a country's literacy and educational levels, the longer its life expectancy, and the higher its average income, the higher it tends to rank on GEM. However, Chile tended to fare a bit worse than expected, and Egypt and Malaysia had higher GEMs than their HDI score would have led us to predict.

Columns 3 and 4 in Table 5.2 are more straightforward and tell us about the influence and representation of women in national politics. They show what portion of the seats in parliament and what percentage of the nation's cabinet ministers were women at the time the United Nations Development Program collected the data. Undoubtedly, there have been changes since then, particularly in the percentage of women holding cabinet posts, since that is a more volatile figure. Norway's parliament, with more than 36 percent women, far surpasses the United States and Japan, as do the other Nordic countries (Denmark, Finland, Iceland, and Sweden). Surprisingly, Singapore also has substantially higher female representation than do the United States and Japan. But, interestingly, with the notable exception of Egypt, there is less of a difference in female parliamentary representation than one might expect between the United States and Japan (highly modern countries), on the one

TABLE 5.2   Measures of Gender Empowerment

Country	Gender Empowerment Measure (Rank)	Percentage of Women as National Parliament Members	Percentage of Women as Cabinet Ministers
Norway	.836 (1)	36.4%	42.1%
United States	.738 (10)	13.8	31.8
Japan	.520 (31)	10.8	5.7
Singapore	.509 (35)	26.0	5.7
Malaysia	.503 (38)	14.5	——
Mexico	.507 (37)	15.9	11.1
Chile	.445 (49)	8.9	25.6
Philippines	.470 (46)	11.8	——
Egypt	.425 (64)	2.4	11.1

Source: United Nations Development Programme, *Human Development Report, 2001* (New York: Oxford University Press, 2001), pp. 214–217, 226–229. Reprinted by permission.

hand, and the developing nations, on the other. Looking at female representations in the cabinet—i.e., positions of considerable power in most governments—women have reached almost full equality in Norway (which also had a woman prime minister at the time), with 42.1 percent of ministerial seats (Sweden's cabinet was over half women). Women were also well represented in the U.S. cabinet appointed by President Bill Clinton, and, despite their rather low representation in Chile's parliament, they fared well in its cabinet, appointed by a socialist president who is committed to greater gender equality. Note, too, that while women were well represented in the Malaysian and Philippine parliaments, they were insignificant in the respective cabinets where the real power lies. In general, as of 1998, female participation in Third World cabinets ranged from 2 percent in the Middle East to 8 percent in Latin America.

Colonialism, Modernization, and the Economic Status of Women

How is the status of women altered when developing areas are colonized by Western powers and when they make the transition from traditional to modern societies? Westerners often associate traditional religious and cultural values with rigid social and economic systems relegating women to an inferior rank. This concept may lead us to assume that the imposition of European colonialism in Africa and Asia and the subsequent spread of modernization and Western ideas offered women greater opportunities and improved their social standing. But while modernization theory would have us believe that urbanization, industrialization, and the diffusion of Western values and lifestyles have an emancipating effect, "feminist scholars [often oriented toward dependency theory] have produced a wealth of literature that maintains that political and economic modernization have had overwhelmingly negative effects on women."[6]

Although the status of women in precolonial Africa varied greatly, oftentimes the consequence of European colonialism was to undermine women's position in society. It must be remembered that colonial rule was introduced at a time (the nineteenth century) when Victorian England and other European societies had rather restricted views of women's roles.[7] Consequently, many colonial administrators in Africa and Asia treated women less equitably than traditional institutions had. In some West African cultures, for example, women had served at times as chiefs or had held other important political positions. However, as the influence of traditional leadership posts declined under colonialism and then decreased further after independence, these women lost their authority to male-dominated colonial or national governments. Among the Nigerian Ibo, women had exercised significant political power before British colonialism. Colonial administrators, however, viewed politics as "a man's concern" and, consequently, downgraded women's political influence.[8]

The commercialization of agriculture reduced women's economic power as well. In Asia and Africa, commercialization often involved the government granting legal titles to the land that frequently transferred farm land that had been controlled by women to male ownership.[9] In addition, as families moved from subsistence agriculture (for family consumption) to commercial agriculture, and as commercial plantations were developed by foreigners, men were more likely to do the farming than before. Commercialization also made farmers more dependent on the state for credit and for technical training. In both the colonial era and in the early decades of independence, women found themselves frozen out of such aid. In Uganda, for example, even though women farmers had first begun commercial cotton cultivation, the British administrator in charge of agriculture declared in 1923 that "cotton growing [can] not be left to the women and old people."[10] Consequently, as new agricultural technologies were introduced, they were taught to men only, ultimately driving women off the land. After independence, a similar pattern continued in most of Africa and Asia. Government extension agents offered modern technologies, credits, and other assistance fairly exclusively to men. Foreign aid programs were generally no less sexist. When a Taiwanese foreign aid team went to Senegal to improve rice cultivation, they only trained men, even though women did most of the rice cultivation. As a result, the men ignored the instructors, the women were not taught, and the new techniques never took hold.[11]

Just as modernization theorists and radical feminists differ on their views of colonialism, they also disagree on how contemporary modernization has affected the lives of Third World women. Modernization theory contrasts the egalitarian values of modern culture with the allegedly sexist perspectives of traditional societies. Radical feminists, many of whom subscribe to dependency theory, counter that industrialization, urbanization, and the spread of world capitalism frequently disadvantage women in the LDCs. How do we reconcile these opposing viewpoints? As with so many other factors discussed in this text, the evidence suggests that modernization affects women's status positively over the long run, but often has adverse effects in the short-to-medium terms. If we examine current data, it is obvious that more modern countries (as measured by education, literacy, and per-capita income), such as Denmark and Canada, have smaller gender gaps than do LDCs with regard to education, employment, and political influence. Economic growth eventually creates new opportunities for women. And expanded educational systems offer women new opportunities while changing societal values and gender roles in the direction of greater equality. For example, in East Asia, the region of the world that has experienced the fastest economic growth in the past 50 years, women's share of the labor force grew in seven of eight high-growth countries (all but Thailand) and rose substantially in four (Singapore, South Korea, Malaysia, Indonesia). Elsewhere, high-growth nations experienced narrowing gender gaps in average years of education.

But as we have noted, the transition to modernity often imposes particular hardships on women in its initial stages. Because Third World women are now more likely to be suffering the short-term effects of economic growth, neoliberal economic reforms, and other consequences of modernization, the sections below focus on these problems. However, in the long run, modernization offers women the best hope for equality. The task is to reduce the short-term pain and increase the likelihood of long-term gain.

Women in the Countryside

Agriculture is a major area of female employment in the developing world. United Nations data on Sub-Saharan Africa, for example, suggested that about 60 to 70 percent of all food production and 50 percent of all animal husbandry is done by women.[12] Other country-specific studies in Africa have shown a smaller, but still significant, female contribution to family farming. Ester Boserup's landmark research indicated that women contributed approximately 40 percent of family farm labor in Ghana, Sierra Leone, and Liberia. In the North African countries of Algeria and Tunisia, women also did 40 percent of the labor on family farms, while another 20 percent was performed jointly by men and women. In Asian nations such as Thailand and South Korea, women contributed close to half of all family farm labor, but the proportion was much lower in Taiwan, India, and the Philippines. By contrast, Latin America's share of farm labor carried out exclusively by women was much lower, generally below 10 percent. But in countries such as Chile, Cuba, Costa Rica, El Salvador, and Mexico, 54 to 69 percent of the labor was contributed jointly by men and women.[13] A more recent study suggests that, in one form or another, women contributed more than 60 percent of agricultural labor in Africa and Asia and 40 percent in Latin America.[14]

But despite women's importance in agriculture, "too little attention has been given by researchers and administrators or planners to women and the roles they play in rural society."[15] Even though male "heads of household" are increasingly employed off the family farm, leaving its cultivation to their wives, government planners have generally clung to "the myth of the ever-present male head."[16] Consequently, rural agricultural development workers have neglected female farmers. Meanwhile, as early as the 1970s, a United Nations study of Kenya estimated that 525,000 rural households were headed by women whose husbands had migrated to urban areas.[17]

In the years since the United Nations' Decade for Women (1975 to 1985), international agencies and Third World governments have developed greater consciousness of the role of women in rural development. Significantly, the 1985 conference (in Nairobi, Kenya) concluding the Decade for Women was the second largest U.N. conference ever held. At the United Nations, the World Bank, the United States' Agency for International Development (AID), and many nongovernmental organizations (NGOs), rural development programs that had previously focused narrowly on agricultural production have given way to integrated rural development programs (IRDPs) designed to promote agricultural production, education, sanitation, and health care simultaneously. Increasingly, these programs have recognized the need to address the role of rural women. AID established an office for Women in Development to better address women's needs in U.S. foreign aid projects. The results of these efforts have been mixed. Some projects have been very successful; others suffered from poor planning or misunderstanding of the cultural milieu. Thus, for example, one study of an IRDP project in India found that its effectiveness was diminished by the absence of female administrators and by inadequate early educational opportunities for women participants.[18] Cornelia Butler Flora's survey of projects designed to generate income for rural women in Latin America found that the programs often produced low-paying jobs with limited economic benefit for the women who were employed. Still, despite the weak economic record of these projects, Flora argues that they are potentially valuable since the women's organizations they establish can serve as the basis for political and social mobilization.[19]

Ultimately, the only way women are likely to make their governments more responsive to their demands will be through political mobilization and pressure. In many LDCs, there are signs of progress. For example, many agencies involved in population control now recognize that merely making family planning services available will not get the job done. Rather, reducing fertility rates requires increasing educational and occupational opportunities for women. In fact, that connection was a central theme in discussions of population control at the 1994 United Nations Conference on Population and Development.

Urbanization and the Status of Women

The harmful effects of early modernization on women have not been limited to agriculture. In her study of Ghana's Ga tribe, Claire Robertson found that women's status declined when their families moved to the capital city and entered a more modern, urbanized environment. Although there previously had been considerable economic cooperation between spouses in fishing and farming villages, it was less common among urban migrants. In the cities, men had greater access to education and to higher-paying jobs, giving them a level of economic security that they had not heretofore enjoyed. Women tended to be more dependent on their husbands and to own less of the family's property than they had before migrating.[20]

In much of Latin America, women constitute the majority of migrants to urban centers. Once there, they often are only able to secure employment in low-end jobs. Indeed, the most common type of employment among women migrants is domestic service, for which they generally receive the legal minimum wage or lower and are often mistreated. Mexican census figures in the 1970s indicated that 25 percent of all women in the nation's work force were either maids in private homes or cleaning women in commercial establishments and hotels, though that percentage has likely declined somewhat since.[21] A second important area of employment is in the informal sector, including street vending and working in "sweat shop" industries that defy legal regulation. While some informal-sector workers manage to earn higher incomes than blue-collar laborers do in the formal (regulated and taxed) economy, many others fall below the poverty line. Finally, in newly industrializing countries, women are frequently employed in low-wage, labor-intensive manufacturing. However, over time, as factories become more technologically sophisticated and as wages rise, the percentage of female employees tends to decline.[22]

In East Asia, the industrial boom of the 1980s to late 1990s created new jobs for women, particularly in labor-intensive industries such as apparel and electronics. Firms in those industries often prefer to hire young unmarried women for several reasons: many of the jobs require manual dexterity, a skill that employers associate with women; because they are not the principal breadwinner in their family, young women are often willing to work for lower wages; and, finally, women are less likely to join unions or to strike. The region's recent economic crisis has brought about numerous plant closings and layoffs. Women are often the first fired, since most employers believe that men need their jobs more in order to support their families. The crisis has also forced many poor and middle-class families to pull their daughters out of school in order to save the costs of school uniforms, educational fees, or tuition. Consequently, Indonesian girls are six times more likely than boys to drop out of school before the fourth grade.[23]

Throughout the developing world, women have fewer educational opportunities than men, a deficit that then limits their occupational chances. All too often, poverty and the lack of vocational skills force desperate women into prostitution to support themselves or their children. Despite Thailand's economic boom from the mid-1960s to mid-1990s, rural poverty drove many young female migrants to work in Bangkok's thriving "sex tourism" industry. A study of Manilla (the Philippines) and Bangkok (Thailand) revealed that 7 to 9 percent of female employment in those two cities was "prostitution related."[24] Since that study was conducted prior to the 1990s financial crisis, those percentages are surely higher today. Some desperately poor families in that region have sold young daughters to brothels or given them as collateral for loans. In the squatter settlements of Kenya's capital, Nairobi, impoverished women are rarely equipped to gain employment in the economy's modern sector. Consequently, illegal brewing of beer and prostitution are the two major sources of female employment.[25]

A more hopeful consequence of modernization is indicated in research on the South Asian labor market that shows that increased education has given poor urban women a vehicle for improving their jobs and incomes.[26] Spurred on by the United Nations' Decade for Women, India's Ministry of Labor, with assistance from the International Labor Organization and the Swedish government, began an extensive vocational training program for urban women.[27]

Within the middle and upper-middle classes, women's educational and occupational opportunities are more comparable to those of men with the same social status. There are, however, interesting differences between countries and regions. A number of years ago, Ester Boserup presented data on the proportion of people between the ages of 15 and 24 who were still in school (essentially high school and university). Not surprisingly, the overall rate of school attendance in individual countries was linked to the nation's level of economic development. In other words, more economically developed countries like Costa Rica, Singapore, and South Korea had higher *overall* rates of high school and university attendance than did poorer nations. However, cultural rather than economic factors seemed to determine what proportion of these students were women. In Latin American nations, about half of the student population was female, regardless of whether the country was more developed (Venezuela, Panama) or comparatively poor (Honduras, El Salvador). In Asia, women made up nearly half of the 15-to-24-year-old students in the Philippines and Hong Kong, but under one-third in India, Malaysia, and Indonesia. The proportion of women among students attending high school or college in Africa and the Middle East was generally quite low, frequently less than 25 percent. As a consequence of these educational patterns, women in Latin America constitute a far higher percentage of all professionals than they do in other parts of the Third World.[28] However, female professionals in the region usually work in traditional nurturing professions such as teaching and nursing. In the most modernized countries, such as Chile, Argentina, and Uruguay, they are significantly represented in other fields, such as university teaching, medicine, and law. Over half of all Argentine doctors, for example, are female.[29]

Women and Economic Crises

During the 1980s, Africa, Latin America, and parts of Asia suffered harsh economic declines from which some nations have not yet fully recovered. A severe debt crisis in Latin America forced most of the region's governments to impose painful economic stabilization and adjustment programs that sharply reduced living standards (see Chapter 10). Similar debt problems compounded by civil war and drought devastated much of Africa. Then, in the late 1990s, Thailand, Malaysia, Indonesia, South Korea, and other parts of East and Southeast Asia, which until then had boasted the world's most dynamic economies, experienced a severe economic downturn. In many ways women suffered disproportionately from these economic crises. As men lost their jobs or suffered declining real wages,[30] women already immersed in housework and child care were forced to seek outside jobs to supplement their family's income. In Tanzania, for example, real wages declined 65 percent between 1974 and 1988. By the end of that period, an average worker's *monthly wage* could feed a family of six for only *three days*. Thus, only if mothers and sisters (who had previously not worked outside the home) earned additional income could the family avoid starvation. Consequently, there was a dramatic surge in the number of urban women starting small businesses or otherwise entering the informal sector. One survey indicated that in a typical low-income family in Dar es Salaam, the nation's capital, only 10 percent of earnings came from wages in the formal sector, while the remaining 90 percent came from the informal sector, much of it earned by women.[31]

Conditions were similar in Nicaragua, which endured a devastating civil war along with Latin America's most severe economic crisis in the 1980s. In the capital city, Managua, the number of women working increased significantly. They have been employed principally in the informal sector for two reasons: first, just as in Tanzania, real wages in the formal sector had collapsed, so that a monthly wage could not support a family, and women had to supplement their household's income; second, it is relatively easy to combine informal activities such as street vending with housework and child care. It is common, for example, to see female street vendors in Latin America caring for their children while working at their stalls. Although most women in the informal sector elsewhere are supplementing their husbands' incomes, this has not been the case in Nicaragua. Even in normal times, many Nicaraguan mothers are single (divorced, separated, or never wed), and in the 1980s many more were widowed by the country's civil war. Consequently, a large portion of the women in Managua's informal sector are their family's primary breadwinners.[32]

The Tanzanian and Nicaraguan experiences have been repeated recently in Indonesia, Thailand, and other parts of the developing world. While the increased female participation in the work force associated with economic crises can be viewed as a liberating factor (giving women a more pivotal economic role in the family and bringing them into greater contact with the outside world), it also brings women problems not shared by men. The most obvious and widespread difficulty is "the double day." Poor women with families generally find that when they begin gainful employment (often out of necessity), they must still put in long hours at home cleaning, cooking, shopping, and caring for their children, with limited help from their husbands or partners. Cuba is the only nation in the world whose laws require both spouses to share housework equally but, as one might expect, compliance is fairly spotty. There is, however, one group of women in the Third World who have an advantage over their First World peers in pursuing their careers. Middle- and upper-class women often benefit from the ready availability of poorly paid domestic servants to care for their children and their homes while they work in the professions or in business. In such cases, one woman's poverty becomes another's career advantage.

WOMEN AND POLITICS

Many of the same traditions and prejudices that have undermined women's socioeconomic positions in the Third World have also disadvantaged them politically. In Latin America, for example, women won the right to vote substantially later than they did in industrial democracies. Whereas the United States and most European democracies legalized female suffrage in the years immediately following World War I,[33] only 7 of 20 Latin American countries allowed women to vote before the close of World War II. Ecuador was the first nation in that region to extend the franchise (1929) and Paraguay the last (1961).[34] In Africa and Asia the situation was different. Since most of the countries in those regions achieved independence in the decades after World War II when female suffrage was a universally accepted principle, women were normally enfranchised from the onset. Saudi Arabia remains a notable exception, with women still unable to vote. Given the low number of democratically elected governments in Asia and Africa until recently, however, the franchise was often of no great value to women (or to men). Today, women generally continue to vote at a lower rate than men, but that gender gap is narrowing.[35]

In many parts of Africa, Asia, and the Middle East, traditional cultural values have limited women's participation in the political system.[36] One study of transitional Hindu families in India (partly traditional and partly modernized) revealed an important generational difference between women who had completed a university education at the time of national independence and their more traditional mothers. The women analyzed in this study were the daughters of Westernized fathers who had worked for the Indian civil service and who had been quite politically involved. Their mothers, on the other hand, generally spoke no English, believed in female submissiveness, and were quite apolitical.[37] In contrast, the university-educated daughters were far more politically involved than their mothers. In the absence of such educational opportunities, political participation levels remain low for the majority of poor women in South Asia, the Middle East, and much of Africa, who lack the resources available to women from more affluent families.

Indeed, social class is important in predicting a woman's political involvement. Among highly educated, Westernized women born to elite Third World families, political involvement may be as great as, or greater than, that of their cohorts in the Western world. It is worth noting, for example, that all the countries of the Indian subcontinent—India, Pakistan, and Bangladesh—as well as neighboring Sri Lanka have had female prime ministers, a record not nearly equaled by North America or Western Europe. Until the 1980s, the percentage of women in the Indian parliament was higher than in the U.S. Congress, though that has since changed drastically. In Africa, elite women have been slow to attain cabinet-level positions but have been quite visible in United Nations delegations. Thus, for example, the first women to serve as president of the General Assembly and the first to preside over the Security Council were both from Africa.[38]

Middle-class women have also benefited in many ways from elements of a Western lifestyle. For example, the greater availability of birth control devices "has ruptured [women's] previously existing physiological fatalism," enabling them to work outside the home and involve themselves in political movements.[39]

⟹ But modernization has not always been politically beneficial to the mass of underprivileged Third World women. Indeed, in Africa, while traditional cultures often included women's organizations and production techniques that bound women together, increased modernity (including urbanization and the decline of the extended family) often deprived women of the organizational foundations they had previously enjoyed. In Nigeria, Africa's most populous Sub-Saharan nation, women in the urban informal sector have been less prone to demonstrate politically since independence than they were under colonial rule.[40] Throughout the developing world, the mechanization and commercialization of agriculture and the accompanying decline of traditional labor relations have frequently deprived rural women of their specialized labor functions. In doing so, these changes may, at least temporarily, reduce women's political influence.

In short, because the developing world encompasses so wide a variety of cultural traditions, and because social change has impinged so differently on the various social classes and sectors within individual nations, there can be no simple generalizations about the way in which modernization has influenced the political status of Third World women. Modernization theory would lead us to expect that more socioeconomically developed countries would be quicker to grant political rights to women than their poorer counterparts would. If we look at Latin America, however, we find that there is only a mild correlation between a country's literacy rate or its GNP per capita and the year in which it enfranchised women.[41] Thus, the spread of education alone does not seem to guarantee women greater political equality. It does appear, however, that in countries such as China, Costa Rica, and Cuba, extensive mass educational programs coupled with conscious efforts to change traditional values have contributed to greater political opportunities and equity for women.[42]

Women's Political Activism at the Grass-Roots Level

Perhaps women most powerfully influence Third World politics when acting through grass-roots organizations in their own neighborhoods and communities. Community-based groups afford them opportunities for participation and leadership that are usually lacking at the national or regional level. Moreover, for poor women who lack day care and who often cannot travel far from home, neighborhood or village organizations have the obvious advantage of close physical proximity. Most important, many of the issues that these associations focus on—housing, health care, clean drinking water, and education—are of particular interest to women. Hence, many traditional women who were not normally politically oriented or who would never consider political-party activity are attracted to these groups because of their obvious relevance to their lives.

Since the 1970s, grass-roots organizations representing poor and middle-class women have emerged in various parts of the Third World. Some represent women exclusively, while others include members of both sexes but are led by women or contain women's wings.[43] Jana Everett studied a number of Indian community groups in urban and rural settings, finding both similarities and differences. In both areas, the organizations were initially led by politically experienced, middle-class women committed to organizing the poor. Subsequent interviews of the low-income women who joined these groups showed that their activity had increased their political awareness, confidence, and assertiveness. Thus, as in grass-roots movements generally, activism frequently induces broader participation in the political system.

Beyond these similarities, however, the tactics and goals of urban and rural groups often differed. The Self-Employed Women's Association (SEWA) of Madras and the Annapurna Mahila Mandal of Bombay (named after the Goddess of Food) represented urban women engaged in home-based production, street vending of food, and other informal-sector activities. Serving extremely poor women who were unable to secure government services, their tactics were quite moderate and peaceful. To begin with, they operated through normal patron-client relations, working within the system to seek government help. Their objectives were also fairly conventional, including enforcement of minimum-wage laws and securing loans for women with very small businesses who had previously been unable to obtain credit from private banks or government agencies.

In contrast, Everett's examination of six organizations representing the rural poor (including underprivileged tribal people) uncovered more militant activity. For example, at an early training session for women in a Bhil tribal organization, members complained about alcoholism among the men in their villages and the associated wife beatings. Emboldened by their own discussions, the women spontaneously marched to an illegal liquor still and smashed it. They then encircled the local police inspector to protest his failure to take action against illegal liquor production.[44]

In general, rural grass-roots groups are more likely than urban organizations to stage protest demonstrations or other direct action and more prone to demand some form of economic redistribution, such as land reform. Armita Basu's study of women's rural protest in the Indian state of Maharashtra found evidence of equal militancy. After a woman was unable to get help from the police against a local landlord who had beaten her severely for reprimanding him for abusive behavior, a crowd of 300 women and 150 men "smeared his face with cow dung . . . and paraded him through the surrounding villages."[45] The rural women's greater militancy likely resulted from the more repressive political atmosphere in which they operated. Village political and economic elites are usually less willing than their urban counterparts to allow the poor to act through normal political channels. So more radical tactics must be employed.

Social movements often develop as a response to a particular crisis or danger. For example, the 1985 earthquake that destroyed large sections of Mexico City had a particularly devastating effect on seamstresses in the city's apparel industry. The quake hit early in the morning when most people had not yet left home for work, but since seamstresses work longer hours, many of them were trapped under rubble at their places of employment. To their horror, some found that their employers were more interested in saving their sewing machines than in bringing out trapped employees. The clothing workers subsequently formed their own labor union led by women from their ranks, independent of the government-affiliated federation to which most Mexican unions belong. With more honest leadership than is typically found in the Mexican labor movement, the union not only bargains with employers and the government for better working conditions but also provides day care and related services for its members.

In Latin America, one of the major catalysts for the grass-roots political activity that sprang up during the 1970s and 1980s was opposition to the authoritarian military governments that swept the region at that time. In Argentina, Brazil, Chile, and Uruguay, bureaucratic-authoritarian (BA) regimes halted the electoral process, banned political party and union activity (particularly by the Left), and arrested, tortured, and killed large numbers of suspected "subversives" (see Chapter 9). At the same time, a major debt crisis in the 1980s, coupled with harsh government economic remedies, produced the worst recession since the 1930s and resulted in a precipitous decline in popular living standards (Chapter 10). In all these countries, women played an important role in anti-authoritarian social movements that helped pave the way for the restoration of democracy.

The women's movement in these countries incorporated three types of political organizations, all primarily urban based. First, it included feminists primarily from middle- or upper-middle-class families, with a heavy represen-

tation of professional women, many of whom had been active in leftist political parties but had become disillusioned by the Left's lack of concern for
women's issues. Second, neighborhood organizations represented women from
the country's urban slums. In the face of the severe economic crisis, self-help
groups had been formed for activities such as communal kitchens and infant
nutrition centers. Though not previously highly politicized, over time members
of these grass-roots groups often expanded their initial goals to demand more
equitable distribution of state resources and the return of democratic government. Finally, a third movement sought to stop or uncover government violations of human rights. Organizations such as Argentina's famed "Mothers of
the Plaza de Mayo," who regularly marched in defiance of government rules to
demand an accounting of their missing children and grandchildren, continue to
do so today, some two decades after the fall of the dictatorship. Responding to
wide-scale imprisonments, torture, disappearances, and death-squad assassinations, women formed a major component of the human rights movement. Of
the three strands of the women's movement, this was the most socially integrated, joining activists from both the middle class and working class. Often
human rights groups were linked to the Catholic church or to Christian organizations such as Base Communities.[46]

One of the most important women's political movements emerged in
Brazil. Several factors contributed to this phenomenon. First was the rapid
expansion of women's educational opportunities, beginning in the early 1960s
prior to the military takeover, and continuing through the 1980s. Between 1969
and 1975, the number of men attending Brazilian universities doubled, while
the number of women increased five-fold. By 1980, nearly half of all university
students in the country were female. Women also constituted a growing proportion of the nation's professionals, with their numbers swelling from 19,000
in 1970 to more than 95,000 in 1980.[47] Often paid significantly less than their
male counterparts, they were the nucleus of new feminist movements. Their
leaders were highly politicized and had usually worked with leftist political
parties. During the intense military repression of the late 1960s, a number of
them were forced into exile, often leaving for Western Europe or Chile, where
they were exposed to more sophisticated feminist organizations. When Brazil's
political system began to open up in the mid-1970s, they returned home to
organize there.

In the absence of democratic elections, grass-roots movements such as
tenants' associations offered one of the only means by which the urban poor
might pressure the government. In slums and shantytowns throughout the
country, radical priests, nuns, and parishioners (often committed to liberation
theology) organized Christian Base Communities that combined Catholic
beliefs and social activism. Leftist activists also helped organize the poor. A
study of neighborhood grass-roots movements in São Paulo, Brazil's largest
city, revealed that most of the members and leaders were women.[48] Typically,
such organizations focused on their members' economic needs—jobs, health
care, and food—and had little initial concern with feminist issues. Indeed,

Church leaders were usually hostile to feminism, and most leftist groups were rather indifferent, viewing gender divisions as secondary to class conflict. In time, however, many poor women came to share their middle-class counterparts' concerns about questions of sexuality, household equality, and protection against abuse by husbands and partners.

In the late 1970s, the women's movement's third strand emerged, concerned with government violations of human rights. Freed political prisoners, political party activists (frequently from the Left), and progressive elements of the Catholic church all played leadership roles. Interestingly, this was one of the only areas in which women's groups had an advantage over parallel groups led by men. Because the government viewed women as inherently less political than men, they allowed their human rights groups greater freedom than other protest movements had.

When the Brazilian military government engineered a transition to democracy in the 1980s, women politicians were very active in the major opposition party, the PMDB. Female voters were also an important base of party support. Yet the restoration of Brazilian democracy removed some of the motivation for unity among disparate wings of the women's movement and presented them with new challenges. As middle-class activists became more involved with political parties in the new democratic order, they tended to lose their contacts with community groups representing the urban poor. Indeed, in many Latin American nations, the restoration of democracy had the ironic effect of demobilizing women.

Finally, an interesting vehicle for grass-roots political activity has emerged in India, Bangladesh, Pakistan, and other South Asian nations in recent years. These countries have experienced a growing politicization of religion—Hindu, Muslim, and Sikh—in the past decades (see Chapter 3). A number of religiously based political parties have gained considerable strength. On the one hand, these religious parties and interest organizations tend to uphold a fairly traditional view of women, promoting the roles of mother and wife over others and endorsing a certain degree of passivity among women. Yet for a variety of reasons, many women have joined these religiously linked political parties and movements, not the least of which is the higher degree of piety often found among women. In some senses, these movements have challenged any feminist agenda and promoted a more restricted role for women. On the other hand, the religious parties have helped mobilize and politicize many women who had formerly been politically inactive. Moreover, once they joined these parties in large numbers, women have often pushed them into a more progressive position regarding gender roles.[49]

Women as Political Leaders

In political systems throughout the world (except perhaps Scandinavia), women are severely underrepresented in political leadership positions. The Third World is surely no exception. During the mid-1980s, for instance, women constituted only 6 percent of the national legislators in Africa and only 2 percent of all cabinet members. Throughout the developing and developed world, "United Nations surveys repeatedly show that even in countries where women are active professionally, their level of responsibility as policy makers and planners is low."[50] Furthermore, an examination of the small number of women who have reached high leadership positions reveals that they have tended to hold posts popularly associated with female qualities. For example, most of the African women who held cabinet posts in the 1980s were in charge of education, women's affairs, health, or social welfare—areas traditionally viewed as compatible with women's "nurturing role."[51]

In her study of Chilean and Peruvian female political leaders, Elsa Chaney discovered a pattern common to much of Latin America. Female political leaders were forced to legitimize their activism outside the home by presenting themselves as *supermadres* ("supermothers") who were using their political position to nurture their constituents (their extended family). That image had been painted eloquently years earlier by Argentina's legendary political leader, Eva Perón (Evita):

> In this great house of the Motherland [Argentina], I am just like any other woman in any other of the innumerable houses of my people. Just like all of them I rise early thinking about my husband and about my children. . . . I so truly feel myself the mother of my people.[52]

Chaney's survey of 167 Chilean and Peruvian female political officials showed that half of them felt that certain government posts (such as education and health) were more appropriate for women, while others should be held by men (finance and defense, for example). Only 13 percent of the women politicians interviewed believed that gender was irrelevant to the type of political post one holds, while another 37 percent were ambivalent.[53] Of course, it is not only in developing nations that women tend to be restricted to political positions associated with their gender stereotypes. Until fairly recently, women cabinet members in the United States normally held such posts as Labor, Education, and Health and Human Services. Recent appointments of women to the powerful positions of U.S. attorney general, U.S. secretary of state, and Canadian defense minister constitute important breakthroughs in this regard.

Another factor limiting female political leaders is a somewhat permeable "glass ceiling" that tends to concentrate them at lower levels. Thus, for the most part, women are more likely to get elected to local or state legislatures than to the national parliament. There are, of course, some notable exceptions to this rule. Despite the generally inferior status of women in India, many of them in the country's Westernized, upper-caste elite have achieved considerable political success. During the 1960s and 1970s, the percentage of women in the Indian parliament was 2.5 to 4 times as high as the proportion of women in the U.S. House of Representatives (a situation that no longer holds).[54] In 1993 India passed a constitutional amendment mandating that one-third of the seats in all local assemblies (village councils, etc.) be reserved for women; the amendment does not apply, however, to the national parliament.[55]

But the ability of women to rise to the top of the political system in South Asia is striking, particularly when one considers their generally lamentable position in society as a whole. All three nations on the Indian subcontinent, along with closely neighboring Sri Lanka, have had women prime ministers. The most prominent member of this group was Indira Gandhi, who served twice as prime minister and dominated Indian politics from 1966 until her assassination in 1984, when she was succeeded by her son Rajiv. In recent decades, women have been prime ministers or presidents in Pakistan (Benazir Bhutto), Sri Lanka (Prime Minister Sirimavo Bandaranaike and now her daughter, President Chandrika Kumaratunga), and Bangladesh (Prime Minister Khaleda Zia and her successor, Sheik Hasina Wazed). Prominent female leaders elsewhere in Asia include former Filipino president Corazón Aquino and current president Gloria Macapagal Arroyo, former Turkish prime minister Tansu Ciller, Indonesian president Megawati Sukarnoputri, and Burmese opposition leader Aung San Suu Kyi, winner of the 1991 Nobel Peace Prize. No other Third World region matches Asia's array of women leaders, but Latin America has produced Eva Perón, current Panamanian president Mireya Elisa Moscoso Rodríguez, as well as former presidents Isabel Perón (Argentina), Violeta Chamorro (Nicaragua), and Ertha Pascal-Trouillot (who served very briefly as Haiti's provisional president).

Two cautions must be raised regarding the political success of these leaders. First, virtually all of them emerged from a tiny elite of highly educated, upper-class women from powerful families. Thus, for example, Pakistan's Benazir Bhutto and Burma's Aung San Suu Kyi were educated, respectively, at Harvard and Oxford universities. Second, in almost all cases they were the wives, widows, or daughters of charismatic national leaders: Indira Gandhi was the daughter of India's first prime minister, Jawaharal Nehru, a legendary figure who led his nation for 15 years; similarly, Aung San Suu Kyi is the daughter of Myanmar's most revered independence leader; Indonesian president Megawati Sukarnoputri is the daughter of the country's founding father; Filipino president Gloria Macapagal Arroyo is the daughter of a respected former president; and Benazir Bhutto is the daughter of another former Pakistani prime minister (executed by the military). A shocking number of women heads of government in the developing world are the widows (or daughters) of assassinated political leaders. Sri Lankan prime minister Sirimavo Bandaranaike was the widow of a slain prime minister, and the country's current president, Chandrika Kumaratunga, endured the political assassinations of both her father and her husband (thirty years apart). Former president Corazón Aquino, hero of the Filipino democracy movement, is the widow of an assassinated opposition leader. Bangladesh's most recent prime ministers are, respectively, the widow and daughter of assassinated heads of government. And former Nicaraguan president Violeta Chamorro is the widow of a famed newspaper editor whose assassination helped spark the Nicaraguan Revolution.[56]

This does not imply that these women lacked political ability or leadership qualities. Indira Gandhi was widely recognized as one of the world's most accomplished political leaders, and Violeta Chamorro helped heal the wounds of her country's civil war.[57] After Sirimavo Bandaranaike succeeded her assassinated husband as Sri Lanka's prime minister, she went on to dominate that country's political system for the next three decades. Current Philippine president Gloria Macapagal Arroyo was a university economics professor before entering politics. What the evidence demonstrates, however, is that no matter how highly skilled Third World women may be, they have been able to reach the top of their political system only as successors to their fathers or husbands.[58] For now, then, the glass ceiling remains in place for most Third World women in politics, with the notable exception of this elite minority.

Women and Revolutionary Change

The political, economic, and social changes brought about by revolutions in the LDCs often present women with rather unique opportunities that merit special attention here. For one thing, revolutions tend to alter or tear down many of the traditional social structures and values that had previously oppressed women. When the communists came to power in China, for example, they eliminated the last vestiges of foot binding for young women and prohibited the sale of women and girls as wives, concubines, or prostitutes.[59] In addition, most revolutionary armies and parties create social structures that are open to women and present greater opportunities for upward mobility. For example, women held important military command positions in both the Nicaraguan Sandinistas and the Salvadorian FMLN during their guerrilla struggles.

Indeed, because of their need for soldiers and their willingness to violate traditional gender roles, many guerrilla armies include significant numbers of women. For example, in the Eritrean People's Liberation Front (EPLF), which carried out a 30–year struggle for independence from Ethiopia, women constituted some 30 percent of the army and 11 percent of the delegates to the First EPLF Congress.[60] Similarly, it is estimated that women constituted 20 to 30 percent of the Sandinista forces in Nicaragua, perhaps 25 percent of Uruguay's Tupamaros, and a significant proportion of the FMLN guerrillas in El Salvador.[61] Because guerrilla armies such as the Sandinistas continued to play a central political role in society after the revolutionary party took power, their high level of gender integration had long-term consequences that transcended the military struggle.

After the communist victory in China, Party Chairman Mao Zedong and the All-China Women's Federation assigned women an important role in rebuilding the nation's economy.[62] Consequently, many women who had long been confined to their homes entered the industrial work force, not because of a feminist agenda but because the government needed to reconstruct an economy devastated by three decades of war. But while the opportunity to work outside the home was obviously beneficial, women failed to attain the occupational equality called for by the government. In both collective farms and industry, they continued to hold less-skilled, lower-paying jobs than men.

Radical regimes such as those in China, Vietnam, and Cuba emphasize the transformation of traditional cultural values through education and propaganda. Combating long-standing prejudices against women is a part of that process. But even these societies find it difficult to eradicate long-standing sexist attitudes. China's 1950 Marriage Law decreed that women could wed only of their own free will and granted women equal rights within the family, but enforcement of the Marriage Law has been considerably less than perfect, especially in rural areas. Furthermore, during the Maoist era (1949–1976) the government's commitment to these new values varied considerably, as the country swung between periods of ideological fervor and eras of pragmatism. During radical phases, such as the Great Leap Forward and the Cultural Revolution, state policy supported female liberation and lambasted traditional Chinese prejudices toward women. Following these periods of mass mobilization and turmoil, however, when party leaders wished to restore stability, the government reverted to more traditional values, extolling the importance of motherhood and the family.

Since the late 1970s, Deng Xiaoping's pragmatic state policies have stressed economic growth more than gender equality. As many Chinese factories begin to abandon their policy of guaranteed lifetime employment (the "iron rice bowl") in their quest for higher efficiency, women are likely to be the first workers to be fired, though it is also true that women are disproportionately employed in the thriving industrial export sector.[63] Nothing more clearly shows the enduring influence of sexism in Chinese culture, however, than the question of population control. Troubled by the country's enormous population (more than 1.2 billion people at the start of the twenty-first century), the government has been pressuring the Chinese people to have only one child per family. In rural China, where girls are considered less desirable than boys, this has apparently led to significant infanticide against female babies by parents who want their single child to be a boy.[64] In addition, girls represent a disproportionate share of the abandoned children in rural orphanages.

The Cuban revolutionary government has very actively sought to improve the status of women and combat traditional male values of machismo. In 1960 the Federation of Cuban Women (FMC) was founded to mobilize women behind the revolution and give them a voice in the political process. Since the federation's longtime leader, Vilma Espín, is Fidel Castro's sister-in-law as well as the wife of Cuba's second most powerful leader, Raúl Castro, the FMC had a direct line to the center of power. Espín, a graduate of the Massachusetts Institute of Technology (MIT), also had a distinguished career as a guerrilla officer in Cuba's revolutionary struggle. Officially representing 70 percent of Cuban women, the FMC successfully encouraged many of them to seek employment and to participate politically. Thus, from 1970 to 1979 the proportion of women in the work force rose from 17.8 percent to 30.9 percent, with impressive gains in the professions.[65] In the political sphere, women have been particularly active in the neighborhood-based Committees for Defense of the Revolution (CDR). The CDRs (to which some 80 percent of Cuba's adults belong) promote revolutionary values, including gender equality. Some men who refuse to let their wives work or who don't put in their share of the housework find themselves denounced for machismo at CDR meetings (perhaps by their wives or even their mothers) and castigated by their peers for their nonrevolutionary values. By the early 1980s, women represented half the local CDR leaders, 46 percent of the leaders of labor union locals, and 22 percent of the delegates to the National Assembly (the Cuban national congress).[66]

But revolutions are no panacea for women's problems. Often radical rhetoric exceeds actual accomplishments. Cuba, like China, demonstrates that even egalitarian revolutions fail to achieve full gender equality. Thus, despite their prominence in local CDR and labor unions, Cuban women have rarely penetrated the top ranks of national political leadership, such as the State Council (in effect, the president's cabinet) or the Central Committee and the Politburo of the Communist Party. An analysis in the early 1980s showed that only 8.9 percent of Central Committee members were female.[67] Similarly, while Cubans pay lip service to the Family Code, few men live up to its requirement that spouses share equally in domestic tasks. Change has been limited by ingrained male attitudes and most women's obvious reluctance to complain to the local CDR (composed of their neighbors) about their husband's noncompliance with the law. As one sympathetic observer noted, "It must take an extremely confident woman to bring her husband to public censure for failure to honor the code."[68] Chauvinist attitudes linger there as they do in other revolutionary societies.

THE STATUS OF WOMEN: THE ROLES OF MODERNIZATION, GLOBALIZATION, AND REGIME TYPE

Our analysis to this point reveals that the political and economic status of Third World women is anything but uniform. Their position varies considerably from region to region and country to country. Within individual countries, a woman's situation differs according to her social class or ethnicity. Three factors seem particularly relevant in this regard: the prevailing cultural values, the level of socioeconomic modernization, and the type of political regime in place.

Religious and other cultural factors ultimately set boundaries on Third World women and influence the opportunities available to them. This is most manifestly true in Islamist (fundamentalist) states such as Afghanistan, Iran, and Sudan, as well as in conservative Islamic nations such as Saudi Arabia. In the most extreme example, Afghanistan's Taliban government prohibited female employment outside the home and virtually confined women to their households. In doing so, they denied one of the world's poorest nations a substantial part of its small core of teachers and health care workers. While educational and professional opportunities exist for a female elite in Iran and Saudi Arabia, most women are marginalized from the mainstream of economic life. Political leadership in all these countries is an exclusively male preserve. Cultural restraints are more subtle in East Asia, but Ester Boserup found that even in modern societies such as Singapore and Hong Kong, women had lower than expected rates of university attendance.[69]

Contrary to modernization theory but in line with radical feminist analysis, socioeconomic modernization often has had an adverse effect on women in the LDCs in the short to medium run. In Africa, for example, the commercialization and mechanization of agriculture have frequently benefited male cultivators disproportionately at the expense of women farmers. In East and Southeast Asia, rapid industrialization based on cheap labor has led to higher wages for some female laborers and exploitation of others.[70] Yet while the initial effects of modernization often negatively impact poor women, over time its longer-term influence is generally beneficial. A growing middle class, wider educational opportunities, and higher rates of literacy enable women to become more aware of their rights and opportunities and increase their capacity to defend them. Socioeconomic development also tends to create more egalitarian values within society as a whole. It should be noted that the more modernized nations of Latin America—including Argentina, Chile, Mexico, and Uruguay—have the largest number of female political leaders and professionals.

And like other political movements carried globally by the mass media and scholarly publications, the feminist movement has extended itself into the Third World through the demonstration effect. In many developing nations, women's rights movements have grown where none existed or were even conceivable a decade or two earlier. Women in more traditional societies like Bolivia or Jordan are influenced by the women's movements that were first born in more progressive societies such as Chile or Lebanon. In each case, however, the movement has taken on a distinct character, distinguishing itself from Western feminism. The women's movement was born in the Western world a mere three to four decades ago, and one can only speculate on its influence in the Third World three decades from now.

Finally, the status of women is strongly influenced by the type of political regime and economic system that prevails in their country. Women seem to fare poorly under right-wing, authoritarian military regimes such as those that dominated much of South America in the 1970s and early 1980s and to benefit from leftist regimes. Ironically, however, while women suffered under the former military dictatorships in Chile, Argentina, and Brazil, they gained considerable political experience in social movements committed to guaranteeing human rights and providing food and services for the poor. Revolutionary regimes, with their ideological commitment to equality, have often championed women's rights. However, while the revolutionary process has benefited many women in countries such as China, Vietnam, Cuba, and Nicaragua, obvious gender inequalities remain in those societies. To some extent, this inequality reflects the heritage of deeply entrenched cultural values as well as continued male dominance of the political system. It also stems from the Marxist belief that all societal inequalities—whether tied to gender, race, religion, or the like— are derived from class divisions. Hence, there is a tendency to underestimate gender-based injustices and to erroneously assume that, in time, the eradication of capitalism will inevitably end serious sexism.

Since full gender equality does not exist even in most advanced industrial democracies (only small, northern European democracies such as Iceland, the Netherlands, Finland, Denmark, Norway, and Sweden come close), it seems unlikely that the process of socioeconomic modernization or the spread of democratic norms will automatically bring gender equality to the developing world. Economic development can be expected to produce both negative and positive consequences. In the short run, economic modernization, particularly in agriculture, will likely adversely affect many low-income women. In countries suffering severe economic difficulties such as debt crises or those suffering internal strife, women will doubtless continue to bear an unequal burden. And the spread of Islamic fundamentalism in many parts of the Middle East and Africa does not bode well for women's rights in those regions.

CONCLUSION: DEMOCRACY AND THE ROLE OF WOMEN IN SOCIETY

Since democratic ideology endorses equal opportunity for political participation and equal rights for *all* citizens, in theory it should follow that the spread of democracy during the final decades of the twentieth century should have advanced the cause of women. Yet the preceding discussion of revolutionary regimes such as China's and Cuba's revealed that some nondemocratic governments have a stronger record of accomplishment than their democratic counterparts in the pursuit of gender equality. They and other revolutionary regimes have established quotas for female participation in the national legislature, improved the legal status of women, banned oppressive traditional customs (the binding of Chinese women's feet, for example), and, at least on the surface, seemed to include women's rights in the new revolutionary political culture. Thus, a good case can certainly be made, for example, that the communist governments of China, Cuba, and Vietnam advanced the cause of gender equality more effectively than did the democratic governments of Brazil, India, or Thailand. Ironically, the transition from communism to democracy in Eastern Europe produced a precipitous drop in the percentage of women elected to parliament.[71]

Of course, most authoritarian governments are not radical and are not committed to women's rights. In non-leftist authoritarian systems, we see little state commitment to greater gender equality. In Afghanistan, the Taliban revolutionary government pursued a very reactionary form of Islamic fundamentalism that denied women even the right to work or to pursue an education and kept them veiled and confined to their homes much of the time.[72] Authoritarian Islamist regimes in Iran and Sudan also heavily restricted women. Elsewhere, in countries such as Chile, Nigeria, and Pakistan, repressive military dictatorships neither restricted the role of women in society nor made any particular effort to improve their status.

What effect on women's status did the wave of LDC democratization have in the closing decades of the twentieth century? As we have seen, women played an important role in the restoration of democracy in a number of Latin American countries, including Chile, Brazil, and Argentina. Often they were able to demonstrate in the streets when men could not. Yet the return of democracy allowed the newly restored political parties (dominated by men) to retake center stage in the political arena and, unintentionally or not, to push "new social movements" and other grass-roots groups (where women had a much larger role) to the sidelines. During the restoration of democracy in the 1990s, the percentage of women in the Chilean parliament and in cabinet posts, while high by Third World standards, was no better than it had been prior to the military dictatorship. On the other hand, the country's socialist and social democratic parties, which have governed the country since 1999, have now established 20 to 25 percent quotas for female representation in all party organizations and committees.[73] Bang-Soon L. Yoon examined the effects of democratization on gender politics in South Korea. There too women had played an important role in the mass protests that helped build democracy, working particularly through their labor unions. Yet the establishment of democracy in the late 1980s and early 1990s failed to raise the comparatively small percentage of women in the National Assembly, judiciary, and bureaucracy.[74] At the same time, however, perhaps spurred on by emerging women's groups, the South Korean National Assembly has become more receptive to legislation advancing the causes of women, such as the Equal Employment Acts (1989 and 1995), the Child Care Act (1990), and the Law on Prevention of Family Violence and Protection of Victims (1997).

On a worldwide basis, the data indicate that the countries with the highest Gender Empowerment Measures (GEM) were Western democracies, most notably countries in northern Europe; countries with the lowest GEM scores were less likely to be democratic. But most of that difference can be attributable to the differences in socioeconomic development: countries with the highest educational, literacy, urbanization, and industrialization levels (Western Europe, North America, and Oceania) were more democratic and also stronger on measures of gender equality. The poorest and least developed countries in Africa and South Asia scored poorly on measures of both democracy and gender equality.

As I have suggested, if we look only at Third World countries, the relationship between democracy and gender equality is not clear. Some democracies, such as Chile and Uruguay, have relatively higher levels of equality (as measured by GEM scores), while other democracies, such as India, fare poorly. Similarly, authoritarian nations, such as Cuba, score very well, while others, such as Egypt and Saudi Arabia, do poorly. There is every reason to believe that in the long run, democratic government will give women greater opportunities as they become able to organize politically, lobby political leaders, and use other democratic rights. But the third wave makes clear that democracy offers no quick fix for gender inequality.

DISCUSSION QUESTIONS

1. Explain how the focus of research on gender in the developing world has moved from the study of oppression to the study of empowerment. What does this change reflect?
2. What occupations attract the highest proportions of Third World women? Why do many women gravitate toward those occupations?
3. Discuss the ways in which modernization has affected women of differing social status in distinct ways.
4. What is the most common characteristic of female heads of government in the Third World? To what extent has their assumption of power substantially improved the status of other women in their nations?
5. Discuss the reasons why Latin American women organized grass-roots political and social movements in the 1980s. What social classes were most mobilized in this period, and what issues motivated mobilization of different classes?
6. Compare the records of Third World democracies to that of authoritarian LDCs insofar as they promote gender equality in politics and the workplace.

NOTES

1. The informal sector, which includes a large number of street vendors and small businesses, is the part of the economy that is "unregulated by the institutions of society [most notably the state], in a legal and social environment in which similar activities are regulated" and taxed. In other words, the informal sector encompasses otherwise legal activities (not criminal operations or prostitution) but operates outside the spheres of tax collection, government labor and safety regulations, and the like. In many developing countries, it represents 30 to 50 percent of the work force. See Manuel Castells and Alejandro Portes, "World Underneath: The Origins, Dynamics and Effects of the

Informal Economy," in *The Informal Economy: Studies in Advanced and Developing Economies*, ed. Alejandro Portes, Manuel Castells, and Lauren A. Benton (Baltimore, MD: Johns Hopkins University Press, 1989), p. 12. Of course, men constitute much of the informal sector, but women are disproportionately represented.

2. *New York Times*, December 30, 1993, p. 5.

3. Arturo Escobar and Sonia E. Alvarez, eds., *The Making of Social Movements in Latin America: Identity, Strategy and Democracy* (Boulder, CO: Westview Press, 1992); June Nash, "Women's Social Movements in Latin America," *Gender and Society* 4, no. 3 (September 1990): 338–353.

4. Women also could not work even if the family had no male breadwinner.

5. The World Bank, *Engendering Development* (New York: Oxford University Press and the World Bank, 2001), p. 58.

6. Sonia E. Alvarez, *Engendering Democracy in Brazil: Women's Movements in Transition Politics* (Princeton, NJ: Princeton University Press, 1990), p. 4, fn. 2.

7. Paul Cammack, David Pool, and William Tordoff, *Third World Politics: A Comparative Introduction* (Baltimore, MD: Johns Hopkins University Press, 1988), pp. 184–193.

8. Leith Mullings, "Women and Economic Change in Africa," in *Women in Africa: Studies in Social and Economic Change*, ed. Nancy J. Hafkin and Edna G. Bray (Stanford, CA: Stanford University Press, 1976), pp. 239–264.

9. Margo Lovett, "Gender Relations, Class Formation, and the Colonial State in Africa," in *Women and the State in Africa*, ed. Jane L. Parpart and Kathleen A. Staudt (Boulder, CO: Lynne Rienner Publishers, 1989), pp. 37–39.

10. Ester Boserup, *Women's Role in Economic Development* (London: George Allen and Unwin, 1970), p. 54.

11. Ibid., p. 55.

12. Cited in Esther Trenchard, "Rural Women's Work in Sub-Saharan Africa and the Implications for Nutrition," in *Geography of Gender in the Third World*, ed. Janet Henshall Momsen and Janet G. Townsend (Albany, NY: SUNY Press, 1987), p. 155; and Marie-Angélique Savané, "Women and Rural Development in Africa," in *Women in Rural Development: Critical Issues* (Geneva: International Labour Office, 1980), p. 27. The findings of any given study are undoubtedly less precise than its tables may suggest, since female labor participation in developing nations is hard to measure and varies considerably from place to place. Yet the research generally shows similar patterns.

13. Boserup, *Women's Role*, pp. 27–28. For other estimates, see Joan Mencher, "Women in Agriculture," in *Food Policy: Framework for Analysis*, ed. Charles K. Mann and Barbara Huddleston (Bloomington, IN: Indiana University Press, 1986), p. 39.

14. A. Bandarage, "Women in Development: Liberalism, Marxism and Marxism-Feminism," *Development and Change* 15, no. 3 (1984).

15. Nici Nelson, *Why Has Development Neglected Rural Women?* (Oxford, England: Pergamon Press, 1979), p. 4.

16. Ibid., pp. 45–47.

17. Savané, *Women in Rural Development*, p. 27.

18. Leena Mehendale, "The Integrated Rural Development Programme for Women in Developing Countries: A Case Study," in *Women, Development and Survival in the Third World*, ed. Haleh Afshar (New York: Longman, 1991), pp. 223–238.

19. Cornelia Butler Flora, "Income Generation Projects for Rural Women," in *Rural Women and State Policy: Feminist Perspectives on Latin American Agricultural Development*, ed. Carmen Diana Deere and Magdalena León de Leal (Boulder, CO: Westview Press, 1987), pp. 212–238.

20. Claire Robertson, "Ga Women and Socioeconomic Change in Accra, Ghana," in *Women in Africa*, pp. 111–133.

21. Gloria González Salazar, "Participation of Women in the Mexican Labor Force," in *Sex and Class in Latin America*, ed. June Nash and Helen I. Safa (New York: J. F. Bergin Publishers, 1980), p. 187.

22. Heleieth I. B. Saffioti, "Technological Change in Brazil: Its Effect on Men and Women in Two Firms," in *Women and Change in Latin America*, ed. June Nash and Helen I. Safa (South Hadley, MA: Bergin & Garvey Publishers, 1985), pp. 110–111; Commack, Pool, and Tordoff, *Third World Politics*, pp. 195–196.

23. *The New York Times*, June 11, 1998.

24. Cited in Alan Gilbert and Josef Gugler, *Cities, Poverty and Development: Urbanization in the Third World*, 2d ed. (New York: Oxford University Press, 1992), p. 104, fn. 29.

25. Nici Nelson, "How Women and Men Get By: The Sexual Division of Labour in the Informal Sector of a Nairobi Squatter Settlement," in *The Urbanization of the Third World*, ed. Josef Gugler (New York: Oxford University Press, 1988), pp. 183–203.

26. Shahnaz Kazi, "Some Measures of the Status of Women in the Course of Development in South Asia," in *Women in Development in South Asia*, ed. V. Kanesalingam (New Delhi, India: Macmillan India Limited, 1989), pp. 19–52.

27. Mary C. Muller, "Vocational Training for Women of India," in *Third World at the Crossroads*, ed. Sheikh R. Ali (New York: Praeger, 1989), pp. 87–94.

28. Boserup, *Women's Role*, pp. 119–128.

29. It should be noted, however, that in countries such as Argentina and Russia where women constitute a high proportion of the medical profession, medicine is not nearly as lucrative an occupation as in the United States. The most financially rewarding jobs in Argentina, such as business executives, are still largely male.

30. *Real wage* is a measure of the purchasing power of individual or family earnings. It factors in earnings and changes in the cost of living. Thus, if an employee receives a 10 percent salary increase during the year, but prices increase by 15 percent during that period, he or she has experienced a 10 percent increase in wages but a 5 percent decline in *real* wages.

31. Aili Mari Tripp, "The Impact of Crisis and Economic Reform on Women in Urban Tanzania," in *Unequal Burden: Economic Crisis, Persistent Poverty, and Women's Work*, ed. Lourdes Benería and Shelley Feldman (Boulder, CO: Westview Press, 1992), pp. 163–166.

32. Paola Pérez-Alemán, "Economic Crisis and Women in Nicaragua," in *Unequal Burden*, pp. 239–247.

33. Only Finland and Norway granted women the vote prior to World War I. Female suffrage was enacted in the United States in 1920 at about the same time as in most West European democracies. On the other hand, women were not able to vote in Swiss national elections until 1972, nor in the small European state of Liechtenstein until 1986.

34. On women's suffrage in Europe and the United States, see Vicky Randall, *Women and Politics: An International Perspective*, 2d ed. (Chicago: University of Chicago Press, 1987), pp. 5, 51, 209–211; on Latin America, see Jane Jaquette, "Female Political Participation in Latin America," in *Sex and Class in Latin America*, p. 223; also, Francesca Miller, *Latin American Women and the Search for Social Justice* (Hanover, NH: University Press of New England, 1991), pp. 96–101.

35. World Bank, *Engendering Development*, p. 57.

36. See, for example, Ellen Gruenbaum, "Sudanese Women and the Islamist State," in *Women and Power in the Middle East*, ed. Suad Joseph and Susan Slyomovics (Philadelphia: University of Pennsylvania Press, 2001), pp. 115–125. Other chapters in

the volume paint a less pessimistic picture, such as the one on Palestinian women in the political system and workplace.

37. Rama Mehta, *The Western Educated Hindu Woman* (New York: Asia Publishing House, 1970), pp. 16–32.

38. Judith Van Allen, "Memsahib, Militante, Femme Libre: Political and Apolitical Styles of Modern African Women," in *Women in Politics*, ed. Jane S. Jaquette (New York: John Wiley and Sons, 1974), p. 310.

39. Lourdes Arizpe, "Foreword: Democracy for a Small Two-Gender Planet," in *Women and Social Change in Latin America*, ed. Elizabeth Jelin (London and Atlantic Highlands, NJ: Zed Books, 1990), p. xv.

40. Nina Mba, "Kaba and Khaki: Women and the Militarized State in Nigeria," in *Women and the State in Africa*, p. 86.

41. Jaquette, "Female Political Participation," p. 223.

42. See, for example, JoAnn Aviel, "Changing the Political Role of Women: A Costa Rican Case Study," in *Women in Politics*, pp. 281–303.

43. See, for example, Amy Conger Lind, "Power, Gender and Development: Popular Women's Organizations and the Politics of Needs in Ecuador," in *The Making of Social Movements*, pp. 134–149.

44. Jana Everett, "Incorporation versus Conflict: Lower Class Women, Collective Action, and the State in India," in *Women, the State and Development*, ed. Sue Ellen M. Charlton, Jana Everett, and Kathleen Staudt (Albany: State University of New York Press, 1989), p. 163.

45. Armita Basu, *Two Faces of Protest: Contrasting Modes of Women's Activism* (Berkeley: University of California Press, 1992), p. 3.

46. Jane S. Jaquette, "Introduction" in *The Women's Movement in Latin America: Feminism and the Transition to Democracy*, ed. Jane S. Jaquette (Boston: Unwin Hyman, 1989), p. 6. This section draws heavily on Jaquette's book and Alvarez, *Engendering Democracy in Brazil*.

47. Sonia E. Alvarez, "Women's Movements and Gender Politics in the Brazilian Transition," in *The Women's Movement in Latin America*, pp. 19–20; see also Alvarez, *Engendering Democracy in Brazil*.

48. Teresa Pires de Rio Caldeira, "Women, Daily Life and Politics," in *Women and Social Change in Latin America*, pp. 47–79.

49. Patricia Jeffery and Amrita Basu, ed., *Appropriating Gender: Women's Activism and Politicized Religion in South Asia* (London: Routledge, 1998).

50. Elsa M. Chaney, *Supermadre: Women in Politics in Latin America* (Austin: University of Texas Press, 1979), p. 4.

51. Jane L. Parpart and Kathleen A. Staudt, "Women and the State in Africa," in *Women and the State in Africa*, p. 8.

52. Quoted in Chaney, *Supermadre*, p. 21.

53. Ibid., p. 141.

54. Manjulika Koshal, "Indira Gandhi as Head of Government," in *Asian Women in Transition*, ed. Sylvia A. Chipp and Justin J. Green (University Park, PA: Pennsylvania State University Press, 1980), p. 253. It should be noted that women were highly under-represented in both bodies, just less so in India for that period.

55. Suranjana Gupta, "Transforming Governance Agendas: Insights from Grass-roots Women's Initiatives in Local Government in Two Districts in India," in *Gender, Globalization, and Democratization*, ed. Rita Mae Kelly et al. (Lanham, MD: Rowan & Littlefield, 2001), pp. 195–204.

56. It is worth noting a similar pattern in the United States until recently. Vicky Randall points out that between 1917 and 1976, 73 percent of female senators and 50 percent of women congressional representatives were the widows of men who had held seats. See *Women and Politics*, p. 132.

57. To be sure, some of the aforementioned group, most notably Isabel Perón, were far less capable.

58. Of course, it is also true that until the 1970s, almost all women governors and senators in the United States were the widows of men who had formerly held those posts. Only relatively recently have American women attained those positions totally on their own.

59. Delia Davin, "Chinese Models of Development and Their Implications for Women," in *Women, Development and Survival*, p. 32.

60. National Union of Eritrean Women, "Women and Revolution in Eritrea," in *Third World: Second Sex*, ed. Miranda Davis (London: Zed Press, 1983), p. 114.

61. *Envio* (Managua) 6, p. 78, quoted in Mary Stead, "Women, War and Underdevelopment in Nicaragua," *Women, Development and Survival*, p. 53; Randall, *Woman and Politics*, p. 61.

62. Bee-Lan Chan Wang, "Chinese Women: The Relative Influences of Ideological Revolution, Economic Growth and Cultural Change," in *Comparative Perspectives of Third World Women: The Impact of Race, Sex and Class*, ed. Beverly Lindsay (New York: Praeger, 1980), pp. 99–104; see also Delia Davin, "Chinese Models of Development," in *Women, Development and Survival*.

63. *New York Times*, May 11, 1993.

64. *New York Times*, April 25, 1993 and July 21, 1993. Thus, demographers have found a higher than normal ratio of male births to female births reported to the government. Some of the discrepancy may be caused by girls being born and not reported, but part is probably due to female infanticide.

65. Isabel Larguia and John Domoulin, "Women's Equality in the Cuban Revolution," in *Women and Change in Latin America*, pp. 344, 363.

66. Ibid., p. 360. There is an extensive literature on women in revolutionary Cuba, most of it written from a strongly prorevolutionary perspective. See Margaret E. Leahy, *Development Strategies and the Status of Women* (Boulder, CO: Lynne Rienner Publishers, 1986), pp. 91–116; Lois M. Smith and Alfred Padula, "The Cuban Family in the 1980s," in *Transformation and Struggle: Cuba Faces the 1990s*, ed. Sandor Halebsky and John M. Kirk (New York: Praeger, 1990), pp. 176–188; and Max Azicri, "Women's Development through Revolutionary Mobilization," in *The Cuba Reader: The Making of a Revolutionary Society*, ed. Philip Brenner et al. (New York: Grove Press, 1989), pp. 457–470. For a different viewpoint, see Julie Marie Bunck, "The Cuban Revolution and Women's Rights," in *Cuban Communism*, 7th ed., ed. Irving Louis Horowitz (New Brunswick, NJ: Transaction Publishers, 1989), pp. 443–465.

67. Randall, *Women and Politics*, p. 103.

68. Johnetta Cole, "Women in Cuba," in *Comparative Perspectives of Third World Women*, p. 176.

69. Boserup, *Women's Role*, pp. 119–128.

70. Linda Y. C. Lim, "Capitalism, Imperialism and Patriarchy: The Dilemma of Third World Women in Multinational Factories," in *Women, Men and the International Division of Labor*, ed. June Nash and María Patricia Fernández-Kelly (Albany, NY: SUNY Press, 1983).

71. World Bank, *Engendering Development*, p. 58.

72. For personal accounts by Afghan women, see Deborah Ellis, *Women of the Afghan War* (Westport, CT: Praeger, 2000).

73. Georgina Waynlen, "Women's Activism, Authoritarianism, and Democratization in Chile," in *Gender, Ethnicity and Political Ideologies*, ed. Nickie Charles and Helen Hintjens (London and New York: Routledge, 1998), p. 159.

74. Bang-Soon L. Yoon, "Democratization and Gender Politics in South Korea," in *Gender, Globalization, and Democratization*, pp.174–176.

chapter 6

Agrarian Reform and the Politics of Rural Change

When we speak of "the people" of Africa and Asia, in large part we are talking about the peasantry—poor farmers living in a traditional culture. Despite substantial urbanization in recent decades (see Chapter 7), much of the developing world remains primarily rural. According to one estimate, half of all Third World families earn their livelihood from agriculture.[1] And it is in the countryside where some of the worst aspects of political and economic underdevelopment prevail. In nations as distinct as China and Mexico, rural annual incomes are only 20 to 25 percent as high as urban earnings. Sharp urban-rural gaps also exist in literacy, health care, and life expectancy. Rural villagers are less likely than their urban cousins to have safe drinking water, electricity, or schools.

While the proportion of the Third World's total population living in the countryside is generally substantially higher than in the First World, it varies greatly from country to country: from under one-third in Venezuela, Argentina, Brazil, and Zambia to two-thirds or more in Malaysia, Yemen, Bolivia, China, India, and much of Africa. In all, more than one billion of these rural people live in "absolute poverty," defined as suffering from inadequate housing, pervasive illiteracy, malnutrition, and high rates of infant mortality.[2] And in the world's poorest nations—including Malawi, Rwanda, the Congo, Bangladesh, and Haiti—the portion of rural inhabitants living in absolute poverty exceeds 80 percent.[3]

Given the size of the agricultural sector, we should not be surprised to find that it contributes a larger share of the Gross Domestic Product (GDP) than it does in industrialized nations. Thus, agriculture constitutes 35 percent of

GDP in the poorest Third World nations, 22 percent in middle-level LDCs, and 10 percent in the more advanced developing countries, compared to only 3 percent in highly industrialized countries.[4] At the same time, however, the farm population's per-capita output is far lower than the urban sector's.

In most of the developing world, political and economic power is concentrated in the cities. Consequently, government policy—on issues ranging from social expenditures to agricultural pricing—has a predictable urban bias. As noted in Chapter 1, modernization theory argues that as countries develop, modern values and institutions will spread from the cities to the countryside, and the gap between the two will narrow. Conversely, dependency theorists maintain that the links between urban and rural areas replicate the exploitative international relationship between the industrialized core (the First World) and the periphery (the LDCs).[5] What is certain is that resolving the political and economic tensions *between* urban and rural areas and reducing the vast inequalities *within* the countryside, the major foci of this chapter, remain among the foremost challenges facing most developing nations.

RURAL CLASS STRUCTURES

Within the countryside, there are generally substantial disparities in access to, and ownership of, farm land. Particularly in Latin America and parts of South Asia, agricultural property tends to be concentrated in a relatively small number of hands. These inequalities have contributed to rural poverty and created rigid class systems in countries such as El Salvador, Colombia, the Philippines, and parts of India. African nations—with notable exceptions such as Zimbabwe, South Africa, Morocco, and Kenya—have a more equitable pattern of land distribution, though they still suffer from sharp urban-rural gaps and intense rural poverty. Farm land is most equitably distributed in East Asia (excepting the Philippines).

At the apex of the rural class system stand the large and powerful land owners, sometimes known as the *oligarchy*. Major Filipino sugar growers and Argentine cattle magnates, for example, have historically exercised considerable political power in national politics. In El Salvador, the most influential coffee producers long dominated the country's political system in conjunction with the armed forces. Land concentration has been most intense in Latin America, with its tradition of large estates (*latifundia*) dating back to the Spanish colonial era and the early years of independence. In the Philippines, Sri Lanka, Pakistan, and Bangladesh, along with parts of India, Indonesia, and Thailand, reactionary landed elites have also contributed to rural backwardness and poverty.

In recent decades, the economic and political power of rural landlords has declined considerably in many LDCs. In industrializing nations such as Mexico, Brazil, and Thailand, the economic importance of agribusiness has diminished relative to the industrial and commercial sectors. Consequently, many wealthy land-owning families have diversified into other parts of the economy or have left agriculture entirely. In other countries, agrarian reform has weakened, or even destroyed, the power of the rural oligarchy.[6]

These changes have been most sweeping and often brutal in countries that have experienced peasant-based revolutions or agrarian reform imposed from above. Following China's revolution, for example, the nation's landlords were stripped of their wealth, while untold thousands were executed. After the communist victory in Vietnam, landlords were sent to prison camps for "political reeducation." Elsewhere, in nonrevolutionary societies such as Peru and South Korea, comprehensive but peaceful agrarian reforms have also undermined the landed aristocracy.

At the local and regional levels, however, landlords in Latin America and many parts of Asia continue to exercise considerable influence. For example, upper-caste farmers in the Indian state of Bihar and cattle barons in the Brazilian interior retain virtually unchallenged local power. At times they have intimidated, or even murdered, peasant organizers and union leaders without fear of legal sanctions. Such was the fate of Chico Mendes, the celebrated Brazilian union leader who had organized Amazonian rubber-tree tappers against the powerful cattle ranchers who were clearing the forest and destroying the local habitat. Despite his impressive international stature (he was honored, for example, by Turner Broadcasting and various U.S. senators) and his links to U.S. environmental groups, Mendes was murdered by hired gunmen. Only after a sustained international outcry were his murderers brought to trial.

On the rung beneath the landed elite in rural society, we find middle-sized landlords and "rich" peasants. The second group (sometimes called *Kulaks*) consists of peasants who, unlike smaller landlords, still work on the land. But, unlike poorer peasants, *kulaks* are sufficiently affluent to hire additional peasant labor to work with them. While neither middle-sized landlords nor rich peasants belong to the national power elite, they exercise considerable local political influence in countries such as India.[7] Indeed, in much of Asia, where the biggest agricultural holdings are not nearly as large as those in Latin America, middle-sized landlords are a potent political force. Together with rich peasants, they are often village political leaders. Moreover, their influence is magnified further by extended family networks.

Finally, at the bottom of the socioeconomic ladder, the rural poor—including peasants who own small plots of land, tenant farmers, and farm workers—are generally the Third World's most impoverished and powerless group. *Peasants* are defined as family farmers (mostly poor) who maintain a traditional lifestyle distinct from that of city dwellers. Because many of them are illiterate or semiliterate and lack familiarity with the commercial or legal systems, peasants generally lack the means to transport their crops to market themselves, lack ready access to credit, and don't know how to deal with legal proceedings that involve them. Consequently, they depend on merchants, money lenders, lawyers, and government bureaucrats, all of whom frequently exploit them. Their links to the outside world—including the government, the military, the church, and the market economy—are largely controlled by individuals and institutions outside the peasants' community.[8] Thus, as Eric Wolf has noted, "Peasant denotes an asymmetrical structural relationship between the producers of surplus [peasants] and controllers [including landlords, merchants, and tax collectors]."[9]

Poor peasants may be further subdivided into two subgroups: those who own small plots of land for family cultivation (smallholders) and the landless. The ranks of the landless, in turn, include tenant farmers (who enter into various types of rental arrangements with landlords) and hired farm laborers. It should be noted that these categories are not mutually exclusive. Smallholders, for example, may also supplement their incomes by working as farm laborers or renting land as tenants. Generally, it is the landless who constitute the poorest of the rural poor. While they represent a mere 10 percent of all agricultural families in countries such as Kenya and Sierra Leone, their numbers rise to 25 to 35 percent in Mexico, Peru, Turkey, and Cameroon, and to 50 to 70 percent in India, Bangladesh, Pakistan, the Philippines, Iraq, the Dominican Republic, and Brazil.[10] Not surprisingly, in much of Asia and Latin America, where concentration of land ownership and associated peasant landlessness are particularly notable, the issue of land reform has been at the center of rural politics.

PEASANT POLITICS

Despite their vast numbers, peasants usually play a muted role in Third World politics. Because most LDCs don't have competitive national elections, those numbers do not readily convert into political influence. The peasantry's political leverage is also limited by their poverty, lack of education, dependence on outsiders, and physical isolation from each other and from the centers of national power. Cultural values stressing caution and conservatism may further constrain peasant political behavior. Karl Marx's analysis of nineteenth-century European rural society questioned the peasants' capacity for political change and questioned their revolutionary potential. Writing on the French peasantry, he derided their alleged lack of solidarity and class consciousness, and disparagingly referred to them as a "sack of potatoes." Dismayed by their apparent conservatism, he dismissed the peasantry as "the class that represents the barbarism in civilization."[11] In the twentieth century, Robert Redfield's classic study of Third World peasants portrayed them somewhat similarly. "In every part of the world," he argued, "generally speaking, peasants have been a conservative factor in social change, a brake on revolution."[12]

Indeed, over the years a number of influential anthropological studies have depicted peasant political culture as fatalistic and atomized. Hence, it is claimed, they doubt the capacity of collective political action to better their own fate.[13] Discussing the reaction of Indian villagers to local government authorities, Phyllis Arora describes a sense of powerlessness resulting in political apathy. "Helplessness is . . . evoked by the presence of the district officer. The

peasant tends to feel that all he [or she] can do before such authority . . . is petition for redress of grievances. . . . In the ultimate analysis, however, . . . the peasant feels at the mercy of the whims of the [political] authorities."[14] More
recently, Western journalists, visiting peasant communities in China at the time
of massive urban student demonstrations, were struck by the villagers' lack of
political involvement and their insularity from national political debate.[15]

No doubt, there often is an underlying conservatism in Third World
rural society. To some extent, this conservatism may reflect a suspicion of outside values—a distrust often grounded in religious beliefs and other long-
standing traditions. Indeed, the maintenance of a distinct peasant culture
depends, to some extent, on the rejection of external influences. But it is
important to recognize that often peasant suspicions of social change are both
understandable and rational. Struggling on the margins of economic survival,
the rural poor have often found that the commercialization and mechanization of agriculture, as well as other aspects of rural modernization, have
affected them adversely. In rural Pakistan, for example, the introduction of
tractors improved the output and income of the farmers who could afford
them. As a consequence, however, many poorer tenant farmers were forced
off the land, and the net result was to increase the concentration of farm property into fewer hands.[16] Parallel examples abound from elsewhere in the
developing world. For example, when convinced by outside organizers to
challenge local injustices, peasants often find themselves ruthlessly
repressed. Small wonder, then, that they are often suspicious of change,
including any challenge to the power structure.

This does not mean, however, that they are incapable of standing up to
landlords and government authorities who wrong them. Far from it.
Examples of peasant resistance are commonplace, ranging from the most
restrained to the most radical. James C. Scott has demonstrated that many
peasants in Southeast Asia who appear to accept the established order actually engage in unobtrusive "everyday forms of resistance," such as theft and
vandalism against their landlords, foot dragging, and false deference.[17]
Elsewhere, peasants have presented their political demands more openly and
aggressively. Since the mid-1990s, in the Mexican state of Chiapas, the
Zapatista rebels, drawn from the area's indigenous communities, have accelerated the nation's democracy movement and forced the government to the
negotiating table. Similarly, peasant demonstrators and voters have been a
force for change in parts of India. And, contrary to Marx's expectations, the
supposedly conservative peasantry was a critical actor in most twentieth-century revolutions. In the Marxist revolutions that swept Russia, China,
Vietnam, and Cuba, as well as in Bolivia's and Mexico's noncommunist insurgencies, peasants played a decisive role.[18] More recently, they have been the
backbone of guerrilla movements in the Philippines, Afghanistan, Cambodia,
Colombia, El Salvador, and Peru.

The role of the peasantry in revolutionary movements will be examined
in greater detail in Chapter 8. For now, however, suffice it to say that peasants

are neither inherently conservative nor intrinsically radical. Rather, they vary considerably in their ideological propensities and their capacity for collective political action. To understand why so many peasants accept the political status quo, while others choose to resist or even rebel, we must first examine the relationship between the powerful and the weak in the countryside. Although landlords in traditional settings frequently exploit their tenants or neighboring smallholders, mutually understood boundaries normally limit the extent of that exploitation. Links between landlords and peasants are usually grounded in long-standing patron-client relationships involving reciprocal obligations. Despite the landlords' superior power, these relationships are not always exploitative. For example, land owners frequently provide their tenants with land and financial credit in return for labor on their estate. And they may fund religious festivals or serve as godparents for their tenants' children.

As long as landlords and other members of the rural power elite fulfill their obligations, peasants generally accept the traditional order despite its many injustices. However, should rural modernization and the commercialization of agriculture induce rural patrons to cease discharging their traditional responsibilities, the peasantry may conclude that the previously existing "moral economy" has failed them.[19] Eric Wolf has noted that the transition from feudal or semifeudal rural relations to capitalist economic arrangements frequently strips the peasantry of the certainty and protection afforded them by the old order. The result is often rural upheaval. Thus, he argues, the origins of communist revolutions in China, Vietnam, Cuba, and other Third World nations could be found in the threat that the growth of rural capitalism posed to the peasants' traditional way of life.[20] This in no way suggests that rural modernization and the transition to capitalism *always* radicalize the peasantry or drive them to revolutionary activity. But when peasants feel that their traditional way of life is threatened, they will resist change or at least try to channel it into forms more beneficial to their interests. How effectively they engage in collective political action and how radical or moderate their demands are depend on a variety of factors: the extent to which they perceive themselves to be exploited; how desperate their economic condition is; the degree of internal cohesion and cooperation within their communities; their ability to form political linkages with peasants in neighboring villages or in other parts of the country; the extent to which they forge political ties with nonpeasant groups and leaders; the type of outside groups with whom they ally (be it the Catholic church in the Philippines or Maoist revolutionaries in Peru); the responsiveness of the political system to their demands; and the variety of political options that the political order affords them.

The last two factors suggest that the probability of radical peasant insurrection depends as much on the quality of a country's political system as it does on the nature of the peasantry. Given a meaningful opportunity to implement change peacefully, peasants rarely opt for revolution. Rebellion—which brings obvious danger to their own lives and the lives of their families—is an act of desperation entered into only when other options are unavailable. It is largely for that reason that no democratic political system has ever been toppled by a revolutionary insurgency.

In recent decades, the spread of the mass media throughout the countryside, increased rural educational levels, and the broadening of voting rights in many LDCs (such as extension of the vote to illiterates) have greatly increased the political influence of peasant voters in democratic and semidemocratic countries. In countries such as India, South Korea, Nicaragua, and Ecuador, politicians must now take the interests of the rural poor more seriously. With rising educational levels and more information at their disposal, peasants can more effectively press their demands. Still, such voting power is of little use in the single-party or no-party governments that still predominate in Africa, the Middle East, and much of Asia. And even in competitive party systems, the peasantry's political power is not proportional to the group's size.

Ultimately, the range of peasant political activity runs the gamut from the far Left to the far Right, from peaceful to violent. As Samuel Huntington has noted, "The peasantry . . . may be the bulwark of the status quo or the shock troops of revolution. Which role the peasant plays is determined by the extent to which the existing system meets his immediate economic and material needs as he sees them."[21] In India, many peasants vote for the BJP—the conservative Hindu fundamentalist party (see Chapter 3). In Latin America, on the other hand, peasants often vote for moderately left-of-center candidates from the Social Democrats, Christian Democrats, and populists. And in countries such as China, Vietnam, Nicaragua, and Peru, many peasants have supported revolutionary insurrections. Whatever their political bent, the peasants' economic and political concerns usually revolve around four broad issues: crop prices (what they are paid for their harvest), consumer prices, taxes, and the availability of land.[22] The issue of land has been the most volatile and the most critical to the political stability of many Third World nations, and it is to this issue that we now turn our attention for much of this chapter.

THE POLITICS OF AGRARIAN REFORM

In many areas of the Third World where land ownership is highly concentrated, the issue of agrarian reform has been at the top of the rural political agenda. To be sure, the pressure for such reform has waxed and waned, and other models of rural development have become more popular in recent decades. Still, the issue of agrarian reform lingers. Normally, it involves redistribution of farm land from landlords to landless peasants or to smallholders who need larger plots to support their families. In other instances, it entails distribution of public property, including previously uncultivated lands. To stand a real chance of increasing agricultural production, improving rural living standards, and establishing political stability, however, government land redistribution must be accompanied by supplementary aid to its program beneficiaries. This aid includes technical assistance on agriculture, commercial credit, transportation, and enhanced access to markets. Unfortunately, agrarian reform programs often fail to provide this additional support in sufficient quantities. Furthermore, the amount of land distributed is frequently inadequate to meet the peasants' needs. Thus, with notable exceptions such as Japan, Taiwan, and South Korea, land reform programs have often fallen short of their goals.

Patterns of Land Concentration

At the start of the twenty-first century, perhaps 100 million rural families (some 500 million people) in the developing world earn most of their income on land they do not own.[23] In addition, millions of land-owning peasants lack sufficient land to support their families adequately. In countries such as Bangladesh, Rwanda, El Salvador, and Peru, the ratio of rural families to arable land is so high that even an equitable distribution of farm land would fail to meet all the peasantry's needs. But in many LDCs, landlessness and land shortages are primarily attributable to the concentration of agricultural land in a small number of hands.

Maldistribution of land is most pronounced in Latin America, where large estates, sometimes measuring thousands of acres, contain a substantial proportion of the region's farm land. In Brazil, for example, a mere 2 percent of the nation's farms, each exceeding 1,000 hectares (2,500 acres),[24] contains 57 percent of all farm land.[25] Vast cattle and citrus estates have been cut out of the Amazonian interior, some covering several hundred thousand acres. In the Dominican Republic, where holdings are not nearly as vast, farms more than 50 hectares in size constitute less than 2 percent of the nation's agricultural units; nevertheless, they control more than 55 percent of the country's farm land. The largest of these estates—those exceeding 500 hectares—represent a mere 0.1 percent of all Dominican farms but possess 27 percent of the nation's agricultural land. At the other end of the spectrum, peasant smallholders (owning units of five hectares or less) own nearly 82 percent of the country's farms, but merely 12.2 percent of its area.[26] Similar patterns prevail in much of Latin America. Prior to the 1979 Sandinista revolution, an astounding 43 percent of Nicaragua's rural families were landless. Yet a mere 2 percent of the rural population owned 36 percent of the land, including about one-fifth of Nicaragua's farm land that belonged to the ruling Somoza family.[27]

With different historical traditions and far higher population density, Asia does not have agricultural estates of the same magnitude. In nations such as Indonesia, India, and Pakistan, farm holdings rarely exceed 50 hectares.[28] Still, in many cases a high proportion of agricultural land is concentrated in relatively few hands. For example, in Bangladesh, one of the world's most densely populated countries, the largest farms are relatively small, rarely exceeding five to ten hectares. Yet less than 3 percent of the nation's rural households control more than 25 percent of the nation's farm land. In the Philippines, virtually identical data show 3.4 percent of the country's farms accounting for 26 percent of the land.[29]

The Case for Agrarian Reform

Given the powerful vested interests opposing land redistribution, supporters of agrarian reform have needed to justify their objectives on a variety of grounds, including social justice and equity, greater political stability, improved agricultural productivity, economic growth, and preservation of the environment. An examination of each of these arguments reveals the complexity of the debate.

Social Justice   Because of the concentration of agricultural holdings in Latin America and parts of Africa and Asia, a *prima facie* case can be made for some type of land redistribution based on social justice and human rights.[30] As noted, the millions of rural families with little or no land are generally among the poorest of the Third World's poor. They are frequently trapped in a web of poverty, malnutrition, and illiteracy from which there is rarely escape. Usually they are politically powerless as well, controlled by landlords, local political bosses, the police, or the military. For them, agrarian reform is a fundamental step toward achieving greater political and socioeconomic justice.[31]

Political Stability   From the perspective of government policy makers, perhaps a more compelling potential benefit of agrarian reform has been curtailing peasant unrest. Samuel Huntington has most starkly linked reform to political stability:

> Where the conditions of land tenure are equitable and provide a viable living for the peasant, revolution is unlikely. Where they are inequitable and where the peasant lives in poverty and suffering, revolution is likely, if not inevitable, unless the government takes prompt measures to remedy those conditions.[32]

Indeed, statistical analyses indicate that the likelihood of revolutionary activity in developing countries increases where there is high inequality of land ownership and where there is a significant proportion of landless peasants.[33]

Without the threat of peasant unrest, however, policy makers have tended to be relatively indifferent to the injustices of land tenure patterns. Throughout the Cold War, for example, the United States tended to press its allies in Asia and Latin America for agrarian reform only when it was apprehensive about political instability and the prospect of communist revolution. Following World War II, the U.S. occupation command oversaw a major land reform in Japan designed to help establish stable democracy. Shortly thereafter, American support contributed to Taiwan's and South Korea's highly successful agrarian reforms. During the 1960s, in the wake of the Cuban revolution, the Kennedy administration formulated the Alliance for Progress for Latin America, which strongly articulated the desirability of land reform in the region, though it achieved only limited success in that regard. During the 1980s, the United States encouraged agrarian reform in El Salvador, again with mixed results. Almost all of these cases had one thing in common: the United States' desire to forestall peasant insurrection and communist insurgency. However, whenever the peasantry was not mobilized or where pro-U.S. dictators dominated the political system (such as Paraguay's Alfredo Stroessner and the Philippines' Ferdinand Marcos), the United States was rather indifferent to rural inequality.

Productivity   One of the most hotly debated results of land reform is its effect on agricultural productivity. Opponents of reform maintain that land redistribution lowers agricultural output, thereby diminishing food supplies for the cities and curtailing export earnings. Citing "economies of scale," they argue that large agricultural units are generally more productive because they can be more easily mechanized and can use rural infrastructures (such as irrigation or roads) more effectively. Second, they insist that peasant cultivators have less education and know-how than large land owners and are, consequently, less productive farmers. Thus, one of Ecuador's most powerful and most progressive land owners (and a former national president) told me that he had voluntarily given some of his land to the peasants on his estate but, unfortunately, had found them incapable of using it properly. Finally, some critics contend that if large agro-export estates were divided into small plots, peasants would switch to cultivation of subsistence food crops (i.e., they would grow more food for their family's consumption and less for the domestic or export markets), thereby denying the country much-needed food and foreign exchange.

Advocates of agrarian reform counter that smallholders are actually the more efficient producers. Although a growing number of land owners currently study agricultural sciences and employ modern productive techniques, many of the landed elite still farm their land ineffectively. For example, in Latin America, where land is an important source of prestige and political power, many landlords own more than they can efficiently cultivate. Peasant cultivators, on the other hand, tend to farm their plots very intensively because their families' living standards depend on raising productivity. This does not mean that small, peasant-run units are *always* more efficient. The comparative productivity of large and small farms varies according to their owner's farming skills and training. Land reform in Taiwan, South Korea, and Japan did not reduce production because the tenant farmers on the estates being divided already had substantial decision-making responsibility over agricultural production prior to the reforms. Consequently, they were well qualified to use the land efficiently as soon as it was distributed to them. Conversely, Latin American peasants farming on large units as tenants or wage laborers had been more tightly controlled and permitted less managerial authority. Consequently, land transfers there sometimes caused short-term declines in efficiency.[34] The beneficiaries of land reform may require supplemental government assistance as they are transformed into land owners.

The comparative efficiency of landlords and smallholders also varies according to which crop or animal is being raised. For example, production of meat, wheat, or sugar is more likely to benefit from economies of scale (that

is, output per acre will usually rise significantly as the result of capital investment). On the other hand, most of the grains, tubers, fruits, and vegetables
that constitute the core of Third World food consumption, along with some
exports such as coffee, do best with labor-intensive cultivation on small farm
units. These variations notwithstanding, data collected in Asia and Latin
America fairly consistently reveal that labor-intensive smallholders typically
have higher yields per acre than do large-scale, capital-intensive (mechanized) producers.[35] For example, a study of Brazilian agriculture found that
the larger the farm, the lower its output per hectare of land and per input of
capital investment such as machinery.[36] Similar relationships have been discovered in countries as diverse as Colombia, Malaysia, the Philippines,
Pakistan, and India.[37]

The economic efficiency of small farms may surprise many Americans
accustomed to believing that larger units are inherently more productive. But
in underdeveloped rural societies with a surplus of labor (i.e., many people
who are underemployed and who will work for low wages), it is cost effective
to use family or hired labor intensively. Out of economic necessity, peasant cultivators work hard, exploiting their own family labor. On the other hand, most
large estates are farmed by tenants or hired laborers, neither of whom gain
from raising productivity. That difference in motivation helps explain why the
agricultural yields of peasant land owners in Japan, South Korea, and Taiwan
and of near-owners in China are generally over twice as high as those of
Filipino tenant farmers with comparable plots of land but less motivation to
raise productivity.[38]

In recent decades, the disparity between large and small units in agricultural productivity has diminished somewhat. By using more advanced technology such as high-yield seeds and complementary irrigation, some large
farmers have narrowed the efficiency gap.[39] But even were the disparity eliminated entirely, smallholding operations would still be more productive to society in another way. Owners of larger farms generally need to import a portion
of their machinery, fuel, and chemicals, thereby expending some of the country's valuable foreign exchange. On the other hand, peasant farms draw upon
family labor, a cheap input found in abundance. It is for this reason that the former president of the Overseas Development Council argued that "a land and
capital scarce (but population plentiful) country should favor 40 two-and-a-
half acre farms over a single-owner 100-acre farm in order to make optimum
use of available land, labor and capital."[40]

Economic Growth In addition to its positive effect on agricultural productivity, land redistribution often brings broader benefits to the economies of
developing areas. Several countries that have implemented extensive agrarian
reforms, such as Bolivia and Cuba, have slowed the tide of peasant migration
to the cities. Giving peasants an economic stake in the countryside has reduced
rural-to-urban migration, thereby alleviating the tremendous strain on
resources in many Third World cities (see Chapter 7).

When successfully implemented, land reform improves the living standards of the rural poor. As their purchasing power increases, they consume more of their country's manufactured goods, thereby stimulating industrial growth.[41] It is no coincidence that Japan's, Taiwan's, and South Korea's postwar economic booms followed closely on the heels of agrarian reform.[42] In South Korea, for example, the expansion of rural purchasing power helped stimulate the nation's electronics industry, setting the stage for subsequent export. Today, more than 90 percent of South Korea's rural families (almost all of them peasant smallholders) own television sets, and many of them have now switched to color sets. That affluence contrasts starkly with the poverty that pervades Third World rural areas outside of East Asia.

Agrarian reform has also contributed to relatively high income equality in Japan, Taiwan, and South Korea (though other factors contributed as well). That equality and pervasive purchasing power, in turn, have been a significant ingredient in the region's dramatic economic development. In contrast, Latin America's concentrated pattern of farm land ownership is partly responsible for its highly inequitable distribution of income, extensive rural poverty, reduced consumer market, and lower economic growth.

Environmental Preservation   Another, relatively new argument for agrarian reform in some regions relates to environmental preservation. Each year in Brazil, an area of the Amazonian tropical forest approximating the size of New York State is destroyed as trees are deliberately burned to clear land for ranching or farming. The fires are so vast that they are believed to contribute to the *greenhouse effect* on world climate (see Chapter 10). The enormous loss of trees also diminishes the Amazonian jungle's contribution to the world's oxygen supply. Although a substantial portion of this burn-off is caused by large-scale farmers and ranchers, peasant settlers also contribute. Driven out of the nation's poorest regions by desperation, land-hungry peasants colonize the jungle in search of a better life. Once there, they discover that cleared jungle soil quickly loses its nutrients. Consequently, they must soon move on, clearing yet more forest land. Agrarian reform in Brazil's unforested regions would reduce landlessness and give tenant farmers a greater stake in the land they farm, thus reducing migration to the Amazonian basin.

Similar arguments have been advanced for land reform in other parts of the world. Although Bangladeshi farmers benefit from the country's very fertile soil, the nation's intense population pressure and its concentrated land ownership have forced many poor farmers to push the frontiers of farming beyond their ecologically desirable limits. In their search for farm land, landless peasants often move to unsafe coastal regions not suitable for habitation. There they fall victim to the typhoons that periodically sweep across the region, killing thousands of people. Only recently have government policy makers in countries such as this and international aid agencies begun to relate agrarian reform to ecological issues. In time, that linkage may become more apparent.

TYPES OF AGRARIAN REFORM

A variety of forces have brought about agrarian reform. At times agrarian reform has followed foreign occupation or pressure; sometimes it has resulted from peasant-based revolutions; and some reform programs have been introduced by moderate governments anxious to garner peasant support and maintain political tranquility. In each case, the underlying forces that stimulated reform have influenced the type of program that emerges.

Externally Imposed Reform

The most successful externally imposed agrarian reforms occurred in East Asia after World War II. In Japan, the U.S. occupation command limited land ownership to 10 acres, transferred 41 percent of the country's farm land from landlords to tenants, and controlled rents for the remaining tenants. The number of landless was reduced from 28 percent to 10 percent of the rural population, making the countryside a bastion of stability.[43] In Taiwan and South Korea, U.S. pressure encouraged similar reforms designed to avert rural unrest. Ownership was limited to small parcels, and about one-third of each country's farm land was transferred to tenants, some 60 percent of whom became land owners.[44] In all three nations, the transformation of rural society was tremendously successful, raising agricultural productivity, improving rural living standards, and strengthening political stability. Consequently, East Asia's agrarian reforms are widely used as benchmarks to evaluate programs elsewhere in the world.

In view of these impressive early achievements, it is striking how ineffective later U.S. pressures have been in stimulating Third World agrarian reform. In retrospect, it appears that there were three unique conditions in postwar East Asia that have not been replicated subsequently. First was the depth of American commitment to reform. Fearing that agrarian revolutions would spread from China to other Far Eastern nations, U.S. policy makers at the start of the Cold War pushed hard for land reform as the best way to contain communism. A second unique condition was the enormous leverage that the United States could exert on those East Asian governments at the time. The Japanese were under U.S. military occupation, while the South Korean and Taiwanese governments were deeply beholden to the United States for shielding them militarily. In subsequent years, the United States lacked comparable influence. Although it later favored land reform in South Vietnam and Central America, it was unwilling or unable to exert sufficient pressure on their conservative governments to achieve effective programs.

This situation leads us to East Asia's last unique characteristic: its landowning elites were so weakened at the end of World War II that they were ill equipped to defend their own interests. The situation was most stark in Japan following its surrender to U.S. forces at the close of the war. As the occupying power, the United States could impose its will on the country's previously powerful rural landlords. Moreover, key Japanese political leaders working with the U.S. high command concurred that agrarian reform was necessary.[45] In South Korea, the landlord class had collaborated with Japan during its years of occupation. Hence, when Japanese colonial rule ended at the close of World War II, the Korean landed elite had little legitimacy or political influence. And in Taiwan, the Nationalist Party government recognized that its earlier failure to implement agrarian reform on the Chinese mainland had contributed to the communist victory there. Now, driven from the mainland to Taiwan and prodded by the United States, the government was ready to modernize the countryside.

In the decades that followed, U.S. efforts on behalf of land reform were far less effective. In Southeast Asia and Central America, big landlords were important figures in their nations' power structures capable of obstructing rural reform. At the same time, when peasant unrest developed in countries such as South Vietnam and El Salvador, the United States lacked the leverage or the will to promote real reform in the face of determined opposition by conservative elites.

Revolutionary Transformation

From the Mexican and Chinese revolutions through more recent insurgencies in the Philippines and El Salvador, most twentieth-century insurrections were peasant based. Consequently, a fundamental rallying cry in both Marxist revolutions (China, Vietnam, Cuba, and Nicaragua) and non-Marxist upheavals (Mexico, Bolivia, and Algeria) was agrarian reform. In the 1930s and 1940s, for example, the Chinese communists gained considerable peasant support by transferring land to the rural poor. Following their victories in Nicaragua, Vietnam, and Cuba, revolutionary parties in those countries also implemented radical agrarian reforms.

After coming to power in 1949, the Chinese communists distributed almost half of the country's arable land to about 60 million peasant households, comprising over half the nation's population. Like the U.S.-sponsored reforms in East Asia (Japan, South Korea, and Taiwan), China's agrarian reform initially disbursed the land to peasant smallholders. But soon convinced that privately owned peasant plots would reintroduce rural inequalities and class divisions, the government pressured the peasantry to join state-sponsored cooperatives. As a consequence, by 1956 almost 90 percent of all farm families had relinquished their property rights and joined Agricultural Producer Cooperatives (APCs).[46]

Because they have fully vanquished the rural upper class, revolutionary governments are more free to redistribute large quantities of land. In countries such as Cuba, Nicaragua, and Vietnam, property belonging to the defeated rural aristocracy was either converted to state farms or distributed to peasant smallholders. Similarly, following their anticolonial revolutions, Algeria and Kenya redistributed farm land belonging to ousted European settlers. In Mexico, some 40 percent of peasant families benefited from agrarian reform, receiving more than 40 percent of the country's agricultural and forest areas. Eighty percent of Bolivia's farm land was transferred to three-fourths of its rural families.[47]

Revolutionary agrarian reform programs are more likely to introduce collective or cooperative farms than the peasant smallholdings promoted in the East Asian model, though many have sponsored a mixture of both. While even some non-Marxist revolutions have distributed land through cooperatives (Mexico, for example), communist regimes have been most committed to collective farming. Some revolutionary governments, such as Cuba's, have kept private farming alongside the larger collectivized sector but have continued encouraging or pressuring (but not forcing) peasant owners to sell their property to the state. Others, however, harshly repressed peasants resisting forced collectivization, often with tremendous loss of life. Eric Wolf points out the irony of forced collectivization in countries such as the Soviet Union (where, under Joseph Stalin, millions died of state-enforced famine), China, Vietnam, and Ethiopia. Peasants, he notes, supported and fought for radical revolutions in hopes of getting plots of land for their families. Yet after risking their lives to bring the revolution to power, they were often coerced into collectivizing their farms.[48]

China illustrates the dangers of forced collectivization, not only when the peasants are coerced into joining collective farms but years after. As we have noted, a brief period of family farming soon gave way to collectivized farming. The process reached its apex during the Great Leap Forward (1958 to 1961), when huge agricultural communes were created. Overcentralization of decision making and poorly informed government policies caused huge declines in the availability of food. In the massive famine that resulted, some 20 to 25 million people died of starvation or disease.[49] Though the government then backed away from the commune experiment, collective farming was emphasized again during the Cultural Revolution (1966 to 1976).

Several factors underlie the communists' preference for collective farming, whether on state farms or on cooperatives under state direction. Fundamentally, it is because farming decisions are more easily controlled by the state. Government administrators can determine which crops are grown and what price they are sold for. Collectivization has also been seen as a tool for eradicating the peasantry's individualistic tendencies. Arguing that private farming inevitably leads to inequalities between villagers and gives peasants a bourgeois mentality, communist governments have generally dismissed family farms as capitalistic, at least until recently.[50] Finally, supporters of collectivized agriculture maintain that large, centrally controlled farms are more efficient than smallholdings. In fact, large state farms *are* often more efficient in one area—government delivery of social services and some agricultural inputs. In other words, it is generally somewhat easier to deliver clean water, medical care, education, and tractors to large collective farms than it is to provide these items to widely scattered private farms. But when it comes to the critical issue of agricultural production, there is no basis to the claim that large state farms are more efficient. Quite the opposite. For example, official production data from Cuba, Ethiopia, Nicaragua, and China demonstrate that, for most crops, private peasant plots have *higher* yields per acre than collective farms do.[51]

In fact, peasant plots are generally more productive than collective farms for the same reason that they tend to outperform large private farms in capitalist LDCs. Because their family income is so closely tied to greater productivity (that is, their standard of living is tied directly to how much they produce per acre), peasant smallholders are more motivated to work intensively. On the other hand, employees on state farms receive essentially the same wage no matter how hard they work. Small wonder that the Cuban government has admitted that the average state farm worker actually works on the job about half of his or her eight-hour day and spends the remaining time taking breaks or, in some cases, illegally working for nearby private farmers.

Faced with growing evidence that peasant smallholdings are more productive than collective farms, several communist governments have set aside their ideological preferences and accepted more pragmatic solutions. When Deng Xiaoping succeeded Mao Zedong as China's political leader, he introduced the "Responsibility System," which essentially transferred China's communes back to peasant-controlled, effectively private farms.[52] In what amounted to a second agrarian reform (or as one expert called it, "a second revolution"), large communal farms were broken up and distributed to the peasants living on them. The ensuing "unleashing [of] the entrepreneurial talents of China's peasants" led to striking gains in farm productivity. From 1980 to 1984 alone, the value of agricultural output rose an astonishing 40 percent.[53] That surge was a major factor contributing to a spectacular improvement in rural living standards during the past two decades. More recently, other Marxist or reformed Marxist regimes in Asia, including Vietnam and Mongolia, have also decollectivized agriculture.

In Nicaragua, Sandinista agrarian reform officials initially considered state farms to be the best production units. They saw peasant-run cooperatives as next best and ranked private smallholdings last. Not surprisingly, surveys showed that the peasants' preferences were exactly the opposite. During the economic crisis of the 1980s, the government, which was generally more pragmatic and less ideologically rigid than most Marxist regimes, began to admit that peasant farms were more efficient. Moreover, as it fought a bitter civil war with the Contras (U.S.-backed anti-revolutionary guerrillas), the government realized that giving land to family farms would give peasant recipients incentive to support the Sandinista army. Consequently, the regime altered its priorities to accommodate peasant preferences.[54] Cuba never eliminated private farming but used various incentives and pressures to convince growing numbers of peasants to sell their farms to the state. During the country's severe economic crisis in the 1990s, however, Castro's government converted many of Cuba's centrally run agricultural cooperatives into units based on family-run farms.

Moderate Reformism

Most agrarian reform programs are not caused directly either by foreign intervention or by revolution. Egypt, Iran, India, Bangladesh, Zimbabwe, Chile, Venezuela, and Peru have redistributed agricultural land in a variety of ways. In each case, however, the government introduced reform as a means of soliciting peasant support. Following the Cuban revolution, the United States and various Latin American governments concluded that rural reform was needed in the region in order to contain the spread of peasant unrest. Colombia, Chile, Venezuela, and Peru all enacted moderate land reform programs in the 1960s. Twenty years later, the challenge of guerrilla insurgency prompted limited agrarian reform in El Salvador.

Elsewhere, the driving force for change has been the enfranchisement of growing numbers of peasants, due either to the abolition of literacy requirements for voting or rising rural literacy rates. Once minor players in the electoral process, peasants have often been transformed into an important voting constituency wooed by competing political parties. Running on platforms calling for agrarian reform, Chile's Christian Democratic Party, Peru's *Acción Popular*, and Venezuela's *Acción Democrática* all won national elections with the help of broad peasant support. Once in office, all these governments introduced land reforms of varying size.[55] Similarly, in Asia, some mix of incipient rural unrest and electoral politics contributed to agrarian reforms in the Philippines and parts of India, including the states of Kerala and West Bengal.[56]

Moderate reformism has one obvious advantage. It is relatively free of the violence and excesses often associated with revolutionary programs. But with rare exceptions, its scope is far more limited than either externally induced redistribution or revolutionary change. In Latin America, for example, the most extensive land redistribution followed revolutions in Cuba, Bolivia, Nicaragua, and Mexico.[57] By comparison, most moderate reform in the region has been more modest. Similarly, reformism in Asia (Bangladesh, Thailand, the Philippines, and India) has also produced meager results when compared to revolutionary land redistributions in China and Vietnam.

Reformism generally produces a less sweeping agrarian transformation because, unlike revolutionary change or the postwar situation in East Asia, it must deal with landed elites who are still strong enough to limit the scope of change.[58] For example, reformist programs generally grant monetary compensation to landlords who have lost property. This means that the scope of land redistribution is limited by the scarcity of government funds. In addition, bureaucratic hangups and court challenges frequently slow the pace of agrarian reform to a crawl.

One notable exception to this pattern took place in Peru from 1968 to 1979. There, a sweeping reform was implemented in the absence of either external pressure or internal revolution. A left-of-center, nationalist military government led by General Juan Velasco expropriated most of the country's large agricultural and ranching estates, turning them over to the peasants and farm laborers who had been working there. Because of its unique powers, the military regime was able to sweep aside objections from the nation's rural oligarchy, a group despised by Velasco and his team. In all, approximately 40 percent of the country's farmland was transferred to 30 percent of all peasant families.[59] Initially, most of the land was organized as cooperatives, but subsequently, as administration and labor problems arose, most of the co-ops were subdivided and converted to peasant family smallholdings.[60] Ultimately, however, the military's agrarian reform failed to reduce Peru's pervasive rural poverty. What it did accomplish, however, was to destroy the once-considerable power of the land-owning class and thereby radically transform the country's political and economic structure. The virtually unchallenged power of a military dictatorship (however benign), like the might of a revolutionary regime, allowed the government to ignore the demands of the rural aristocracy in a way which a democratic government could never get away with. No other military government in Latin America, however, has been equally dedicated to comprehensive rural change.[61]

In contrast, democratic governments, no matter how committed to helping the peasantry, can't launch that type of frontal assault on the landed elite. For example, Venezuela's democratically elected *Acción Democrática* government, elected with strong backing from peasant voters, introduced a relatively ambitious agrarian reform. But because of political and financial restraints (the landlords' political power, the limited resources to pay landlords for their property), much of the land transferred was previously uncultivated public property in the nation's jungle regions. Although this transfer permitted the government to sidestep landlord objections, it meant that much of the land turned over was of marginal quality and not easily accessible. Moreover, since this colonization of new land often involved clearing tropical forest, it posed serious environmental dangers.

THE LIMITS OF AGRARIAN REFORM

While the experiences of Taiwan, South Korea, Cuba, and China demonstrate how agrarian reform can improve peasant living standards substantially, few programs elsewhere have matched their success. Peru illustrates how even sweeping change initiated by a well-intentioned government may not achieve its objectives. The proportion of national farm land turned over to the peasantry was quite high compared to other agrarian reforms in Latin America; it even compared well with revolutionary transformations such as Cuba's, Mexico's, and Nicaragua's. Powerful Andean and coastal landlords who had once dominated the countryside were stripped of their land and the accompanying power. Yet these radical changes failed to improve peasant living standards as had been expected.

To be sure, there was progress in Peru in some respects. Previously isolated peasants entered the mainstream of economic life, villagers were absorbed into the national culture, and literacy rates improved. Yet now, three decades after the reform began, there still has not been an improvement in agricultural production or rural living standards. Indeed, in many regions those have declined. Moreover, ironically, the reform beneficiaries who gained the most—coastal sugar workers—already lived better than most of the rural poor had prior to the reform. On the other hand, the country's poorest peasants gained little. Peasant disillusionment and dashed hopes contributed to the rise of the Maoist Shining Path guerrillas in the 1970s. By the mid-1980s, much of the countryside was being brutalized by the Shining Path and the Peruvian armed forces. Thus, this highly ambitious agrarian reform, once viewed as Peru's salvation, failed to achieve the social justice or the peace it was designed to create. There were multiple reasons for these failures. Because of its inept administrative and political style, the government often alienated the very peasants it wished to help. For example, the military organized peasant federations to mobilize rural support for the agrarian reform and to open channels of communication between the government and the rural poor. However, military officers are more prone to give orders than to consult with peasants. Increasingly, peasants voiced the opinion that their old masters (the neofeudal hacienda owners) had been removed only to be replaced by new masters (military-government bureaucrats).

But even if the program had been better executed, expropriating the nation's largest haciendas and plantations wouldn't have provided enough land to satisfy the peasants' needs. The ratio of rural families to arable land in Peru is not as favorable as in many other Latin American countries. Ultimately, less than one-third of the rural families in need received any land, and the poorest of the poor were frequently overlooked.[62] Even the program's beneficiaries generally discovered that their added land was insufficient to alleviate their deep poverty. While the government had narrowed appreciably the gap between rich and poor in the countryside, it had done nothing to bridge the more important gulf between rural and urban living standards. As in most LDCs, Peru's economic structure had long favored the urban population over the rural. Third World governments typically spend far more on education, health care, and other services in the cities than in rural areas. As we'll discuss later in this chapter, they often impose price controls on food that keep costs down for urban consumers but reduce rural incomes. The average income of Peru's city dwellers is several times that of the rural population (even considering the huge number of urban poor). Consequently, a substantial improvement in peasant living standards is impossible without a shift of wealth and government resources from urban areas to the countryside. Given the tremendous political clout of the urban upper class, middle class, and organized working class, this shift was something not even the Peruvian armed forces were prepared to make. Absent such a transfer, one World Bank economist noted, agrarian reform merely redistributed poverty. Finally, whatever modest gains had been achieved were wiped out with Peru's economic collapse in the 1980s and continuing problems since.

Revolutionary agrarian reforms have limitations as well. Mexico still suffers from substantial rural poverty and landlessness, despite an agrarian reform that affected half the nation's peasants and a similar proportion of agricultural land. Beginning in the 1930s, reform beneficiaries were organized into *ejidos*, cooperative units designed to channel state aid to the peasantry and increase their productivity. Following World War II, however, government agricultural policy changed in favor of larger commercial farms, while failing to channel adequate credits, infrastructure, or technology to the *ejidos*. Since much of the Mexican countryside is arid, the absence of government irrigation projects was particularly devastating for poor farmers. As a consequence, poor farmers were even less able to compete in the marketplace. Many lost their farms and poured into the nation's cities or across the border to the United States. Since 1970, the government has developed several programs designed to bolster peasant agriculture. While these programs have had some positive impact, they were cut short after 1982 by the country's debt crisis and severe economic recession.[63] Current government policy encourages the privatization of the *ejidos'* communal property. Ultimately, this may benefit the most productive peasants, who will be able to buy and sell land more readily, but it may also force less competitive peasants off their farms into Mexico's already overcrowded cities.

The shortcomings of Peru's and Mexico's efforts do not mean that agrarian reform is valueless. Rather, they indicate that redistribution of land must take place in a proper political setting and must be supported by additional government measures if it is to be effective. Evidence from South Asia and Latin America indicates that successful reform programs usually require some degree of peasant organization and mobilization.[64] If pressured by peasant organizations, the state is more likely to provide land recipients with needed technical assistance, infrastructure, education, and financial credit. Government also needs to allow peasants a fair price for their crops.[65] The administrative apparatus governing reform must be simple, and peasant beneficiaries must be given a strong role in the decision-making process. In countries where the landed elite maintain substantial political power, landlords losing property must receive reasonable payments if the program is to be politically viable. At the same time, peasant beneficiaries must be asked only to pay an amount they can sustain if the program is to be economically feasible for them.[66] Where possible, Third World governments must reduce the tremendous gap that typically separates urban and rural living standards.

Even the most intelligently executed reform programs, however, will not be equally successful in each country. As we saw, in nations such as Peru, El Salvador, and Bangladesh, there simply isn't enough quality land to fully satisfy peasant needs. In such cases, alternative employment needs to be created for the rural poor in other sectors of the economy. Ultimately, each nation's agrarian reform package must be carefully designed to meet its own specific needs.

OTHER APPROACHES AND ISSUES

Since the 1970s, agrarian reform has lost much of its allure, with a few notable exceptions, such as Nicaragua and, to a more limited extent, El Salvador. Critics on the Right have long believed it undermines allegedly more efficient, large-scale agribusiness. Critics on the Left have found the fruits of moderate reformism disappointing, claiming that it has benefited capitalists and state bureaucracies more than it has the peasantry.[67] And powerful urban interests fear agrarian reform will curtail agricultural production. In many ways, rural pressure for reform has diminished. Increasing numbers of peasants have migrated to the cities, no longer demanding change in the countryside (see Chapter 7). Most governments now attach less importance to peasant agriculture than to large, export-oriented commercial farming, which earns the nation foreign exchange. While modest land redistribution programs continue in some LDCs, for now at least, efforts at rural reform have shifted to other issues and other types of programs.

Integrated Rural Development

As interest in agrarian reform has diminished, a number of Third World governments have turned to Integrated Rural Development (IRD), a potentially less conflictual means of raising agricultural productivity and improving rural living standards. The underlying purpose of IRD is to channel a consolidated package of government assistance programs to selected peasant communities. That package may include agricultural inputs (e.g., seeds, fertilizers), technical assistance, credit, public health services, education, irrigation, and other infrastructure. The objective is to transform traditional peasants and the rural unemployed into efficient producers. During the 1970s and 1980s, the World Bank, the U.S. Agency for International Development (AID), and other international donors enthusiastically supported IRD programs in countries such as India, Colombia, and Mexico. In some cases, including South Korea and Nicaragua, IRD supplemented land reform. More frequently, however, it served as a substitute, enabling centrist governments to assist a portion of the peasantry without alienating powerful landed interests.

Critics of IRD have charged that its primary objective is not to help the rural poor but rather to establish strong state control over the peasantry.[68] Whatever its impetus, Integrated Rural Development has had a mixed record of success. In India, for example, a large program was established aimed at giving poor peasants subsidized credits to buy dairy cows. Unfortunately, the program was undermined by corruption and poor distribution of aid.[69] Even critics of Mexico's SAM program (Mexican Food System) concede that it helped many peasants. However, much of its funds earmarked for the rural poor ended up in the hands of large producers, ultimately creating more competition for small farmers. Similar criticisms were leveled against Brazil's Integrated Rural Development program, *Polonordeste*.[70]

Colombia undertook one of Latin America's most ambitious IRD programs. Like many others, it was designed to raise food production by providing infrastructure, credit, and agricultural inputs to small farms. Peasant producers were encouraged to join marketing cooperatives. While the program seemed to increase food supplies for Colombia's cities, its benefits for the rural poor were small. Indeed, in its second phase it concentrated on peasants with larger plots, dropping those with the smallest holdings. In her analysis of the Colombian program, Nola Reinhardt found it to be of some benefit to the peasants it served. But, she argued, Integrated Rural Development alone cannot raise rural living standards substantially, particularly those of the very poor. To achieve that, needy peasants must be given access to more land through some type of agrarian reform.[71]

In recent years, some governments and nongovernmental organizations (NGOs) have pursued a variant of IRD known as Micro-Enterprise Development. The goal of these projects is to help peasants develop self-sustaining systems of farming that draw upon, but preserve, the area's natural resources. Poor farmers living in or near ecologically fragile zones are particularly targeted. In one of the more well-known enterprises, the World Wildlife Federation has helped peasants in Brazil's Amazonian jungle to sell the nuts they harvest to American candy and ice cream manufacturers such as Ben and Jerry's. It is hoped that the profits yielded by the nuts will convince the peasants to preserve the local forest rather than clear it for cultivation.

Crop Pricing

In addition to the problem of access to land, peasants often suffer from unfavorable government price policies. Anxious to assure a supply of cheap food for their urban populations, many governments, particularly in Africa and the Middle East, have imposed price controls on basic commodities such as rice, potatoes, sugar, and milk. Price controls are also meant to promote industrialization by providing workers with cheap food, thereby helping employers to keep wages down and permitting more capital investment.[72] But by holding crop prices below their free-market levels, these controls have further impoverished peasant producers.

In Africa, governments also commonly control the price of export crops, extracting the difference between what they pay farmers and the higher world-market price as a de facto tax. One early study found that African farmers often received less than two-thirds, and in some cases less than half, of the value of their export crops.[73] Although designed to provide the urban poor and the middle class with cheaper food and to generate government revenues from exports, price controls ultimately have perverse effects. They particularly damage poor farmers and reduce the supply of basic foods by creating disincentives to production. In Egypt, for example, when the government controlled the price of basic food grains, large landlords either evaded government controls or, more commonly, reduced the supply of badly needed grains by switching to other, uncontrolled crops. Peasants were less capable of switching crops and thus suffered declining incomes.[74] Throughout Africa, price controls have reduced food output by driving many farmers out of business and reducing production incentives for the rest. For more than two decades, per-capita food production has declined, and the continent has become increasingly dependent on food imports and foreign aid. While there is no single cause for that deterioration, one study of African famine argues that government price controls and inefficient government bureaucracies have aggravated the problem.[75] Other research indicates that agricultural production was stronger in Zimbabwe than in the neighboring countries of Mozambique, Tanzania, and Zambia because only in Zimbabwe were farmers paid the market price for their crops.[76]

Unfortunately, once governments embark on the path of commodity price regulation, they are soon caught in a conflict between short-term political pressures and long-term production needs. The immediate effect of price deregulation is a sharp increase in food prices. Governments that have tried this tactic (often in response to external pressures) frequently faced urban protests and riots by irate urban shoppers. Not surprisingly, until recently, few administrations have been willing to risk such unrest, particularly since the urban middle class, a group adversely affected by price hikes on food, is usually a vital pillar of government support. In the long run, however, better crop prices should stimulate greater food production, ultimately leading prices to decline again, though not necessarily to their prior low. Thus, as many developing nations are introducing neoliberal economic policies (eliminating government economic intervention), more and more are eliminating price controls (see Chapter 10).[77]

CONCLUSION: DEMOCRACY AND RURAL REFORM

For decades government development policies in most LDCs have emphasized industrial growth and urban modernization, often to the detriment of the rural sector. In many cases the consequences have been stagnant agricultural production, rising food imports, rural poverty, and heavy rural-to-urban migration. In some instances, rural poverty has led to peasant insurrection. Most notably in Latin America, pro-urban government biases, along with the forces of capitalist development, have driven many peasants into the rural or urban working class in a process known as *proletarianization*.[78] Pessimistic scholars have predicted the inevitable spread of large mechanized farms to the detriment of peasant family farming.

More recently, research in countries such as Bolivia, Ecuador, and Colombia has revealed that, in at least some regions, innovative peasants have adapted skillfully to the forces of rural capitalism and modernization. Many have taken advantage of new commercial opportunities to compete successfully in the marketplace.[79] In Africa and Asia, peasant smallholders remain an even greater component of rural society. Rather than abandoning the peasantry as a relic of history, Third World governments and international agencies should seek balanced economic and political development that gives proper weight to the rural sector and its peasant population.

The relationship between democracy and rural reform is somewhat paradoxical. On the one hand, democratic governments such as Venezuela, which carried out agrarian reform and other forms of assistance to the rural poor, broadened their base of political support. As we noted earlier, experts such as Samuel Huntington argued during the Cold War that agrarian reform was a Third World nation's best defense against revolution. However, the fact remains that most of the major land reforms in the past century were not carried out by democratic governments. Revolutionary regimes in China, Vietnam, Mexico, Bolivia, Cuba, and Nicaragua introduced some of the most far-reaching reforms. Other significant redistribution of land took place under military governments in Peru and Egypt. South Korea's and Taiwan's reforms were implemented by authoritarian governments under pressure from the United States. By contrast, in democratic countries such as Brazil, India, and, more recently, the Philippines, landlords are sufficiently powerful as a lobbying group and pillar of major political parties that they can block substantial reform laws from becoming law.

With the threat of communist revolution no longer facing most developing nations, the prospect of major land redistribution in the Third World currently seems remote. But if the LDCs are to prevent unmanageable rural-to-urban migration, rural violence, and related disruptive forces, their governments will have to find other ways to improve the lives of the rural poor.

DISCUSSION QUESTIONS

1. Third World peasants have frequently been described as conservative or apolitical, yet they have been major players in revolutionary movements. How can those two images be reconciled?
2. What are the major arguments that have been raised for and against agrarian reform programs in the developing world?
3. Describe the different types of agrarian reform programs that have been introduced. Briefly discuss some of the advantages and disadvantages of each type of reform.
4. How have government crop-pricing policies often disadvantaged the rural producer and inhibited production?

NOTES

1. This figure is extrapolated from Prosterman and Riedinger's estimate in the mid-1980s that 60 percent of the developing world's population was agricultural at that time. Roy L. Prosterman and Jeffrey M. Riedinger, *Land Reform and Democratic Development* (Baltimore, MD: Johns Hopkins University Press, 1987), p. 1.

2. Published statistics on the proportion of rural poverty in any country are usually imprecise. They often vary greatly from study to study and should be treated as edu-

cated estimates designed to serve as guideposts. Occasionally the data clash with the "common sense" observations of experts who have studied the region. In the decade since these U.N. data were collected, the populations of most of the countries studied have increased appreciably, the percentages of their populations living in the country-side have dropped sharply in some cases, and the actual number of persons living in rural poverty (as opposed to the percentage) has risen.

3. Figures are extrapolated from earlier data in M. Riad El-Ghonemy, *The Political Economy of Rural Poverty* (London: Routledge and Kegan Paul, 1990), pp. 302–303, 17–19. The data were adapted from the United Nations Food and Agricultural Organization, *The Dynamics of Rural Poverty* (Rome: 1986).

4. Merilee S. Grindle and John W. Thomas, *Public Choices and Policy Change: The Political Economy of Reform in Developing Countries* (Baltimore, MD: Johns Hopkins University Press, 1991), p. 46.

5. Alain de Janvry, *The Agrarian Question and Reformism in Latin America* (Baltimore, MD: Johns Hopkins University Press, 1981), pp. 7–60.

6. The terms *agrarian reform* and *land reform* are often used interchangeably. Technically, land reform refers only to the redistribution of land to needy peasants or laborers. Agrarian reform is a broader term that encompasses financial and technical aid, infrastructure, and the like that are normally needed to go with land redistribution if it is to be effective.

7. Marcus Franda, "An Indian Farm Lobby: The Kisan Sammelan," in *The Politics of Agrarian Change in Asia and Latin America*, ed. Howard Handelman (Bloomington: Indiana University Press, 1981), pp. 17–34.

8. George Foster, "Introduction: What Is a Peasant?" in *Peasant Society*, ed. Jack Potter, George Foster, and May Diaz (Boston: Little, Brown, 1967); Teodor Shanin, "The Nature and Logic of the Peasant Economy," *Journal of Peasant Studies* 1, nos. 1–2 (1974).

9. Eric R. Wolf, *Peasants* (Upper Saddle River, NJ: Prentice Hall, 1966), p. 10.

10. Prosterman and Riedinger, *Land Reform and Democratic Development*, p. 41.

11. Karl Marx, *Capital*. Quoted in Teodor Shanin, "Peasantry as a Political Factor," *Sociological Review* 14 (March 1966): 6.

12. Robert Redfield, *Peasant Society and Culture: An Anthropological Approach* (Chicago: University of Chicago Press, 1965), p. 77.

13. See, for example, Oscar Lewis, *La Vida* (New York: Random House, 1966); George M. Foster, "Peasant Society and the Image of the Limited Good," *American Anthropologist* 67 (April 1965): 293–315.

14. Phyllis Arora, "Patterns of Political Response in Indian Peasant Society," *Western Political Quarterly* 20 (September 1967): 654.

15. See, for example, *New York Times*, July 4, 1993.

16. Ronald J. Herring and Charles R. Kennedy, Jr., "The Political Economy of Farm Mechanization Policy: Tractors in Pakistan," in *Food, Politics and Agricultural Development: Case Studies in the Public Policy of Rural Modernization*, ed. Raymond F. Hopkins, Donald J. Pachula, and Ross B. Talbot (Boulder, CO: Westview Press, 1979), pp. 193–226.

17. James C. Scott, *Weapons of the Week: Everyday Forms of Peasant Resistance* (New Haven, CT: Yale University Press, 1986).

18. One of the most insightful books on the role of the peasantry in twentieth-century revolutions is Eric R. Wolf, *Peasant Wars of the Twentieth Century* (New York: Harper & Row, 1969).

19. James C. Scott, *The Moral Economy of the Peasant: Rebellion and Subsistence in Southeast Asia* (New Haven, CT: Yale University Press, 1976); James C. Scott and Benedict J. Kirkvliet, *How Traditional Rural Patrons Loose Their Legitimacy* (Madison: University of Wisconsin, Land Tenure Center, 1975).

20. Wolf, *Peasant Wars*.

21. Samuel P. Huntington, *Political Order in Changing Societies* (New Haven, CT: Yale University Press, 1968), p. 375.

22. Ibid.

23. That is probably a conservative estimate based on figures presented a decade ago in Roy L. Prosterman, Mary N. Temple, and Timothy M. Hanstad, "Introduction," *Agrarian Reform and Grassroots Development: Ten Case Studies,* ed. Prosterman, Temple, and Hanstad (Boulder, CO: Lynne Rienner Publishers, 1990), p. 1.

24. Hectares, rather than acres, are the standard measurement of farm land area in most of the world. One hectare is equivalent to 2.47 acres.

25. Anthony L. Hall, "Land Tenure and Land Reform in Brazil," in *Agrarian Reform and Grassroots Development*, p. 206.

26. Carrie A. Meyer, *Land Reform in Latin America: The Dominican Case* (New York: Praeger, 1989), p. 38.

27. Rupert W. Scofield, "Land Reform in Central America," in *Agrarian Reform and Grassroots Development*, pp. 154–155.

28. D. P. Chaudhri, "New Technologies and Income Distribution in Agriculture," in *Peasants, Landlords and Governments: Agrarian Reform in the Third World*, ed. David Lehmann (New York: Holmes and Meier, 1974), p. 173; Howard Handelman, "Introduction," *The Politics of Agrarian Change*, p. 4.

29. F. Tomasson Jannuzi and James T. Peach, "Bangladesh: A Strategy for Agrarian Reform," and Jeffrey Riedinger, "Philippine Land Reform in the 1980s," in *Agrarian Reform and Grassroots Development*, pp. 84, 91.

30. Henry Shue, *Basic Human Rights: Subsistence, Affluence and U.S. Foreign Policy* (Princeton, NJ: Princeton University Press, 1980). For a discussion of the moral issues, see Joseph S. Nye, Jr., "Ethical Dimensions of International Involvement in Land Reform," in *International Dimensions of Land Reform*, ed. John D. Montgomery (Boulder, CO: Westview Press, 1984), pp. 7–29.

31. Keith Griffin, *Land Concentration and Rural Poverty*, 2d ed. (London: Macmillan, 1981), p. 10.

32. Huntington, *Political Order*, p. 375.

33. Bruce M. Russet, "Inequality and Instability: The Relation of Land Tenure to Politics," *World Politics* 16 (April 1964): 442–454; Prosterman and Riedinger, *Land Reform*, p. 24.

34. William Thiesenhusen, "Introduction," *Searching for Agrarian Reform in Latin America*, ed. William Thiesenhusen (Boston: Unwin Hyman, 1989), p. 18. An advocate of agrarian reform in Latin America, Thiesenhusen does not imply that peasants in that region are ill-equipped to receive land.

35. Ibid., pp. 16–20; Peter Dorner, *Latin American Land Reforms in Theory and Practice* (Madison: University of Wisconsin Press, 1992), pp. 21–29; R. Albert Berry, "Land Reform and the Adequacy of World Food Production," in *International Dimensions*, pp. 63–87.

36. William C. Thiesenhusen and Jolyne Melmed-Sanjak, "Brazil's Agrarian Structure: Changes from 1970 through 1980," *World Development* 18 (1990): 393–415.

37. Albert R. Berry and William R. Cline, eds., *Agrarian Structure and Productivity in Developing Countries* (Baltimore, MD: Johns Hopkins University Press, 1979).

38. Riedinger, "Philippine Land Reform," p. 19.

39. Dorner, *Latin American Land Reforms*, pp. 23–25; Berry, "Land Reform," p. 72; Michael R. Carter and Jon Jonakin, *The Economic Case for Land Reform: An Assessment of 'Farm Size/Productivity' Relations and Its Impact on Policy* (Madison: University of Wisconsin, Department of Agricultural Economics, 1989), quoted in Dorner, *Latin American Land Reform*.

40. James Grant, "Development: The End of Trickle Down," *Foreign Policy* 12 (Fall 1973): 43–65.

41. Bruce F. Johnston and John W. Mellor, "The Role of Agriculture in Economic Development," *American Economic Review* 51 (September 1961): 566–593.

42. Dorner, *Latin American Land Reforms*, pp. 29–31.

43. Ronald P. Dore, *Land Reform in Japan* (London: Oxford University Press, 1959); Mikiso Hande, *Modern Japan* (Boulder, CO: Westview Press, 1986), pp. 347–348.

44. Shirley W. Y. Kuo, Gustav Ranis, and John C. H. Fei, *The Taiwan Success Story: Rapid Growth with Improved Distribution in the Republic of China, 1952–1979* (Boulder, CO: Westview Press, 1981); Gregory Henderson, *Korea: Politics of the Vortex* (Cambridge, MA: Harvard University Press, 1968).

45. Dore, *Land Reform in Japan*, pp. 147–148.

46. John W. Bruce and Paula Harrell, "Land Reform in the People's Republic of China: 1978–1988," Land Tenure Center Research Paper No. 100 (University of Wisconsin-Madison, 1989), pp. 3–4; Vivienne Shue, *Peasant China in Transition—The Dynamics of Development Toward Socialism, 1949–56* (Berkeley: University of California Press, 1980).

47. Thiesenhusen, *Searching for Agrarian Reform*, pp. 10–11.

48. Wolf, *Peasant Wars*.

49. Harry Harding, *China's Second Revolution* (Washington, DC: Brookings Institution, 1987), p. 12; Suzanne Ogden, *China's Unresolved Issues* (Englewood Cliffs, NJ: Prentice Hall, 1989), pp. 46–50; Nicholas Lardy, *Agriculture in China's Modern Economic Development* (Cambridge, England: Cambridge University Press, 1983).

50. There are exceptions to this pattern, particularly outside the Third World. Poland and Yugoslavia, for example, did not collectivize agriculture during the communist era. Cuba and especially Nicaragua had private farms alongside a larger collectivized sector.

51. For a crop-by-crop analysis of state and private sector farm productivity in Cuba, see Nancy Forster, "Cuban Agricultural Productivity," in *Cuban Communism*, 7th ed., ed. Irving Louis Horowitz (New Brunswick, NJ: Transaction, 1989), pp. 235–255.

52. Nicholas Lardy, "Agricultural Reforms in China," *Journal of International Affairs* (Winter 1986): 91–104. The program was announced in 1978 but was not implemented for two years.

53. Harding, *China's Second Revolution*, p. 106.

54. Forrest D. Colburn, *Post-Revolutionary Nicaragua: State, Class and the Dilemmas of Agrarian Policy* (Berkeley: University of California Press, 1986), and Laura J. Enríquez, *Harvesting Change: Labor and Agrarian Reform in Nicaragua* (Chapel Hill: University of North Carolina Press, 1991), offer contrasting analyses.

55. David Lehmann, "Agrarian Reform in Chile, 1965–1972: An Essay in Contradictions," in *Peasants, Landlords*, pp. 71–119; Marion R. Brown, "Radical Reformism in Chile: 1964–1973," in *Searching for Agrarian Reform*, pp. 216–239.

56. Riedinger, "Philippine Land Reform," and Ronald Herring, "Explaining Anomalies in Land Reform: Lessons from South India," in *Agrarian Reform and Grassroots Development*, pp. 15–75; K. N. Raj and Michael Tharakan, "Agrarian Reform in Kerala and Its Impact on the Rural Economy," and Ajit Kumar Ghose, "Agrarian Reform in West Bengal," in *Agrarian Reform in Contemporary Developing Countries*, ed. Ajit Kumar Ghose (New York: St. Martin's Press, 1983), pp. 31–137.

57. Thiesenhusen, "Introduction," *Searching for Agrarian Reform*, pp. 1–41; Meyer, *Land Reform in Latin America*, p. 4. Thiesenhusen and Meyer each calculate the percentage of farm land redistributed and the percentage of rural families benefiting. Although they use somewhat different time periods and Meyer analyzes a wider sample of nations, they arrive at very similar rankings.

58. de Janvry, *The Agrarian Question*.

59. Howard Handelman, "Peasants, Landlords and Bureaucrats: The Politics of Agrarian Reform in Peru," in *The Politics of Agrarian Change*, pp. 103–125; Cristóbal Kay,

"The Agrarian Reform in Peru: An Assessment," in *Agrarian Reform in Contemporary Developing Countries*, pp. 185–239.

60. Michael Carter and Elena Alvarez, "Changing Paths: The Decollectivization of Agrarian Reform Agriculture in Coastal Peru," in *Searching for Agrarian Reform*, pp. 156–187.

61. Agrarian reforms enacted by the Ecuadorian and Panamanian militaries were far more modest.

62. Howard Handelman, "Peasants, Landlords and Bureaucrats," pp. 103–125; Kay, "The Agrarian Reform in Peru," pp. 185–239.

63. Merilee S. Grindle, *Searching for Rural Development: Labor Migration and Employment in Mexico* (Ithaca, NY: Cornell University Press, 1988); Grindle, "Agrarian Reform in Mexico: A Cautionary Tale," in *Agrarian Reform and Grassroots Development*, pp. 179–204; Steven E. Sanderson, *The Transformation of Mexican Agriculture* (Princeton, NJ: Princeton University Press, 1986); Frank Meissner, "The Mexican Food System (SAM)—A Strategy for Sowing Petroleum," and M. R. Redclift, "The Mexican Food System (SAM)—Sowing Subsidies, Reaping Apathy," *Food Policy* 6, no. 4 (November 1981): 219–235.

64. Ronald J. Herring, "Explaining Anomalies in Agrarian Reform: Lessons from South Asia," in *Agrarian Reform and Grassroots Development*, p. 73.

65. Thiesenhusen, "Conclusions," in *Searching for Agrarian Reform*, pp. 483–503.

66. Prosterman and Riedinger, *Land Reform and Democratic Development*, pp. 177–202.

67. de Janvry, *The Agrarian Question*; Merilee S. Grindle, *State and Countryside: Development Policy and Agrarian Politics in Latin America* (Baltimore, MD: Johns Hopkins University Press, 1986).

68. Grindle, *State and Countryside*.

69. Demetrios Christodoulou, *The Unpromised Land: Agrarian Reform and Conflict Worldwide* (London: Zed Books, 1990), pp. 204–205.

70. Grindle, *State and Countryside*, pp. 160–174.

71. Nola Reinhardt, *Our Daily Bread: The Peasant Question and Family Farming in the Colombian Andes* (Berkeley: University of California Press, 1988), pp. 219–224.

72. Charles Harvey, ed., *Agricultural Pricing Policy in Africa* (London: Macmillan, 1988), p. 2.

73. Robert H. Bates, *Markets and States in Tropical Africa: The Political Basis of Agricultural Policy* (Berkeley: University of California Press, 1981), p. 29; see also Michael J. Lofchie, *The Policy Factor: Agricultural Performance in Kenya and Tanzania* (Boulder, CO: Lynne Rienner Publishers, 1989), pp. 57–59.

74. Marvin G. Weinbaum, *Food, Development, and Politics in the Middle East* (Boulder, CO: Westview Press, 1982), p. 61.

75. Michael F. Lofchie, "Africa's Agricultural Crisis: An Overview," and Robert H. Bates, "The Regulation of Rural Markets in Africa," in *Africa's Agrarian Crisis: The Roots of Famine*, ed. Stephen K. Commins, Michael F. Lofchie, and Rhys Payne (Boulder, CO: Lynne Rienner Publishers, 1986), pp. 3–19, 37–54.

76. Harvey, *Agricultural Pricing Policy*, pp. 236–245; Lofchie, *The Policy Factor*.

77. Neoliberalism rejects much of the state intervention in the economy that was prevalent in many developing economies and instead favors free-market mechanisms. For a more extensive discussion of these issues, see Chapter 10.

78. de Janvry, *The Agrarian Question*; David Goodman and Michael Redclift, *From Peasant to Proletarian: Capitalist Development and Agricultural Transitions* (Oxford, England: Basil Blackwell, 1981).

79. This is most impressively demonstrated in Nola Reinhardt, *Our Daily Bread*. See also Lesley Gill, *Peasants, Entrepreneurs and Social Change: Frontier Development in Lowland Bolivia* (Boulder, CO: Westview Press, 1987).

chapter 7

Rapid Urbanization and the Politics of the Urban Poor

Each day, in the villages of Kenya, Morocco, Egypt, and Colombia, hundreds, sometimes thousands, of young men and women pack up their meager belongings and board buses, trucks, or trains for the long trip to Nairobi, Casablanca, Cairo, or Bogotá. Often they travel alone, sometimes with family or friends. They are a part of one of the largest and most dramatic tides of human migration in world history. Despairing of any hope for a better life in the countryside and seeking new opportunities for themselves and their children, millions of villagers leave the world they have known for the uncertainties of the city. In Africa, these legions of migrants have been augmented by millions of refugees fleeing civil war and famine.

Most maintain·close links with their rural roots long after they have migrated. Some come intending to accumulate savings and eventually return to their villages. "Others alternate between city and country in a permanent pendular pattern."[1] Indeed, in many parts of West Africa and Southeast Asia, more than half the urban migrant population is temporary, including those who repeatedly circulate between village and city.[2] In contrast, Latin America's cityward migrants tend to settle permanently. But whatever their initial aspirations, they continue to crowd the urban slums and shantytowns they have come to call home. Swelled by both internal population growth and the influx of migrants in recent decades, many Third World cities have mushroomed in size and will continue to do so in the coming years (see Tables 7.1 and 7.2). In the past half century, the magnitude of that expansion has placed tremendous strains on the developing world's larger cities. In

TABLE 7.1   Percentage of the Population in Urban Areas, 1970–2015

Country	Percentage Urban 1970	Percentage Urban 1995	Percentage Urban 2015 (estimate)
Ethiopia	9%	15%	26%
Morocco	35	42	64
Mozambique	6	34	52
Bangladesh	8	18	31
Thailand	13	20	29
Chile	75	84	87
Honduras	29	44	56
Mexico	59	73	78

Source: United Nations Development Programme, *Human Development Report, 1998* (New York: Oxford University Press, 1998), pp. 174–175. Reprinted by permission.

Latin America, national capitals such as Caracas (Venezuela) and Lima (Peru) were doubling their populations every 12 to 15 years. African cities, though starting from a smaller base, expanded at an even faster pace. Kinshasa (Congo) grew by nearly 600 percent between 1960 and 1983; Dar es Salaam (Tanzania) by 550 percent; and Abidjan (Côte d'Ivoire) by more than 800 percent.[3] In the Middle East, Baghdad's population soared by nearly 700 percent between 1950 and 1975.

In 1970, Third World cities contained 675 million people. That figure reached 1.9 billion by the year 2000 and is expected to be some four billion in 2025.[4] There is some debate among demographers as to what proportion of that growth has been caused by internal (natural) increase and what percentage has resulted from rural-to-urban migration. The evidence indicates that about half the urban population explosion has come from each of those two sources, with a higher propor-

TABLE 7.2   Population of Third World Cities, 1995–2015

City	Population 1995	Population 2015 (estimate)
Mexico City	16,562,000	19,180,000
Tegucigalpa	995,000	2,016,000
Santiago	4,891,000	6,066,000
Cairo	9,690,000	16,530,000
Casablanca	3,101,000	4,835,000
Addis Ababa	2,431,000	6,578,000
Lagos	10,287,000	24,640,000
Bangkok	6,547,000	9,844,000
Dhaka	8,545,000	19,486,000

Source: United Nations Development Programme, *Human Development Report, 1998* (New York: Oxford University Press, 1998), pp. 174–175. Reprinted by permission.

tion attributable to migration in Africa and a greater percentage to natural increase in Asia.[5]

Latin America (consisting of South America, Central America, Mexico, and the Caribbean) is by far the most urbanized region in the developing world. By 1990 the portion of its population living in cities (72 percent) virtually equaled that of the First World, and it likely surpassed the developed world by the start of this century. With some 17 million people today, Mexico City is already one of the world's largest metropolitan areas (Table 7.2), and Sao Paulo (Brazil) and Buenos Aires (Argentina) are not far behind. To be sure, poorer Central American countries such as Honduras are still less than half urban, but in Chile, 85 percent of the population currently lives in cities (Table 7.1).

African and Asian cities encompass a considerably smaller percentage of their region's total population (35 to 40 percent), but they have grown at a more rapid rate in recent decades. In 1960, Casablanca (Morocco) and Cairo (Egypt) were the only cities on the African continent with populations of more than one million. Twenty-three years later, nine cities exceeded that size, with four of them surpassing two million.[6] As Table 7.2 indicates, African cities such as Addis Ababa (Ethiopia) are growing at an enormous rate, and Lagos's (Nigeria) metropolitan area will soon have a population of almost 25 million. In Africa, the proportion of people residing in cities varies considerably from country to country. At one end of the spectrum, Ethiopia is only a bit over 15 percent urban. But urbanization is far more advanced in North African countries such as Morocco, with about 45 to 50 percent of its population currently living in cities (Table 7.1).

Asia still remains predominantly rural. For example, the cities of Indonesia, India, and Pakistan contained only about 30 percent of the nation's population in the early 1990s.[7] Yet megacities such as Jakarta (Indonesia), Karachi (Pakistan), and New Delhi, Bombay, and Calcutta (all in India) have populations exceeding 10 million. During the second half of the twentieth century, the populations of their metropolitan areas leapfrogged past New York, London, and Los Angeles. While Bangladesh is now only about 20 to 25 percent urban, its primary city, Dhaka, will see its population more than double from 1995 to 2015, reaching an expected level of nearly 20 million (Tables 7.1 and 7.2).

THE POLITICAL CONSEQUENCES OF URBAN GROWTH

Surprisingly, the Third World's enormous percentage rate of urban growth since the middle of the twentieth century is not without precedent. According to one estimate, the proportion of the LDCs' total population living in cities grew from 16.7 percent in 1950 to 28.0 percent in 1975. But from 1875 to 1900, the West's urban population increased from 17.2 to 26.1 percent, a change of similar magnitude.[8] What makes the current urban explosion unique, however, is the sheer volume of people involved. Third World populations are much larger today than were populations in nineteenth-century Europe and North America, and they are growing at a more rapid rate. It is one thing for a nineteenth-century

First World city to grow from 80,000 to 400,000 people in a 25-year period. It is quite another for Seoul (South Korea) to mushroom from one million to nearly seven million or for Kinshasa (Congo) to spiral from 400,000 to more than 2.5 million in the same period of time. Massive population shifts such as these obviously pose especially daunting challenges in urban housing, sanitation, education, and transportation.

This chapter examines two important aspects of urban politics in the developing world. First, it looks at the problems that exploding urban populations present to political leaders and government planners. Specifically, it asks how poor countries can provide the needed jobs, housing, sanitation, and other urban services. What is the government's role in those areas, and how does state policy interact with private sector activity and self-help efforts? Second, we examine the political attitudes and behavior of city dwellers in the LDCs, focusing particularly on the politics of the urban poor. To what extent do urban shantytown and slum dwellers have political orientations that are distinct both from those of the rural poor and those of the urban middle and upper classes? Is rapid urbanization likely to contribute to political development, or does it carry the seeds of political instability?

THE STRUGGLE FOR EMPLOYMENT

Contemporary Third World urbanization differs from the West's earlier experience not only in magnitude but also in terms of its economic contexts. The nineteenth-century urban revolution in Europe and North America occurred at the dawn of unprecedented industrialization and economic growth. Modern capitalism was coming of age and could accommodate, indeed needed, the wave of migrant and immigrant laborers. By contrast, the formal economies of most contemporary LDCs have failed to provide sufficient employment to their growing urban work force.

To be sure, many do find jobs, and some low-income workers achieve impressive upward mobility. For example, one study of Howrah, an industrial city in West Bengal, found that "several hundred men who started with almost nothing now own factories large enough to employ twenty-five [or more] workers," placing them "among the richest people in the community."[9] Similar examples can be found in much of the developing world. But these cases are exceptional. Economic survival remains an ongoing struggle for most of the urban poor. Even during Mexico's economic boom in the 1960s and 1970s, the country's expanding modern sector was able to provide new employment for only about half the people seeking to enter the urban work force. The debt crisis and severe recession that gripped Africa, Latin America, and parts of Asia in the 1980s exacerbated the problem, as industrial employment in many countries plummeted. Hyperinflation in many Sub-Saharan African countries has meant that even people who are regularly employed rarely have salaries or wages high enough to support their families.

For those unable to find work in the formal sector of the urban economy (i.e., factories, civil service, modern commercial enterprises) and for those whose formal-sector paychecks cannot feed or house their families, the answer normally has been employment in the informal economy. As noted in Chapter 5, that sector is defined as the part of the economy that is "unregulated by the institutions of society [most notably the state], in a legal and social environment in which similar activities are regulated" and taxed.[10] A large proportion of the workers in the informal economy are self-employed in occupations ranging from recycling garbage to shoe shine boys, street vendors, mechanics, electricians, plumbers, and drivers of unlicenced taxis.

Of course, informal sector activity is not limited to the developing world. In recent years, cities like New York, Los Angeles, and Milan have seen substantial expansion in the number of unlicenced street vendors, underground garment manufacturers, and other illegal or unlicenced activities. In the Third World, however, the informal economy represents a far greater proportion of all urban employment. During the 1970s, for example, it constituted some 35 percent of the urban work force in Malaysia; 44 percent in Nairobi (Kenya); 45 percent in Jakarta (Indonesia); and 60 percent in urban Peru.[11] Those percentages rose significantly as a result of the economic crises of the 1980s and late 1990s.

In the vast garbage dumps of Cairo, hordes of entrepreneurs can be found sifting through the refuse looking for marketable waste. At night, on the streets of Rio de Janeiro (Brazil) and Port-au-Prince (Haiti) thousands of prostitutes search for customers. On the commercial boulevards of Manila and Mexico City, an army of street vendors sells food, household appliances, and bootleg audiotapes. In Lagos (Nigeria) and Lahore (Pakistan), shoemakers and carpenters, working out of their homes, sell their wares to appreciative clients. All belong to the informal economy. While it was once assumed that people working in this sector were particularly impoverished, we now know that their earning power varies greatly, and that some have higher incomes than factory workers.[12] To cite one admittedly atypical example, during Nicaragua's runaway inflation in the 1980s, street vendors selling Coca Cola earned more in a few hours than government white-collar employees made in a week. A more representative study of Montevideo (Uruguay) found that laborers in the formal and informal sectors made fairly comparable incomes.[13]

The informal economy's merits and faults have been debated extensively. Critics point out that its workers are not protected by minimum wage laws and lack access to government health and welfare programs, since people normally enroll in these programs through their legal jobs. Proponents respond that the informal economy not only employs vast numbers of people who would otherwise have nothing, but it also contributes a substantial proportion of the Third World's consumer goods and services. In a book that has been very influential in Latin American political circles, Peruvian author Hernando de Soto argues that Third World governments should cease trying to regulate and license the informal sector and instead allow it to flourish and expand.[14]

While the informal sector represents concrete, small-scale efforts by the poor (and not-so-poor) to create employment, the government's involvement in the job market has usually been more indirect. Only in communist countries such as China and Cuba is the state the primary urban employer. Because they consider employment to be a fundamental worker's right, until recently many communist governments created as many jobs as necessary to achieve full, or nearly full, employment, no matter how economically inefficient that might be. Often they also restricted rural-to-urban migration, prohibiting people from moving into cities unless they already previously had employment lined up there (though these regulations have been totally ineffective in China as of late). Governments in capitalist LDCs, on the other hand, reject the role of "employer of last resort" and do not limit urban migration. They may occasionally institute public works projects specifically designed to create employment, but such efforts are normally quite limited.

Instead, nonsocialist, Third World governments primarily influence urban employment indirectly through their broader national macroeconomic policies.[15] In their efforts to stimulate economic growth, they hope to generate employment over the long run. Two areas of economic policy particularly influence job creation: industrialization strategy and the containment of inflation. Differences in government industrialization policies led to very different employment outcomes in Latin America and East Asia.

Starting as early as the 1930s and 1940s, some Latin American governments began stimulating economic development through import-substituting industrialization (ISI).[16] The governments of Argentina, Brazil, and Mexico, for example, created tariff walls and fiscal stimuli to nourish local industries that produced consumer goods for the domestic market. Items such as clothing, appliances, and sometimes even automobiles, which had previously been imported, were instead manufactured locally. One of ISI's many goals was to create industrial employment for the urban working class. Consequently, from the 1940s into the 1970s, labor unions and industrialists, despite their differences on a host of other issues, united behind state policies supporting ISI.

Many comparatively well-paid blue-collar jobs were created, but their number was still rather small relative to the vast army of unskilled laborers. Domestic markets simply weren't large enough to generate a sufficient number of industrial jobs, and the region's highly protected industries, facing little external competition, had few incentives to improve product quality or manufacturing efficiency. As a consequence, their products were unable to compete in the international market. By the late 1970s, Latin America's industrial economies began to stagnate.

In contrast, East Asian governments in Hong Kong, Singapore, South Korea, Taiwan, Thailand, and Malaysia, which had first stimulated industrialization through import-substituting policies (ISI), soon lowered or removed protective tariffs, forcing domestic manufacturers to compete with foreign imports. That competition forced firms to produce goods whose quality and price made them competitive, not only at home but in the export market.

Though the East Asian export-led model was initially based on the exploitation of a poorly paid work force, the region's labor-intensive industries eventually generated so many jobs that they drove up local wage scales. More recently, Latin American countries such as Brazil, Chile, Colombia, and Mexico have sought to emulate East Asia's export-led model, with some degree of success.[17] But while these countries have increased their industrial exports considerably in the past 20 years, job creation has still lagged behind because Latin American export industries tend to be more capital-intensive and less labor-intensive.

Beginning in the early 1980s, many LDCs faced the dual problems of rampant inflation and stagnant economic growth. Because solutions to each of those problems often conflicted, at least in the short run, governments had to decide which challenge to tackle first and how to confront it. Encouraged or pressured by the International Monetary Fund (IMF), the World Bank, and private lenders, many heavily indebted African and Latin American countries adopted macroeconomic policies designed to slash inflation rates first. To do so, they reduced (or tried to reduce) large budgetary and trade deficits by slashing government spending and public sector employment, devaluating the national currency, and privatizing state enterprises (selling them to private investors). More recently, East and Southeast Asian governments have been forced to devalue their currencies as well.

Although stabilization and adjustment policies such as these may be beneficial in the long run (their record is somewhat mixed), they always drive unemployment up sharply in the short run. And while austerity programs in countries such as Argentina, Ghana, Morocco, and Peru have curtailed inflation, they have been slow or unable to reinvigorate employment. Since the late 1990s, government economic adjustment policies in Thailand, Indonesia, and Malaysia have caused substantial unemployment and declining living standards.

Government policy also affects the urban employment market in yet another important way, by expanding or contracting state bureaucracies and semi-autonomous, state-owned enterprises known as *parastatals*. Throughout Africa, government bureaucracies and parastatals have traditionally employed far more people than they needed. Ten people often do the work of six. They have been overstaffed for two important political reasons: they provide work for potentially volatile white- and blue-collar workers unable to find jobs in the weak private sector, and they are a source of patronage for government or party supporters. For example, at the start of the 1990s, some 40 percent of all government employees in Sierra Leone were "ghosts," employees on the government payroll who never showed up for work. The government's inclination to hire an excessive number of bureaucrats, pervasive throughout the Third World, primarily benefits the urban middle class rather than the poor, who lack the necessary education for these positions. However, parastatals (including agricultural marketing operations, electric power plants, telephone companies, railroads, and other state enterprises) employ both blue- and white-collar workers, thereby benefiting working-class and middle-class constituencies.

Since the early 1980s, the IMF and other international lenders have induced debt-ridden African governments to pare their payrolls substantially. As a result, Uganda fired some 20,000 ghosts from government employment, while Ghana dropped 11,000.[18] Austerity measures in Latin America have also required sharp cuts in government employment. Many parastatals have been sold to private investors, who have no incentives to maintain unneeded workers. Following the sale of Mexico's state steel industry, for example, the new private owners laid off more than half the industry's workers.[19]

Thus, for the foreseeable future, a shrinking state sector will offer no relief for the growing number of urban job seekers. Quite the contrary. For decades, the expansion of labor-intensive, export-oriented industries provided substantial private sector employment in East and Southeast Asia. Since 1997, however, the region's economic crisis has led to widespread plant closings. Industrial exports in Latin America tend to be more capital-intensive and, hence, have generated less employment. In Africa, where economic performance in the 1980s and much of the 1990s was particularly disastrous and the size of the industrial sector remains fairly limited, the informal sector will probably provide a growing proportion of urban jobs.

THE STRUGGLE FOR HOUSING AMONG THE URBAN POOR

Of all the problems facing the urban poor, particularly the waves of new immigrants, none is more serious than finding adequate housing. With many metropolitan areas doubling in size every 10 to 20 years, private sector housing cannot possibly expand fast enough to meet the need. Moreover, most of the new homes and apartment houses built for sale or rental by private firms are designed for the middle and upper classes, while poorer people are relegated to old tenement housing. Low-income housing is not profitable enough to attract new private sector investment. Many Third World governments have invested in public housing, but little of it reaches the poor. So, lacking enough options in either the private or state sectors, a large segment of the urban poor live in squatter settlements and other forms of "self-help" (occupant-built) housing referred to in the literature as "spontaneous shelter."[20] Many others crowd into existing urban slums. The poorest city dwellers, lacking even the resources to rent or build, are left homeless, residing in doorways, unused construction material, or the like.

In all, the total number of shantytown residents, slum dwellers, and homeless account for over half the inhabitants of Third World cities. A 1990 United Nations report on "Shelter and Urbanization" estimated that 100 million people worldwide are homeless. In Cairo, several hundred thousand people with nowhere else to go live in cemetery tombs. Half the population of Ankara (Turkey) and about one-third the inhabitants of Manila and São Paulo live in squatter settlements and other forms of spontaneous shelter. For many of these people, sanitary conditions are particularly problematic. A recent

United Nations report calculated that close to 20 percent of the Third World's urban population has no access to clean water, and almost 30 percent lack sanitation facilities. Although the proportion of city dwellers lacking those vital services has fallen somewhat, their absolute numbers have risen as a result of rapid urban growth. Less than one-third of the inhabitants of São Paulo and New Delhi are served by sewage systems, while in Karachi that portion drops to 20 percent. Tap water is equally hard to come by, reaching only half the population of Acapulco and one-third of Jakarta. Those who lack running water must either purchase it from private vendors (water tankers) at high prices or drink unsafe water. An estimated 100,000 inhabitants of Bangkok (Thailand), for example, obtain their drinking water from canals and other waterways that are dangerously polluted by industrial and human waste.[21] In light of these conditions, LDCs have sought an appropriate state response.

Public Housing and the Role of the State

Governments throughout the developing world have constructed public housing as a means of alleviating housing shortages. In China, workers in state enterprises are assigned apartments linked to their employer. Cuba's revolutionary regime has built large apartment blocks housing 25,000 to 40,000 persons on the outskirts of its largest cities.[22] During Venezuela's petroleum boom, the government constructed as many as 34,000 urban housing units annually.[23] In the 1960s and 1970s, various African governments established housing agencies with far more limited resources. One of the continent's most ambitious programs was in the Côte d'Ivoire, where some 40,000 units were constructed during the 1970s, almost all in the capital city of Abidjan. By the close of that decade, the Kenyan government was building more than 3,000 units annually.[24]

In time, however, it has become clear that public housing cannot provide sufficient shelter for the poor and, indeed, sometimes worsens their plight. In the capital cities of India, Senegal, and Nigeria, for example, government housing projects have often been designed to eradicate urban blight. Prior to their construction, "unsightly" squatter settlements or slums have been demolished so that the city could become more aesthetically pleasing to the political elite, urban planners, middle-class residents, and foreign tourists. But rarely do the slum dwellers who have been evicted from their homes subsequently secure residence in the newly constructed public housing projects. Even those who are given alternate housing are usually relocated on the edges of town, far removed from their workplace. Diana Patel describes how Zimbabwe's government periodically ousted the same squatters from their settlements in different parts of the nation's capital, in effect "chasing them around town." Government planners, viewing these shacks through middle-class lenses, believed that unless the squatters could afford "decent" urban housing with plumbing and multiple rooms for their families, they would be better off returning to the countryside.[25]

Even when new public housing projects are not built on the ruins of shantytowns and slums, they usually don't help the needy. In order for the government to recoup its costs, it must sell or rent the individual housing units for more than the urban poor can afford to pay. Consequently, the state is faced with two options: it must either heavily subsidize rents and mortgages to bring the unit costs down to a level that the poor can afford, or it must rent or sell the dwellings to those who can better afford them, namely the middle class.

Despite its obvious attraction as a welfare measure for the poor, subsidized housing has several drawbacks. First, it is simply too costly for most developing nations to sustain, whatever the government's priorities may be. Following the Cuban revolution, the government committed itself to a variety of programs designed to serve workers and the urban poor—including public health, education, and housing. "Early housing policies reflected Fidel Castro's belief that nothing was too good for the working class."[26] Housing projects such as Santiago's José Martí provided schools, day-care centers, theaters, clinics, and stores for its 40,000 inhabitants. But by lavishing excessively "luxurious" housing on early recipients, the government soon ran out of funds for the many others needing shelter. Thus, the East Havana project, planned for 100,000 dwelling units, ultimately contained only 1,500. Even though it lacked adequate resources itself, the government discouraged or prohibited private and self-help housing (i.e., units built by the owner) until recently.[27] Not surprisingly, Cuba, like most Marxist regimes, has suffered chronic housing shortages.[28]

Second, subsidized housing almost invariably becomes a political plum, with dwellings allocated on the basis of political connections (rewarding government or party activists) rather than need. Political patronage plays an important role in housing allocation, with policemen, government bureaucrats, teachers, and activists in the ruling party being the first served.[29] For both these reasons, residents in state housing generally come from the middle class. They not only can better afford the rents, thereby reducing, but not eliminating, the size of government housing subsidies, but they also have the political influence to acquire this valuable resource.

Two of the few cities to construct extensive working-class public housing are Singapore and Hong Kong. But they are extremely atypical cases in two respects. First, they are so densely populated, with no land area on which to expand, that high-rise projects are the only possible housing solution. Second, they are probably the Third World's most affluent cities and, hence, can afford the cost of extensive subsidized housing. With the exception of the oil-rich Gulf states, other developing nations lack the resources to make a serious dent in their housing shortage. Consequently, most analysts feel that limited state funds would be better spent helping a larger number of beneficiaries in a less costly way.

Spontaneous Housing

For years, many social scientists and urban planners have maintained that the most effective remedy for housing shortfalls in Third World cities is spontaneous (or self-help) shelter—the very shantytowns and squatter settlements that are so frequently viewed as a blight. In cities throughout the developing world, the poor have built their own homes, often with hired or volunteer assistance. While living in these dwellings, many proprietors, particularly in Africa, also rent space to tenants. In some cases, the owners are squatters, living on land that has been occupied illegally, though often with the compliance of government authorities.[30] Other residents, living in so-called "pirate settlements," have purchased their lots from land speculators but lack legal titles because their community doesn't have basic urban services such as water or otherwise fails to conform to government zoning requirements.[31]

Spontaneous housing may consist of a few isolated homes or a community of many thousands. For example, on the dried-up marshlands outside Mexico City, the municipality of Netzahualcóyotl began as a pirate settlement in the 1940s. Though lightly settled until the 1960s, it housed 600,000 people by 1970.[32] A tenants' strike eventually induced the government to provide badly needed urban services and grant the squatters legal title to their homes. Elsewhere, up to 40 percent of Nairobi's population and one-fourth to one-third of the inhabitants of Jakarta, Karachi, and Lima live in squatter settlements.[33] These homes, argues John F. C. Turner, have erroneously been viewed as a problem, when in fact they are a major part of the solution to urban housing needs.[34] Rather than build public housing, he insists, Third World governments can serve many more people by removing legal and political obstacles to spontaneous housing settlements and helping residents upgrade the dwellings they have built.

Self-built homes have several important advantages over public housing.[35] First, they actually serve the poor, whereas most public housing does not. Second, they afford occupants the opportunity to upgrade their homes continuously. For example, in Lima's vast network of shantytowns, one can observe many wood and straw shacks whose owners are building brick walls around them, slowly constructing a better home as funds become available. Third, precisely because they are user-built, these homes better address the needs and desires of their residents than do units built by government planners. Finally, squatter settlements have the "churches, bars and neighborhood stores that help create a sense of community" that is too often lacking in large, impersonal, public housing projects.[36] Given these advantages, proponents of spontaneous housing argue that the state's most constructive role would be to end squatter evictions and instead grant them land titles and other assistance needed to improve their homes.

Sites-and-Services Programs

Many planners who favor a more active role for the state view the Turner thesis as a convenient excuse for governments that don't wish to spend funds on the poor. Championing self-help housing, charge these critics, merely perpetuates the status quo and allows the state to direct its limited housing resources toward the middle class.[37]

By the 1970s, however, many Third World governments, the World Bank, and other foreign aid donors were pursuing a middle ground between providing expensive, fully built public housing units and a policy of laissez faire (i.e., letting the poor build their own shelters). In countries as diverse as Colombia,

India, Malawi, and Turkey, the state has sold or rented parcels of land to the poor with basic services such as running water, sewage, and electricity. Purchasers then build their own homes on the sites as they do with spontaneous housing. In some cases, governments provide credit, technical assistance, or low-cost construction materials.[38]

These "sites-and-services" programs have several obvious advantages. First, they allow the government to steer self-built housing to locations that are safer and more environmentally sound. By contrast, unregulated spontaneous shelter in Caracas (Venezuela) illustrates the dangers of unzoned squatter settlements. There, more than half a million people live on precarious hillsides in shacks that are sometimes washed away during the rainy season by mudslides. Second, in contrast to many sprawling squatter settlements, residents of sites-and-services locations have electricity, sanitation, and other needed services from the outset. Finally, although occupants must purchase their sites, the lots are far more affordable than are fully built state housing units. The government can further assist residents by providing cheaper credit and construction materials.

Critics of sites-and-services programs note, however, that even these relatively inexpensive lots are too costly for the poorest of the poor. While conceding that the communities developed on these sites are often healthier, safer, and more aesthetically pleasing, some scholars contend that the tradeoff is building fewer homes for the very poor. In addition, they charge that these programs skim off relatively better off and talented residents from unaided slums and shantytowns, thereby leaving the older communities bereft of leadership. Finally, they note that governments are likely to locate sites-and-services projects in remote areas of town in order to remove the poor from downtown business areas. As a consequence, residents are far removed from their jobs and from important urban facilities.[39]

Such criticisms notwithstanding, we have seen that sites-and-services programs have some clear advantages over unaided spontaneous shelter and are clearly more beneficial to the poor than is fully built public housing. Unfortunately, many of these programs have not been self-financing (i.e., government income from the rent or sale of lots has not covered costs). Consequently, during Africa and Latin America's economic crisis in the 1980s and the East Asian crisis of the late 1990s, governments often abandoned them, once again leaving the poor to fend for themselves. Finally, both sites-and-service programs and unregulated squatter settlements have faced a growing obstacle in recent years; as a consequence of increasing urban sprawl, cities have ever-diminishing space available for any type of self-built housing.[40]

THE POLITICS OF THE URBAN POOR: CONFLICTING IMAGES

How do the urban poor react politically to their daily struggle for jobs and shelter? The politics of the urban poor, like those of the peasantry, have been depicted in sharply conflicting manners.[41] When political scientists first noted

the sweep of cityward migration and urban growth in the developing countries, many of them viewed the sprawling slums and squatter settlements as
potential hotbeds of unrest or even revolution. In one of the most influential
early works on Third World politics, James Coleman warned, "There exist in
most urban centers . . . elements predisposed to anomic activity."[42] Samuel
Huntington maintained that urban migrants themselves were unlikely to challenge the existing order, but their children certainly might: "At some point, the
slums of Rio and Lima . . . are likely to be swept by social violence, as the children of the city demand the rewards of the city."[43] And economist Barbara
Ward, taking note of shantytown poverty and the rise of radical urban movements, insisted,

> unchecked . . . left to grow and fester, there is here enough explosive material to
> produce . . . bitter class conflict . . . erupting in guerrilla warfare, and threatening,
> ultimately, the security even of the comfortable West.[44]

As we shall see, the urban poor have, indeed, been important participants
in several recent Third World revolutions. In addition, rioting over food prices
and bus fares has shaken Algiers, Caracas, Santo Domingo, and other cities. But
the urban conflagrations that many expected have rarely happened. Most of the
poor have shunned violence. And voters in the slums and squatter settlements
of the LDCs have been as likely to support right-wing or centrist political candidates as radicals.

Initial expectations of a violent or radicalized urban lower class were
based on a set of premises that has generally proven erroneous. To be sure,
many urban migrants came to the cities with raised expectations and height-
ened political sensitivities. When their hopes for a better life were not satisfied, many scholars predicted they would likely erupt in fury against the
system, or at the least support the most radical political parties. But horrendous as the slums of Cairo, Calcutta, or Karachi may appear to the Western
observer, migrants usually find them preferable to their previous conditions
in the countryside. In fact, the urban poor are far more likely than their rural
counterparts to enjoy electricity, sewage, access to tap water, and educational
opportunities for their children. In many countries, urban migration also
allows people to escape from semifeudal social controls or ethnic civil war.
Small wonder that surveys of migrants in Ankara, Baghdad, Bogotá, Mexico
City, Rio de Janeiro, and other cities indicate that most respondents feel better off in their urban hovels than they had been in their rural villages.[45] A
study of 13 low-income neighborhoods in Bogotá (Colombia), Valencia
(Venezuela), and Mexico City revealed that between 64 and 76 percent of the
respondents believed that their settlement was "a good place to live," while
only 11 to 31 percent felt they lived in a "bad place."[46] Undoubtedly, the
severe economic recession during the 1980s that sharply lowered urban living
standards in Africa and Latin America and the more recent economic crisis in
Asia gave slum dwellers a more jaundiced view of their condition. Yet survey

research indicates that even when the urban poor do not feel their own lives have improved, most remain optimistic about the future and about prospects for their children.[47]

When early expectations of urban radicalism and violence rarely materialized, some scholars reached diametrically opposite conclusions. For example, based on his studies of low-income neighborhoods in Mexico and Puerto Rico, anthropologist Oscar Lewis concluded that most of the urban poor are prisoners of a "culture of poverty." Lewis described a sub-proletariat that lacks class consciousness, economic and political organization, or long-term aspirations. While distrustful of government, they feel powerless and fatalistic about effecting change. The culture of poverty, Lewis argued, is inherently apolitical and, hence, quite unlikely to generate radical or revolutionary activity.[48]

A related body of literature described the urban poor as "marginal"— outside the mainstream of the nation's political and economic life. Consequently, it was argued, there is a political vicious cycle in which the poor's exclusion leads to increased apathy on their part, which, in turn, further isolates them. They demonstrate a "lack of active participation due to the fact that . . . marginal groups make no decisions; they do not contribute to the molding of society."[49] Like the victims of Lewis's culture of poverty, marginals allegedly show little class consciousness or capacity for long-term collective action.

Just as initial predictions of radicalism and violence among the urban lower class proved to be greatly exaggerated, so too did assertions that the poor were invariably apathetic and fatalistic. To be sure, most low-income communities are not very politicized. In his study of the poor in Guatemala City, Bryan R. Roberts found that "they claim to avoid politics in their local work, and to them the term 'politician' is synonymous with deceit and corruption."[50] This perception is not the result of apathy or fatalism, however, but stems rather from the realistically "perceived impracticality of changing the existing order" in most Third World countries[51] or, in the case of Guatemala, from a repressive political climate. On the other hand, when given the opportunity to organize (i.e., when their political activity is not repressed) and when there is a realistic chance of attaining some benefits from the political system, many low-income communities, or at least an activist minority within them, have seized the opportunity. Studies of Caracas, Lima, and Rio, for example, reveal a number of poor neighborhoods with extensive political cooperation and organization. Moreover, their community leaders often have a keen sense of how to manipulate the political environment.

In time, social scientists came to question the concepts of marginality and the culture of poverty.[52] Clearly, a more nuanced view of Third World urban politics requires us to ask: Under what circumstances do the urban poor organize politically? What goals do they seek, and how do they pursue them? What factors determine whether their political organization is peaceful or violent, conservative or radical, reformist or revolutionary?

FORMS OF POLITICAL EXPRESSION AMONG THE URBAN POOR

Political scientists have long understood that the urban poor tend to be better informed and more active politically than their rural counterparts. Indeed, early scholarship on Third World politics used a nation's level of urbanization as an indicator of its degree of political participation.[53] City dwellers have higher levels of literacy than peasants do, greater exposure to the mass media, and more contact with political campaigns and rallies. But this does not mean that most residents of poor urban neighborhoods are highly politicized. To the contrary, many of them are uninterested, apathetic, or even fatalistic about political events.[54] Nor does it even mean that political activists in the community are radical, indignant about their economic conditions, or interested in insurrectionary activity. What it does mean is that the urban poor generally vote in higher numbers than the peasantry. And it means that many low-income neighborhoods and communities, having intelligently assessed what kinds of benefits they can reasonably hope to extract from the political system, have organized to secure them. Contrary to initial expectations that the disoriented and frustrated urban poor would riot and rebel, they have tended, instead, to be rather pragmatic and careful in their political behavior.

Individual Political Behavior

For most slum and shantytown dwellers, opportunities for individual political activity are rather limited. Voting has had limited political impact in most developing nations. In Africa, the Middle East, and much of Asia, fairly contested elections, at least until recently, have been rare. Many African and Middle Eastern regimes engage in nonparticipatory politics designed to exclude the masses. After an authoritarian interlude, democracy has gradually returned to most of Latin America and it has tentatively started in parts of Africa, but its relevance to the poor remains unclear.

An alternative, often more fruitful, type of individual political activity takes the form of *clientelism*. As Josef Gugler and others have noted, members of the urban lower class seek to advance their interests by attaching themselves to a patron within the government or within a powerful political party, faction, or movement.[55] Clientelism (i.e., patron-client relationships) involves "the dispensing of public resources as favors . . . by political power holders/seekers and their respective parties, in exchange for votes or forms of popular support." While offering concrete advantages to the less-powerful partner (the client), it is at its heart "a strategy of elite controlled political participation fostering the status quo."[56] Among the urban poor, potentially frustrated or radicalized individuals and groups can be co-opted into the political system with the lure of immediate, if limited, gains.

Patron-client relations, of course, were typical of American big-city political machines in the late nineteenth and early twentieth centuries. Political parties aided recently arrived immigrants or Black migrants from the South by offering them jobs, Christmas turkeys, or assistance with local authorities, all in exchange for their support at the polls. Today, in countries throughout Africa, the poor attain credit, employment in parastatals, and the like by supporting the governing political party or local government strongman. Elsewhere, even in countries with competitive elections, such as India, Uruguay, and the Philippines, political bosses garner votes and volunteers primarily through patronage.

For most of the urban poor, however, collective rather than individual activity appears to be the most productive form of political participation. Many low-income neighborhoods have organized rather effectively to extract benefits from the political system. Not surprisingly, one of their most common objectives is to secure land titles for their homes along with basic services such as sanitation, sewage, tap water, education, and paved streets.

Collective Goals: Housing and Urban Services

On the outskirts of Lima, Peru, several million people live in squatter communities once known as *barriadas* and more recently called *pueblos jóvenes* ("young towns"). Typically, these settlements were born out of organized invasions of unoccupied land, either government property or land whose ownership had been in dispute:

> Some invasions involve relatively small groups of families who join together on an informal basis shortly before the occupation of the land. Others involve hundreds of families and are planned with great care. The leaders of these invasions often organize well before the invasion occurs and meet many times to recruit members, choose a site and plan the occupation itself.[57]

Although these land seizures were obviously illegal, David Collier found that nearly half of them (involving more than 60 percent of Lima's squatter population) were conducted with explicit or tacit government approval.[58] While the authorities didn't want this phenomenon to get out of hand, they understood that permitting a controlled number of invasions onto low-value land (much of it public) enabled the poor to build their own homes with little cost to the state and defused a potentially explosive situation. There were political benefits to be gained as well. By protecting the invaders from police eviction, a political leader or governing party could garner future electoral support from that community. In many cases, squatters also paid off local authorities prior to their invasions.

When Peru's leftist military regime seized power in 1968, it was anxious to mobilize the urban poor but, at the same time, to reduce spontaneous grassroots political activity. The generals issued an urban reform law legalizing most existing squatter communities. They also tried to mobilize, yet control, the poor through SINAMOS, a state-controlled political organization for the rural and urban masses. However, they took a tougher stance against new land invasions. Henry Dietz's study of six poor neighborhoods in Lima demonstrates that community leaders in several locations were quite adept at moving from pre-military, competitive electoral politics to the new rules of enlightened authoritarianism.[59] Mobilized neighborhoods used an impressive array of political tactics to secure assistance from the military regime. These tactics included working through SINAMOS, enlisting the aid of a sympathetic Catholic bishop whom the church had assigned to the shantytowns, gaining the support of foreign nongovernmental organizations (NGOs), publishing letters in leading newspapers, pressuring local government bureaucrats, and directly petitioning the president.

Lima's squatter settlements have long attracted the interest of political scientists and anthropologists because of their unusually high level of political activity. But research elsewhere in Latin America has found similar ties between poor neighborhoods and the state.[60] For example, in her study of low-income neighborhoods in Mexico City, Susan Eckstein describes how powerful community leaders tied themselves to the then-ruling party (the PRI) and became the links between the government and the grass roots. Because these community organizations were controlled from the top down and tended to be short-lived, Eckstein is skeptical about how much the poor really gained by operating through Mexico's clientelistic system. Still, she concedes that over the years poor neighborhoods have successfully petitioned the government for water, electricity, local food markets, schools, public transportation, and the like.[61] Following the National Action Party's presidential victory in 2000 and Mexico's transition to democracy, Mexico's low-income neighborhoods have been forced to establish new clientelistic relationships.

The politics of low-income neighborhoods throughout the developing world tends to resemble Peru's and Mexico's in two important respects: the scope of their demands and their relationship to the national political system. Studies of urban politics in India, Pakistan, the Philippines, and other LDCs repeatedly show the demands of the poor to be quite limited and pragmatic.[62] At times they are defensive, simply asking not to be evicted from illegal settlements. Frequently, their political objectives focus on housing. But, as John Turner suggested, squatters and slum dwellers rarely want the government to build homes for them, desiring instead the means to do it themselves.[63] Some neighborhoods may ask for a medical clinic, a market, or a preschool lunch program. None of these objectives, however, involve a fundamental challenge to the political system or a major redistribution of economic resources.

Such limited demands are intimately related to the structure of political organization in low-income neighborhoods. Political inputs from the poor are filtered through patron-client linkages to the state, powerful political parties, or political bosses. Organizations may be based in particular neighborhoods; they may be tied to ethnic, religious, or racial identities; or they may simply be formed around powerful political figures. In the slums of Madras, India, where politics is closely linked to the film industry, clientelistic organizations grow out of local fan clubs for politically active movie stars.[64] Whatever its base, patron-client politics inherently reinforces the status quo. In return for votes or other forms of political support, the state delivers some of the goods or services that residents need. In many cases, a neighborhood's rewards are very paltry. Elsewhere, political systems are far more generous. In either case, however, the state engages in "divide and rule" politics, as poor urban districts compete with each other for limited government resources.[65]

Critics of clientelistic politics point out that the benefits that accrue to slums and shantytowns are limited. While some communities gain water, electricity, or clinics, many others are left out. Moreover, even successful neighborhoods find it difficult to maintain pressure on the system for extended periods of time because their political organizations generally atrophy after a number of years. Consequently, as Alan Gilbert and Peter Ward charge, "The main aim of community-action programs is less to improve conditions for the poor . . . than to legitimate the state . . . to help maintain existing power relations in society."[66] As an alternative to clientelism, its critics favor a more independent, and perhaps more radical, form of mobilization that would raise the urban poor's political consciousness and, hopefully, lead to more sweeping redistributive policies benefiting far more people.

Other analysts, however, have a more positive view of clientelism. While recognizing its shortcomings, they insist that the limited benefits that it brings are clearly better than nothing. Viewed in the broader context of society's tremendous inequalities, paved streets, clean drinking water, a clinic, or a food market may not seem like sufficient gains to a middle-class observer. But they are usually greatly appreciated by the low-income neighborhoods that need them badly. A radical regime might redistribute more to the poor, but that is not a viable option in most LDCs.[67]

The benefits of clientelism vary from country to country, depending on the nature of its political system and the state of the economy. In open and democratic systems or even in quasi-democratic governments, the poor have broader opportunities to organize, demonstrate, petition, and vote. Clearly, their capacity to demand rewards from the state is greater than under authoritarian regimes. At the same time, the benefits clientelistic systems can allocate to low-income neighborhoods are constrained by the state's economic resources. During their petroleum booms, the Mexican and Venezuelan governments could be more generous to the urban poor. Even in more difficult economic times, the Mexican government has used revenues from the sale of state enterprises to finance public works projects in urban slums. Conversely, the impoverished dictatorships of Sub-Saharan Africa have neither the economic resources nor the political will to aid their slums and squatter settlements.

During the 1980s, a number of independent grass-roots organizations emerged in the poor neighborhoods of Brazil, Chile, Mexico, and several other Latin American countries. Known as "new social movements," they avoided clientelistic linkages with the government or political parties, keeping independent even of leftist parties. For example, following Mexico City's immense earthquake in 1985, slum dwellers, frustrated by the ineptitude of the government's reconstruction efforts, formed an effective network of self-help associations. In Monterrey, radicalized squatters in the community of *Tierra y Libertad* (Land and Liberty) hijacked several buses, forcing the public transport company to extend its routes further into their neighborhood.[68] Ultimately, however, these independent movements had limited longevity. By the early 1990s they were being overshadowed by President Carlos Salinas's public works network for poor neighborhoods known as the National Solidarity Program. Using traditional clientelistic techniques, his administration won the support of the poor by establishing new schools, clinics, and the like through government-affiliated neighborhood groups.

Whatever the merits or limits of clientelism, its scope and range refute prior assumptions about the politics of the urban poor. On the one hand, the sometimes delicate and complex patron-client negotiations that they often require demonstrate that many neighborhood leaders are more politically skilled than most outside analysts had assumed. While many slum dwellers suffer from fatalism and excessive individualism, others are capable of sophisticated political organization and tough bargaining with the state. On the other hand, the poor rarely engage in the kind of revolutionary activity, violent upheavals, or radical politics that some political scientists had expected. During the 1980s, when living standards declined precipitously in much of the Third World, there was some increase in protest activity.[69] But the extent of rioting and social unrest remained surprisingly limited. Similarly, the slums of Bangkok have remained politically peaceful despite Thailand's current severe economic crisis. To be sure, the recent sharp decline in Indonesia's economy produced widespread urban rioting that toppled the Sukarno dictatorship in 1998. But it was university students, not the poor, who demonstrated against the government. Jakarta's slum dwellers more often vented their anger, instead, against the affluent Chinese minority.

Radical Political Behavior

While most of the Third World's urban poor have favored moderate and pragmatic forms of political expression, there have been important exceptions. In some countries, such as Chile in the early 1970s and Peru in the 1980s, they have voted in substantial numbers for Marxist political candidates. And in a few cases, urban slum and shantytown dwellers have been important players in revolutionary upheavals. In 1970, Salvador Allende, candidate of Chile's leftist Popular Unity (UP) coalition, became the developing world's first democratically elected Marxist president. Allende received considerable electoral support in the *campamentos* (squatter settlements) that ring the capital city of Santiago. In addition, a number of *campamentos* were organized by the UP or by the MIR (Leftist Revolutionary Movement), a movement to the left of the UP that periodically engaged in armed action.[70] In 1983, the poor of Lima played a major role in electing a Marxist mayor, Alfonso Barrantes. These examples, as well as the Communist Party's electoral successes in several Indian cities, indicate that the poor do support radical political parties under certain circumstances. Those parties must have a realistic chance of winning at the local or national level and, with it, the possibility of delivering benefits to their supporters. Thus, even radical voting is often based on very pragmatic calculations. Not long after supporting Barrantes for mayor, Lima's poor rejected him for the post of national president, seeing even his moderate Marxism as not viable at the national level.[71]

More often, the urban poor are attracted to charismatic populists (left- or right-wing) such as the current president of Venezuela, Hugo Chávez. Squatters or slum dwellers are even less likely to embrace urban guerrillas or other revolutionary movements. Teodoro Petkoff, a former leader of the Venezuelan communists' urban guerrilla wing in the early 1960s, noted that even residents of Caracas's poor barrios who belonged to leftist unions rejected the guerrillas. Blue-collar workers often elected communist union representatives in those days, Petkoff observed, because they felt that union militants would deliver more at the bargaining table. But when it came to voting for national office, Caracas's poor were more prone to support the two mainstream parties (Social Democrats and Christian Democrats) or even the former right-wing dictator, all of whom had a better track record of delivering rewards to their supporters.[72] Talton Ray's study of barrio politics explains why residents were unlikely to support the armed insurrection of the Armed Forces of National Liberation (Fuerza Armada de Liberación Nacional/FALN):

> The FALN's urban guerrilla warfare proved to be a grave tactical error . . . [creating a] mood of revulsion . . . in the barrios. Terrorist activities struck much too close to home. . . . Almost all of the murdered policemen [killed by the FALN] were barrio residents.[73]

More recently, Peru's *Sendero Luminoso* (Shining Path) guerrillas had some success in the shantytowns of Lima. However, in view of Sendero's terror and intimidation tactics against both the peasantry and the urban poor, there is every reason to believe that the group inspired more fear and acquiescence than support. When the popular vice-mayor of one of Peru's largest and most radical shantytowns, Villa El Salvador, tried to keep the Shining Path out of her community, she was brutally assassinated. In any event, Sendero activists in both the countryside and urban slums have more often been students and teachers, rather than the poor themselves.

This is not to suggest that the urban poor never support revolutions. Josef Gugler notes that during the second half of the twentieth century, in four of the Third World's revolutions—Bolivia, Cuba, Iran, and Nicaragua—the cities played a central role.[74] However, in all but Nicaragua, where the urban poor's mass demonstrations were crucial, social classes other than the very poor took the lead in the cities: miners, blue-collar workers, artisans, the lower-middle class, and the national police in Bolivia; students and university graduates in Cuba; theological students and petroleum workers in Iran. In contrast, Douglas Butterworth's study of the former inhabitants of a Havana slum, *Las Yaguas*, found that most were barely aware of Fidel Castro's existence during his rise to power.[75]

CONCLUSION: FUTURE URBAN GROWTH AND DEMOCRATIC POLITICS

While the rate of Third World urbanization has slowed somewhat, absolute increases in city populations will be greater than ever in the coming decades (Table 7.2). Thus, governments will have to heed urban needs, including those of the poor. Still, even with the best-intentioned public policies, developing economies will be hard pressed to provide sufficient jobs, housing, sanitation, and social services. Economic crises such as Latin America's and Africa's in the 1980s and East Asia's in the late 1990s have made the task all the more difficult. Urban crime, pollution, and AIDS will add tremendously to the burdens on the political-economic systems.

Given the current weakness of the radical Left, however, and the tendency of the poor to engage in adaptive behavior, urban discontent is more likely to express itself in occasional rioting than in mass insurrection or revolution. Perhaps the one exception may be in the Middle East, where the urban poor and perhaps the middle class may turn to Islamic fundamentalism, as many have already done in Iran, Algeria, and Egypt. It is worth noting that Turkey's large fundamentalist party receives its greatest support from recently arrived urban migrants. Elsewhere, crime and drug usage are more likely than radical politics to threaten stability in the proximate future. In the long run, Third World governments may be able to cope with these problems if they can generate sustained economic growth. In the short term, however, the possibility of increased state repression persists in many countries as the military and middle class become fearful of urban crime and disorder.

I have noted previously that poor urban neighborhoods generally receive more government assistance from democratic governments than from authoritarian ones. In countries where there has been an enduring transition to democracy, the urban poor will have to refine their strategies for securing state resources. By the same token, if newly democratic governments are to endure, they will need to become more responsive to the poor and more cognizant of the vast inequalities that plague Third World cities. Studies of urban slums and shantytowns generally suggest that while the poor are not as radical or even potentially radical as once thought, they are not necessarily committed to democratic values either. Democratic governments will have to prove to them that they are as helpful as prior authoritarian regimes. And political institutions of all kinds need to spread democratic cultural values.

DISCUSSION QUESTIONS

1. How have Third World governments been involved in providing urban housing? To what extent have such efforts benefited or hurt the urban poor?
2. Describe the advantages and limitations of spontaneous housing. In what ways are sites-and-services programs an improvement over spontaneous housing? Are there disadvantages to sites-and-services programs?

3. Discuss the political orientations of the urban poor.
4. Discuss the role of clientelism or patron-client relationships in the politics of the urban poor.
5. Is rapid urban growth (linked to migration) beneficial or harmful for developing democratic government?

NOTES

1. Stella Lowder, *The Geography of Third World Cities* (New York: Barnes and Noble, 1986), p. 19.

2. Sally Findley, "The Third World City," in *Third World Cities*, ed. John Kasarda and Allan Parnell (Newbury Park, CA: Sage Publications, 1993), pp. 14–16.

3. R. A. Obudho, "Urbanization and Urban Development Strategies in East Africa," in *Urban Management*, ed. G. Shabbir Cheema (New York: Praeger, 1993), figures extrapolated from Table 4.2, p. 84.

4. Cheema, "The Challenge of Urban Management," in *Urban Management*, p. 2.

5. David Drakakis-Smith, *Urbanization, Housing and the Development Process* (New York: St. Martin's Press, 1980), p. 6; Samuel Preston, "Urban Growth in Developing Countries," in *The Urbanization of the Third World*, ed. Josef Gugler (New York: Oxford University Press, 1988), pp. 14–15, using earlier data, indicates a higher percentage of increase due to natural growth; Findley, "The Third World City," p. 15, using more recent data, indicates a higher percentage of increase due to migration.

6. Obudho, "Urbanization and Urban Development Strategies," p. 84.

7. Alan Gilbert and Josef Gugler, *Cities, Poverty and Development*, 2d ed. (New York: Oxford University Press, 1992).

8. John V. Graumann, "Orders of Magnitude of the World's Urban and Rural Population in History," *United Nations Population Bulletin* 8 (1977): 16–33, quoted in Preston, "Urban Growth," p. 12.

9. Raymond Owens, "Peasant Entrepreneurs in an Industrial City," in *A Reader in Urban Sociology*, ed. M. S. A. Rao, Chandrashekar Bhat, and Laxmi Narayan Kadekar (New Delhi, India: Oriental Longman, 1991), p. 235.

10. Manuel Castells and Alejandro Portes, "World Underneath: The Origins, Dynamics and Effects of the Informal Economy," in *The Informal Economy: Studies in Advanced and Developing Economies*, ed. Alejandro Portes, Manuel Castells, and Lauren A. Benton (Baltimore, MD: Johns Hopkins University Press, 1989), p. 12.

11. Om Prakash Mathur, "Managing the Urban Informal Sector," in *Urban Management*, p. 179. The data are drawn from International Labor Organization (ILO) studies.

12. Gilbert and Gugler, *Cities, Poverty and Development*, p. 98. Gugler argues that the composition of the informal economy is so diverse that it is not clear whether it can really be referred to as a single sector.

13. Alejandro Portes et al., "The Informal Sector in Uruguay," *World Development* 14 (1986), pp. 727–741.

14. Hernando de Soto, *The Other Path* (New York: Harper & Row, 1989), translated from the Spanish edition.

15. Dennis Rondinelli and John Kasarda, "Job Creation Needs in Third World Cities," in *Third World Cities*, pp. 92–120.

16. Macroeconomic policy will be discussed in far greater detail in Chapter 10. The reader wishing to better understand the economic analysis offered briefly in this section is referred to that chapter.

17. Stephan Haggard, *Pathways from the Periphery* (Ithaca, NY: Cornell University Press, 1990).

18. Richard Sandbrook, *The Politics of African Economic Recovery* (New York: Cambridge University Press, 1993), pp. 60–61.

19. *New York Times,* October 27, 1993.

20. While squatter settlements or shantytowns can accurately be called poor neighborhoods, not everyone living in them is poor. Data from Istanbul, Rio, Caracas, and elsewhere show that some shantytown residents are white-collar workers or well-paid blue collars. Some better-off residents live there because rents elsewhere are too high. Others have enjoyed upward mobility since settling there but stay because of attachments to friends and community.

21. Statistics in the preceding paragraphs come from Om P. Mathur, "forward" in Kamlesh Misra, *Housing the Poor in Third World Cities* (New Delhi, India: Concept Publishing Company, 1992), pp. 6–8; Gilbert and Gugler, *Cities, Poverty and Development,* p. 115.

22. Fred Ward, *Inside Cuba Today* (New York: Crown, 1978), pp. 36–38.

23. Howard Handelman, "The Role of the State in Sheltering the Urban Poor," in *Spontaneous Shelter,* ed. Carl V. Patton (Philadelphia: Temple University Press, 1988), pp. 332–333.

24. Richard Stern, "Urban Housing in Africa: The Changing Role of Government Policy," in *Housing Africa's Urban Poor,* ed. Philip Amis and Peter Lloyd (Manchester, England: Manchester University Press, 1990), pp. 36–39.

25. Diana Patel, "Government Policy and Squatter Settlements in Harare, Zimbabwe," in *Slum and Squatter Settlements in Sub-Saharan Africa,* ed. R. A. Obudho and Constance Mhlanga (New York: Praeger, 1988), pp. 205–217.

26. Handelman, "The Role of the State," p. 339.

27. Some experts call Cuba's construction of microbrigade housing (houses built by teams of worker volunteers) self-help. But they are built by groups under state direction who don't design the homes and don't conform to much of the self-help model discussed later in the chapter.

28. Gilbert and Gugler, *Cities, Poverty and Development,* p. 139.

29. Susan Eckstein, *The Poverty of Revolution: The State and the Urban Poor in Mexico,* 2d ed. (Princeton, NJ: Princeton University Press, 1988); Henry Dietz, *Poverty and Problem Solving Under Military Rule* (Austin: University of Texas Press, 1980), p. 41; Howard Handelman, *High-Rises and Shantytowns* (Hanover, NH: American University Field Staff, 1979), p. 17; B. Sanyal, "A Critical Look at the Housing Subsidies in Zambia," *Development and Change* 12 (1981): 409–440.

30. David Collier, *Squatters and Oligarchs* (Baltimore, MD: Johns Hopkins University Press, 1976).

31. Gilbert and Gugler, *Cities, Poverty and Development,* p. 123.

32. Alan Gilbert and Peter Ward, *Housing, the State, and the Poor* (New York: Cambridge University Press, 1985), pp. 86–87.

33. Diana Lee-Smith, "Squatter Landlords in Nairobi," in *Housing Africa's Urban Poor,* p. 177; Douglas Butterworth and John Chance, *Latin American Urbanization* (New York: Cambridge University Press, 1981), p. 147; Collier, *Squatters and Oligarchs,* pp. 27–28.

34. John F. C. Turner, "Barriers and Channels for Housing Development in Modernizing Countries," *Journal of the American Institute of Planners* 33 (May 1967): 167–181; John F. C. Turner and Robert Fichter, eds., *Freedom to Build* (New York: Macmillan, 1972); see also William Mangin, "Latin American Squatter Settlements: A Problem and a Solution," *Latin American Research Review* 2, no. 3 (1967): 65–98.

35. Gilbert and Gugler, *Cities, Poverty and Development,* pp. 117–130; Carl Patton, "Prospects for the Future," in *Spontaneous Shelter,* pp. 348–355.

36. Handelman, "The Role of the State," p. 328.

37. Peter Nientied and Jan van der Linden, "Approaches to Low-Income Housing in the Third World," in *The Urbanization of the Third World*, pp. 138–156; R. Burgess, "Petty Commodity Housing or Dweller Control? A Critique of John Turner's Views on Housing Policy," *World Development* 6 (1978): 1105–1133.

38. Handelman, *High-Rises and Shantytowns*; A. A. Laquian, "Whither Site and Services," *Habitat* 2 (1977): 291–301; Thomas Pennant, "The Growth of Small-Scale Renting in Low-Income Housing in Malawi," in *Housing Africa's Urban Poor*, pp. 196–200.

39. Ernest Alexander, "Informal Settlement in Latin America and Its Policy Implication," in *Spontaneous Shelter*, pp. 131–133; Drakakis-Smith, *Urbanization, Housing and the Development Process*, pp. 141–142; Jorge Hardoy and David Satterthwaite, *Shelter, Need and Response* (New York: John Wiley, 1981); Lisa Peattie, "Some Second Thoughts on Sites-and-Services," *Habitat International* 6 (Winter 1982): 131–139.

40. Gilbert and Ward, *Housing, the State and the Poor*.

41. Joan Nelson, *Access to Power* (Princeton, NJ: Princeton University Press, 1979), chap. 4; Howard Handelman, "The Political Mobilization of Urban Squatter Settlements," *Latin American Research Review* 10, no. 2 (1975): 35–72; Gilbert and Gugler, *Cities, Poverty and Development*, chap. 7.

42. James Coleman, "Conclusion: The Political Systems of Developing Nations," in *The Politics of Developing Areas*, ed. Gabriel Almond and James Coleman (Princeton, NJ: Princeton University Press, 1960), p. 537. Anomic activity is action not governed by social practices and values.

43. Samuel Huntington, *Political Order in Changing Societies* (New Haven, CT: Yale University Press, 1968), p. 283.

44. Barbara Ward, "Creating Man's Future Goals for a World of Plenty," *Saturday Review* 9 (August 1964): 192.

45. Joan Nelson, *Migrants, Urban Poverty, and Instability in Developing Nations* (Cambridge: MA: AMS Press and the Harvard University Center for International Affairs, 1969), pp. 18–20; Eckstein, *The Poverty of Revolution*, p. 41.

46. Gilbert and Ward, *Housing, the State and the Poor*, p. 215.

47. Ibid., pp. 57–61.

48. Oscar Lewis, *The Children of Sanchez* (New York: Random House, 1961), and *La Vida* (New York: Random House, 1966).

49. Jorge Giusti, "Organizational Characteristics of the Latin American Urban Marginal Settler," *International Journal of Politics* 1, no. 1 (1971): 57.

50. Bryan R. Roberts, *Organizing Strangers: Poor Families in Guatemala City* (Austin: University of Texas Press, 1973), p. 299.

51. Alejandro Portes and John Walton, *Urban Latin America* (Austin: University of Texas Press, 1976), p. 108.

52. Janice Perlman, *The Myth of Marginality* (Berkeley: University of California Press, 1976); William Mangin, "The Role of Regional Associations in the Adaptation of Rural Migrants to Cities in Peru," in *Contemporary Cultures and Societies of Latin America*, ed. Dwight Heath and Richard Adams (New York: Random House, 1974).

53. Karl Deutsch, "Social Mobilization and Political Development," *American Political Science Review* 55 (September 1961): 493–514; Daniel Lerner, *The Passing of Traditional Society* (Glencoe, IL: Free Press, 1958).

54. Of course, even in highly educated industrial democracies such as the United States, many citizens are also apolitical. Moreover, that political apathy extends to members of the middle class.

55. Gilbert and Gugler, *Cities, Poverty and Development*, pp. 180–187; S. N. Eisenstadt and L. Roninger, *Patrons, Clients and Friends* (New York: Cambridge University Press, 1984).

56. A. Bank, "Poverty, Politics and the Shaping of Urban Space: A Brazilian Example," *International Journal of Urban and Regional Research* 10, no. 4 (1986): 523.

57. Collier, *Squatters and Oligarchs*, p. 41.

58. Ibid., p. 44.

59. Dietz, *Poverty and Problem-Solving under Military Rule.*

60. Wayne Cornelius, *Politics and the Urban Poor in Mexico* (Stanford, CA: Stanford University Press, 1975); Gilbert and Ward, *Housing, the State and the Poor*, pp. 189–196.

61. Eckstein, *The Poverty of Revolution*, chap. 3.

62. Frans Schuurman and Ton van Naerssen, *Urban Social Movements in the Third World* (New York: Routledge, 1989).

63. Turner, "Barriers and Channels."

64. Joop de Wit, "Clientelism, Competition and Poverty: The Ineffectiveness of Local Organizations in a Madras Slum," in ibid., pp. 63–90.

65. Jan van der Linden, "The Limits of Territorial Social Movements: The Case of Housing in Karachi," in *Urban Social Movements*, p. 101.

66. Gilbert and Ward, *Housing, the State and the Poor*, p. 175.

67. Marxist governments often redistribute significant resources to the poor soon after taking power. However, with the notable exception of China, leftist regimes generally have a poor record of economic growth. In Nicaragua, for example, the urban poor benefited initially from Sandinista welfare programs but then saw their standard of living deteriorate sharply due to the U.S.-backed Contra war as well as to poor economic management by the Sandinistas. In other revolutions, such as Cuba's, China's, or Vietnam's, where counterrevolutionary activity has been less extreme, experts differ sharply regarding how the urban poor have fared in the long run.

68. Vivien Bennet, "The Evolution of Popular Movements in Mexico Between 1968 and 1988," in *The Making of Social Movements in Latin America*, ed. Arturo Escobar and Sonia Alvarez (Boulder, CO: Westview Press, 1992); Menno Vellinga, "Power and Independence: The Struggle for Identity and Integrity in Urban Social Movements," in *Urban Social Movements*, pp. 151–176.

69. Susan Eckstein, *Urbanization Revisited: Inner-City Slum of Hope and Squatter Settlement of Despair* (Storrs: University of Connecticut and Brown University Occasional Papers in Latin American Studies, 1989), p. 14.

70. Handelman, "The Political Mobilization of Urban Squatter Settlements: Santiago's Recent Experience," *Latin American Research Review* 10, no. 2 (1975): 35–72.

71. Henry Dietz, "Political Participation in the Barriadas: An Extension and Reexamination," *Comparative Political Studies* 18, no. 3 (1985): 323–355.

72. My own conversations with Petkoff in 1976 and 1978. Petkoff left the Communist Party to help found a democratically oriented Marxist party called MAS. He was subsequently elected to Congress on the MAS ticket and in the late 1990s held a powerful cabinet position.

73. Talton Ray, *The Politics of the Barrios of Venezuela* (Berkeley: University of California Press, 1969), pp. 132–133.

74. Josef Gugler, "The Urban Character of Contemporary Revolutions," in *The Urbanization of the Third World*, pp. 399–412.

75. Douglas Butterworth, *The People of Buena Ventura* (Urbana: University of Illinois Press, 1980), pp. 19–20.

chapter 8

Revolutionary Change

Revolutions, however one may be tempted to define them, are not mere changes.[1]

The opening decades of the twentieth century ushered in the Mexican and Russian revolutions. The closing decades witnessed the collapse of Soviet communism, the transformation of the Chinese and Mexican revolutions, and the weakening of Cuba's revolutionary government.[2] No era in world history has encompassed more revolutionary upheaval. Yet as the twenty-first century begins, the force that had once promised, or threatened, to transform the face of the Third World appears to be spent, at least for the time being.

Karl Marx, the foremost prophet of revolution, expected these upheavals to take place in industrialized European nations where the organized working class would rise up against the oppressive capitalist system. Instead, modern revolutionary movements have been largely a Third World phenomenon, fought primarily by the peasantry. And even Europe's internally generated communist revolutions—Russia and Yugoslavia—occurred in countries where capitalism and industrialization were relatively underdeveloped. The remaining communist regimes in Eastern Europe were installed by Soviet military intervention, not through indigenous uprisings.

In the Third World, the appeal of revolutionary change has been its promise of rapid and sweeping solutions to the problems of underdevelopment. It pledged to end colonial rule, terminate dependency, protect national sovereignty, reduce social and economic inequalities, accelerate economic development, mobilize the population, and transform the political culture. Not surprisingly, many of the LDCs' poor and oppressed, along with numerous intellectuals and alienated members of the middle class, have found revolutionary platforms and ideologies quite appealing.

Some revolutionary governments—in China, Cuba, and Mexico, for example—were able to deliver on a number of their promises. Under Mao Zedong's leadership, the Chinese Communist Party redistributed land to the peasantry, industrialized the economy, and transformed the country into a world power. Fidel Castro's government implemented extensive land reform, a vast adult literacy campaign, and significant public health programs. Mexico's revolutionary party reestablished national sovereignty over the country's natural resources, initiated agrarian reform, and transformed the nation into a Third World industrial power.

Often, however, these gains have come at great cost, including political repression, considerable human suffering, and rampant corruption. As a result of their revolution, the Chinese people now enjoy far better medical care, more education, and better living conditions than ever before. At the same time, however, some thirty million people starved to death in the 1950s due to the mistaken experiments of Mao's Great Leap Forward. Millions more suffered humiliation, imprisonment, or death (for some 400,000 people) during the ultra-radical period called the Cultural Revolution (1966 to 1976). Most communist governments have had their *gulags* for real and imagined political opponents. In Vietnam, many suspected dissidents were sent to "reeducation" camps, and in Cuba a smaller, but still significant, number were imprisoned.

In the most unfortunate cases—Angola, Mozambique, Kampuchea (Cambodia)—huge portions of the population died as the result of civil war or the regime's brutality, with little or nothing positive to show for it.[3] In Kampuchea, the fanatical Khmer Rouge government killed more than a million people, including much of the country's educated class, while accomplishing nothing for its people. Over the years, even some of the more idealistic revolutionary regimes were transformed into corrupt bureaucracies, run by a new generation of opportunistic *apparatchiks* (party or government bureaucrats) who had never risked anything for the revolution's ideals.

After examining the meaning of revolution and classifying different types of twentieth-century revolutions, this chapter will discuss the causes of revolutionary upheavals, their principal sources of leadership and support, and the policy objectives of their leaders once in power.

DEFINING REVOLUTION

Scholars have argued endlessly about what constitutes a revolution and whether particular upheavals such as the American Revolution or Iran's Islamic Revolution were, in fact, true social revolutions.[4] Thus, Chalmers Johnson notes, "half the battle will lie in answering the question, 'What is revolution?'"[5] In its broadest and least precise usage, the term is applied to any nonlegal, nondemocratic, or violent overthrow of government. Peter Calvert offers perhaps the most open-ended definition when he maintains that revolution is "simply a form of governmental change through violence."[6] Such a definition, however, seems too loose since it encompasses military coups and other upheavals that do little more than change the heads of government. Most scholars insist on a more rigorous definition, arguing that revolutions must involve fundamental political, economic, and social change. Samuel P. Huntington has suggested:

> A revolution is a rapid, fundamental, and violent domestic change in the dominant values and myths of society, in its political institutions, social structure, leadership and government activity and policies. Revolutions are thus to be distinguished from insurrections, revolts, coups and wars of independence.[7]

Unfortunately, the distinctions that Huntington proposes in the last sentence are not always easily made. For example, many "wars of independence" (sometimes called "wars of national liberation") such as Algeria's and Angola's are generally considered authentic social revolutions because they ushered in fundamental societal change.[8] On the other hand, Theda Skocpol accepts Huntington's starting definition but narrows it by claiming that "social revolutions are accompanied and in part effectuated through [massive] class upheavals."[9] She adds:

> Social revolutions are set apart from other sorts of conflicts . . . by the combination of two coincidences: the coincidence of societal structural change with class upheaval; and the coincidence of the political with social transformation.[10]

Skocpol concedes that according to her more restrictive, class-based definition, only "a handful of successful social revolutions have ever occurred." The most clear-cut cases are the three she has studied in great detail: France (1789), Russia (1917), and China (1911 to 1949). Other, less restrictive definitions of revolution would apply to Mexico, Bolivia, Cuba, Nicaragua, Algeria, Ethiopia, Mozambique, Angola, Eritrea, Vietnam, Cambodia, Turkey, and Iran, among others. What is common to all of them is that insurgency brought sweeping changes to the country's political, economic, and social systems.

It is because revolutions involve a fundamental transfer of political and economic power, rather than a mere change in political leaders (as is the case in most military coups), that they are invariably violent. Not surprisingly, government officials and social classes that have long held (and often abused) power and that now face uncertain futures normally fight bitterly to stay on top. Should the revolutionaries triumph, old elites will be removed from power, new ones will be installed, and at least in some respects, there will be a broadening of political, economic, and social participation to include those further down the social ladder. This does not imply that revolutionary governments are democratic. They virtually never are. But they are usually more broadly participatory and egalitarian than the regimes that they toppled.

I classify as a revolution any insurgency that brings about these kinds of comprehensive political and socioeconomic changes. The upheaval may be rooted in class struggles (China and Nicaragua), as Skocpol insists, or, contrary to Huntington, it may be a war of national liberation (Algeria and Angola), as long as it overturns critical political and economic institutions and changes the country's underlying power structure. In fact, the borderline between national-ist and class-based revolutions is often difficult to discern. The Vietnamese rev-olution most clearly combined anticolonial and class struggle.[11] But even primarily class-based revolutions, such as China's, Mexico's, Cuba's, and Nicaragua's, had important nationalist, anti-imperialist components to them.

Revolutions may be Marxist (China, Russia, Vietnam, Kampuchea, and Cuba), partially Marxist (Nicaragua), or non-Marxist (Mexico, Bolivia, Libya, and Iran). Marxism was particularly appealing to many revolutionaries because it promised the redistribution of economic resources, the ideological rigor, and the new set of political myths that they sought. But the revolution-ary's vision of social justice need not be tied to communism. It may also come from nationalism, Islam, or a number of other ideologies or religions.

Revolutions generally come to power either through mass uprisings fea-turing strikes, protest marches, and street riots (Russia, Bolivia, and Iran), or through guerrilla warfare (China, Vietnam, and Cuba), or through a combina-tion of both (Nicaragua). There have also been a few elite revolutions in which military officers or upper-level bureaucrats have overthrown the regime and instituted far-reaching socioeconomic changes that far transcended the objec-tives of mere coups.[12] Primary examples include Mustafa Kemal Ataturk's revolt in Turkey in 1919, Gamal Abdel Nasser's officers' revolt in Egypt in 1952, and Peru's "revolution from above" in 1968, all led by progressive military offi-cers (see Chapter 9).

UNDERLYING CAUSES OF REVOLUTION

Just as experts have failed to agree on a common definition of revolution, they have also been divided on the causes of revolutionary insurrection. Some theo-ries focus on broad historical trends, including changes in the world order that their proponents believe make revolution likely or even inevitable. Other explanations center on weaknesses in the *ancien régime* (the outgoing political system), examining factors that caused the prerevolutionary state to fall. And yet others focus on the major players in Third World revolutions, particularly the peasantry, seeking the factors that cause them to revolt.

Inexorable Historical Forces

Karl Marx viewed revolution as an unstoppable historical force growing out of class inequalities that are rooted in the unequal ownership of the means of pro-duction. Those who command the economic system, he argued, control the state as well. Over time, however, subordinate classes will become alienated from the political-economic system and will attain sufficient political skills and vision (class consciousness) to overthrow the existing order. Thus, Marx maintained, the 1640 British Revolution (or Civil War) and the French Revolution (1789) were each led by the ascendent *bourgeoisie* (property owners, including capitalists) who toppled the old order controlled by the aristocracy and landed oligarchy. Both revolutions were part of a broader European transition from agrarian feudalism to industrial capitalism. Although Marx believed that this new capitalist order presented a more advanced and more productive historical stage, he maintained that it depended on the exploitation of the working class (proletariat). In time, he predicted, as the exploitation of the proletariat became more apparent and as workers developed sufficient class consciousness, they would eventually overthrow capitalism and install revolutionary socialism.[13]

More than any other revolutionary theorist, Marx influenced the course of history, since most of the twentieth century's major revolutionary leaders—including V. I. Lenin, Mao Zedong, Ho Chi Minh, Ché Guevara, and Fidel Castro—believed fervently in his ideology. His writings evoked the centrality of class struggle in most revolutionary movements. But as even sympathetic analysts have noted, "He was, first and foremost a nineteenth-century man" whose ideology was closely linked to the era in which he lived.[14] "Marx's theoretical approach," wrote one contemporary Marxist sociologist, "enabled him to explain the past but failed him in his predictions."[15] Indeed, *no* country has ever had the succession of revolutions that he predicted, first capitalist, then socialist.[16] Instead, the major locus of modern revolution has been the Third World—not advanced capitalist nations—and the major protagonists have been peasants rather than industrial workers.

Mao Zedong, the father of the Chinese Revolution, accepted Marx's view of revolution as part of a historical dialectic.[17] Like other Third World Marxists, he viewed capitalist exploitation and the resulting class conflict as the root cause of communist upheavals. However, the Chinese Communist Party's military defeats in the 1920s convinced him that its orthodox commitment to proletariat revolution was not viable in a country in which the working class constituted such a small percentage of the population. Consequently, he reinterpreted Marxist revolutionary strategy to make it more applicable to China and other parts of the developing world. Mao developed a theory of peasant-based struggle and a military strategy designed to encircle and conquer China's cities following a period of protracted rural guerrilla conflict.[18] The success of his strategy in the world's most populous country and its widespread application elsewhere in the Third World made Mao the most influential twentieth-century practitioner of revolutionary warfare.

In Vietnam and Cuba, Ho Chi Minh and Ché Guevara refined Mao's vision of "peoples' war" to make it more compatible with conditions in Southeast Asia and Latin America. While all of them demonstrated that communist revolutions could take place in countries that are not highly industrialized (Cuba came closest to Marx's ideal), they still adhered to Marx's theory of history and his vision of class struggle.

Regime Decay

Even before the collapse of the Soviet bloc, it had become obvious that there was no *inevitable* march toward revolution and that, in fact, successful revolutions are rather rare and unique. Theta Skocpol argues that neither the repression of the masses nor the skills of revolutionary leadership alone can bring about successful social revolutions. These factors may be necessary, but they are not sufficient. Rather, true revolutions succeed only when the state is undermined by international pressures such as war, economic competition, or an arms race. Modernization of Britain and other European powers, she contends, created severe military and economic pressures on less developed countries within and outside Europe. Some of those states, such as royalist France, czarist Russia, and imperial China, were less able to adjust to these challenges and, hence, became more susceptible to revolutionary challenges.[19]

In the Russian case, excessive military entanglements, foreign indebtedness, and a disastrous entry into World War I undermined the czarist state. Successive military defeats in two wars—first by the Japanese (1905) and then by the Germans (1917)—did in the regime. Similarly, China's Manchu dynasty, having been fatally weakened first by European and then Japanese imperialism, was toppled easily by Guomindang (Nationalist) forces in 1911. Elsewhere, stronger regimes were able to withstand comparable challenges, but the Russian and Chinese states were too weak to marshal sufficient economic and military resources. Ultimately, peasant rebels led by "marginal elites" (university students and middle-class professionals alienated from the system) toppled the old order.[20] Ironically, just as military competition undermined the czarist government and set the stage for the Russian Revolution, some 70 years later the Soviet-American arms race weakened the Soviet Union and contributed to its collapse.

Thus, Skocpol and others have argued that the primary factor contributing to revolutionary transformation is not the revolutionaries' strategy, tactics, or zeal, but rather the internal rot of the decaying old order. For example, Japan's invasion of China prior to World War II undercut the legitimacy of the Guomindang (Nationalist) government. The Japanese occupation demonstrated that the Nationalists were too corrupt and incompetent to resist a foreign threat, while the Chinese Communist Party's People's Liberation Army was far more effective in that regard. When the Chinese revolutionary war resumed after World War II, many of the areas in which the communists won major military victories were the same ones in which they had organized mass resistance against the Japanese.[21]

In fact, military defeats have frequently delegitimatized the regime in power, setting the stage for subsequent revolutions. Thus, the destruction of the Ottoman empire in World War I and the Japanese capture of British, French, and Dutch colonies in Asia (Burma, Vietnam, and Indonesia) during World War II all undermined the imperial or colonial governments and led, respectively, to the "Young Turks" military revolt in Turkey and independence movements in South and Southeast Asia.[22] Similarly, Egypt's defeat in a war with Israel (1948–1949) helped precipitate Colonel Nasser's revolution from above.

War has the additional effect of disrupting peasant life, forcing many of them to seek physical protection and a new social structure from the revolutionary forces. For example, in accounts of life in rural China during its civil war and the Japanese invasion, "one is struck by the number of peasants . . . who had their routines upset through the [war-related] death of their kin before they joined revolutionary organizations."[23]

But governments may be undermined by factors other than military defeat. In Cuba and Nicaragua, prolonged dictatorships became obscenely corrupt. Fulgencio Batista rose from the rank of army sergeant in 1933 to become Cuba's dominant political actor over the next two decades. Under his administration and those of others he dominated, corruption infested all ranks of government. Batista's links to the American mafia helped turn Havana into a playground for affluent tourists seeking gambling and prostitution. For decades, members of the ruling Somoza dynasty commandeered a huge share of Nicaragua's economy, while their personal army, the National Guard, engaged in petty graft like intercepting and selling United States relief supplies sent after the nation's capital (Managua) was leveled by an earthquake.

A further factor undermining the legitimacy of both dictatorships was their subservience to the United States and their breach of national pride. Because both countries that had been occupied for years by the American military early in the twentieth century and had subsequently remained in the American sphere of influence, this was a particularly sensitive issue. Nicaragua's hated National Guard was first headed by Anastasio Somoza, Sr., during the U.S. Marine occupation. Decades later, in the years preceding their revolution, Nicaraguans derisively referred to President Anastasio Somoza, Jr., a graduate of West Point, as "the last Marine." In both Cuba and Nicaragua, the combination of rampant corruption and blatant affronts to nationalist sensibilities united people across classes lines—from peasants to students to businesspeople—against the government. Lacking any real commitment to the regime, Batista's undisciplined army offered surprisingly little resistance to Fidel Castro's rather small guerrilla force. In Nicaragua, the National Guardsmen, knowing that they faced popular retribution if they lost power, put up a stronger fight against the Sandinista revolutionaries but also fell relatively quickly.[24]

Revolutionary opportunities may also develop when the economy deteriorates, standards of living decline, and the government is unable to meet longstanding economic responsibilities to its population. For example, support for China's Guomindang government was eroded by runaway inflation. Declining living standards helped spark the Kenyan rebellion against British colonialism. Thus, maintains Charles Tilly, one cause of revolution is "the sudden failure of government to meet specific obligations which members of the subject population regarded as well established and crucial to their welfare."[25]

While Skocpol, Tilly, and others emphasize the decay of state authority at the *national* level, revolutions can also be linked to the breakdown of authority at the *grass-roots* level. We observed earlier (Chapter 6) that a web of patron-client relationships linking peasants to their landlords and other local power brokers helps maintain stability in the countryside. Peasants will tolerate considerable injustice if the local landlord or the village political boss compensates by providing villagers with needed benefits: secure access to land, credit, protection from the police, and the like. However, if the expansion of market forces makes rural patrons unwilling or unable to continue providing benefits that peasants had come to expect, then their authority will likely break down. At this point, the state may try to replace the traditional patrons by providing social services such as credit, technical assistance, schools, and clinics. If, however, government authorities also fail to satisfy the peasants' needs, the rural poor may turn to revolutionary groups as their new patrons and protectors.

Challenge from Below

While revolutionary movements generally succeed only against discredited or weakened governments, they must also mount a well-organized and politically coherent challenge from below. Without that, the old regime, weak though it may be, will either cling to power (the Third World has many incompetent and discredited governments that linger on) or the society may collapse into disorder or even anarchy.

Charles Tilly contends that three things must happen before a revolutionary movement can succeed: First, the revolutionaries must establish themselves as an "alternative sovereignty"; that is, the rebel leadership must convince its would-be supporters that it can function as a viable alternative government. Second, significant portions of the population must support that revolutionary alternative. Finally, the established government must be unable to suppress the revolutionary opposition.[26] Following the collapse of Russia's czarist regime, the Bolsheviks (Communist Party) established a network of workers' soviets (local political committees) to challenge the sovereignty of Alexander Karensky's moderate provisional government. Asia's protracted guerrilla wars also illustrate the phenomenon of alternative sovereignties. During the Chinese Revolution, the People's Liberation Army (the Communist Party's military arm) controlled "liberated zones" in which the communists distributed land to the peasants, organized support, and demonstrated their ability to govern. The same was true of South Vietnam's National Liberation Front (Viet Cong).

Knowing these broad preconditions for successful revolutionary activity, we still must ask what causes a revolution to break out in a particular place and time? Samuel Huntington maintains that the probability of a successful insurrection is determined by the balance of power between the capabilities of government political institutions, on the one hand, and the level of anti-government political and social mobilization, on the other. Most revolutions, he notes, occur neither in highly traditional societies nor in very modern ones. Rather, they are most likely to erupt in modernizing countries—those in transition from traditional culture to modernity.[27] As greater urbanization, increased education and literacy, and expanded mass media communication stimulate mass political mobilization, civil society (the network of organized groups independent of government control) makes increased demands on the political system. Unless appropriate institutions capable of accommodating this increased political participation can be created in a timely fashion, the system will become overloaded and, hence, more unstable.

Huntington then distinguishes two distinct revolutionary patterns: a *Western* model in which "the political institutions of the old regime collapse . . . followed by the mobilization of new groups into politics and then by the creation of new [revolutionary] political institutions" (i.e., regime decay precedes a full challenge from below); and an *Eastern* revolutionary model that "begins with the mobilization of new groups into politics and the creation of new [revolutionary] political institutions and ends with the violent overthrow of the political institutions of the old order." The French, Russian, and Mexican revolutions fit the Western model, while communist revolutions in China and Vietnam followed the Eastern model.[28]

James C. Davies shifts attention from the broad historical-social forces that make revolution possible to the question of why particular individuals choose to join a revolt or a revolution. He asserts that, contrary to what we might expect, people rarely rebel when they are experiencing prolonged or permanent suffering. "Far from making people revolutionaries, enduring poverty makes for concern with one's solitary self or solitary family, at best a resignation, or mute despair at worst."[29] To uncover the source of political upheavals, Davies combines economic and psychological explanations. Unlike Marx, Skocpol, or Tilly, his analysis lumps mass revolutions together with local uprisings and military "revolutions from above." Drawing upon historical data ranging from Dorr's Rebellion (an 1842 uprising in Rhode Island) to the Egyptian military revolution of 1952, he concludes that each upheaval was preceded by a period of sustained economic growth followed by a sharp downturn. A diagram of that growth and subsequent downturn (Figure 8.1) produces what Davies called the "J-curve."[30] As a country's economy grows for a period of time, he suggests, people's expectations rise correspondingly (parallel to the long side of the J). However, those expectations continue to rise even after the economy enters a downturn. What emerges is "an intolerable gap between what people want and what they get."[31] Davies argues that the American and French revolutions, the American Civil War, the rise of German Naziism, student unrest in the United States during the 1960s, and the African-American civil rights movement can all be explained by economic J-curves as well.[32]

Using twentieth-century data from 17 LDCs, Raymond Tanter and Manus Midlarsky confirmed Davies's thesis in Asia and the Middle East but not in

FIGURE 8.1 Davies's Psychological Model Showing the Gap
Between People's Expectations and Economic Reality

Latin America. Interestingly, their Asian and Middle Eastern cases also indicated that the higher the rate of economic growth prior to a downturn and the
sharper the slide immediately preceding a revolution, the longer and more violent the upheaval will be.[33]

Davies's theory is one of the most influential, psychologically based explanations of revolutionary behavior. There is, however, an important limitation to
his findings. His conclusions were based entirely on countries in which revolts or
revolutions had taken place. That raises the question of whether there are countries that experienced a J-curve in their economies (growth followed by a downturn) yet did not have social upheavals. In fact, Davies admits that there are. For
example, he notes the absence of mass unrest in the United States during the
Great Depression, a devastating economic downturn. The same holds true for
many Latin American countries that enjoyed strong economic growth in the
1960s and 1970s followed by a precipitous decline in the 1980s. Argentina had a
comparable cycle in the 1990s to 2001. Thus, as Davies concedes, his theory iden-
tifies common but not sufficient conditions for unrest. Although a J-curve often
leads to revolution, it is not an inevitable predictor of mass insurrection.

Ted Gurr has also developed a psychological model examining the gap
between people's expectations and reality. Like Davies, he tries to explain all
types of civil violence, not just revolution. Gurr argues that "the necessary pre-
condition for violent civil conflict is relative deprivation defined as [the] actors'
perception of the discrepancy between their value expectations [i.e., what people believe they deserve from life] and value capabilities . . . conditions that
determine people's perceived chances of getting . . . what they . . . expect to
attain."[34] In other words, *relative deprivation* is the gap between what people
want or expect from life and what they actually get.

Unlike Davies's theory, however, Gurr's notion of relative deprivation is
not solely economic. Thus, he posits that there will be civil unrest if many people are deprived of something they have come to expect, or if they have suffered a blow to their status and their preferred social order. For example,

although Westerners admired the Shah of Iran's attempts to modernize the dress and status of Iranian women (removing the veil), many of these changes violated the "preferred social order" of the nation's Shi'ite majority. This, as we have seen, helped set the stage for the Islamist revolution. Furthermore, adds Gurr, the closer people are to attaining their goals, the greater will be their frustration if they fail to achieve them. Note, for example, the growing frustration of Palestinians as the peace process between Israelis and the PLO has seemingly broken down and with it their dreams of a Palestinian state.

Finally, Gurr maintains that the type of civil violence that a country experiences will depend on which segments of society are experiencing relative deprivation. If the poor alone feel frustrated, there may be political "turmoil" (spontaneous, disorganized violence) but not a revolution. Only if important portions of the middle class and the elite—more educated and politically experienced individuals who can provide political leadership—also suffer relative deprivation can there be revolutionary upheaval (organized, instrumental violence).

Causes of Revolution: A Summary

None of the theories of revolution discussed above offers a single "correct" explanation. For one thing, they often focus on different aspects of the question. For example, while Gurr and Davies ask why individuals join revolts or revolutionary movements, Skocpol focuses on the international economic and military factors that have weakened the state prior to successful revolutionary insurrections.

Clearly, revolutions are never inevitable and, in fact, successful ones are rare. While the causes of unrest may lie in relative deprivation and the regime's loss of legitimacy, the ultimate success or failure of revolutionary movements also depends on the relative military and political capabilities of the contending forces. Only by comparing the political-military strength of those who rebel with the state's capacity to defend itself can we understand why some revolutionary movements succeed while others fail.

As we have seen, major revolutions often occur after a country has been defeated or badly weakened in war (Russia, China, Turkey, and Egypt) or after its government has been ousted temporarily (Europe's colonial regimes in Asia during World War II). They may also take place when a government is particularly corrupt (Cuba and Nicaragua) or subservient to foreign powers (China, Mexico, and Nicaragua). In all of these cases, the incumbent regime lost its legitimacy (what the Chinese and Vietnamese called "the mandate of heaven"). Thus, the Russian czarist and Chinese Guomindang governments both fell when they showed themselves to be incapable of defending their people's sovereignty. Similarly, Cuba's President Batista lost his legitimacy when he turned Havana into "the brothel of the Caribbean." So did the Shah after his Westernization program offended Iran's Islamic mullahs. British, French, and Dutch colonial rule in Asia was secure as long as the indigenous population believed that Europeans were more powerful than they were and also better equipped to govern. When the Japanese ousted the colonial governments of Burma, Malaysia, Vietnam, and Indonesia, they demonstrated that Asians could defeat Europeans militarily. Once the European powers lost their aura of invincibility, they were unable to restore colonial rule after World War II.

Finally, the very authoritarianism of many Third World governments may ultimately undermine them. Cuba's Fulgencio Batista, the Shah of Iran, and Nicaragua's Anastasio Somoza illustrate that point. Because their governments had never been legitimized through free and honest elections, they could not convincingly claim to represent the people. Ignoring that fact during the Cold War, the United States frequently supported authoritarian governments in countries such as El Salvador, Nicaragua, Chile, Zaire (Congo), South Korea, Iran, and Pakistan. Responding to criticisms by human rights groups, Washington argued that, whatever their faults, these repressive governments were the last remaining fire walls against communist subversion and the rise of totalitarianism. Yet history shows that having a democratic government offers the best inoculation against revolution. Indeed, no established democracy has ever been toppled by a revolution.[35]

LEVELS OF POPULAR SUPPORT

Ché Guevara, the leading military strategist of the Cuban Revolution, observed that those who undertake revolutions either win or die. Though perhaps overstating his point, Guevara's remark highlights the tremendous risk revolutionary fighters take, be they poor peasants or radicalized university students. Rebels almost always face superior fire power and a range of repressive state institutions (police, military, special intelligence units, etc.). Not surprisingly, most of the time the insurgents lose. One study counted 28 guerrilla movements in Latin America from 1956 to 1990. Of them, only two succeeded (Cuba's July 26 movement and Nicaragua's Sandinistas).[36] Asia and Africa are also littered with the corpses of dead revolutionaries and failed insurgencies. Even victorious revolutions, such as Vietnam's and China's, leave behind vast numbers of fallen rebel fighters and supporters. Those who survive often return home to devastated villages and suffering families. Not surprisingly, then, individual peasants, workers, students, and professionals do not take lightly the decision to join a revolutionary force.

What portion of the population must support a revolution if it is to succeed? What type of people are most likely to join the movement? The answer to the first question is ambiguous. There is no fixed or knowable percentage of the population that must support an insurrection in order for it to triumph. Following World War II, a majority of Ukrainians probably favored a separatist movement fighting Soviet control, yet that uprising was still crushed by the powerful Soviet army. On the other hand, insurgencies elsewhere have succeeded with the active support of less than 20 percent of the civilian population.

Any evaluation of popular sentiment during a revolutionary upheaval should identify at least five different groups: First, there are those who strongly support the government and believe that their own fates are linked to the regime's survival. Government officials, military officers, land owners, and businesspeople with close links to the state normally fall in this category. It may also include ethnic groups tied to the regime (such as the Hmong people of Laos), people ideologically committed to the political system, and an assortment of others with a vested interest in preserving the status quo.

A second group in society also supports the government but more conditionally. For example, during the 1960s, most Venezuelans supported the government's battle against Marxist guerrillas. Even though many of them shared the guerrillas' condemnation of Venezuela's severe inequalities, sprawling urban shantytowns, and rural poverty, they were repelled by the rebels' use of violence and their failure to work within the country's recently achieved democratic framework.[37] Because the government's public support was broad but thin (i.e., many Venezuelans were conditional supporters), it could easily have lost its advantage had it used the repressive anti-guerrilla tactics so widely employed elsewhere in Latin America.

A third, often critical, segment of the population supports neither the revolutionaries nor the government. Its members are generally alienated and probably dislike both sides. In the1980s and 1990s, many Peruvian Indian peasant communities were victimized by the *Sendero Luminoso* (Shining Path) guerrillas, an extremely fanatical and brutal Maoist movement. At the same time, these same villagers were often also brutalized by the Peruvian army, which flagrantly violated the peasants' human rights. Not surprisingly, most peasants feared and hated both sides. Caught in the middle, they avoided taking sides for their own preservation, though many others joined government-supported defense militias.

A fourth group—drawn primarily from peasants, workers, urban poor, and alienated members of the middle class who sympathize with the revolutionary cause—includes people who occasionally lend support to the insurgents. For example, sympathetic peasants in China, Cuba, and Vietnam offered intelligence information, food, and shelter to rebel guerrillas. In countries such as China and El Salvador, where the guerrillas controlled "liberated zones" for extended periods of time, these support networks were very extensive. In other countries where the revolution was fought primarily through urban street protests rather than guerrilla war (Iran) and in revolutions with important urban and rural components (Mexico, Nicaragua), revolutionaries depended on the sympathy and occasional support of the urban poor, workers, and the middle class.

Finally, there is a relatively small portion of the population that fully involves itself in the revolutionary struggle. In Cuba, Mexico, and Nicaragua, for example, committed students, teachers, and professionals assumed leadership positions. Many peasants (including women and teenagers) in China, Vietnam, and El Salvador provided the revolution's foot soldiers. Given the enormous risks involved for the participants and their families, it is not surprising that only a small portion of the people took up arms. Some peasants joined out of desperation, because their village had been destroyed by the armed forces or because they feared being drafted into an army they despised. Others were attracted by the revolutionaries' promises of a more just social order.

One can only guess the proportion of a country's population in each of these five groups at a particular point in time. Public opinion surveys in countries that are divided between warring factions are unlikely to elicit honest responses. But we do know that if they are to succeed, revolutionary movements must attract a core of firmly committed activists willing to risk their lives for the cause, as well as a larger circle of sympathizers. How large their numbers must be depends on the extent of government decay and loss of legitimacy. It also depends on how well-armed government troops are, how committed they are, how effectively they fight, and how much foreign support the government has. Fidel Castro's small rural force of only a few hundred troops (supported by a number of urban guerrillas) defeated Batista's much larger but dispirited army. On the other hand, El Salvador's FMLN—a far larger and better-equipped guerrilla army—could not unseat a government that was bolstered by extensive American economic and military aid. Yet even the United States' commitment of massive military assistance and hundreds of thousands of U.S. troops could not save the South Vietnamese government from the Viet Cong and its North Vietnamese allies.

The people in the second category (mild government supporters) and the third (neutrals) are equally important targets for any revolutionary movement. In developing countries with substantial urban populations, a government can maintain power in the face of considerable peasant unrest and rural guerrilla activity as long as it controls the cities and retains the support of the urban middle class, particularly civil servants, businesspeople, and professionals. These middle-class groups are not normally radical, but they can become disenchanted with particularly corrupt, repressive, or ineffectual regimes. In Iran, the tide turned in favor of the revolutionary mullahs when Tehran's bazaar shopkeepers lost confidence in the Shah's government.

Nicaragua's revolution also illustrates this point. Because the Somoza family had expropriated such a large share of the national economy, its greed not only damaged the poor but hurt the business community as well. As the Sandinista uprising spread and as the National Guard became increasingly repressive, Nicaragua's business community became increasingly alienated from the government. Prominent business leaders—including the head of the country's Coca Cola bottling plant, the nation's most prominent publishing family, and the directors of several important banks—demanded Somoza's resignation and organized business shutdowns to express their opposition. While most of these people were wary of the Sandinista movement (which made no secret of its leftist ideology), they shared its desire to oust the Somoza regime.[38]

While flying from Panama to Miami during the height of the insurrection, this author found himself seated next to the chief executive of an important Nicaraguan agrochemical plant. In the course of our conversation about events back home, he declared, "Somoza has to go. He's too damned corrupt and he's wrecking the country." "But what if reformist business leaders such as yourself have to share power with the [Marxist-oriented] Sandinistas after he falls?" I asked.[39] "I don't like those guys," he said, "but if sharing power with them is what it takes to get rid of Somoza, then we'll have to do it." In the face of such broad ideological and cross-class opposition to the government, it was just a matter of time before the Somoza regime fell.

In short, if a revolutionary movement is to gain power, there must be wide-scale disaffection with the government, a disaffection that reaches beyond the ranks of the poor and the oppressed to the heart of the middle class and the business community. It is neither likely nor necessary for a large portion of those groups to actively support the insurrection. For the revolution to succeed, it is only essential that some of them, including a highly committed core, do so, while many others, like the Nicaraguan business executive on the plane, simply cease supporting the government.

PEASANTS AS REVOLUTIONARIES

Let us now turn our attention to the ranks of committed revolutionary supporters, particularly the last group, revolutionary activists. With rare exception, Third World revolutions have been fought primarily by peasants. The Chinese Red Army and the Viet Cong, for example, consisted overwhelmingly of the rural poor. Indeed, almost all African and Asian revolutionary movements have been overwhelmingly rural in character. And even in Latin America's revolutions, where the urban populations often played key roles, peasants still were very important. Consequently, it is important to ask, "What factors induce peasants to risk joining a revolution, and what types of peasants join?"

Why Peasants Rebel

In our analysis of Third World rural society (see Chapter 6), we noted that traditional peasant culture tends to be rather conservative. Since early economic modernization frequently affects them negatively, they have good reason to cling to tradition. But the intrusion of market forces into their communities sometimes so unsettles their world that it radicalizes them as they struggle to protect what they have. On the one hand, increasing numbers of subsistence farmers (peasants producing primarily for their family's consumption) in a modernizing economy are induced or pressured to enter the commercial market for the first time. Once involved in commercial agriculture, however, they must deal with fluctuations in the price of their crops, including volatile shifts that they are ill-equipped to handle.

At the same time, rural landlords, whose precapitalist exploitation of local peasants had been somewhat constrained by their neofeudal obligations, now viewed their tenants merely as factors of production in the new market economy. In Latin America, many landlords who had previously funded their peons' *fiestas* or lent them money when they were ill concluded that such expenditures were no longer financially prudent in the more competitive market environment. Other landlords entering the commercial market decided to mechanize production and evict tenant farmers from their land.

For all of these reasons, rural society's transition from neofeudal to capitalist production precipitated many of the twentieth century's Third World revolutions.[40] James Scott notes that the pain that peasants suffered during that transformation was not merely economic or physical but also involved *moral pain*. To be sure, the precapitalist rural order had its share of grave injustices, but those inequities were somewhat mitigated by a web of reciprocal obligations between landlords and peasants and among peasants. It is the collapse of that "moral economy," Scott argues, that drives many peasants to revolution.[41] Similarly, Eric Wolf insists that in countries as disparate as Cuba, Mexico, Algeria, Vietnam, and China, most peasant participants in revolutionary movements were not trying to create a new socialist order. Rather, they were seeking to restore the security of their old way of life.

Which Peasants Rebel

Even in a single country or region, peasants are not a homogeneous mass. Some of them, called *kulaks*, own larger plots of land and employ other peasants to work their farms with them. Others are landless or own extremely small plots. And still others work as wage laborers on large estates or rent parcels of land from the landlord, paying their rent in cash, labor, or sharecropping.[42] Each group has distinct political and economic needs.

Those peasants most threatened by the economic modernization of the countryside are the ones most likely to join local revolts or broader revolutionary movements. Analyzing data collected from 70 developing nations over a 22-year period, Jeffrey M. Paige found that the peasant groups most likely to join insurgencies are sharecroppers (tenant farmers who pay the rent on their plot of land by turning over a percentage of their crop to the landlord) and wage laborers (who work for landlords who, in turn, lack financial resources outside of their land).[43] Not only are these peasants particularly vulnerable to changing economic conditions, but their landlords are also less likely to grant them financial concessions because they depend exclusively on their farm land for their incomes. Research on Latin American guerrilla movements reveals that squatters (poor farmers illegally occupying land) and other peasants who face eviction from the land they cultivate are also more prone to rebel.[44]

But even peasants with more secure access to the land feel threatened by declining crop prices. For example, in Peru's Ayacucho province, the birthplace of the Shining Path guerrilla movement, peasants experienced declining terms of trade for two decades; that is, the cost of the goods they consumed had been rising faster than the price of the crops that they sold. Caught in an ongoing financial squeeze, they felt increasingly insecure and, hence, became more receptive to the Shining Path's appeals.[45]

All of the peasants who are prone to support revolutions, then, have one element in common—they are threatened by the prospect of losing their land and/or their livelihood. Conversely, the most conservative peasants are those with secure title to their land holdings and relatively stable prices for their crops. It is for this reason that many analysts maintain that the best protection against rural revolution is an agrarian reform program that distributes land, secure titles, and support services to the peasantry.

Peasant insurrections are also more likely to develop in areas that already had historical traditions of rebellion. For example, the revolutionary forces in China, Vietnam, Cuba, Mexico, and Nicaragua all received their greatest support in regions that had traditions of peasant resistance, what one author calls a "rebellious culture."[46] Fidel Castro's home province of Oriente, known as "the cradle of the Cuban Revolution," had a long history of unrest dating back to nineteenth-century slave revolts against their owners and against Spanish colonial rule. China's Hunan province (Mao Zedong's home) and the area around the Sandinista stronghold of León also had rebellious traditions. Some revolutionary movements take root in areas without a record of prior rebellions but with a tradition of lawlessness and hostility toward the legal authorities. For example, Mexican revolutionary leader Pancho Villa operated in a region known for cattle rustling and other forms of social banditry, and Villa himself was a bandit turned revolutionary. Similarly, Castro's July 26 guerrillas based themselves in the Sierra Maestra mountains, a region with a history of smuggling, marijuana production, and banditry.

REVOLUTIONARY LEADERSHIP

Although peasants furnish the foot soldiers for revolutions, they rarely provide their highest leaders. They may stage spontaneous uprisings or even more extensive revolts on their own, but they usually lack the organizational and political skills needed to conduct a broader social revolution. Consequently, both the upper echelons and the middle ranks of revolutionary leadership are usually occupied by people with more education and greater political experience. To be sure, there are exceptions to that rule. Mexico's Emiliano Zapata was a horse trainer from a peasant family and only learned to read when he was an adult.[47] More recently, the Colombian Revolutionary Armed Forces (FARC) guerrillas in Colombia have largely been led by peasants.[48] Ultimately, however, their lack of political experience usually proves costly. For example, Villa and Zapata jointly conquered Mexico City, the nation's capital, but then left it because neither man was equipped to run the country.

More typically, then, the top revolutionary leadership comes from middle-class or even upper-class backgrounds. In Latin America, for example, "they are drawn disproportionately from the intelligentsia, not only highly educated, but also largely involved in the production of theories."[49] Trained as a librarian, China's Mao Zedong was the son of a rural grain merchant. In Vietnam, Ho Chi Minh, the son of a rural school teacher, practiced a number of professions, including photography, while living in Paris and becoming a French Communist Party activist. Fidel Castro received a law degree at the University of Havana, where he was a leader in student politics. His father, a Spanish immigrant, had started life in Cuba as a worker, but he eventually became a well-to-do land owner. Castro's comrade, Ché Guevara, was a doctor whose mother came from an aristocratic Argentine family and whose father was an architect. Similarly, most of the nine *comandantes* who directed the Sandinista revolution came from solid middle- or upper-class families and were well educated. For example, President Daniel Ortega and his brother, Defense Minister Humberto Ortega, were the sons of an accountant-businessman. Luis Carrión, the son of a millionaire, had attended an American prep school. Only one *comandante*, Henry Ruiz, came from a poor urban family, and none were of peasant origin.[50] Finally, a Vietnamese Communist Party study of nearly 2,000 party activists (conducted after World War II, at the start of their long revolutionary struggle) revealed that 74 percent of them were either intellectuals or were from bourgeois families, while only 7 percent were workers, and 19 percent came from peasant families.[51] These are noteworthy statistics for a party trying to speak for the country's peasantry and working class.

Not surprisingly, a larger number of lower-ranking revolutionary leaders are of peasant or working class background. The rural poor have been most broadly represented at all leadership levels in Asian nations such as China, Vietnam, and Kampuchea, where they account for most of the country's population. Both during their two-decade revolutionary struggle and once in power, the Chinese Communist Party and the Red Army provided peasant activists with unprecedented opportunities for upward mobility. Virtually from the date of its formation, the party offered peasants and children of peasants—heretofore at the bottom of the social ladder—preference for admission. And as late as 1985, decades after the communists took power, one-third of all Communist Party members were peasants (some 25 percent of whom were illiterate).[52] Similarly, many of the lower- and middle-level guerrilla leaders in El Salvador and Peru were of peasant origin, although they had often left their villages to become teachers, health workers, or the like.

The educational and social gap separating aspiring revolutionary leaders and the peasant rank-and-file can be a considerable problem unless the leaders have a firm understanding of local peasant culture. Although Mao Zedong became an urban intellectual, his rural upbringing had given him an understanding of village culture. Fidel Castro was certainly no peasant, but his childhood on his father's farm had familiarized him with the region's rural poor.

And in Venezuela, several of the FALN commanders were sons of local land-lords who traded on their father's patron-client ties to the local peasants.[53]

On the other hand, aspiring guerrilla activists who come to the country-side from the city, from other regions of the country or other countries, or from other ethnic backgrounds are often rejected by the rural poor. Given their history of exploitation, peasants tend to be understandably wary of outsiders. The wider the linguistic, cultural, or racial gaps between would-be revolutionary leaders and the local villagers, and the greater the peasants' prior suspicion of outsiders, the harder it is for organizers to break through the wall of distrust. In Cuba, where racial and ethnic divisions were relatively less severe, Ché Guevara—a White, urban, middle-class Argentinian—was accepted by the peasants of the Sierra Maestra. So when Guevara later ventured to Bolivia to spread the revolution, he may have been ill-prepared for the substantial mistrust its Aymara Indian peasants felt toward White outsiders such as him. There he was killed by an antiguerrilla unit of the Bolivian armed forces, which was aided by the CIA and by local villagers who saw no reason to risk their safety for an outside agitator. Similarly, Hector Béjar, a failed Peruvian guerrilla leader, later wrote candidly in his memoirs about how he—a coastal, White journalist and poet—was unable to gain the trust of the highland Indians whom he had hoped to lead.[54]

REVOLUTIONARIES IN POWER

While many comparative studies have examined the causes of revolution, there is less cross-national research on the *policies* revolutionary regimes implement once in office. Perhaps guerrilla fighters in the hills have inspired more interest and romanticization (or fear) than have revolutionary bureaucrats in the corridors of power. The record suggests that Third World revolutions in the developing world have accomplished more than their detractors admit but less than their supporters claim.

A primary objective of Marxist and many non-Marxist revolutionary governments alike has been greater socioeconomic and political equality. That quest usually begins with the struggle for power itself, when revolutionary leaders use egalitarian appeals to garner support from downtrodden peasants and workers. Recognizing the critical importance of that support, Mao Zedong wrote that the peasantry is to the guerrilla army what the water is to fish. To win their loyalty, the Red Army treated China's peasants with greater respect than other military forces or governments had.[55] Similarly, in Cuba, "the army's brutal treatment of the peasants" contrasted with "Castro's policy of paying for the food purchased from the peasants . . . and putting his [mostly urban] men to work in the . . . fields."[56]

Once in power, revolutionary governments continue to emphasize equality. In addition to redistributing land and other economic resources, they introduce egalitarian cultural and psychological reforms as well. For example, at meetings of Cuba's Committees for the Defense of the Revolution (CDRs), men may be pressured to share household tasks with their spouses. Efforts at economic and social egalitarianism have been more limited in non-Marxist revolutions. Still, insurgencies such as Bolivia's and Mexico's have somewhat improved the social status of their rural populations, including indigenous peoples.

As we have seen, revolutions open up new channels of upward social mobility for peasants and workers who previously had few such opportunities. To be sure, most of the higher government and party posts are still held by people from middle-class backgrounds. Nor do many party members from ethnic minorities hold the most powerful political positions. Thus, for example, there have been relatively few Blacks in Cuba's Communist Party politburo nor ethnic minorities in China's. But many revolutionary activists from humble backgrounds *do* hold lower- and mid-level political positions that they could never have attained under the old order. Revolutionary parties and mass organizations such as Mexico's National Peasant Confederation and Cuba's CDRs may give peasants and workers a greater sense of participation in the political system.

Finally, revolutions usually decrease their nation's level of economic inequality, though the degree of change varies from country to country. Agrarian reform programs in China, Vietnam, Bolivia, Cuba, Mexico, and Nicaragua redistributed land from the rural oligarchy to the peasantry.[57] Many Marxist regimes provided guaranteed employment, state-supported medical care, subsidized housing and food, and other egalitarian measures, while at the same time establishing more equitable income distribution than in other LDCs at comparable stages of economic development. On the other hand, more moderate revolutions in Bolivia and Mexico failed to reduce economic inequality.

To be sure, notable inequalities persist even in radical revolutionary societies. Disparities between rural and urban populations may be reduced but not eliminated. As China implements free-market reforms, the gap between its coastal cities and the rural interior has become particularly pronounced. In Cuba and Vietnam, professionals and skilled workers still earn much higher salaries than peasants or unskilled blue-collar workers do, even though that gap frequently has narrowed. At the same time, a new form of inequality often seeps in, as newly entrenched party and government officials begin to appropriate special perquisites for themselves and their families. Many years ago, Milovan Djilas, a disillusioned former leader of Yugoslavia's communist government, complained about the rise of a "new class" in revolutionary regimes, an elite of party officials who enjoy special privileges and a better standard of living.[58] Today in China, the foremost Communist Party leaders are well-known for their lavish lifestyles, while the children of the party cadre are despised for their arrogance and corruption. Still, in spite of these phenomena, revolutionary governments such as Cuba's and Vietnam's have reduced the general level of societal inequality.

Another major revolutionary objective has been mass political mobilization. As Samuel Huntington notes, "a full-scale revolution . . . involves the rapid and violent destruction of existing political institutions, the mobilization of new groups into politics, and the creation of new political institutions."[59] Thus, in China, Vietnam, Cuba, and Nicaragua, government incentives and pressures have induced a large portion of the population to join revolutionary support groups.[60] At one time, close to 90 percent of Cuban adults belonged to their neighborhood Committees for the Defense of the Revolution (CDRs). In the 1980s, substantial portions of the Nicaraguan population joined Sandinista Defense Committees (CDSs).

At its best, mass political mobilization has increased the government's capacity to build the economy by mobilizing volunteer labor or spreading labor discipline. At times, revolutionary support groups have also helped combat sexism, racism, and criminality. At worst, these groups have been used as vigilantes against alleged counterrevolutionaries and as agents of thought control. At CDR meetings, members are familiarized with the current government political line, encouraged to volunteer for projects such as planting neighborhood gardens, and imbued with greater revolutionary consciousness.[61] But in Mao Zedong's China, mass mobilization often involved brutal political campaigns that called upon citizens to root out and punish alleged enemies of the revolution. Hundreds of thousands were persecuted, jailed, or killed in the government's Anti-Rightist Campaign (1957) and its Cultural Revolution (1966–1976).[62]

Mass mobilization can be used either to activate citizens who support the revolution's goals or to isolate and persecute those who do not. Most revolutionary regimes are led by a dominant party, such as the Chinese Communist Party or the Mexican PRI, which stands at the center of the mobilization process. Opposition parties are either prohibited or are only tolerated in a weakened condition. Among Marxist governments, only Nicaragua's Sandinistas allowed themselves to be voted out of office. Elsewhere, a number of non-Marxist revolutionary parties have lost favor over time. They may resort to fraud when faced with the prospect of losing (Mexico until 2000), cancel elections that the opposition is expected to win (Algeria), or hand over the reins of power and become just another competing party (Bolivia and, very recently, Mexico).

In short, while revolutionary regimes claim to speak for the people and often do in many respects, we have noted that they are hardly ever democratic. Because they view themselves as the *only* legitimate voice of the popular will and the *only* representatives of the general good, most radical regimes tend to regard opposition groups as enemies of the people who should not be afforded political space. Nicaragua's Sandinista government, a rare exception, allowed opposition parties and interest groups to function, though they were occasionally harassed. Although the opposition newspaper, *La Prensa*, was periodically censored or briefly shut down, it continued to vigorously, and sometimes outrageously, attack the government right up to the time its publisher, Violeta Chamorro, became the nation's president. For the most part, however, even communist governments that have opened up their economies to free-market reforms (China and Vietnam) have maintained their repressive political structure and remained intolerant of opposition voices.

While the first generation of revolutionary leaders often comes to power full of idealism, either its own members or the generation that succeeds it generally succumbs in some way to the corruptions of power. In Vietnam and China—where the large private sector still depends on the government for licenses, raw materials, and the like—bribing the right state official is a necessity for doing business.[63] Cubans, who once felt that their revolutionary officials had a higher standard of honesty than preceding governments, were shocked by the "Ochoa affair," which revealed that high-ranking military and security officers were involved in the drug trade. Government corruption on a lesser scale has since become far more pervasive as a result of the severe economic scarcities of the 1990s. And after the Sandinistas left office, disillusioned Nicaraguans learned that top party officials had kept for themselves some of the luxurious mansions that had been confiscated from the Somoza regime. It is not that revolutionary regimes are more corrupt than other Third World governments; often they are less so. It is just that their followers, many of whom made considerable sacrifices for their cause, had expected more.

CONCLUSION: REVOLUTIONARY CHANGE AND DEMOCRACY

Throughout the twentieth century, revolutionary movements had a tremendous influence on the developing world. That influence was most pronounced in Asia, where the Chinese Revolution transformed the lives of one-fifth of humanity and where revolutionary conflicts in Vietnam, Laos, and Cambodia involved France and then the United States in major wars. Elsewhere in Asia, failed communist insurgencies affected the Philippines and Malaysia. Most of Africa's revolutions have been wars of national liberation from European colonialism (Algeria, Kenya, and Namibia among others) or secessionist wars (Biafra, Eritrea, and southern Sudan). Class-related revolutions in Africa (such as Ethiopia's and Libya's) were generally initiated from above by military officers. Latin America had two non-Marxist insurrections (Bolivia and Mexico), two Marxist revolutions (Cuba and Nicaragua), and a number of unsuccessful revolutionary movements (Argentina, Colombia, El Salvador, Guatemala, Peru, Uruguay, and Venezuela). Both the revolutions and the failed insurgencies had spillover effects in neighboring countries. For example, the Cuban Revolution spawned various agrarian reform programs elsewhere in Latin America, most designed to avert "another Cuba." The Nicaraguan Revolution inspired both agrarian reform and intensified government repression in neighboring El Salvador. But, as we enter the twenty-first century, the appeal of revolution, particularly the Marxist variety, has waned considerably. Indeed, today's world is a veritable graveyard of failed insurrections. The Soviet Union, once the fountainhead of communism, lies in ruins, and its most important successor state, Russia, struggles to overcome the errors of its Marxist-Leninist past. Communism is equally discredited in most of Eastern and Central Europe, where it held sway until recently. Cuba's government, like Nicaragua's before it, has seen its impressive initial gains in education, health care, and social equality somewhat eroded by its deteriorating economy. And in many other recently fallen or still-surviving Marxist and neo-Marxist revolutions, the scorecard of successes and failures is far more disheartening. Countries such as Afghanistan, Angola, Cambodia, Ethiopia, Mozambique, and Myanmar have suffered enormous devastation with little or nothing to show for it.

Evaluating the quality of revolutionary change in the more successful revolutions is not easy, for it is influenced by the analyst's ideological lens and by the difficulty of isolating the effects of revolutionary policy from a host of other overlapping factors. For example, critics of the Chinese Revolution argue that the socioeconomic gains attained under Mao were achieved in spite of his radical policies, not because of them. They further insist that the country's rapid economic growth under Deng Xiaoping demonstrates the advantages of free-market reforms. Others maintain that Cuba's substantial gains since its revolution in health care and education have been no more impressive than Costa Rica's and were only accomplished with the benefit of massive Soviet aid.

On the other hand, more sympathetic observers note that Cuba achieved impressive social gains in the face of the U.S. economic embargo, and that the American-backed Contra war (coupled with a trade embargo) destroyed the Nicaraguan revolution's earlier economic and social accomplishments. China's market-based economic boom, others insist, could never have been achieved without the educational gains produced under socialism. Neither side can prove that it is right nor can it undermine the other side's arguments because too much of their arguments are tied to unprovable causal relationships or are based on speculation about how things might have been had history been different.

In any event, it is likely that the age of revolution is drawing to an end in the Third World. The demise of Soviet and Eastern European communism exposed more clearly the deficiencies of Marxism-Leninism. So too have China's and Vietnam's introduction of free-market (capitalist) components into their economic systems.[64] As communism has been discredited even among some of its once-fervent adherents, its capacity to attract new revolutionary adherents, including people willing to risk their lives fighting for Marxist-Leninist ideals, has diminished sharply. Marxist ideology, once chic among Third World intellectuals and political activists, has become far less fashionable.[65] At the end of the 1980s, facing defeat by its mujahadeen opponents, Afghanistan's People's Democratic Party renounced its Marxist ideology in a failed effort to maintain power. One of its leaders dismissed the party's long-standing communist stance by claiming that it had been adopted at "a time when Marxism-Leninism was quite in fashion in underdeveloped countries." In Angola, where the governing party made a similar ideological conversion, the president explained that continuing to support the Marxist-Leninist model "would be rowing against the tide [of capitalist democracy]."[66] Similar transformations have occurred within Nicaragua's Sandinista party and El

Salvador's FMLN, both former revolutionary movements that subsequently transformed themselves into democratic socialist political parties. In his 2001 campaign for the presidency, Sandinista leader Daniel Ortega insisted that Jesus Christ, not Marx, was his first inspiration when he led the country's revolution more than 20 years earlier. Modifying his leftist views, he declared that "in this new context, to which we had to adjust, the market economy plays its role."[67]

How many revolutionary upheavals will take place in the coming years is hard to predict, and the answer is partly a matter of semantics (that is, how we choose to define a revolution). However, now that colonialism has come to an end in Africa and Asia, there are few possibilities for wars of national liberation as we have known them. There still may be other mass-based revolutions in societies that suffer from severe socioeconomic inequalities, sharp rural-urban divisions, or repressive governments. But, as we have noted, the collapse of the Soviet bloc, the abandonment of Marxist economics in China and, to a lesser extent, Vietnam, the failure of the Nicaraguan revolutionary government, and Cuba's current economic crisis have all substantially diminished the appeal of revolutionary Marxism. Thus, El Salvador's FMLN guerrillas ended their 12-year struggle, signed a peace treaty that promised some of the reforms that they had long fought for, and converted themselves into one of the leading political parties in the congress. Marxist guerrilla groups continue to battle in Colombia (where their considerable income from cocaine trafficking, kidnapping, and extortion help make them a formidable military force), Nepal, and a few other places. But very few seem to have much likelihood of success.

Based in the impoverished southern Mexican state of Chiapas, the Zapatista (EZLN) insurgents have attracted considerable support from Mexicans of all social classes. But the Zapatistas have expressed their desire to work within a democratic political framework, and they have not carried out any armed attacks since the first few days of 1994 when they burst onto Mexico's political scene. In 2001, Mexico's president presented the congress with a peace package that appeared acceptable to the EZLN, but which the legislation failed to pass. While the peace process remains on hold, nobody, including the rebels' supporters, believes Zapatistas could topple the government, nor do they appear to want to. In short, most internal wars in the coming decades will almost surely be ethnically based, involving secessionist rebellions or movements seeking greater rights for their ethnicity (Chapter 4). Insurgencies of this type are most likely to occur in Africa as well as Southeast and South Asia. Conceivably, there also will be scattered uprisings by indigenous peoples (Indians) in Latin America, as there already have been in Bolivia, Ecuador, and Peru. Whether these struggles can properly be called revolutions, however, is debatable. They satisfy neither Huntington's nor Skocpol's definitions. Hence, it is probably more accurate to call them civil wars, secessionist rebellions, or ethnic conflicts rather than revolutions. Successful revolutions, in the sense that Skocpol or even Huntington define them, appear unlikely in the foreseeable future.

DISCUSSION QUESTIONS

1. What are some of the major factors that have led to the collapse of state power and the rise of revolutions?
2. What factors account for the declining likelihood of further Third World revolutions?
3. Discuss some of the psychological theories of revolution (i.e., the theories of James C. Davies or Ted Robert Gurr).
4. What segments of the population are more likely to support revolutionary movements, and how much support do such movements need in order to succeed?
5. Discuss some of the major accomplishments and failures of revolutionary governments.

NOTES

1. Hannah Arendt, *On Revolution* (New York: Viking Press, 1963), p. 13.

2. China's Leninist regime remains in place, but the principles of Marxist economics and class politics have been abandoned.

3. In Angola and Mozambique, most of the killing was carried out by counterrevolutionary forces. For the hundreds of thousands of innocent civilians butchered, however, it mattered little which side killed them.

4. One classical study of historical change argues that the American War of Independence was not a revolution. See Barrington Moore, Jr., *The Social Origins of Dictatorship and Democracy* (Boston: Beacon Press, 1966), p. 112. For a contrary view, see J. Franklin Jameson, *The American Revolution Considered as a Social Movement* (Boston: Beacon Press, 1956), pp. 16–20, 32–35.

5. Chalmers Johnson, *Revolution and the Social System* (Stanford, CA: Hoover Institution, 1964), p. 2.

6. Peter Calvert, "Revolution: The Politics of Violence," *Political Studies* 15, no. 1, (1967): 2; and *Revolution and Counter Revolution* (Minneapolis: University of Minnesota Press, 1990).

7. Samuel P. Huntington, *Political Order in Changing Societies* (New Haven, CT: Yale University Press, 1968), p. 264. A similar definition was offered decades earlier in Sigmund Neumann, "The International Civil War," *World Politics* 1, no. 3 (April 1949): 333–334, fn. 1.

8. Norman R. Miller and Roderick R. Aya, *National Liberation: Revolution in the Third World* (New York: Free Press, 1971).

9. Theda Skocpol, "France, Russia, China: A Structural Analysis of Social Revolutions," *Comparative Studies in Society and History* 18, no. 2 (1976): 176.

10. Theda Skocpol, *States and Social Revolutions: A Comparative Analysis of France, Russia and China* (Cambridge, England: Cambridge University Press, 1979), p. 4.

11. John Walton distinguishes between the handful of "great revolutions" that satisfy Skocpol's definition and a larger number of "national revolts" that are based on class and nationality and that he feels are not particularly distinguishable from social revolutions. John Walton, *Reluctant Rebels* (New York: Columbia University Press, 1984), pp. 1–36.

12. Ellen Kay Trimberger, "A Theory of Elite Revolutions," *Studies in Comparative International Development* 7, no. 3 (1972): 191–207; Ellen Kay Trimberger, *Revolution from Above: Military Bureaucrats and Development in Japan, Turkey, Egypt and Peru* (New Brunswick, NJ: Transaction Books, 1978).

13. Karl Marx and Frederick Engels, *Manifesto of the Communist Party* (New York: International Publishers, 1948).

14. A. S. Cohan, *Theories of Revolution* (London: Thomas Nelson and Sons, 1975), p. 72.

15. Irving M. Zeitlin, *Marxism: A Re-examination* (Princeton, NJ: Princeton University Press, 1967), p. 142.

16. In other words, no Marxist revolution has taken place in a country where capitalism was entrenched. By the end of the twentieth century, in a complete turnabout of Marxist theory, communist regimes in the Soviet Union and Eastern Europe were falling to capitalism. It is still too early to know what form that transition will ultimately take.

17. Marx's use of "dialectic," which he drew from the German philosopher G. W. F. Hegel, indicated that major ideas or historical forces (the thesis) are inevitably opposed by opposing ideas or forces (the antithesis), and out of this struggle emerges a "synthesis" that draws upon both sides.

18. Stuart R. Schram, *The Political Thought of Mao Tse-tung* (New York: Praeger, 1969).

19. Skocpol, *States and Social Revolutions*.

20. Skocpol, "France, Russia, China."

21. Chalmers Johnson, *Peasant Nationalism and Communist Power* (Stanford, CA: Stanford University Press, 1962).

22. Johnson, *Revolution and the Social System*.

23. Joel Migdal, *Peasants, Politics and Revolution* (Princeton, NJ: Princeton University Press, 1974), p. 252.

24. Ramón L. Bonachea and Marta San Martín, *The Cuban Insurrection, 1952–1959* (New Brunswick, NJ: Transaction Books, 1974); Jorge L. Domínguez, *Cuba: Order and Revolution* (Cambridge, MA: Belknap Press of Harvard University Press, 1978), pp. 93–95; John A. Booth, *The End and the Beginning: The Nicaraguan Revolution* (Boulder, CO: Westview Press, 1982).

25. Charles Tilly, *From Mobilization to Revolution* (New York: Addison-Wesley, 1978), pp. 204–205.

26. Charles Tilly, "Does Modernization Breed Revolution?" *Comparative Politics* 5, no. 3 (April 1974): 425–447.

27. Huntington, *Political Order in Changing Societies*, p. 265.

28. Ibid., p. 266. Not all Asian revolutions followed the Eastern model, nor did all Latin American insurgencies conform to the Western model. The collapse of the Chinese imperial regime in 1911 fit the Western model, while the Cuban Revolution (1959) followed the Eastern model, at least in part.

29. James C. Davies, "Toward a Theory of Revolution," *American Sociological Review* 27, no. 1 (February 1962): 7.

30. More precisely, the economic pattern he describes can be graphed as the letter "J" tipped over (Figure 8.1), with the long side representing the period of economic growth and the rounded part depicting the downturn.

31. James C. Davies, "Toward a Theory of Revolution," reprinted along with other articles on the causes of revolution in James C. Davies, ed., *When Men Revolt and Why* (New York: Free Press, 1971).

32. Ibid., and James C. Davies, "Revolution and the J-Curve," in *Violence in America: Historical and Comparative Perspectives, A Report Submitted to the National Commission on the Causes and Prevention of Violence*, ed. Hugh Davis Graham and Ted Robert Gurr (New York: New American Library, 1969), Vol. 2, pp. 547– 577.

33. Raymond Tanter and Manus Midlarsky, "A Theory of Revolution," *Journal of Conflict Resolution* 11, no. 3 (1967): 264–280.

34. Ted Robert Gurr, "Psychological Factors in Civil Violence," *World Politics* 20, no. 2 (1967–1968): 252–253; see also Ted Robert Gurr, *Why Men Rebel* (Princeton, NJ: Princeton University Press, 1970).

35. The only case where a communist regime replaced a democratic government is in post-war Czechoslovakia. But that communist government took power through a Russian-backed coup, not through revolutionary insurgency.

36. Timothy P. Wickham-Crowley, *Guerrillas and Revolution in Latin America* (Princeton, NJ: Princeton University Press, 1992), p. 312. Revolutions and guerrilla wars are not synonymous, of course. In recent decades, however, virtually all revolutionary struggles have been fought by guerrillas in Latin America and other parts of the Third World.

37. One defining event, a guerrilla attack on a tourist train, alienated most Venezuelans. Ultimately, several guerrilla leaders renounced violence and, following a government amnesty, entered electoral politics. Teodoro Petkoff, a former guerrilla who has since enjoyed a distinguished career as a congressman, cabinet minister, and presidential candidate, told me in a 1978 interview that the Left's violent tactics had been a major error and had cost it considerable support.

38. Booth, *The End and the Beginning*.

39. Such an alliance was being discussed in the U.S. press and government circles. Neither Nicaraguan businessmen nor the State Department harbored any illusions that they could keep the *Sandinistas* out of power at that point. However, they and the Carter administration hoped that the *Sandinistas* were not strong enough to hold power on their own. In fact, after the Somoza regime was ousted, the *Sandinista*-led government did initially include progressive business leaders, but they soon parted ways.

40. Eric R. Wolf, *Peasant Wars of the Twentieth Century* (New York: Harper & Row, 1969). For a discussion of similar factors in the capitalist transformation of Europe, see Karl Polanyi, *The Great Transformation* (New York: Rinehart, 1957).

41. James C. Scott, *The Moral Economy of the Peasant: Rebellion and Subsistence in Southeast Asia* (New Haven, CT: Yale University Press, 1976); James C. Scott and Benedict J. Kirkvliet, *How Traditional Rural Patrons Lose Legitimacy* (Madison: University of Wisconsin, Land Tenure Center, 1975).

42. Sharecroppers are tenant farmers who pay their rent by giving the landlord a percentage of their crop.

43. Jeffrey M. Paige, *Agrarian Revolution: Social Movements and Export Agriculture in the Underdeveloped World* (New York: Free Press, 1975), chaps. 1–2.

44. Wickham-Crowley, *Guerrillas and Revolution*, Chap. 6.

45. Cynthia McClintock, "Sendero Luminoso: Peru's Maoist Guerrillas," *Problems of Communism* 32, no. 5 (September–October 1983): 19–34.

46. Wickham-Crowley, *Guerrillas and Revolution*, pp. 246–250; Wolf, *Peasant Wars*.

47. John Womack, Jr., *Zapata and the Mexican Revolution* (New York: Vintage, 1968).

48. Wickham-Crowley, *Guerrillas and Revolution*, p. 145.

49. Ibid., p. 213; Alvin Gouldner, *The Future of Intellectuals and the Rise of the New Class* (New York: Seabury Press, 1979), pp. 53–73.

50. Dennis Gilbert, *Sandinistas: The Party and the Revolution* (New York: B. Blackwell, 1988); for detailed information on the social backgrounds and occupations of a substantial number of Latin American guerrilla leaders, see Wickham-Crowley, *Guerrillas and Revolution*, pp. 327–339.

51. Thomas H. Green, *Comparative Revolutionary Movements* (Upper Saddle River, NJ: Prentice Hall, 1974), p. 18.

52. Of course the percentages of peasants and illiterates in the party were still well below their proportions in the general population, but they were higher than in most LDCs.

53. Wickham-Crowley, *Guerrillas and Revolution*, p. 143.

54. Hector Béjar, *Peru 1965: Notes on a Guerrilla Experience* (New York: Monthly Review Press, 1970).

55. Among the many writings on Maoist ideology and strategy, see Stuart R. Schram, *The Political Thought of Mao Tse-tung* (New York: Praeger, 1963); Arthur Cohen, *The Communism of Mao Tse-Tung* (Chicago: University of Chicago Press, 1964); Cohan, *Theories of Revolution*, pp. 93–110.

56. Sebastian Balfour, *Fidel Castro* (New York: Longman, 1990), p. 49.

57. Peasants have been most pleased when they received individual family plots and far less satisfied when agrarian reform converted the old agricultural estates into cooperatives or state farms.

58. Milovan Djilas, *The New Class* (New York: Praeger, 1957).

59. Huntington, *Political Order in Changing Societies*, p. 266.

60. See, for example, William J. Duiker, *The Communist Road to Power in Vietnam*, 2d ed. (Boulder, CO: Westview Press, 1996).

61. Richard R. Fagen, *The Transformation of Political Culture in Cuba* (Stanford, CA: Stanford University Press, 1969); Domínguez, *Cuba: Order and Revolution*.

62. There is a voluminous literature on the Cultural Revolution. Liang Heng and Judith Shapiro, *Son of the Revolution* (New York: Vintage, 1983), offers a moving personal account of both the Anti-Rightist Campaign and the Cultural Revolution. See also K. S. Karol, *The Second Chinese Revolution* (New York: Hill and Wang, 1974); Jean Esmein, *The Chinese Cultural Revolution* (New York: Anchor Books, 1973); and Lowell Dittmer, *Liu Shao-ch'i and the Chinese Cultural Revolution* (Berkeley: University of California Press, 1974).

63. Liang Heng and Judith Shapiro, *After the Nightmare* (New York: Collier, 1986).

64. Nicholas Nugent, *Vietnam: The Second Revolution* (Brighton, England: In Print Publishers, 1996), Chaps. 5–6.

65. On this theme, see Forrest Colburn, *The Vogue of Revolution in Poor Countries* (Princeton, NJ: Princeton University Press, 1994).

66. Both quotations come from Colburn, *The Vogue of Revolution*, p. 89.

67. *The New York Times*, September 6, 2001.

chapter 9

Soldiers and Politics

During the years I was in the State Department, I was awakened once or twice a month by a telephone call in the middle of the night announcing a coup d'état in some distant [Third World] capital with a name like a typographical error.[1]

Even the most advanced governments are occasionally headed by men emerging from the ranks of the military. American president Dwight Eisenhower, French president Charles de Gaulle, and Israeli prime minister Ariel Sharon all used distinguished military careers as stepping stones to the leadership of their nations. But each of them entered politics as a private citizen, having first retired from the armed forces. Moreover, their accessions to high office were achieved through democratic elections.

What has distinguished Third World politics is the extent to which the military has intruded either as a dominant interest group or as the governing power. Unlike their counterparts in industrial democracies, soldiers in the LDCs often reject the dividing line between military and political activity. A pronouncement by the Indonesian armed forces prior to their assumption of power in the 1960s illustrates that perspective well:

> The army, which was born in the cauldron of the Revolution, has never been a dead instrument of the government, concerned exclusively with security matters. The army, as a fighter for freedom, cannot remain neutral toward the course of state policy, the quality of government, and the safety of the state.[2]

To be sure, there are countries such as India, Malaysia, Kenya, Tunisia, Mexico, and Costa Rica where the military has not penetrated deeply into politics for decades. But until recently such restraint has been the exception rather than the rule. Indeed, the military's political involvement in most of the Third World has been so pervasive that it has been a defining characteristic of political under-development. The wave of democratic transitions during the closing decades of the twentieth century has diminished the military's political influence in many LDCs, especially in Latin America. Still, in numerous developing countries, the armed forces retain considerable political power.

George Ball's frequent experience with coups d'état as a high-ranking official in the Kennedy and Johnson administrations was not unique. One study of military intervention revealed that 59 LDCs experienced 274 attempted coups between 1946 and 1970. Twenty-three of those countries were subjected to five or more takeover attempts in little more than two decades. Bolivia and Venezuela led the way with 18 coups each.[3] In the three decades since that study, the annual roll call of attempted and successful coups in the developing world has continued, rising at times in one region, abating at other times in another. Only since the 1980s has the rate of new military takeovers diminished.

Starting in Egypt with North Africa's first coup d'état in 1952, and then with General Mobutu's 1960 takeover in the Congo (Kinshasa), the first in Sub-Saharan Africa, that continent's politics has been especially dominated by the armed forces. From 1958 to 1984, there were more than 62 coups and 60 failed attempts in Sub-Saharan Africa, affecting more than 80 percent of the nations in that region.[4] In 1982 to 1983 alone, Upper Volta (now Burkina Faso) experienced three military takeovers in only nine months! On average during the 1980s, 65 percent of Africa's population was governed by the armed forces. Noting the absence of electoral change in the region until the 1990s, one observer argued that "coups had become the functional equivalent of elections, virtually the sole manner of ousting incumbent political leaders."[5]

In the second half of the twentieth century, the level of military rule in Latin America rose and fell in regional cycles. After a postwar period of widespread elected government, a wave of military intervention began in the mid-1960s, most notably in Brazil. Subsequently, in Chile and Uruguay, South America's most entrenched democracies were replaced by highly repressive military dictatorships. Indeed, by the mid-1970s, Colombia, Costa Rica, Cuba, Mexico, and Venezuela were the only Latin American nations still governed by civilians.[6] Since the start of the 1980s, another cycle of change has restored elected government throughout the region. But while civilian rule has taken root firmly in some nations, such as Argentina, Brazil, Chile, and Uruguay, the future of democratic government remains less certain in countries such as Guatemala, Haiti, and Paraguay. In much of Central America, the armed forces, though out of the political front line, remain a potent influence behind the scenes.

Although several Islamic nations in North Africa (Algeria, Libya, and Sudan) are controlled to varying degrees by the armed forces or by military strongmen, indirect military dominance is more common in the Middle East. Presidents Husni Mubarak of Egypt and Syria's recently deceased strongman,

Hafez Assad (since replaced by his civilian son), entered politics as military men, while Iraq's Saddam Hussein is a civilian who has adopted military trappings. All three have governed through political parties closely linked to the armed forces. Elsewhere in the region, monarchies in Morocco, Jordan, Saudi Arabia, Kuwait, and the smaller Gulf states have, at least until now, successfully controlled the military.

In Asia, the South Korean army has gradually transferred the reins of government to elected civilians but continues to exercise political influence. Thai military officers, by contrast, have been more reluctant to exit the political arena. Since entering politics in 1932, they have held the prime minister's post some 70 percent of the time. Although active military officers have been constitutionally barred from holding political office since 1983, several retired officers have continued to serve as prime minister.[7] Bangladesh and Pakistan have also alternated between army rule and military-dominated civilian regimes for decades. Myanmar's military regimes have been particularly long-lived and brutal, as was General Suharto's government in Indonesia (finally toppled in 1998 after 33 years in power). By contrast, India, China, Malaysia, and the Philippines have enjoyed uninterrupted civilian government.

While the number of military governments has declined since the 1980s, the armed forces continue to be a powerful political force in much of Africa and the Middle East and wield considerable political influence over a number of civilian governments in Asia and Latin America. Frequently, they are able to veto the decisions of elected civilian officials in particular policy areas. In some countries, military leaders protect their own budget, determine who serves as defense minister, or control military promotions. Elsewhere, the scope of their influence is far greater, including national defense, foreign affairs, and even economic policy. So, although Guatemala has experienced elected government since 1985, the president would still hesitate to pursue a policy that threatens the army's interests. Similarly, when Corazón Aquino served as Philippine president, she regularly consulted on major issues with her military chief of staff, General Fidel Ramos, who later succeeded her as president.[8]

In order to examine military involvement in Third World politics, this chapter explores a series of interrelated questions: What accounts for the high level of armed-forces involvement? Why have countries such as India, China, Malaysia, Costa Rica, and Tanzania been able to establish greater civilian control, while so many other developing nations have failed? How do the structures of military regimes differ from one another? What does the military hope to accomplish when it seizes power? How successful has it been in achieving its political and economic goals? Is military rule generally beneficial or detrimental to economic and political development? What factors have increasingly induced military regimes to step down in recent decades? And what political role do the armed forces continue to play after they have been forced from the center of political power?

THE CAUSES OF MILITARY INTERVENTION

Two alternative perspectives have been formulated to explain the frequency and nature of military intervention in developing countries. The first focuses on the internal characteristics of the armed forces themselves. The second stresses the broader political environment in which the generals operate, most notably the weakness of civilian regimes.

The Nature of the Armed Forces

In the past, many political scientists maintained that Third World armies enjoy greater organizational cohesion and clarity of purpose than do civilian political institutions, hence their proclivity to intervene. As one leading analyst concluded, "The ability of officers to intervene in domestic politics and produce stable leadership is [directly] related to internal [military] social cohesion."[9] Stressing the importance of understanding the military's inner workings, scholars examined the officer corps' class origins, educational level, ideological orientations, and internal organization. These factors, they suggested, affect the probability of military involvement in politics and help determine the officers' goals.

Obviously, military politics is greatly influenced by the officers' education and training. In his highly influential book *The Soldier and the State*, Samuel Huntington argued that a country wishing to keep the military out of politics must impart professional values to its officers.[10] Ideally, as military training and techniques become more sophisticated, officers develop specialized and complex military skills, while becoming more politically neutral. Under those circumstances, he claimed, "a clear distinction in role and function exists between military and civilian leaders."[11] But, Huntington warned subsequently, such a division of function will only develop if military training is addressed toward external threats such as war with other nations. Should the focus of military education shift toward internal warfare—controlling guerrilla unrest or other civil insurrection—professionalization will not suffice to keep the military out of politics.[12]

Building on this theme, Alfred Stepan distinguished between "old" and "new" military professionalism. The former, typical of developed countries such as the United States, emphasizes skills appropriate to "external security." As military officers are trained to repel foreign enemies, Stepan agreed, they can be expected to remove themselves from domestic politics. In many developing nations, however, military training (new professionalization) primarily prepares them for internal warfare against class- or ethnically based insurgencies.

Following the Cuban Revolution, Latin American generals and U.S. policy makers shared a common concern over leftist guerrilla movements in the region. Training of Latin American officers at home and in the United States emphasized counterinsurgency techniques as well as "civic action" programs (e.g., road and school construction) designed to "win the hearts and minds" of the local population. American policy makers claimed that such preparation would provide the military with a professional mission and thereby remove it from national politics. Invariably, however, teaching officers to deal with internal security threats involved them in the study of domestic political and economic issues, thereby drawing them into the political arena.[13]

Nowhere was this more evident than in Brazil's Superior War College (ESG) and Peru's Center for Higher Military Studies (CAEM). Offering each country's most capable officers sophisticated courses on domestic political, economic, and social issues, the two academies could not help but politicize their students. As severe inflation and political polarization worsened in Brazil, and as peasant unrest surged in Peru's neofeudal countryside, officers in both armies became convinced that they were more qualified than civilian politicians to solve their country's problems. After seizing power in the 1960s, the generals dramatically restructured the political-economic order in both nations, though their ideologies and programs were diametrically different.

The Nature of Civil Society

Although research into the internal structure and dynamics of the armed forces has been very valuable, it has its limits. Increasingly, scholars have come to understand that the likelihood and nature of military intervention in politics cannot be ascertained merely by evaluating factors such as military cohesion, size, or ideological orientation. There is, for example, surprisingly little correlation between the military's size or firepower and its propensity to topple civilian governments. Indeed, Africa, the region with some of the world's smallest armed forces, has had one of the highest incidence of military rule. West Africa's first coup was carried out in Togo by an army of 250 men and a small number of retirees from the former French colonial force. "In Dahomey, General Sogol, who had come to power [himself] by a coup d'état, was overthrown by sixty paratroopers."[14] Several other takeovers in the region were also executed by small and poorly armed units. In the closing years of the twentieth century, of nearly 45 African countries, 35 had military forces of fewer than 30,000 and 23 of those had fewer than 10,000 men.[15] By way of contrast, the armed forces of China, India, Israel, Sweden, and the United States have never attempted coups despite their large size, strong internal cohesion, and considerable military prowess.

Ultimately, then, the military's propensity to intervene in politics is less a function of its own might than of the weaknesses of civilian political institutions. As Huntington has insisted, "The most important causes of military intervention in politics are not military, but political and reflect not the social and organizational characteristics of the military establishment but the political and institutional structure of society."[16] Hence, it is on the fabric of civil society that the second category of explanatory theories focuses its attention.

If a civilian government enjoys widespread support, maintains stability, and presides over a healthy economy, it is relatively immune to coups.

Conversely, "in times of uncertainty and the breakdown of [civilian political] institutions, soldiers come into their own; when there is no other effective organization of society, even a small, weak army may take command over a large, unorganized mass."[17] In his classic study of civil-military relations, *The Man on Horseback*, Samuel E. Finer maintained that national political cultures could be ranked according to the following three criteria:[18]

1. The extent of public support for the procedures used to transfer political power and for the corresponding belief that only those procedures are legitimate.
2. The degree of public awareness regarding the individuals and institutions holding sovereign authority, and the degree to which the population believes that no other person or group can legitimately hold that power.
3. The strength of civil society. That is, the extent to which the populace is organized into groups such as political parties, labor unions, business associations, or churches that act independently of the government.

The higher a nation's political culture ranks on each of these three dimensions, argued Finer, the lower the likelihood of military interventionism. In short, countries are most capable of maintaining civilian rule when there is a wide consensus on the legitimacy of civilian government along with independent interest groups capable of defending that principle—taking to the streets if need be.

When the government retains widespread citizen loyalty, even if coups are tried they will usually fail. A Second World example demonstrates well what can happen when the civilian government enjoys greater legitimacy than its military opponents. In 1991, when Soviet generals and hardline communist civilian officials staged a coup aimed at ousting Soviet president Mikhail Gorbachev, thousands of civilians joined Russian president Boris Yeltsin in defending the Russian parliament with their bodies. At the same time, key commanders of troops sent to take Moscow and St. Petersburg refused to support the rebellion. Thus, the coup d'état failed badly because Yeltsin and Gorbachev had sufficient legitimacy to survive. In contrast, the legitimacy of civilian regimes in many developing nations is low. Disgruntled military elements are therefore more inclined to overthrow them, while loyalist troops and civilians are less likely to risk their lives defending them.

A variety of factors may either strengthen or undermine a government's legitimacy. From an institutional perspective, civilian regimes stand most firmly when they are supported by broadly based political parties. Where party systems are deeply entrenched in the fabric of society and elicit widespread support, the likelihood of military intervention is greatly diminished.[19] Indeed, a country's susceptibility to coups is less influenced by its level of democracy than by the degree to which its party system penetrates and organizes society. Thus, authoritarian governments in Mexico, Cuba, and China (all dominated by a single party) controlled the military as effectively as did democratic party systems in Venezuela and India. When put under sufficient stress, however, not even a strong party system can fully immunize a political system from military interference. For much of the twentieth century, vibrant, competitive parties in

Uruguay and Chile shielded those countries from the pattern of military takeovers that plagued most of Latin America. By 1973, however, increased class conflict and political polarization had undermined the political order in both countries, ushering in authoritarian military regimes.

Civilian governments are most vulnerable during periods of economic decay (particularly runaway inflation), when they are unable to maintain political stability, or when they are widely perceived as corrupt. All these circumstances undermine their legitimacy and increase popular expectations that military rule can improve the situation. In nations such as Nigeria, Thailand, and Pakistan, soon after seizing power coup leaders declared their intention to root out widespread corruption. Following severe economic and political crises in Argentina, Brazil, Chile, and Uruguay, the new military authoritarian regimes set out to crush leftist movements, restore social order, and reinvigorate the economy.

As modernization theory would lead us to believe, at any point in time countries that are more socioeconomically developed are less likely to suffer military takeovers than their poorer neighbors.

> Countries with per-capita GNPs of $1,000 or more [in 1995 dollars] do not [usually] have *successful* coups; countries with per-capita GNPs of $3,000 or more [normally] do not have coup *attempts*. The area between $1,000 and $3,000 per-capita GNP is where unsuccessful coups occur, while successful coups . . . were in countries with per-capita GNPs under $500.[20]

All of this indicates that a nation's propensity for military intervention correlates strongly with the nature of its political institutions, its political culture, and its level of economic development. Yet these factors alone do not account for all the variations in civil-military relations. Elite values and behavior also play an important role. For example, India and Costa Rica, with political-economic circumstances comparable to those of their neighbors, have far less military intervention. The explanation may lie in the values of their political elites: elected officials and government bureaucrats, along with political party, business, and labor leaders.

India illustrates this point well. Adjoining several countries with histories of military intervention (Pakistan, Bangladesh, Myanmar, Thailand), it has been governed exclusively by civilians since independence. There is little to suggest that the Indian public, largely rural and illiterate, has a political culture more modern or informed than that of its neighbors. It appears, however, that India's political elite subscribes more strongly than do its neighbors to the principle of civilian control.

Sometimes a rapid change in elite values can impact civil-military relations significantly, as long as that elite retains the respect of the population. Venezuela was governed by the military for much of the first half of the twentieth century. From 1959 into the mid-1990s, nearly four decades of elected government transformed the country into one of Latin America's most stable democracies until the legitimacy of its political establishment was undermined in the 1990s.[21] While a number of factors contributed to the prolonged period of civilian dominance, one critical element was a change in the attitudes of political elites following the collapse of Venezuela's first experiment with democracy (1945 to 1948). Recognizing that political polarization had precipitated the 1948 military coup, leaders of the major political parties agreed to moderate their political conflict. In 1958, the principal democratically oriented political parties signed the Pact of *Punto Fijo*, increasing interparty cooperation and setting the basis for civilian political dominance.[22] Viewed as a model for democratic reform in the region, Venezuela was one of the only Latin American countries to avoid military rule in the 1970s and 1980s. Political pacts, somewhat modeled after *Punto Fijo*, were later used to terminate civil wars and establish democratic government in Central America. By the end of the 1980s, however, the combination of deep economic crisis and pervasive government corruption had severely eroded civilian support for the leadership that had dominated Venezuelan politics since the interparty pact. Two unsuccessful coup attempts in 1992 drew considerable popular approval and turned coup leader, Lieutenant Colonel Hugo Chávez, into a national hero, at least among the poor. Elected government has survived, but Chávez, who spent two years in jail for his coup activity, easily won the 1998 presidential elections. The two political parties that had signed the *Punto Fijo* pact and had dominated Venezuelan politics for the next 40 years were practically wiped off the electoral map. Chávez has subverted many of the country's democratic institutions and given the armed forces a much greater foothold in politics. All of this suggests that political pacts are an important, but not necessarily permanent, solution to the problem of military intervention.

PROGRESSIVE SOLDIERS AND MILITARY CONSERVATIVES

Given the disorder and conflict that characterize so many Third World civilian governments, the question arises whether military involvement might bring greater stability and national development, at least in the short run. Once in office, are the generals and colonels likely to be a force for progressive change or defenders of the status quo? Some of the leading early modernization theorists felt strongly that the armed forces could contribute to development. Marion J. Levy was impressed by the military's alleged rationality, disciplined organization, and commitment to modern values. Taking their critics to task, he maintained that the armed forces might be "the most efficient type of organization for combining maximum rates of modernization with maximum levels of stability and control."[23] Lucian W. Pye also saw the military as one of the best-organized major institutions in otherwise "disorganized transitional societies." It was, said Pye, at the forefront of technical training and a leader in imparting the values of citizenship.[24] For Manfred Halpern, the Middle Eastern military was "the vanguard of nationalism and social change."[25]

Positive evaluations such as these predominated in the early moderniza-tion literature.[26] They were based to some extent on an idealized vision of the professional soldier: trained in modern organizational techniques; nationalistic; above narrow tribal, class, and regional interests. At times these writings reflected the authors' strong preference for order and stability, coupled with the assumption that the military could bring order out of chaos. Occasionally, they drew on a few military success stories and projected them on a larger screen. One early model was the Turkish military revolt led by Mustafa Kemal (Ataturk) in 1922. During the next two decades, Ataturk and his followers mod-ernized the country before eventually turning it over to civilian rule.[27] Another frequently cited military reformer was Egypt's Colonel Abdel Gamal Nasser, who rose to power in the 1950s seeking to reform his country's social institu-tions while strengthening its military. Subsequent reformist militaries else-where have often been labeled "young Turks" or "Nasserites."

Over the years a wide array of soldiers have seized power, promising to modernize their country through industrialization, greater labor discipline, expanded education, agrarian reform, or other fundamental changes. Those militaries on the Left, in countries such as Upper Volta, Libya, and Peru, have promoted economic redistribution, greater state intervention in the economy, mass mobilization, and a struggle against imperialism. Conversely, conserva-tive generals in Brazil, Chile, Indonesia, and South Korea repressed mass polit-ical participation while encouraging investment by domestic and multinational corporations.

Why, then, do some military regimes champion the poor, while others support wealthy corporate and land-owning interests? To find the answer, we must examine the class origins of the officer corps, the nation's level of socio-economic development, and the class alliances that emerge in the political sys-tem. Research in various parts of the developing world frequently has shown that officers tend to come from middle-class backgrounds, at least in Asia and Latin America. Typically, their fathers were either officers, shopkeepers, mer-chants, mid-sized land owners, teachers, or civil servants.[28] Not surprisingly, then, military regimes commonly identify with the goals and aspirations of their nation's middle class.

But what are those goals, and what political ideologies and government programs emerge from them? In the least developed Third World countries, officers often view economic elites, including powerful land owners and multinational corporations, as the source of their country's backwardness. The middle class frequently resents those same elites for obstructing its own rise to political and social prominence. In such a setting, both groups may perceive the relatively unmobilized lower class as a potential ally in the bat-tle against the oligarchy. For example, soon after taking power, Peruvian gen-eral Juan Velasco denounced the traditional land-owning class and the country's economic dependency as the sources of Peru's underdevelopment. In the following years, the military's ambitious land redistribution, shanty-town reform, expropriations of property belonging to multinational corporations, expansion of the state economic sector, and mass mobilization greatly altered the country's political and economic landscape. Elsewhere, "General Omar Torrijos of Panama railed against oligarchical control and encouraged the lower class to participate in politics."[29] Muammar Qadhafi's government in Libya and a number of Marxist military regimes in Africa were also cut from similar cloth.

As a country modernizes, however, and as lower-class mobilization intensifies, the military confronts a changing political panorama. Urbanization, the spread of secondary and university education, and the development of more complex economies all enlarge and strengthen the middle class, enabling it to wrest a share of political power from the economic elites. At the same time, industrialization increases the size of the working class and strengthens the trade union movement. Urbanization also creates a growing and sometimes militant shantytown population. And the commercialization of agriculture often triggers unrest in the countryside (see Chapter 6). Not surprisingly, the middle class (having achieved a share of political power) and its military partners now come to see the more activated and politicized lower classes as a threat rather than a useful ally.

If the Left has considerable mass support and there is growing political unrest, the military is even more likely to ally itself with the economic elite and to repress mass mobilization. In Chile, the election of Salvador Allende's Marxist government and the accompanying mobilization of workers, peasants, and urban poor polarized the country along class lines. In nearby Uruguay, the Left's electoral appeal was not as strong, but labor-industrial conflict was intense, and the Tupamaros, a potent urban guerrilla force, were engaged in a campaign of political kidnappings and other forms of violence. In both countries, the perceived threat of mass mobilization and an ascendent Left caused the military to topple long-standing democracies.

In short, then, the more underdeveloped a country is and the weaker its middle class is, the greater its likelihood of having a progressive military.[30] But, notes Eric Nordlinger, "the soldiers who have power in countries with an established middle class . . . act as more or less ardent defenders of the status quo."[31] Similarly, Samuel Huntington observes:

> In the world of the oligarchy, the soldier is a radical; in the middle class world, he is a participant and arbitrator; as mass society looms on the horizon he becomes the guardian of the existing order. . . . The more advanced a society becomes, the more conservative and reactionary becomes the role of the military.[32]

THE GOALS OF MILITARY REGIMES

Having observed the range of ideological orientations among military governments, we now examine these regimes' varying structures and the primary political-economic goals associated with each.

Personalistic Regimes

In the world's most underdeveloped nations—those with low levels of military professionalization, limited citizen participation, extensive political corruption, and little semblance of representative government—military officers frequently seize power for their own personal enrichment and aggrandizement. Their administrations tend to be highly personalistic; that is, they are led by a single charismatic officer with a strong personal following. In order to bolster his support, however, the leader allows some government plunder to pass on to the military or civilian clique surrounding him. "Legitimacy is secured through patronage, clientelistic alliances, [and] systemic intimidation."[33]

In Latin America, personalistic dictatorships have been most common in the less developed political systems of Central America and the Caribbean. One of the most prominent examples was the Somoza dynasty in Nicaragua. As leader of the country's National Guard, General Anastasio Somoza seized power in 1937, primarily seeking his own enrichment. Governing a small and impoverished nation, he amassed several hundred million dollars by using state resources to purchase construction firms, urban real estate, electrical power plants, air and shipping lines, cement factories, and much of the nation's best farm land. Following his assassination in 1956, his political and financial empire passed to his two sons, who ruled the country in succession until the 1979 Sandinista revolution.[34] Other personalistic regimes in the Americas included the Batista government in Cuba (which eventually fell victim to Fidel Castro's revolutionary army) and Alfredo Stroessner's dictatorship in Paraguay. Batista had links to the mafia's gambling and prostitution operations in Havana. Stroessner and his associates enriched themselves by collaborating with international smugglers and drug dealers.[35]

Personalistic military regimes have also been common in Sub-Saharan Africa, sometimes led by upwardly mobile junior officers or even enlisted men such as Ghana's Flight Sergeant Jerry Rawlings and Liberia's Sergeant-Major Samuel Doe. While some, like Rawlings, were well-intentioned, most have done little to develop their countries. The most infamous personalistic dictators in the continent have been Uganda's Idi Amin Dada and the Central African Republic's Jean-Bédél Bokassa. Enamored as much of power as of wealth, Amin played upon and exacerbated Uganda's ethnic divisions during his brutal eight-year reign (1971 to 1979). He not only expelled the country's sizable Asian population but also murdered many thousands of his countrymen, most notably members of the previously influential Langi and Acholi tribes. Seeing enemies at every turn, he even executed one of his wives and had another tortured. In an attempt to maintain absolute control over the armed forces, he purged or executed a large portion of the officers' corps, eventually creating an army composed largely of foreign troops (principally Sudanese and Zairean).[36]

Equally megalomaniac, the Central African Republic's Marshal Bokassa unleashed a reign of death and terror on his country following his seizure of power in 1965. Having plundered the treasury of one of the world's more impoverished nations, he concluded that the presidency was not a sufficiently exalted position, so he lavished millions on his own coronation as the country's new emperor. Ultimately, Amin and Bokassa so outraged the world community that they were ousted through external intervention. Amin fell to a Tanzanian invasion, while Bokassa was toppled by a French-sponsored coup.[37]

Because most personalistic dictators lack a meaningful ideology or policy program to legitimize their regime, they commonly must share some of the spoils of state plunder with their military and civilian supporters in order to maintain themselves in power. For example, Zaire's President Mobutu, once Africa's most enduring military dictator (1965–1997), made himself one of the richest men on earth while opening up the floodgates of corruption to benefit his military and civil service. In this manner, he kept himself in power for three decades while bankrupting the national government and destroying a once-dynamic economy. By the late 1990s, however, as the Zairean economy collapsed, his government unraveled, falling rapidly to a rebel force who, unfortunately, proved just as corrupt once they were in power.[38] In Sierra Leone and Liberia, warlords have seized power with few goals other than looting the country. The Somoza dynasty maintained the critical support of Nicaragua's National Guard by allowing its officers to share in the regime's plunder. In the most egregious example, following an earthquake that devastated the nation's capital, Guard officers appropriated relief supplies sent from the United States and sold them for a profit.[39]

Institutional Military Regimes

As the political and economic systems of many Third World nations modernize, corresponding changes take place in military attitudes and institutions. Selected officers attend advanced military academies at home or abroad. Sometimes they enroll in specialized seminars with civilian leaders, establishing links with politicians, businesspeople, or academics. Through these programs they become more deeply exposed to their country's political and economic problems.

When these "new soldiers" seize power, they are more likely to govern collectively than to vest total authority in the hands of a single leader. To be sure, some institutional military regimes have been dominated by a single figure, such as Libya's Muammar Qadhafi, Indonesia's Suharto, Syria's Hafez Assad, and Chile's Augusto Pinochet. As with purely personalistic dictators, these men may be motivated by "covert ambition, fear, greed and vanity."[40] Still, even in such cases, many officers hold influential government positions, and there is a degree of institutional decision making. Moreover, regime goals are broader than any single leader's ambitions. In Indonesia, for example, active and retired military officers at one time held nearly half the positions in the national bureaucracy and some two-thirds of provincial governorships.[41] In a like manner, the Argentine military dominated top positions in almost all government ministries during its most recent period in office.

Institutional military governments are generally headed by collegial bodies such as Niger's Supreme Military Council or Myanmar's Revolutionary Council. Comparable councils or juntas have governed Algeria, Argentina, Brazil, Ethiopia, Thailand, Uruguay, and a host of other countries.[42] Typically, one active or retired officer serves as president and wields the most power. Often, however, his term of office is limited. For example, presidents of recent military governments in Argentina and Brazil were restricted by their colleagues to a single term. In some countries, including South Korea, Brazil, and Indonesia, the armed forces tried to legitimize their rule by forming a government political party that ran candidates in tightly controlled elections. Commonly, military candidates retire from active duty before standing for office. And in Egypt, Iraq, and Syria, military and civilian elites have joined together to form a ruling political party.[43]

Institutional military regimes can be as repressive and brutal as personalistic dictatorships, sometimes more so. Their day-to-day governing style, however, is more bureaucratic and sophisticated, commonly drawing on the talents of highly trained civilian technocrats.[44] Moreover, unlike purely self-aggrandizing personalistic leaders, they are more likely to support the aspirations of the middle class (from which most officers have sprung), more prone to espouse a coherent political ideology, and more likely to champion nationalistic causes.

Most institutional military governments pursue four broad objectives, or at least profess to do so. First, whatever their real motivations, they usually justify their seizure of power by denouncing the alleged corruption of the government they have ousted. Thus, when Bangladesh's Lieutenant General Husain Muhammad Ershad led a 1982 army coup, he charged that the outgoing administration had "failed totally because of [its] petty selfishness . . . and unbounded corruption."[45] Similar proclamations have been made by incoming military leaders in Uruguay, Pakistan, Thailand, and much of Africa. All promised to clean up the mess.

A second goal—one rarely publicly articulated or acknowledged—is the advancement of military corporate interests. As Ruth First observed in Africa, while coup leaders may claim to have seized power for the good of the nation or other broad political purpose, "when the army acts, it generally acts for army reasons."[46] When officers are unhappy with their salaries, defense budgets, or the level of arms purchases, they usually respond. They also react negatively to civilian government "interference" in military affairs, such as deviating from normal officer promotion practices or lessening the armed forces' autonomy.

Ever since the 1960s—marked by coups in Togo, Ghana, Mali, Congo-Brazzaville, and Algeria—African armies have frequently seized power to protect themselves from competing military units (presidential guards and the like), to increase their troop strength, to raise their salaries, or to augment their budgets.[47] Repeated coups in Bangladesh have been motivated by similar desires for greater military spending and by resentment against civilian interference in military promotions.[48] In Southeast Asia, on the other hand, "neglect of [military] corporate interests" by civilian governments "is often a background factor contributing to a general sense of alienation [among the armed forces] rather than an immediate cause of intervention."[49] Still, army dissatisfaction with defense expenditures contributed to coups in Burma, Thailand, and pre-communist Cambodia, Laos, and South Vietnam. In the last three cases, officers believed their takeovers would increase U.S. military aid.[50]

A third common goal is the maintenance or restoration of order and stability. Institutional coups oftentimes occur when the country has experienced or anticipates civil unrest, guerrilla activity, or civil war. For example, the military first entered politics in South Korea when the administrations of Syngman Rhee and Chang Myon were challenged by student and labor unrest (though other factors also played a role). Thailand's many coups have frequently followed strikes and street demonstrations in Bangkok.

Officers are particularly troubled by radical challenges to the political and economic order and by threats to the safety and integrity of the armed forces. During the early 1960s, Indonesian civilian president Sukarno moved his regime leftward and became increasingly dependent on the country's large Communist Party, much to the discomfort of his conservative military command. In 1965, leftist military officers assassinated Lieutenant General Achmad Yani and five other officers, claiming they had been plotting a coup against Sukarno. The armed forces responded with a massive attack against the communists, eventually killing some half a million alleged party supporters. The ethnic Chinese minority was also targeted. Two years later, army leader General Suharto ousted Sukarno and assumed the presidency, a post he held until 1998.[51] Similarly, in Argentina, Brazil, Chile, and Uruguay, military dictatorships in recent decades were partly inspired by the generals' fear of leftist unions, guerrillas, and radical political parties.[52] In 1992, the Algerian armed forces terminated parliamentary elections that seemed sure to bring victory to the FIS, a group of militant Islamic fundamentalists.

Finally, most institutional military regimes hope to stimulate their nation's economy. As we have noted, coups frequently follow a period of rampant inflation, work stoppages, and economic stagnation. Thus a statistical analysis of military intervention in 38 Sub-Saharan African governments over a two-decade period revealed that coups are most likely to occur after an economic downturn.[53] Similar patterns exist in Asia and Latin America.

Third World militaries are particularly committed to industrialization. From a purely logistical perspective, industrial growth promises to provide them with arms and supplies that now must be imported from abroad. In the least developed countries, such production may be limited to food, uniforms, or rifles. On the other hand, in countries such as Brazil, Indonesia, and South Korea, a highly advanced arms industry produces planes, tanks, and sophisticated weaponry for domestic consumption and export. Even when it has no direct military applicability, industrialization is a source of national pride and international prestige. Small wonder, then, that in Latin America and parts of Asia there has often been a political alliance between industrialists and the armed forces.[54]

Having reviewed the goals of institutional military governments in general, we now focus on two distinct regime types that have received considerable attention in recent years: the bureaucratic authoritarian regime and the revolutionary military regime.

Bureaucratic Authoritarian Regimes Beginning with the Brazilian coup d'état of 1964, through the Argentine military takeovers of 1966 and 1976, to the 1973 coups in Uruguay and Chile, four of the most socioeconomically developed countries in South America succumbed to authoritarian rule. Chile and Uruguay had also been the most long-standing democracies in the region, free of military domination for decades. Thus, the coups contradicted the widely held assumption, noted previously, that both socioeconomic development and the creation of a strong party system would prevent military intervention.

Once in power, these regimes endured longer than did typical military governments in the region, lasting between 12 years (Uruguay) and 21 (Brazil).[55] By South American standards, they were also far more repressive. Political party activity was suspended for extended periods, labor unions and other grass-roots organizations were crushed, strikes were prohibited, and many suspected political dissidents were jailed and often tortured. In Argentina and Chile, thousands of people were murdered, many of them taken from their homes never to be seen again.

In a series of provocative writings, Argentine political scientist Guillermo O'Donnell referred to these military governments as "bureaucratic authoritarian (BA) regimes." Compared to previous military dictatorships, they had a more extensive bureaucratic structure that included like-minded civilian technocrats. They penetrated more deeply into the spheres of civil society, were especially closely linked to multinational corporations (MNCs), and were highly repressive.[56] O'Donnell focused on the closely related economic and political factors that explained the rise of these BA regimes in the most developed area of Latin America. First, he argued, economic growth in these countries had come to a relative standstill because they had developed as far as they could with their available capital and technology. Further growth would require heavy investment in capital goods industries and new technologies, both of which could only be provided by multinational corporations. But MNCs (as well as domestic companies) had been reluctant to invest because of frequent labor conflicts in these countries, civil unrest, and leftist electoral strength. All of these conditions, in turn, resulted primarily from economic stagnation, high inflation, and declining living standards for workers.

The military looked very dimly at the growing radicalism and political polarization of society. In Argentina, Chile, and Uruguay, urban guerrillas added to the perceived threat. The goals of the new BA regimes, then, were to crush leftist unions, political parties, and guerrilla movements; limit wages; create a "stable environment for investment"; and work closely with MNCs and domestic big business to control inflation and reinvigorate the economy. Beyond repressing the Left, the armed forces sought to depoliticize society and exclude the population from political participation for a prolonged period. At the same time, the military wished to extend the role of the private sector and, hopefully, roll back state economic intervention such as welfare programs, minimum wage guarantees, and state ownership. Many of these objectives, of course, were consistent with the goals of other institutional military regimes articulated earlier. They involve, however, a more precise and elaborate "game plan" and a far more sweeping restructuring of society. Despite fears that Latin America's BA regimes might become a model for industrializing LDCs, they proved to be an exception to the general pattern in which military takeovers are more likely in the least economically developed Third World nations.

Revolutionary Military Regimes In a number of developing nations, the military pursued goals diametrically different from the BA regimes' conservative agenda. Rather than excluding much of the population from the political system, they extended political and economic participation to formerly excluded groups. Virtually always, however, that participation was tightly controlled by an authoritarian political structure.[57]

In Africa, various military Marxist regimes laid out a program of cultural nationalism, anti-imperialism, mobilization of the peasantry and working class, nationalization of parts of the private sector, expansion of the state's economic role, and redistribution of the nation's economic resources to the poor.

Revolutionary soldiers have usually been led by radicalized officers from the junior ranks. In a speech outlining the goals of Upper Volta's military government, Captain Thomas Sankara articulated the Marxist rhetoric typical of such regimes:

> The triumph of the Revolution . . . is the crowning moment of the struggle of the Volta People against its internal enemies. It is a victory against international imperialism and its internal allies. . . . These enemies of the people have been identified by the people in the forge of revolutionary action. They are: the bourgeoisie of Volta [and] . . . reactionary forces whose strength derives from the traditional feudal structures of our society. . . . The People in our revolution comprises: The working class . . . the petty bourgeoisie . . . the peasantry . . . [and] the lumpen proletariat.[58]

Similarly radical declarations have been made by military regimes in Ethiopia, the Sudan, Somalia, Congo-Brazzaville, Benin (formerly Dahomey), and Madagascar. Like other African military regimes, however, these governments have been led by men lacking extensive political experience or advanced education, though they tended to be more educated than the officers who preceded them. Consequently, their Marxist ideals were "self-taught, ideologically immature and crude, and riddled with inconsistencies."[59] For some, Marxism simply expressed their strong nationalism and distaste for the European powers that had colonized the continent. For others, revolutionary rhetoric came almost as an afterthought, a means of justifying their seizure of power and authoritarian control. Thus, the government of Colonel Mengistu in Ethiopia, perhaps Africa's most prominent radical military regime, did not embrace Marxism-Leninism until it had been in office for three years. In Dahomey, General Mathieu Kerekou declared his government Marxist and created "revolution committees" simply as a pretext for spying on the civil service.[60]

Outside of Sub-Saharan Africa, leftist but non-Marxist military regimes have arisen in places as disparate as Libya, Myanmar, Panama, and Peru. Peru's military seized power in 1968, seeking to curtail the power of the traditional rural oligarchy and incorporate the peasantry, working class, and urban poor into the political system.[61] Comparable, though far more modest, reform programs were introduced by military regimes in Panama and Ecuador.

THE ACCOMPLISHMENTS AND FAILURES OF MILITARY REGIMES

How successfully have military governments achieved the goals just articulated, and how well have they served their country? Little needs to be said about personalistic military dictatorships. With a few notable exceptions, they rarely make a serious pretext of serving the country. Even when they have some broader goals, their primary objectives tend to be patently self-serving. In short, it would be hard to argue seriously that dictators such as Batista (Cuba), Somoza (Nicaragua), Stroessner (Paraguay), Amin (Uganda), or Bokassa (Central African Republic) contributed to the long-term political or economic growth of their nation. Consequently, the analysis that follows focuses on the record of institutional military governments.

Combating Corruption

Let us look first at the most commonly professed objective of institutional regimes—eliminating government corruption. Because government malfeasance is so pervasive in much of the Third World, denouncing it is a convenient means of legitimizing an extraconstitutional seizure of power. Yet most soldiers in power prove every bit as corrupt as their predecessors, or more so. To be sure, a few military regimes have been quite honest, but they are the exceptions. As one leading scholar has observed:

> Every Nigerian and Ghanaian coup . . . has had as its prime goal the elimination of deeply ingrained corruption from society. Yet, not one military administration has made truly consistent efforts in that direction . . . or for that matter remained immune to it itself. . . . [Elsewhere in Africa] in two . . . military regimes—Guinea and Burkina Faso—nepotism and accumulation of wealth commenced the very day the officers' hierarchy took office.[62]

Ironically, the continent's constant military intervention has tended to increase corruption in the civilian governments that are ousted. "The fear that [civilian] power may not last encourages the incoming politicians to grab what is grabbable."[63] In Asian nations such as Thailand and Indonesia, the military's record has been equally disappointing. Speaking of Southeast Asia, Harold Crouch noted that "often military officers have already become entangled in this web [of corruption] even before the coup takes place."[64] Even within those military governments that avoid gross corruption, the lure of contraband automobiles and tax-supported vacation homes proves irresistible to many officers. In short, even military governments that take office with noble intentions soon become corrupted.

Defending Corporate Interests

When it comes to pursuing their second major objective—advancing their own corporate interests—not surprisingly, military governments have been more successful. But their increased budgetary allocations have come at the cost of badly needed social and economic expenditures. Moreover, even from the armed forces' perspective, seizing power has been a mixed blessing.

Military rule normally leads to increased defense outlays. Typically, there are more armament purchases, higher military salaries, better military housing, and more luxurious officers' clubs. Sometimes the armed forces increase in size. In Asia, military officers have benefited from "lucrative public sector employment, foreign postings, and preferential treatment in the disbursal of governmental contracts."[65] After seizing power in Libya, Colonel Qadhafi sought to insure the military's loyalty by doubling their salaries, making them the highest paid army in the Third World. In their first five years in power, Uruguay's generals raised the military and security share of the national budget from 26.2 percent to more than 40 percent.[66] A parallel "bias in favor of army, police and civil-service salaries and benefits can be observed in practically every military regime in Africa."[67] An analysis of government expenditures in Southeast Asia from 1970 through the early 1980s reveals that military-dominated regimes spent a somewhat higher percentage of their national budget and GNP on defense than civilian governments did.[68]

Even when soldiers are not actually in control of the government, the mere specter of military intervention has often led civilian governments to bestow salary hikes and expensive weapons systems on the armed forces. For example, it would be very imprudent of the civilian governments in the Philippines or Thailand to shortchange military expenditures. Even Malaysia and Singapore, with no history of coups d'état, pay their officers generously to keep them out of politics.[69] Similarly, Colombia and Venezuela, two of Latin America's most long-lived civilian governments (though military involvement in politics has risen sharply in both since the 1990s), have supported healthy defense budgets aimed at keeping the military at bay.

Of course, the military's budgetary gains are frequently the country's loss, especially since few LDCs face a real military threat. Third World military outlays are frequently far higher than the country can afford. As a consequence, they reduce badly needed social and economic investment. Countries in South America that have not fought an international war in decades waste fortunes on naval vessels and state-of-the-art combat jets. In the Middle East, the percentage of GNP allocated to defense is among the highest in the world. And in Africa, home to many of the world's poorest countries, military expenditures are especially out of proportion to economic capacities. Thus, despite having a per-capita GNP less than half of Latin America's, African governments spent one third more per soldier in the 1980s.[70] The continent's defense outlays declined slightly (less than 20 percent) but unevenly from 1991 to 1998, with steeper declines in Sub-Saharan than in North Africa. But they shot up sharply (about 40 percent) from 1998 to 2000, making the region one of the only ones in the world to increase military spending in the decade.[71] Defense consumes a disproportionate share of the GNP and limits expenditures for education, health, and other welfare needs. Military budgets in countries that are engaged in domestic or international warfare—Uganda, Rwanda, Sudan, Angola—are particularly large. In 1996, Angola, one of the world's poorest nations, spent 6.7 percent of its GNP on defense, which was more than twice the worldwide average.[72]

Until the 1990s, only civilian governments with unusually strong control over the armed forces were able to reduce military budgets substantially. As the third wave strengthened the legitimacy and authority of elected governments, however, a number of LDCs made significant cuts in their military establishments. For example, following the restoration of democracy in Argentina, military spending declined by 40 percent from 1983 to 1987 (70 percent if pension expenditures are excluded).[73] From 1985 to 1993, military spending as a share of GNP fell from 2.9 percent to 1.7 percent in Argentina, from 6.8 percent to 2.1 percent in Chile, and from 4.4 percent to 1.6 percent in El Salvador.[74] Similar cuts in both spending and military manpower have taken place elsewhere in Central America as well.

In Africa, Ethiopia slashed the size of its armed forces, Africa's largest, from 438,000 in 1991 to 120,000 in 1996, while Mozambique and Nigeria also made sizable cuts. But, unfortunately, these cuts have been partially offset by sizable troop enhancements in Chad and Sudan.[75] Authoritarian governments such as Iraq's and North Korea's continue their massive military expenditures, and spending remains high in democracies such as India, South Korea, and Taiwan, which fear military threats from their neighbors. But democratization seems to have opened up some important opportunities for reducing military outlays.

Ironically, even for the military, ruling the nation is not without its risks. Although power may enlarge defense budgets, it also tends to reduce institutional cohesion. Generals and admirals squabble over the allocation of resources and over broader policy issues. Even military governments that came to power with considerable popular support usually lose legitimacy over time as they confront difficult economic and social problems. As politically divisive issues arise, they generate splits within the high command of the armed forces.[76] In some regions, most notably Sub-Saharan Africa, internal coups (one faction ousting another) have produced a series of unstable military governments. Elsewhere, the armed forces have returned to the barracks, ceding power to civilians, to avoid further internal divisions. Eric Nordlinger's study of military governments found that they tended to dissolve in five to seven years.[77] Karen Remmer's more recent work on 12 South American military regimes between 1960 and 1990 showed four to be quite durable (12 to 35 years); the remaining eight, however, averaged less than seven years in office.[78]

Establishing Stability

Military officers almost universally react negatively to popular unrest and political instability. For one thing, disorder violates their hierarchical view of society. In some cases, it threatens the interests of groups such as the middle class or industrialists, who are closely allied with the armed forces. In other instances, it poses an imminent danger to the military itself. Military men in Latin America, for example, are keenly aware that Marxist revolutions in Cuba and Nicaragua destroyed the old military establishment. Some of Batista's officers in Cuba faced the firing squad, and many Nicaraguan National Guardsmen were imprisoned or fled the country. In Chile and Brazil, leftist movements threatened the officers' hierarchical control of the armed forces. Similarly, the generals in Algeria felt endangered by the growing strength of Islamic fundamentalism. Even "revolutionary soldiers" in Ethiopia, Libya, and Peru favored discipline and socioeconomic change controlled from the top.

In many respects, military governments are particularly well-suited for controlling civil unrest. They can use force with impunity to combat guerrilla insurrections, disperse street demonstrations, and ban strikes. In a few countries, extensive and sophisticated intelligence agencies like South Korea's KCIA and Chile's DINA have enabled the regime to penetrate deeply into society and control dissent. The Argentine and Uruguayan armies used repressive tactics to crush potent urban guerrilla movements. In Indonesia, the military destroyed one of the world's largest communist parties and decimated various separatist movements.

But these mass movements could only be defeated at a tremendous cost in human suffering. Some 20,000 to 30,000 people died in the Argentine army's "dirty war" against the Left, while many more were imprisoned and tortured. Students and other young people were the primary victims, many of them incorrectly identified as part of the radical opposition. In Chile, thousands of intellectuals and professionals fled the country, devastating one of the Third World's most advanced university systems and artistic communities. Some 3,000 Chileans died; many others were the victims of torture.[79] During Indonesia's "year of living dangerously," perhaps 500,000 communists and ethnic Chinese were massacred, while some 150,000 other people died subsequently (many through starvation) in the army's struggle against East Timorian separatists.[80]

In all, the military's record of providing long-term stability is mixed. In several Asian and Latin American countries, state repression, coupled with technocratic development policies, has either co-opted or decimated opposition groups. In South Korea, sharply improved living standards and gradual political change have opened the way for stable, elected government, though the military remains a force in the background. In Argentina, Chile, and Uruguay, the BA regimes' brutality against radical movements ultimately convinced political leaders on both sides of the ideological spectrum (but especially the Left) to moderate their positions so as not to provoke further armed forces intervention. But these "successes" are the exception. Despite their brute strength, the length of the armed forces' hold on power has been surprisingly limited. One early study of Third World military regimes showed that nearly half of them lasted less than two years.[81] While their longevity has increased since that time, they continue to have a detrimental effect on political development. Military rule, no matter what its accomplishments, only impedes the maturation of political parties and other civilian institutions necessary for long-term stability.

In Africa, more often than not, coups have only led to further coups with no real stability. The brutal regime of Sergeant Samuel Doe exposed Liberia to a devastating civil war and a more sinister dictator who spread bloody conflict to Sierra Leone. Military rule in Ethiopia and the Sudan only exacerbated ethnically based civil wars. In the Middle East and Asia, extended suppression of dissident groups in countries such as Iraq and Myanmar will likely lead to greater upheavals after those regimes fall.[82]

Economic Development

Earlier we noted that coups often follow economic downturns or severe inflation. Consequently, newly installed military governments commonly hope to impose fiscal discipline and thereby revitalize the economy. In South Korea, Indonesia, Brazil, and Chile, for example, conservative military regimes curtailed union activity in order to suppress wage demands. Reduced strike activity and weaker unions were expected to both lower inflation and attract multinational investment.

Proponents of military dictatorships assert that they can more freely make economic decisions consistent with the broad national interest because they need not pander to special interest groups. Critics counter that soldiers are not trained to manage an economy. Even when well-intentioned, they tend to allocate excessive funds to defense and to wasteful chauvinistic projects. Examining the economic performance of military governments provides some evidence to support both sides of this debate. South Korea demonstrates that a military government can oversee a very successful economic development program. Following General Park Chung Hee's seizure of power in 1961, the military governed the country for more than 25 years. During that period the Republic of Korea was transformed from an underdeveloped nation into one of the world's most dynamic industrial economies.[83] Moreover, sustained economic growth was accompanied by very equitable distribution of income.

Consequently, South Korea is now cited, along with Taiwan, Hong Kong, and Singapore, as a model of well-executed economic development.

Elsewhere in Asia, Indonesia's military also presided over rapid economic growth from the mid-1960s to late 1990s. During the 1970s and early 1980s, some of the country's extensive petroleum revenues were plowed back into labor-intensive export industries. At the same time, rural development programs and mass education improved income distribution and, coupled with economic growth, substantially reduced the number of Indonesians living in poverty. Thailand, governed by the military for much of the last 70 years, also participated in East and Southeast Asia's economic boom.[84] However, excessive borrowing, "crony capitalism" (plentiful government loans and contracts to politically connected businesspeople), and corruption brought on a severe financial crisis in East and Southeast Asia beginning in 1998. Sharp declines in production, plant closings, currency devaluations, and inflation all eradicated some of the gains the population had enjoyed in the preceding decades.

Two of Latin America's major bureaucratic authoritarian regimes—Brazil and especially Chile—had relatively successful economic records, though not without problems. After several false starts, Chile's pro-business, export-oriented policies ushered in a period of strong economic expansion with low inflation. Pinochet's achievements, however, followed a period of severe economic hardship, with the poor being forced to bear a disproportionate share of the sacrifice. Under Chile's military government, as with other BA regimes, income distribution deteriorated. After the restoration of democracy in 1990, the civilian governments of Patricio Aylwin and Eduardo Frei maintained high growth rates while using targeted programs to reduce the number of Chileans living in poverty. Antipoverty programs continue under the current presidency of Ricardo Lagos in the face of more difficult economic circumstances.

Brazil's BA regime achieved dramatic economic growth during the late 1960s and 1970s, turning the country into an important industrial power. The benefits of that growth, however, were very poorly distributed, leaving many of the poor worse off. Moreover, Brazil's "economic miracle" was built on excessive foreign borrowing, making the nation the Third World's largest external debtor. Unlike Chile, civilian rule has not improved the economy since the military stepped down in 1985. Initially, continued deficit spending and poor planning brought back the hyperinflation that the generals had vowed to eradicate. Current President Fernando Henrique Cardoso brought inflation under control in the 1990s, but economic growth has been weak and the country's financial structure unstable.

Other Latin American military governments, including the BA regimes in Argentina and Uruguay, generally performed poorly in the economic sphere. They spent excessively on defense, borrowed too much, suffered from corruption, and, even when well-intentioned, lacked a grasp of development economics. In Africa, the armed forces' economic record has typically ranged from poor to disastrous. But if only a few military governments have outstanding records of economic achievement, it is not clear that the military has performed significantly worse than civilian administrations.

Efforts at systematically comparing the economic performance of military and civilian governments throughout the developing world face a number of methodological problems. Most important, it is virtually impossible to control for the myriad of other factors that might explain why one government has performed better than another.[85] When statistical analyses have been made, they tend to find little difference between the economic growth rates of the two types of regimes. Karen Remmer's analysis of Latin America, however, indicates that economies frequently decline right after the military has stepped down, suggesting that they, rather than their civilian successors, are responsible.[86] It is worth noting that the military rulers with the best economic performance—South Korea, Indonesia, and Chile—recognizing the limits of their own skills, pursued the policy recommendations of civilian advisers.[87]

MILITARY WITHDRAWAL FROM POLITICS

Once the armed forces have become entrenched in the political system, dislodging them is often no easy task. Military withdrawal is sometimes induced by domestic unrest, revolution, or external powers. More often, however, the armed forces voluntarily return to the barracks for one or more of the following reasons: they had limited objectives from the outset and, having accomplished their major objectives, decide to withdraw; difficult economic conditions make further governance unpalatable; extended rule threatens internal military cohesion; or the government has become so unpopular that staying in power would undermine the armed forces' legitimacy as an institution.

Many military governments see themselves as caretakers whose task it is to restore stability or solve a particular problem and then return power to the civilians. In Ecuador, for example, the armed forces frequently ousted elected leaders whom they considered too demagogic, too populist, or too incompetent. After ruling relatively briefly, they then voluntarily returned to the barracks.

Since the instigators of institutional coups come to office with expectations of augmented military budgets and accelerated economic growth, their interest in power, not surprisingly, wanes when the economy turns sour. In countries such as Peru, Uruguay, Pakistan, and Thailand, economic downturns have convinced military governments to step down. Economic declines may also aggravate internal divisions within the armed forces.

In Sub-Saharan Africa, governing may also exacerbate ethnic divisions within the army, particularly when officers from one tribe or religion dominate top government positions. For example, in Nigeria, the armed forces' entrance into the political arena unleashed four internal coups in a ten-year span, with ethnic tensions playing a role. Two heads of government and several other senior officers were killed in the military's internal struggles. Fearing a deterioration in military cohesiveness, some military governments may prefer to step down, leaving the county's problems to civilians.

Finally, just as military coups are most likely when civilian governments lack legitimacy, the army is most likely to return to the barracks when its own legitimacy declines. This happens most dramatically when the soldiers are defeated in war. For example, following its humiliating defeat by Britain in the Falklands (or Malvinas) war, the Argentine military regime was forced to return power to an elected civilian government. Similarly, in Pakistan, the military had to hand over power to its leading civilian critic, Zulfiqar Ali Bhutto, after it lost East Pakistan (now Bangladesh) in a war with India.

Of course, there are other ways military regimes lose legitimacy. In Uruguay, economic decay and public revulsion against government repression so weakened the regime that it unexpectedly lost a national referendum that it was sure it could tightly control.[88] Eventually, popular discontent induced the generals to negotiate a return to civilian government. More recently, in Thailand, massive student-led, prodemocracy demonstrations convinced the armed forces to withdraw.

While some combination of these factors accounts for the withdrawal of most military regimes, they do not guarantee that the armed forces will stay in the barracks. Quite the contrary. The soldiers are likely to return. Talukder Maniruzzaman examined 71 instances of military withdrawal from power in the Third World from 1946 to 1984.[89] In 65 percent of these cases, the armed forces were back in power within five years.[90]

Since the early 1980s, however, those military regimes that have stepped down from power have been more prone to remain in the barracks. For example, as of 2001, the Latin American nations of Argentina, Ecuador, Brazil, Guatemala, and El Salvador, all with long histories of armed forces' intervention, have enjoyed anywhere from 12 to 23 years without military rule. In South Korea, decades of military dominance came to an end in 1993.[91] In Africa, military rulers in several countries, including Nigeria, Ghana, Benin, and Congo-Brazzaville, have handed over power to elected civilian governments .[92] Indeed, during the past decade, many military regimes throughout the developing world have been replaced by elected governments. While some of those transitions have already been reversed, many are likely to endure.

In some cases, the military's legitimacy has been undermined by years of repressive or corrupt rule. Thus, Argentina's elected governments since the mid-1980s have been able to reduce the country's formidable armed forces to one-third their previous size. Elsewhere, as in Mozambique, El Salvador, and Nicaragua, peace treaties ending long civil wars have stipulated sharp reductions in the size of the military. In other cases, however, the military has maintained its share of the government budget.

Ultimately, if the armed forces are to acquiesce to their removal from the center of national politics, they will need to find new roles to justify their existence. This is particularly true in countries where there is little external military danger, as in Africa and Latin America, where wars between nation-states, as opposed to civil conflict, have been quite rare. In doing so, however, the military must be careful not to involve itself in tasks that may draw it back into politics—a danger some analysts see in the Latin American military's growing involvement in combating the drug trade.

NEW ROLES FOR THE ARMED FORCES

Many of the proposed "new roles" for the military are not really entirely new. They include combating drug trafficking (in parts of Latin America, the Caribbean, and Asia), antiterrorism activity, emergency relief efforts (following earthquakes, typhoons, hurricanes, and the like), and construction of infrastructure such as roads. With the expansion of the cocaine trade in recent decades, antidrug activity has become particularly important in countries such as Bolivia, Colombia, and Mexico.

Unfortunately, in the past some of these activities have brought as many new problems as solutions. In Mexico, Colombia, the Caribbean, and Central America, antidrug efforts have often corrupted the armed forces, as officers changed from enforcers to well-paid protectors of the drug cartels. In Mexico, for example, there have even been gun fights between antidrug units and other military units that had been paid off to protect drug bosses. Furthermore, the armed forces have often used their mandates to combat terrorism and other forms of internal subversion as carte blanche to violate human rights and crush peaceful and legitimate political opposition groups.

During the Cold War, U.S. training programs for Third World officers overtly stressed democratic norms. However, particularly in Latin America, the training missions' emphasis on combating guerrilla movements and other perceived subversive threats often sent a covert message that these goals might require, and therefore justify, violating human rights and interfering in national politics. With the end of the Cold War, the United States began to exert its tremendous influence abroad, seeking to reorient the political outlook of Third World militaries. During the mid-1990s, for example, the U.S. government directed its military commanders stationed overseas to encourage foreign armed forces "to consider roles . . . that are supportive of civilian control and respectful of human rights and the role of law."[93] During the Clinton administration, the International Military Education and Training program (IMET) developed considerable capabilities in that area.[94] In short, it is critical that the military pursue its new roles in a manner that reinforces, rather than subverts, civilian control over the armed forces and strengthens the military's respect for human rights and civil liberties. This is a task easier said than done.

Finally, one last, new role for Third World militaries needs mention. In recent years countries such as India, Pakistan, Argentina, and Uruguay have supplied United Nations peacekeeping forces in trouble spots such as Bosnia, Cambodia, and Afghanistan. This role represents a very different military activity and holds great promise for supporting international peace efforts. In West

Africa, regional peacekeeping forces have been sent to Liberia and Sierra Leone. But there is some potential for mischief here as regional powers such as Nigeria may use such efforts as a means of extending their own power and pursuing their foreign policy agendas.

CONCLUSION: DEMOCRACY AND THE MILITARY

By definition, the spread of democracy in the LDCs has reduced the number of military governments. But, as we have noted, even in democratically elected governments, the military may exercise considerable political influence or veto power in some policy areas and may remain dangerously independent of civilian control. In Chile, where the military dictatorship was able to dictate the terms of its 1989 withdrawal from office, the new constitution afforded the armed forces considerable power. The armed forces were granted amnesty for most of their human rights violations, including the murder of perhaps 3,000 civilians. The elected civilian president lacked the authority to remove the military's chief of staff, and the armed forces were able to name several members of the nation's Senate. General Augusto Pinochet, the departing dictator, was himself appointed senator for life. It was to be some nine years before a Spanish judge indicted Pinochet for human rights violations, and he was placed under extended house arrest during a medical visit to England. Only then did the Chilean armed forces lose their aura of invincibility, and only then was Chile's civilian government able to more forcefully assert its control over the military and begin more extensive trials for human rights violations. A more direct threat to other newly established democracies comes from actual military attempts to regain power. By one count, there were 30 to 40 such attempts in the 1980s and early 1990s.[95]

If democracy is to be consolidated, it is not enough to just have civilian government. The military must be placed securely under civilian control and the generals must unconditionally accept the authority of democratically elected presidents and prime ministers who play by the rules of the "democratic game" (respecting civil liberties and the legitimacy of political activity by opposition groups). Long accepted in the advanced industrialized democracies and in a small number of LDCs such as India, Costa Rica, and Jamaica, these guidelines have begun to take hold in a growing number of developing nations since the inception of the third wave of democratization. Still, for much of the Third World, much remains to be done to create civil-military relationships that sustain democracy.

Secure, democratic civilian government requires a professionalized military that is committed to staying out of domestic politics. In other words, there must be both "a high level of . . . professionalism and recognition by military officers of the limits of their professional competence" and "subordination of the military to the civilian political leaders who make the basic decisions on foreign and military policy [as well as domestic policy]."[96] Officers must define their professional role in terms of defending the country from potential external threats, recognizing that their involvement in national politics would only divide the armed forces and diminish their professional capacity. But just as military men must keep out of the domain of national politics, civilian political leaders are obliged to respect the domain of the military and not attempt to politicize the armed forces. All too often in the developing world, aspiring political leaders who are unable to gain power through legitimate channels have approached the military for its support. As David Mares has noted, "If civilians are willing to accept democracy as a value, it is hard to see how a professional military would be drawn into politics. And if civilians, especially powerful corporate groups, do not accept the rules of the democratic game, it is difficult to see how democracy could be consolidated whether or not the military intervenes."[97]

Even the most successful military regimes inhibit political development. They do so because their very rationale for seizing power is "the politics of antipolitics."[98] With their hierarchical perspective and their distaste for disorder, soldiers believe in a managed society. Most reject the give and take of political competition and the compromises inherent in politics. Consequently, they

> fail to see the functional aspects of the great game of politics: They severely restrict the free flow of the political process and force would-be politicians into a long period of hibernation. . . . The opportunity for gaining political skills by a people once under a military regime is likely to be continually postponed with the arrival of every new military regime.[99]

DISCUSSION QUESTIONS

1. What factors influence the likelihood of military intervention in Third World politics?
2. What are the major types of military regimes, and what are their goals?
3. What are the major strengths and weaknesses of military governments?
4. What factors induce the armed forces to withdraw from politics?

NOTES

1. George W. Ball, *The Discipline of Power* (Boston: Little, Brown, 1968), p. 231.

2. Harold Crouch, *The Army and Politics in Indonesia* (Ithaca, NY: Cornell University Press, 1978), p. 345.

3. William Thompson, "Explanations of the Military Coup," Ph.D. dissertation, University of Washington, Seattle, 1972, p. 11. Quoted in Amos Perlmutter, *The Military and Politics in Modern Times* (New Haven, CT: Yale University Press, 1977), p. 115.

4. Claude E. Welch, "Military Disengagements from Politics?: Incentives and Obstacles in Political Change," in *Military Power and Politics in Black Africa*, ed. Simon Baynham (New York: St. Martin's Press, 1986), pp. 89–90; Steven Thomas Seitz, "The Military in Black African Politics," in *Civil-Military Interaction in Asia and Africa*, ed. Charles H. Kennedy and David J. Louscher (Leiden, The Netherlands: E. J. Brill, 1991), pp. 65, 67.

5. Samuel Decalo, *Coups and Army Rule in Africa* (New Haven, CT: Yale University Press, 1990), p. 2.

6. Since its 1959 revolution, Cuba's civil-military relations have been somewhat unique. While the government is essentially controlled by civilians, there is a close linkage between the ruling Communist Party and the armed forces, with many military officers holding high party ranks and the party very involved in military policy. Consequently, there is considerable debate among Cuba scholars as to the military's strength relative to the Communist Party.

7. Chai-Anan Samudavanija and Suchit Bunbongkarn, "Thailand," in *Military-Civilian Relations in South-East Asia*, ed. Zakaria Haji Ahmad and Harold Crouch (Singapore: Oxford University Press, 1985), p. 78; Suchit Bunbongkarn, "The Thai Military and Its Role in Society in the 1990s," in *The Military, the State, and Development in Asia and the Pacific*, ed. Viberto Selochan (Boulder, CO: Westview Press, 1991), p. 68.

8. When Aquino's term ended, Ramos was elected as her successor. During his term in office he increased the military's political role. See Jeffrey Riedinger, "Caciques and Coups: The Challenge of Democratic Consolidation in the Philippines," in *Democracy and Its Limits*, ed. Howard Handelman and Mark Tessler (Notre Dame, IN: Notre Dame University Press, 1999).

9. Morris Janowitz, *Military Institutions and Coercion in the Developing Nations: Expanded Edition of the Military in the Political Development of New Nations* (Chicago: University of Chicago Press, 1977), p. 105.

10. Samuel P. Huntington, *The Soldier and the State: The Theory and Politics of Civil-Military Relations* (New York: Vintage Books, 1964).

11. Samuel P. Huntington, "Civilian Control of the Military: A Theoretical Statement," in *Political Behavior: A Reader in Theory and Research*, ed. Heinz Eulau, Samuel Eldersveld, and Morris Janowitz (New York: Free Press, 1956), pp. 380–381.

12. Samuel P. Huntington, "Patterns of Violence in World Politics," in *Changing Patterns of Military Politics*, ed. Samuel P. Huntington (New York: Free Press, 1962), pp. 19–22.

13. Alfred Stepan, "The New Professionalism of Internal Warfare and Military Role Expansion," in *Armies and Politics in Latin America*, rev. edit., ed. Abraham Lowenthal and J. Samuel Fitch (New York: Holmes and Meier, 1986), pp. 134–150. See also Jose Nun, "The Middle-Class Military Coup Revisited," in ibid., pp. 59–95, for similar arguments.

14. Ruth First, *The Barrel of a Gun: Political Power in Africa and the Coup D'état* (London: Allen Lane/Penguin Press, 1970), pp. 208, 4.

15. Michel Louis Martin, "Operational Weaknesses and Political Activism: The Military in Sub-Saharan Africa," in *To Sheathe the Sword: Civil-Military Relations in the Quest for Democracy* (Westport, CT: Greenwood Press, 1997), p. 89.

16. Samuel P. Huntington, *Political Order in Changing Societies* (New Haven, CT: Yale University Press, 1968), p. 194.

17. Robert Wesson, "Preface," *New Military Politics in Latin America*, ed. Robert Wesson (New York: Praeger, 1982), p. v.

18. Samuel E. Finer, *The Man on Horseback: The Role of the Military in Politics*, 2d ed. (London: Penguin Books, 1976), pp. 78–82.

19. Huntington, *Political Order in Changing Societies*.

20. Samuel P. Huntington, "Reforming Civil-Military Relations," in *Civil-Military Relations and Democracy*, ed. Larry Diamond and Marc F. Plattner (Baltimore: The Johns Hopkins University Press, 1996), p. 9. Italics added. Huntington's quotation lacks the modifiers that I have inserted and is correct without them currently. However, during the 1970s countries such as Argentina, Chile, and Uruguay suffered successful coups despite having per-capita GNPs well above $1,000.

21. For a cautiously optimistic look at Venezuelan democracy and the role of the military written only a year before former coup leader Lt. Colonel Chávez's election as president, see Gisela Gómez Sucre and María Dolores Cornett, "Civil-Military Relations in Venezuela," in *Civil-Military Relations: Building Democracy and Regional Security in Latin America, Southern Asia and Central Europe*, ed. David R. Mares (Boulder, CO: Westview Press, 1998), pp. 59–75.

22. Terry Karl, "Petroleum and Political Pacts: The Transition to Democracy in Venezuela," in *Transitions from Authoritarian Rule*, ed. Guillermo O'Donnell, Philippe C. Schmitter, and Laurence Whitehead (Baltimore, MD: Johns Hopkins University Press, 1986), pp. 196–219. See also Felipe Aguero, "The Military and Democracy in Venezuela," in *The Military and Democracy*, ed. Louis W. Goodman, Johanna S. R. Mendelson, and Juan Rial (Lexington, MA: Lexington Books, 1990), pp. 257–276.

23. Marion J. Levy, Jr., *Modernization and the Structure of Societies* (Princeton, NJ: Princeton University Press, 1966), vol. 2, p. 603.

24. Lucian W. Pye, "Armies in the Process of Political Modernization," in *The Role of the Military in Underdeveloped Countries*, ed. John J. Johnson (Princeton, NJ: Princeton University Press, 1962), pp. 69–89.

25. Manfred Halpern, *The Politics of Social Change in the Middle East and North Africa* (Princeton, NJ: Princeton University Press, 1963), pp. 75, 253.

26. One of the most influential was Morris Janowitz, *Military Institutions and Coercion in Developing Nations* (Chicago: University of Chicago, 1977). For a summary of those writings and further references, see Henry Bienen, "The Background to Contemporary Study of Militaries and Modernization," in *The Military and Modernization*, ed. Henry Bienen (Chicago: Atherton, 1971), pp. 1–33; First, *The Barrel of a Gun*, pp. 13–20.

27. Daniel Lerner and Richard D. Robinson, "Swords and Plowshares: The Turkish Army as a Modernizing Force," in *The Military and Modernization*, pp. 117–148.

28. Eric A. Nordlinger, *Soldiers in Politics: Military Coups and Governments* (Englewood Cliffs, NJ: Prentice Hall, 1977), pp. 32–37.

29. Karen L. Remmer, *Military Rule in Latin America* (Boston: Unwin Hyman, 1989), p. 3.

30. It is not invariable that the armed forces of the least developed nations are reform oriented. While the military has often been progressive in the less developed nations of South America, Africa, and the Middle East, it has been quite reactionary in Central America and the Caribbean, where it has been co-opted by the upper class.

31. Eric Nordlinger, *Soldiers in Politics*, p. 173; also Huntington, *Political Order*, chap. 4.

32. Huntington, *Political Order*, p. 221.

33. Decalo, *Coups and Army Rule in Africa*, p. 133.

34. John Booth, *The End and the Beginning: The Nicaraguan Revolution*, 2d ed. (Boulder, CO: Westview Press, 1985).

35. Some personalistic dictators, like Argentina's Juan Perón, have broader social programs. Peronism sought to industrialize the country and benefit the working class. Even benevolent personalistic regimes such as his, however, still suffer from extensive corruption and overconcentration of power in the hands of one person.

36. Decalo, *Coups and Army Rule in Africa*, pp. 139–198.

37. On personalistic dictatorships in Africa, military and civilian, see Robert Jackson and Carl Rosberg, *Personal Rule in Africa* (Berkeley: University of California Press, 1982).

38. David J. Gould, *Bureaucratic Corruption and Underdevelopment in the Third World* (New York: Pergamon Press, 1980), p. xiv; Michael J. Schatzberg, *The Politics of Oppression in Zaire* (Bloomington: Indiana University Press, 1988). Mobutu changed the name of his country from the Congo to Zaire. After he was overthrown, the name was changed back to the Congo.

39. Richard Millet, *Guardians of the Dynasty* (Maryknoll, NY: Orbis, 1977).

40. Decalo, *Coups and Army Rule in Africa*, p. 11. Decalo argues that in Africa personalities, more than broad socioeconomic or political variables, explain military intervention. See also his *Psychoses of Power: African Personal Dictatorships* (Boulder, CO: Westview Press, 1989).

41. Edward A. Olsen and Stephen Jurika, Jr., "Introduction," and Harold W. Maynard, "The Role of the Indonesian Armed Forces," in *The Armed Forces in Contemporary Asian Society*, ed. Edward A. Olsen and Stephen Jurika, Jr. (Boulder CO: Westview Press, 1986), pp. 18, 207–208.

42. In some cases—Liberia, for example—such councils have been mere facades, with one person really in power. Thus, it is not always easy to distinguish between personalistic and institutional military regimes. Ultimately, the determining factor is where real power resides rather than the formal structures.

43. Amos Perlmutter, *Political Roles and Military Rulers* (London: Frank Cass, 1981).

44. Guillermo O'Donnell, *Modernization and Bureaucratic-Authoritarianism: Studies in South American Politics* (Berkeley: University of California Press, 1973).

45. Jeffrey Lunstead, "The Armed Forces in Bangladesh Society," in *The Armed Forces in Contemporary Asian Society*, p. 316.

46. Ruth First, *Power in Africa* (New York: Pantheon Books, 1970), p. 20.

47. First, *The Barrel of a Gun*, p. 429.

48. Craig Baxter and Syedur Rahman, "Bangladesh Military: Political Institutionalization and Economic Development," in *Civil Military Interaction*, pp. 43–60.

49. Harold Crouch, "The Military and Politics in South-East Asia," in *Military-Civilian Relations*, p. 291.

50. Ibid.

51. Crouch, *The Army and Politics in Indonesia*.

52. Remmer, *Military Rule in Latin America*, pp. 3–31.

53. Seitz, "The Military in Black African Politics," in *Civil-Military Interaction*, pp. 61–75.

54. John J. Johnson, *The Military and Society in Latin America* (Stanford, CA: Stanford University Press, 1964); O'Donnell, *Modernization and Bureaucratic-Authoritarianism*.

55. Argentina's two military regimes lasted seven years each (1966 to 1973 and 1976 to 1983), with a three-year hiatus of unstable civilian government. The Pinochet government in Chile lasted from 1973 to 1990. While the Chilean dictatorship was not as long-lived as Brazil's, Pinochet himself ruled far longer than any of the generals in those four countries.

56. Guillermo O'Donnell, "Corporatism and the Question of the State," in *Authoritarianism and Corporatism in Latin America*, ed. James Malloy (Pittsburgh: University of Pittsburgh Press, 1977). The most complete analysis of O'Donnell's rather difficult theories is contained in David Collier, ed., *The New Authoritarianism in Latin America* (Princeton, NJ: Princeton University Press, 1979); and an excellent critique is found in Karen L. Remmer and Gilbert W. Merkx, "Bureaucratic-Authoritarianism Revisited," *Latin American Research Review* 17, no. 2 (1982): 3–40.

57. For a discussion of the difference between inclusionary and exclusionary regimes and their relationship to democracy and authoritarianism, see Remmer, *Military Rule in Latin America*, pp. 6–17.

58. "The Political Orientation Speech Delivered by Captain Thomas Sankara in Ouagadougou, Upper Volta on 2 October, 1983," in *Military Marxists in Africa*, ed. John Markakis and Michael Waller (London: Frank Cass, 1986), pp. 145–153 (selected portions).

59. Samuel Decalo, "The Morphology of Radical Military Rule in Africa," in *Military Marxist Regimes*, p. 123.

60. Thomas S. Cox, *Civil-Military Relations in Sierra Leone* (Cambridge, MA: Harvard University Press, 1976), p. 14.

61. Kevin Middlebrook and David Scott Palmer, *Military Governments and Political Development: Lessons from Peru* (Beverly Hills, CA: Sage Publications, 1975).

62. Samuel Decalo, "Military Rule in Africa: Etiology and Morphology," in *Military Power and Politics in Black Africa*, pp. 56, 58.

63. J. Bayo Adekanye, "The Post-Military State in Africa," in *The Political Dilemma of Military Regimes*, ed. Christopher Clapham and George Philip (London: Croom Helm, 1985), p. 87.

64. Crouch, "The Military and Politics in South-East Asia," in *Military-Civilian Relations*, pp. 292–293.

65. Charles H. Kennedy and David J. Louscher, "Civil-Military Interaction: Data in Search of a Theory," in *Civil-Military Interaction*, p. 5.

66. Howard Handelman, "Uruguay," in *Military Government and the Movement towards Democracy in South America*, ed. Howard Handelman and Thomas Sanders (Bloomington: Indiana University Press, 1981), p. 218.

67. Decalo, *Coups and Army Rule in Africa*, p. 20.

68. Crouch, "The Military and Politics in South-East Asia," p. 306.

69. Harold Crouch, "The Military in Malaysia," in *The Military, the State*, pp. 130–131.

70. Claude E. Welch, Jr., "From 'Armies of Africans' to 'African Armies': The Evolution of Military Forces in Africa," in *African Armies: Evolution and Capabilities*, ed. Bruce E. Arlinghaus and Pauline H. Baker (Boulder, Co: Westview Press, 1986), p. 25.

71. Elisabeth Sköns et al.,"Military Expenditures," in The Stockholm International Peace Research Institute (SIPRI) *Yearbook 2000: Armaments, Disarmament and International Security* (Oxford: Oxford University Press, 2000). Summarized on the SIPRI website (http://www.sipri.se/).

72. *Electronic Mail & Guardian* (Johannesburg, South Africa) October 16, 1997: website. http://www.mg.co.za/

73. J. Samuel Fitch, *The Armed Forces and Democracy in Latin America* (Baltimore, MD: The Johns Hopkins University Press, 1998), pp. 77–78.

74. Juan Rial, "Armies and Civil Society in Latin America," in *Civil-Military Relations*, p. 57.

75. Michel Louis Martin, "Operational Weaknesses and Political Activism," in *To Sheathe the Sword*, p. 89.

76. On the problems soldiers face when trying to govern, see Clapham and Philip, eds., *The Political Dilemma of Military Regimes*, especially chap. 1.

77. Nordlinger, *Soldiers in Politics*, p. 139.

78. Remmer, *Military Rule*, p. 40.

79. Pamela Constable and Arturo Valenzuela, *A Nation of Enemies: Chile under Pinochet* (New York: W. W. Norton, 1991).

80. Of course, many military regimes are not particularly repressive. However, it is precisely those that seize power to restore order in highly polarized societies that normally are the most brutal.

81. R. D. McKinlay and A. S. Cohan, "Performance and Instability in Military and Nonmilitary Regime Systems," *American Political Science Review* 70 (September 1976): 850–864.

82. Both countries have experienced extensive ethnic unrest under semimilitary (Iraq) or military rule. Iraq's Kurdish secession movement was revitalized by the country's defeat in the Gulf War.

83. Jueng-en Woo, *Race to the Swift* (New York: Columbia University Press, 1991).

84. For a somewhat more critical view, particularly of income distribution and welfare in Indonesia, see "Military Regimes and Social Justice in Indonesia and Thailand," in *Civil-Military Interaction*, pp. 96–113; see also the chapters on South Korea, Indonesia, and Thailand in James W. Morely, ed., *Driven by Growth* (New York: M. E. Sharpe, 1992).

85. For a discussion of the problems involved in evaluating the economic performance of Latin America's military governments, see Karen L. Remmer, "Evaluating the Policy Impact of Military Regimes in Latin America," in *Armies and Politics*, pp. 367–385; Remmer, *Military Rule*, chap. 4.

86. Remmer, *Military Rule*, pp. 197–200; Robert W. Jackman, "Politicians in Uniform: Military Governments and Social Change in the Third World," *American Political Science Review* 72, no. 4 (1978): 1262–1275; Seitz, "The Military in Black African Politics."

87. Edward A. Olsen, "The Societal Role of the ROK Armed Forces," in *The Armed Forces in Contemporary Asian Society*, pp. 95–96.

88. Howard Handelman, "Prelude to the 1984 Uruguayan Election: The Military Regime's Legitimacy Crisis and the 1980 Constitutional Plebiscite," in *Critical Elections in the Americas*, ed. Paul Drake and Eduardo Silva (San Diego: University of California Press, 1986).

89. In all of these cases military rulers were succeeded by civilians. There are, of course, also many instances of military governments giving way to other ones as the result of internal coups or other intramilitary conflict.

90. Talukder Maniruzzaman, *Military Withdrawal from Politics: A Comparative Study* (Cambridge, MA: Ballinger Publishing, 1987), pp. 21, 24–25.

91. South Korea's first democratic presidential election had been held in 1987, but the victor, Roe Tae Woo, was a former military strongman. Thus, full civilian government did not come until Kim Young Sam assumed the presidency in 1993. On Korea's transition, see Byung-Kook Kim, "Korea's Crisis of Success," in *Democracy in East Asia*, ed. Larry Diamond and Marc F. Plattner (Baltimore, MD: Johns Hopkins University Press, 1998), pp. 113–132.

92. Michael Bratton and Nicolas van de Walle, *Democratic Experiments in Africa* (New York: Cambridge University Press, 1997), pp. 197–203.

93. Quoted in Louis W. Goodman, "Military Roles Past and Present," in *Civil-Military Relations and Democracy*, p. 32. The discussion that follows of "new roles" for the military draws on Goodman's chapter.

94. Joseph S. Nye, Jr., "Epilogue: The Liberal Tradition," in *Civil-Military Relations*, pp. 153–154.

95. Samuel P. Huntington, "Reforming Civil-Military Relations," p. 8.

96. Ibid., pp. 3–4.

97. David R. Mares, "Civil-Military Relations, Democracy, and the Regional Neighbors," in *Civil-Military Relations*, ed. Mares (Boulder, CO: Westview Press, 1998), p. 18.

98. Brian Loveman and Thomas M. Davies, Jr., eds., *The Politics of Antipolitics: The Military in Latin America*, 2d ed. (Lincoln: University of Nebraska Press, 1989).

99. Ibid., p. 6.

chapter 10

The Political Economy of Third World Development

Virtually every Third World government, except the most corrupt and incompetent, wishes to promote economic development. Economic growth coupled with a reasonably equitable distribution of income offers the promise of improved living standards and, presumably, increased popular support for the ruling regime.[1] It also provides added tax revenues, thereby augmenting government capacity. And economic development can enhance a nation's military strength, diplomatic influence, and international prestige. But the obvious benefits of growth should not obscure the many difficult questions that surround economic development. For example: How is growth to be achieved, and how can the sometimes conflicting goals of economic development be reconciled? How should the inevitable sacrifices required for generating early economic development be shared? How can economic development be achieved without doing irreparable harm to the environment?

The optimism expressed by early modernization theorists regarding Third World economic development seemed ill-founded during the 1980s in the face of sharp economic declines in Africa and Latin America.[2] In South Asia, Sub-Saharan Africa, and other developing regions, the war on poverty often seemed unwinnable. On the other hand, dependency theory's pervasive pessimism about the limits of development in the periphery seemed to have been belied by East Asia's spectacular growth from the 1960s into the 1990s, though that region's deep economic crisis at the close of the 1990s complicated that picture somewhat.

In recent years, scholarship on the Third World has increasingly turned to *political economy*. Martin Staniland defines this field as the study of "how politics determines aspects of the economy, and how economic institutions determine the political process," as well as "the dynamic interaction between the two forces."[3] As such, political economy covers a wide field of inquiry. Staniland notes, for example, that as of the early 1980s, his university's library catalog contained 117 books whose title began with "The Political Economy of. . . ." Since that time, the number has multiplied substantially.

This chapter focuses on several important economic issues: What should the role of the state be in stimulating and regulating economic growth and industrialization in the LDCs? What are the major strategies for development? How should countries deal with the deep economic inequalities that persist, or even increase, during the modernization process?

THE ROLE OF THE STATE

The question of the state's proper economic role has been at the center of political and economic debates for hundreds of years, first in Western industrial economies, and more recently in the Third World. During the sixteenth and seventeenth centuries, major European powers were guided by the philosophy of *mercantilism*, which viewed a nation's economic activity as a means of enhancing the political power of the state and its monarch. Government, consequently, was viewed as "both source and beneficiary of economic growth."[4] That perspective was sharply challenged by the eighteenth-century Scottish political economist Adam Smith, who favored a minimized state that allows market forces a relatively free hand. The following century, Karl Marx, reacting to the exploitative nature of early capitalism, proposed assigning the state a dominant role through ownership of the means of production and the centralized direction of the economy. Finally, in the twentieth century, Sir John Maynard Keynes, responding to the Great Depression, advocated a substantial degree of government economic intervention but rejected Marxist prescriptions for state ownership and centralized planning.

Today, the collapse of the Soviet "command economy" and the poor economic performance of the remaining communist nations (except China and Vietnam, which have largely abandoned Marxist economics) have discredited the advocates of state-dominated economies. At the same time, however, no government embraces full *laissez faire* (i.e., allowing market forces a totally free reign, with no government intervention). All countries, for example, no matter how capitalistic, have laws regulating banking, domestic commerce, and international trade. Most have introduced some environmental regulation. In the real world, then, governments must decide where to position themselves between the extreme poles of laissez faire and a command economy.

For a number of reasons, that choice is contentious in the LDCs. The fragile nature of many Third World economies, their high levels of poverty, their poor distribution of wealth and income, their extreme dependence on international market forces, and their endangered natural environment have encouraged many governments to assume an active economic role. Moreover, many developing nations also lack a strong entrepreneurial class and substantial private capital for investment. As a consequence, their governments have often built the steel mills, railroads, or sugar refineries that the private sector could not, or would not. More recently, governments have been called upon to protect the environment against the ravages of economic development. Not surprisingly, then, state economic intervention traditionally has been more pronounced in Africa, Latin America, and South Asia than in the West. In recent decades, however, a worldwide trend toward "neoliberal" economic policies has sharply reduced government economic intervention in both the developing and developed world.[5]

The pages that follow discuss a number of alternative models prescribing the role of the state in Third World economies, ranging from command economies such as North Korea's to very limited state intervention in Hong Kong. In considering these alternatives, the reader should keep in mind that these are ideal types. Few countries fit any of these models perfectly (Cuba's Marxist government, for example, permits private farming and a number of small businesses), and many nations have tried some mix of these approaches. Other models exist, and the options discussed below are not exhaustive.

The Command Economy

Marxism began as a critique of capitalism in the Western world during the early stages of industrial development. Inherently, argued Marx, capitalism produces an inequitable distribution of wealth and income because those who control the means of production (industrialists, landlords) exploit those who work in them (the working class, peasants). One of Marxism's appeals to its supporters, then, is its *promise of great equality and social justice*. Consequently, it is not surprising that the ideology has appealed to many Third World leaders and aspiring leaders who are troubled by the deep injustices in their own economic systems. That argument is particularly persuasive in Latin America and parts of Africa, which have the greatest disparities between rich and poor. Furthermore, inequalities tend to grow as countries move from the lower to the middle levels of development.[6]

A second assertion made by Third World Marxist regimes is that only they can *free their country from the yoke of dependency*. Since many dependency theorists believe that an exploitative relationship between core industrial nations and peripheral LDCs is an inevitable outcome of capitalist trade and investment, they believe that only a socialist economy can achieve economic independence and development. It is in that spirit that Havana's José Martí airport displays a billboard reading "Welcome to Cuba, the only free territory in the Americas."

Finally, another of communism's appeals has been its belief in *centralized state control over the economy*. A command economy, initially established in the Soviet Union, has two central features. First, the means of production are primarily owned and managed by the state. That includes factories, banks, major trade and commercial institutions, retail establishments, and, frequently, farms. While all communist nations have allowed some private economic activity, the private sector has been quite limited, aside from communist nations such as China, which have largely abandoned Marxist economics in recent years. Second, decisions concerning production are not set by market forces but rather by centralized state plans.

Interestingly, Marxists have viewed market (capitalist) economies as anarchistic because the most fundamental decisions over the allocation of resources and the determination of prices are left to the whims of supply and demand. Adam Przeworski satirizes the orthodox Marxists' attitude toward the mundane organizational schemes of capitalism: People in Britain and the United States get up in the morning and find their newspaper or milk carton already sitting outside their door without even knowing who delivered it. But, Przeworski notes wryly, Marxists continue to insist that the paper or milk carton couldn't possibly be there without a central planner guaranteeing its arrival.[7] In fact, the collapse of Soviet and Eastern European communism revealed the organizational failures of centralized, command economies. As Przeworski maintains, under a centrally planned economy not only would milk delivery deteriorate, but there also would be constant shortages of both cartons and milk.

Indeed, the flaws of command economies are now so obvious as to hide their earlier accomplishments. By being able to dictate the movement of people and resources from one sector of the economy to another, communist countries such as the Soviet Union and China were able to jump-start their industrial takeoffs. During the 1920s and 1930s, "entire industries were created [in the USSR], along with millions of jobs that drew peasants away from the countryside and into higher-paying jobs and higher living standards."[8] Western estimates of Soviet economic performance during its industrialization phase indicate that between 1928 and 1955, GNP grew at a robust average annual rate of roughly 5 percent.[9] During the early decades of its revolution, China also moved quickly from a backward agrarian economy to a far more industrialized society. According to one leading authority, between 1952 and 1975, China's economy grew at an average annual rate of 8.2 percent, while industry surged at 11.5 percent.[10] These rates far exceeded the norms in either capitalist developing nations or industrial democracies.[11] Other analysts believe that China's growth rates could not have been quite that high because of the setbacks of the Great Leap Forward and the Cultural Revolution. Still, all agree that compared to India, Pakistan, and most LDCs, China's growth during that period, just like the Soviet Union's decades earlier, was extremely impressive. Small wonder that the Soviet and Chinese models (though in many ways different from each other after 1966) were attractive to many Third World leaders.

Finally, command economies have generally made great strides toward reducing income inequalities. Indeed, it is here that communist LDCs most clearly outperform their capitalist counterparts. In Cuba, for example, the revolution brought a substantial transfer of income from the richest 20 percent of the population to the poorest 40 percent.[12] The poor also benefited from an extensive land reform program, subsidized rents, and free health care, though some of those gains were undermined in the 1990s, following the loss of Soviet economic assistance. Equality was further advanced through mass adult literacy programs and the expansion of education. Nor was Cuba unique in this respect. Cross-national, statistical comparisons indicate that communist countries as a whole have more equal income distribution than do capitalist nations at similar levels of development.[13]

Eventually, however, the weaknesses of command economies overshadow their accomplishments.[14] In the absence of signals of consumer demand, state planners have little basis for deciding what to produce and how much. Moreover, factory and farm managers in centrally controlled economies are rewarded for meeting their output quotas, with little concern for product quality. Even in the best of circumstances, to be at all efficient, a centralized, command economy would need a highly skilled and honest bureaucracy equipped with sophisticated technology such as computers and accurate consumer surveys. None of these qualities exist in Third World bureaucracies. So, in command economies, inefficient state bureaucracies are given inordinate power and, as Lord Acton warned, "Power tends to corrupt, and absolute power tends to corrupt absolutely."

Analysts of Chinese politics observe that for local entrepreneurs, the price of doing business is bribing government officials (cadres) or their adult children.[15] More generally, command economies are known for their large privileged class of state and party bureaucrats (*apparatchiks*), who enjoy perquisites unavailable to the rest of the population. While the Soviet Union and China enjoyed impressive bursts of growth in the early decades of their revolutions, each eventually ran out of steam as their economies became more complex and, hence, harder to control centrally. Moreover, command economies are more adept at building heavy industries such as steel mills or constructing public works projects—endeavors more typical of early industrialization—than they are at developing sophisticated, high-tech production techniques or producing quality consumer goods. The Soviet Union, for example, turned out impressive military hardware and powerful space rockets but was unable to produce a decent automobile or home washing machine. By the late 1970s (in China) and the 1980s (USSR), with both economies deteriorating, their leaders (Deng Xiaoping and Mikhail Gorbachev) recognized the need to decentralize their economy and reduce state control. China's transition to *market socialism* (a mixture of free market and socialist economics) has been tremendously successful, producing one of the world's fastest growing economies. However, in the Soviet Union and its major successor state, Russia, economic reforms have so far failed to arrest the country's downward slide.

The collapse of Soviet bloc communism and China's remarkable economic transformation have inspired market-oriented reforms in other command economies. Vietnam, for example, has transferred state farm land to the peasantry and freed prices from state controls. Elsewhere in Asia and Africa, governments such as Myanmar and the Congolese Republic have privatized much of the state sector and reduced government economic controls. The end of Soviet aid has undercut some of Cuba's earlier gains in health care, nutrition, and education. Stripped of its primary benefactor, it has been forced to accept certain free-market innovations.

For most former communist nations, the demise of their command economies has so far failed to improve living standards and has often sharply lowered them. In some cases, the economic order previously imposed by government authorities was removed without adequate free-market incentives to replace it. In a sense, the "stick" driving the economy forward disappeared before workable "carrots" had been developed to replace it. Workers who accepted Spartan living conditions in return for guaranteed incomes and social services (what the Chinese call the "iron rice bowl") find themselves stripped of these guarantees with no compensatory gains. Only in China, where many state controls remain in place, has the transition toward free-market economics raised living standards substantially.

Latin America Statism

Even in capitalist Third World countries, the state has often played a major economic role, seeking to be an engine of economic growth. In the period between the two World Wars, many Latin American nations first pursued state-led industrialization. That process accelerated during the Great Depression, when countries in the region had difficulty finding markets for their food and raw material exports and, consequently, lacked foreign exchange for industrial imports. Argentina, Brazil, Chile, Uruguay, and Mexico were among the early leaders in the push toward industrialization.

Unlike communist countries, Latin American nations, with rare exceptions, have left most economic activity in the hands of the private sector and have not imposed centralized control over the economy. But their governments have generally owned strategically important enterprises and have invested in industries that failed to attract sufficient private capital. Consequently, prior to the recent privatization of state enterprises, many of the region's railroads, airlines, petroleum industries, mines, steel mills, electric power plants, telephone companies, and armaments factories were state owned.

Two aspects of state ownership in the region contradict popular stereotypes. First, government takeovers frequently were not opposed by the domestic private sectors. For one thing, many of the most important nationalizations—including the petroleum industries in Mexico and Venezuela, mining in Chile and Peru, and railroads in Argentina—involved companies that had been owned by multinational corporations, not local capitalists. Second, state-owned petroleum industries, railroads, and utilities provided private-sector industries with subsidized transportation, power, and other needed resources. In fact, until the 1980s, conservative governments in the region were as likely to expand government ownership as were left-leaning or populist regimes. For example, during the 1960s and 1970s, Brazil's right-wing military regime substantially increased the size of the state sector.

Along with its ownership of many essential enterprises, the state also played a pivotal role in fomenting private-sector industrial growth. In Latin America's largest economies, the government initiated import-substituting industrialization (ISI) programs in the early to mid twentieth century. ISI (discussed more extensively later in this chapter) sought to replace imported consumer goods with products that were manufactured domestically.[16] Although import-substituting manufacturers were almost always privately owned, government economic policies and programs were essential for stimulating industrial growth. Protective import tariffs, quotas, favorable exchange rates, subsidized loans, and controlled interest rates were all used to promote industrialization.

In Argentina, Brazil, Colombia, Mexico, and elsewhere, these state policies were quite successful. From 1945 to 1970, rates of investment in Latin America were higher than in the Western industrial powers, and from 1960 to 1980, its manufacturing output grew faster as well.[17] Virtually every country in the region began to manufacture basic consumer goods such as textiles, apparel, packaged food, and furniture. Larger nations such as Argentina, Brazil, and Mexico established automotive industries, steel mills, and other heavy industries. Although the largest manufacturing plants were mostly foreign owned, local entrepreneurs also played an important role in the region's industrial expansion. In time, industrialization altered the region's demographic and class structures. Massive rural migration to the cities transformed Latin America into the Third World's most urbanized region (see Chapter 7). Many blue-collar jobs were created, and the size of the middle class expanded substantially.

But hidden beneath these accomplishments, state-sponsored ISI also promoted economic inefficiencies and inequalities. While its nurturing of industrialization was helpful, perhaps necessary, in the early stages of economic development, government protection and stimuli were employed too broadly and too long. Rather than serving as a finely calibrated tool for getting industrialization off the ground, ISI became a politically motivated juggernaut. With industrialists, the middle class, and organized labor all united behind these policies, elected officials were unwilling to wean established industries from government support and protection long after they should have become more self-sufficient. Inefficient domestic industries received excessive protection; trade and fiscal policies designed to promote industrialization often harmed agricultural exports; and the income gap widened both between urban and rural populations and between skilled and unskilled workers.

Mexico illustrates both the initial accomplishments and subsequent weaknesses of statism in the region. From the mid-1930s to 1970, the national government accounted for 35 to 40 percent of the country's total investment.[18] At the same time, the state-owned petroleum and railroad enterprises provided private industry with subsidized energy and transport (i.e., both were priced below their free-market values).[19] Government trade and labor policies protected Mexican companies from foreign competition and held down wages as a means of stimulating further investment. As a consequence, between 1935 and 1970, industrial output grew at an average annual rate of nearly 10 percent, and GNP rose 6 percent annually, making Mexico one of the world's fastest growing economies.[20] During the 1970s and early 1980s, however, the role of the state in the economy took on a life of its own and grew enormously.[21] By the mid-1980s, the government operated nearly 1,200 state enterprises (called *parastatals*). Mexico's "economic miracle" had left the countryside and urban poor behind, creating a highly unequal distribution of income and substantial pockets of poverty. When the state petroleum company discovered vast new oil reserves in the 1970s and the price of petroleum more than tripled, the government came under intense political pressure to use its oil bonanza not just to help the poor, but to provide subsidies for consumers of all classes, further subsidize private industry, and create new jobs in the parastatals. Quite quickly, spiraling government expenditures exceeded new petroleum revenues and contributed to huge fiscal deficits and enormous foreign indebtedness.

Two sources of inefficiency should be noted, both relevant not only to Mexico but to the Third World generally. First, while it is quite possible to run state enterprises efficiently (for example, many of the companies nationalized in the 1980s by France's socialist government were well operated), few Third World governments manage to do so. In the face of high unemployment and underemployment rates, governments are under great political pressure to hire more personnel than the enterprises need. Consequently, most parastatals are substantially overstaffed.[22] At the same time, these enterprises are also under political pressure to sell the public consumer goods and services at highly discounted prices. For example, prior to 1991, Argentineans rode the state railroads for a nominal fee and received highly subsidized electricity. Not many years ago, gas was selling in Venezuela for 22 cents per gallon.[23] Ultimately, the combination of money-losing parastatals, consumer subsidies, and subsidies to private-sector producers helped bankrupt many Latin American governments. By 1982 virtually every government in the region was deeply in debt and experiencing severe fiscal problems.

Another important weakness of Latin America's development model was the inefficiency it encouraged in the private sector. To be sure, governments throughout the world have effectively used protectionist measures to help infant industries get off the ground during the early stages of industrialization. A wall of high tariffs and import quotas largely shields manufacturers of domestic consumer goods from foreign competition. But over time, the level of protection needs to be scaled back or domestic firms will have little incentive to become more productive and internationally competitive. Instead, Latin American protectionism, rather than serving as a temporary stimulus, became embedded in the economy.

Since the 1980s, most Latin American nations, moved by the region's severe debt crisis and economic depression, have sharply reversed their earlier statist policies. In Mexico, the de la Madrid and Salinas administrations (1982 to 1994) shut down or privatized more than 80 percent of the country's 1,155 state enterprises, including the national airline, telephone companies, and banking system.[24] In Chile, the transition to a slimmed-down state was begun by the military dictatorship of General Augusto Pinochet (1973 to 1990). But when democracy was finally restored, the new governing coalition (including the Christian Democratic and Socialist parties) continued many of Pinochet's economic policies, which they had once denounced.

While these reductions in public-sector activity may have been necessary, they were implemented at great human cost. Throughout Latin America, millions of workers lost their jobs, as parastatals were either shut down or were subject to massive layoffs after being privatized. In Mexico alone, an estimated 400,000 jobs were eliminated in the course of the government's economic restructuring. For example, more than half the workers formerly employed in state steel mills lost their jobs when their companies were privatized.[25] Similar layoffs took place in Argentina, Chile, Peru, and Venezuela. At the same time, reduced protectionism in much of the region opened the door to a surge of imported consumer goods, thereby reducing sales and employment by local firms that were unable to compete. Finally, the elimination or reduction of government consumer subsidies sharply increased the cost of many basic necessities, including a variety of foods, gasoline, public transportation, and electricity.

In Mexico and Argentina, just as in Chile, populist and leftist parties that had once been the leading advocates of government economic intervention reluctantly conceded that the state sector had grown too unwieldy and had to be cut back.[26] Excessive government spending, coupled with the state's inability or refusal to make the middle and upper classes pay their fair share of taxes, had resulted in massive fiscal deficits and runaway inflation. Only by substantially cutting budgetary deficits since the 1980s have Latin America's governments been able to control inflation rates that had reached annual rates of 1,000 to 10,000 percent in Argentina, Brazil, Nicaragua, and Peru. The debt crisis and the related economic recession contributed to a sharp decline in Latin American living standards during the 1980s and early 1990s (the "lost decade"). In Peru and Venezuela, for example, real incomes fell by nearly 40 percent.[27] Since that time, the region has experienced moderate growth overall, but countries such as Argentina, Brazil, and Mexico have alternated between periods of growth and years of sharp economic decline.[28]

East Asia's Developmental State

While Latin America has been struggling since the early 1980s, a number of East and Southeast Asian economies have grown at a phenomenal rate during most of that period. South Korea, Taiwan, Hong Kong, and Singapore (known as the "little tigers") and China (now the world's third largest economy) have received the most attention. For one thing, their impact on world trade has been enormous. China is now one of the United States' leading trading partners. But other Southeast Asian economies—Thailand, Malaysia, and Indonesia—have also grown dramatically. From the mid-1960s until the region's recent economic crisis, Taiwan, South Korea, Singapore, Hong Kong, Thailand, Malaysia, Indonesia, and China all grew at annual rates ranging from 4 to 10 percent, and China and South Korea occasionally exceeded 10 percent.[29] In fact, from 1960 to the late 1990s, these economies grew almost three times as fast as Latin America and five times as fast as Sub-Saharan Africa.[30] Moreover, the benefits of East and Southeast Asia's rapid growth were relatively equitably distributed, with a far narrower gap between the rich and poor than one finds in Latin America and Africa.

With the partial exception of Communist China (which has developed a mixed socialist and free-market economy), East and Southeast Asian countries have largely tied their growth to the free market. More so than in other Third World regions, productive capacity has been largely owned by private enterprise, with a relatively smaller state sector.[31] Not surprisingly, this has led conservative economists to hail the East Asian economic miracle as a triumph of unfettered capitalism, a testimony to keeping government out of the economy.[32]

But many scholars specializing in East Asian economies argue that, to the contrary, governments in that region have been key players in stimulating economic growth.[33] Examining the causes of Japan's spectacular postwar economic resurgence, Chalmers Johnson first formulated the notion of the *developmental state*.[34] The meaning of that term is best understood by comparing the role of government in East Asia's high-growth capitalist nations (Japan, South Korea, Singapore, and Taiwan) to its function in Western nations during their early industrial expansions some 150 years before. The early-developing Western nations established *regulatory states* in which "government refrained from interfering in the marketplace, except to insure certain limited goals (e.g., antitrust regulations, protection of consumer rights)," while the East Asian developmental states "intervene actively in the economy in order to guide or promote particular substantive goals (e.g., full employment, export competitiveness, energy self-sufficiency)."[35]

Japan's powerful Ministry of International Trade and Industry (MITI), Johnson notes, directed that country's postwar industrial resurgence. Subsequently, South Korea, Taiwan, Singapore, Indonesia, and other industrializing nations in East and Southeast Asia adopted many aspects of Japan's state-guided, capitalist development model.[36] Typically, each country has a powerful government ministry or agency "charged with the task of planning, guiding and coordinating industrial policies."[37] They include South Korea's Economic Planning Board, Taiwan's Council for Economic Planning and Development, and Singapore's Economic Development Board, all modeled after MITI. Under the developmental state, there is far more extensive and direct government economic intervention than in the West, targeting either whole economic sectors (such as agriculture or industry), whole industries (such as computers, automobiles, and electronics), or particular companies (such as Hundai).[38]

Not all developmental states are the same. For example, the bonds between government and big business are tighter in South Korea than in Taiwan, while state enterprises are more important in Taiwan than in Korea. In Singapore, government control over labor is more extensive than in the other two countries.[39] But in all of them, the state plays an important role, guiding the private sector toward targeted economic activities and stimulating growth in areas that the government wishes to expand. Sometimes government planners will even pressure particular industries or companies to specialize in certain products and abandon others.

For the most part, East Asian state intervention was more indirect than it had been in Latin America, but it was significant nonetheless. Among the tools governments have used to sway private-sector activity are tax policy, control over credit, and influencing the price of raw materials. For example, when the South Korean and Taiwanese governments wished to develop the electronics, computer software, and automobile industries, they intervened aggressively, rather than leaving it to the marketplace. They established related research institutes; granted firms in targeted industries preferential access to credit; temporarily required companies that had been importing targeted products to switch to domestic manufacturers; and offered trade protection to new industries for limited periods of time. South Korea temporarily banned all imports of computers when it promoted that industry, and Taiwan did the same for textiles.[40]

While the East Asian development model's tremendous success won it widespread admiration, some observers are skeptical about its applicability elsewhere. One concern is the model's apparent political requirements. Chalmers Johnson notes that most developmental states have been authoritarian—or what he calls "soft authoritarian"—during their major industrialization push.[41] Other analysts feel that authoritarian or semi-authoritarian rule (including the ability to repress or control labor unions and to direct management) was an essential component of the region's early economic growth. Taiwan and South Korea industrialized under authoritarian governments, though both have subsequently become democracies. The governments of Malaysia, Singapore, and Indonesia have all repressed democratic expression to varying degrees. Since its return to Chinese rule, Hong Kong, a former British colony, has curbed its brief experiment with democracy. Of course, Japan, the original developmental state, is a democracy, but since the 1950s, its government has been largely dominated by one political party (the Liberal Democrats). Thus, we are left to wonder how the developmental state would perform under the democratic pressures now spreading across the Third World.

Another important question is the transferability of East Asian political and economic practices to other parts of the Third World.[42] The developmental state seems to require qualities that are in short supply elsewhere in the developing world: a highly skilled government bureaucracy and close cooperation between business, labor, and agriculture. In Indonesia, for example, a team of skilled government economists known as "the Berkeley Boys" (most of them had doctoral degrees from the University of California at Berkeley) oversaw that country's economic development. Similarly, South Korea's highly trained state technocrats worked closely with the country's dominant business conglomerates (*chaebols*), such as Hundai and Samsung.[43] Similar cooperation between sophisticated government planners and big business, unchallenged by a relatively docile working class, has contributed to the economic surges elsewhere in East and Southeast Asia. Outside of Asia, however, only Chile's "Chicago Boys" (economists trained at the University of Chicago) brought a comparable set of skills and similar cooperation with the business community.

Some have argued that East Asia's Confucian culture—featuring nationalism, close cooperation between different sectors of society, and a strong work ethic—has been a critical ingredient in the region's rapid economic growth.[44] If that is true, then a development model that has worked in that part of the world may not transfer well to other cultures. Of course, similar cultural explanations have been put forth to explain the West's economic takeoff. Long ago, Max Weber credited the birth of capitalism to the Protestant work ethic. But such cultural explanations have always aroused considerable controversy. Critics point out, for example, that not all of Asia's star economic performers have Confucian cultures. Rapidly growing Malaysia and Indonesia, for example, are predominantly Muslim. A more telling criticism of the cultural thesis points out that Confucian culture has been around for centuries, while the East Asian economic "miracle" is only a few decades old.[45] Ironically, before the region's takeoff, some Western scholars attributed East Asia's poverty, in part, to Confucian culture.

In fact, it is implausible that there is something so uniquely Asian about the developmental state that it cannot be reproduced elsewhere. But few African, Latin American, or Middle Eastern nations currently offer promising conditions for its growth. Most still lack both a highly professional, merit-based bureaucracy and a spirit of cooperation between key economic actors that would allow them to replicate the East Asian model. And even in Asia, the economic crisis of the late 1990s revealed serious weaknesses in the developmental state model. In countries such as Indonesia, intense government involvement in the economy helped create "crony capitalism" in which the government provided well-connected investors with insider opportunities. Elsewhere, excessive government regulation stifled competition within the private sector. As we shall see shortly, the developmental state has been fine-tuned since East Asia's financial crisis.

The Neoclassical Ideal

Quite unlike the preceding models, the neoclassical ideal assigns government a very limited economic role.[46] The state, it argues, should provide certain fundamental "public goods" such as national defense, police protection, a judicial system, and an educational system. It can also supply physical infrastructure, including sewers and harbors, when it is not feasible for private capital to do so, and perhaps allocate enough resources to the very poor to meet their basic needs.[47] But, say neoclassical analysts, most Third World governments have injured their economies by moving far beyond that limited role. These critics attribute Africa's and Latin America's economic development problems to excessive state intervention, at least in the past, while they credit East Asia's success to their governments' allegedly limited role.

Neoclassical economists insist that free-market forces should determine production decisions and set prices without government interference. Consequently, they have criticized government policies designed to stimulate industrial growth in the LDCs: protective tariffs and import quotas that restrict free trade and thereby drive up prices to the consumer; artificial currency exchange rates that distort the prices of exports and imports; state subsidies to producers and consumers; and government controls on prices and interest rates. All of these measures, argue the neoclassicists, distort the choices made by producers, consumers, and governments. Only when these artificial constraints are removed will the economy "get prices right" (i.e., let them be determined by free-market forces).

During the past two decades the neoclassicists (also known as neoliberals) have largely won the debate against advocates of extensive state intervention. As we have observed, governments throughout Africa and Latin America have liberalized their economies in recent years, deregulating the private sector, removing trade barriers, and freeing prices. Government subsidies for industry and for consumers have been reduced, often out of financial necessity. And many state enterprises have been privatized. In part, these changes resulted from pressures that international lending agencies such as the World Bank and the International Monetary Fund (IMF) have exerted on the LDCs. But they have also sprung from the growing conviction of Third World governments that earlier statist models have failed. Still, the growing consensus that government intervention had gotten out of hand does not mean that the neoclassical model has triumphed. While conservative economists and politicians often depicted the East Asian economic miracle as proof positive of what free enterprise can do if government doesn't intervene in the economy, leading specialists on the region such as Stephan Haggard and Alice H. Amsden disagree. They insist that government intervention has been a fundamental ingredient of industrial growth in that region.[48] Far from "following the market," Robert Wade maintains, the state has actively "governed the market."[49] So, while the neoclassicist's criticisms of statist policies ring true, they take their case too far in prescribing a hands-off state.

In fact, the only East Asian economy that has nearly conformed to the neoclassical model has been Hong Kong's, and the city's recent absorption into Communist China does not seem to have altered that. As the least regulated economy in the area, it is often cited as a success story for unrestricted capitalism. But Hong Kong is such a unique case that it may not offer many lessons for other countries. For one thing, it is rather small and it consists mostly of a single city with no rural population to speak of. Like Singapore, it hasn't had to deal with rural poverty or the related problems that are so daunting in most Third World countries. Initially, its wealth was tied to its location as a major port for Asian trade and an outpost of the British Empire. Other LDCs obviously don't enjoy such benefits.

Some of the strongest criticisms of neoclassical economics have come from environmentalists. From their perspective, even a modified policy of laissez faire, acknowledging some state responsibility for the environment, is totally inadequate. As Richard Albin notes, "The idea that private interest, operating within unfettered markets, will tend to produce a close approximation of the socially optimal allocation of resources, was close to the truth when output (population, too) was so much smaller."[50] But, he argues, as world population and pollution reach dangerous levels, society can no longer afford to let free-market mechanisms allocate penalties for pollution. Such remedies would come far too late. Further discussion of economic growth and the environment follows later in this chapter.

Finding a Proper Role for the State

Political scientists and economists will long continue to debate the state's proper role in Third World economies. As time goes on, new models will undoubtedly emerge. Still, some areas of agreement have emerged in recent decades. On the one hand, the level of government intervention in both the command economies and Latin American statism was surely excessive. At the same time, the extremely limited government role advocated by the neoclassicists is unrealistic and inadequate in most countries. East Asia's developmental state model has been the most successful, at least until the late 1990s. But it is unclear whether it can be replicated elsewhere. Indeed, a model that succeeds in one country or region will not necessarily work in another. Countries vary greatly in size, human capital, natural resources, and the like. Thus, cookbook formulas will likely prove inadequate. Finally, new crises—such as the oil shocks of the 1970s, the Latin American and African debt crises of the 1980s, the Asian financial crisis of the 1990s, and perhaps international terrorism in the first decade of the twenty-first century—force planners to alter and adapt development models.

INDUSTRIALIZATION STRATEGIES

Since the time of Britain's industrial revolution, governments have equated industrialization with economic development, economic sovereignty, and military strength. Latin America's largest countries launched their major industrialization drives in the 1930s. Following World War II, a number of newly independent Asian and African countries also developed their industrial capacities. Steel mills and auto plants became symbols of national prestige.

Neoclassical economists frequently criticized industrialization, arguing that each country should specialize in economic activities for which it has a "comparative advantage." That is, it should produce and export those goods it can provide most efficiently and cheaply relative to other nations. Based on that argument, neoclassicists maintained that most Third World nations should abandon plans for industrialization and concentrate, instead, on the production and export of raw materials or agricultural products.[51] Rather than manufacture goods such as cars, washing machines, or fertilizers, they insisted, countries such as Sri Lanka or Kenya would be better off increasing tea or coffee exports, where they have a comparative advantage, so that they could use those earnings to import manufactured products. Similarly, they contended that it made little sense for Ghana to build steel mills or for Uruguay to manufacture refrigerators. Still, many LDCs have been reluctant to depend fully on revenues from the export of "primary goods," in part because agricultural and raw-material prices are so volatile. One possible solution (easier said than done) is to pursue balanced growth, including some industrial development (presumably manufacturing products such as Indonesian wicker furniture, which draw on local natural resources and can be exported), while still stressing traditional primary goods production and export.

Industrializing nations have generally pursued two alternative strategies: import-substituting industrialization (ISI) and export-oriented industrialization (EOI). In the first case, as we have seen, LDCs reduce their dependency on manufactured imports by producing more of them at home. While ISI has been most closely identified with Latin America, it is a strategy that has been used, at least initially, in most of the developing world. While ISI focuses on producing consumer goods for the home market, EOI stresses industrial development tied to exports. Although EOI has been most closely associated with East and Southeast Asia, it is a strategy now widely embraced in Latin America and other parts of the Third World. Starting later, Latin American and other developing areas have yet to catch up with Asia's export capabilities. One is much more likely to find shirts, blouses, slacks, or Nike running shoes in American department stores that are manufactured in Singapore, Sri Lanka, Indonesia, or Thailand than similar products from Honduras, Brazil, or Colombia.

Import-Substituting Industrialization (ISI)

National economic policies are partly the product of deliberate choice, partly the result of political and socioeconomic opportunities and constraints. As we have seen, ISI emerged as a development strategy in Latin America during the 1930s as the worldwide depression sharply reduced international trade.[52] Because the industrialized nations of North America and Europe curtailed their consumption of Third World primary goods (Uruguayan wool, Argentinian beef, or Brazilian coffee), Latin America was denied the foreign exchange needed to import manufactured products. But while it was initiated as a response to the international economic crisis, ISI was subsequently transformed into a long-term strategy for industrial development. With substantial unemployment at home and their urban populations pressing for economic growth, government leaders faced a political imperative to industrialize. Nationalist presidents such as Argentina's Juan Perón and Brazil's Getúlio Vargas forged populist coalitions of industrialists, blue-collar workers, and the urban middle class, all committed to industrialization.

As we have seen earlier, in order to protect embryonic domestic industries from foreign competition, consumer imports were generally subjected to protective quotas and tariffs. At the same time, however, planners also wanted to facilitate other types of imports, namely capital equipment (primarily machinery) and raw materials needed by domestic manufacturers. To reduce the cost of those imports, governments overvalued their own currencies.[53] Eventually, most Latin American countries established multiple currency exchange rates, with differing rates for transactions tied to either imports, exports, or other financial activities. To further encourage industrial development, governments also offered domestic manufacturers tax incentives, low interest loans, and direct subsidies.[54]

Because of ISI's impressive record in Latin America from the 1940s into the 1970s, the strategy was emulated in many parts of Africa and Asia, sometimes with comparable success. Turkey, for example, enjoyed strong ISI growth before shifting to EOI during the 1980s.[55] Even East Asia's highly admired industrial export miracle was preceded by a period of ISI. By the 1970s, however, the ISI strategy undermined Latin America's economies. As John Sheahan notes, "It fostered production methods adverse for employment, hurt the poor, blocked the possible growth of industrial exports [and] encouraged high-cost consumer goods industries."[56]

To understand how poorly Latin America's newly industrialized countries (NICs) fared in international trade relative to their East Asia counterparts, it is useful to compare Mexico (one of the region's major industrial powers) with East Asia's "little tigers" (South Korea, Taiwan, Hong Kong, and Singapore). Mexico has a larger population than the other four combined. It also has a considerable geographic advantage over them, being located thousands of miles closer to the United States, the world's largest importer. Yet as of the mid-1980s (prior to NAFTA), the combined value of manufactured exports of all four little tigers was 20 times as high as Mexico's.[57]

Overvalued currencies and export taxes put traditional primary goods exporters at a competitive disadvantage, thereby depriving the country of needed foreign exchange revenues. At the same time, because local consumer-goods manufacturers were allowed to import capital goods cheaply, the region never developed its own capital-goods industry and, instead, imported manufacturing technologies that were inappropriate to local needs. Subsidized imports of machinery and heavy equipment encouraged capital-intensive production (i.e., using relatively advanced technologies and machinery while employing fewer workers) rather than the labor-intensive manufacturing common to Asia. The ISI model of industrialization benefited a small, relatively well-paid "labor elite" (i.e., skilled unionized workers employed in highly mechanized factories). But it failed to provide enough jobs for the region's unemployed and underemployed.

Ironically, although ISI was originally designed to make Latin America more economically independent, in the end it merely replaced dependence on consumer-goods imports with dependence on imported capital goods, foreign technologies, and overseas bank credit. Traditional primary exports were allowed to languish, while little was done to develop new manufactured exports. Increased balance of trade deficits contributed to Latin America's spiraling foreign debt, leading eventually to a major debt crisis and an economic depression in the 1980s.[58] The crisis, in stark contrast to East Asia's prosperity at that time, induced Latin American governments to abandon their inwardly oriented economic policies as they tried to emulate East Asia's export-driven model. The North American Free Trade Agreement (NAFTA) between Mexico, Canada, and the United States is the most dramatic manifestation of that region's move toward EOI.[59] Chile, once among the most inward-looking economies in the hemisphere, was at the forefront of export manufacturing and free trade.[60]

Export-Oriented Industrialization (EOI)

East Asia's NICs initiated their industrialization drive through import substitution, just as their Latin American counterparts had done years earlier. Soon, however, they diversified into manufacturing for export. Early protectionist measures were phased out, thereby forcing local companies to become more competitive. State planners shaped the market, pressuring manufacturers and offering them incentives to export. By 1980, manufactured goods constituted more than 90 percent of all South Korean and Taiwanese exports but represented only 15 percent in Mexico and 39 percent in Brazil.[61] Fueled by their dynamic industrial export sectors, East Asia's booming economies became the envy of the developing world.

There are a number of explanations for East Asia's decision to stress manufactured exports and for Latin America's initial failure to do the same. For one thing, the East Asian industrialization drive began in the 1960s, a period of unprecedented expansion in world trade, inspired by the GATT, the General Agreement on Trade and Tariffs, and the West's economic boom. The opportunities offered by outwardly oriented growth were more obvious to government policy makers at that time. Conversely, the expansion of Latin American industrialization began during the Great Depression, a period of greatly restricted world trade. Indeed, it was their very inability to export traditional products at that time that inspired Latin American nations to turn initially to ISI. In retrospect, Latin America should have moved to EOI after World War II, but ISI seemed to be working so well until the mid-1970s that there was little incentive to change. Ironically, one reason why East and Southeast Asian countries chose EOI is that their economic opportunities seemed more limited than Latin America's. Because of their smaller populations, Hong Kong, Singapore, and Taiwan (though not

South Korea) saw ISI, which relied upon the domestic market, as less feasible for them than for larger countries like Mexico, Argentina, Brazil, and Colombia.[62] Furthermore, with fewer agricultural goods or raw materials to export, East Asians turned a weakness into a strength by emphasizing manufactured exports.

The final factors that distinguished East Asia from Latin America were the influence of U.S. advisers and the differing training and economic orientation of government technocrats. During the decades after World War II, Latin America's government planners who shaped industrial policy were strongly influenced by the United Nations Economic Commission for Latin America (ECLA), a vigorous advocate of ISI. Until the 1980s, Latin American intellectuals remained very committed to economic nationalism and the need to limit U.S. influence. On the other hand, because of Taiwanese and South Korean military and political dependence on the United States during the postwar decades, their leaders were far more receptive to American policy advisers advocating EOI. East Asian economic planners often received their graduate training at American universities, where they were inculcated with the values of free trade. It was not until the 1970s and 1980s that the so-called "Chicago Boys" as well as other American-trained economists favoring free trade began to direct economic policy in Latin America.[63]

EAST AND SOUTHEAST ASIA'S ECONOMIC CRISIS

For decades, East and Southeast Asia seemed to be doing everything right economically. The developmental state and the EOI strategy produced phenomenal growth and comparatively equitable income distribution. China, using a more centrally planned industrialization strategy and far more state ownership, pursued EOI with equal success. But for countries like Indonesia, Malaysia, South Korea, and Thailand, the bubble burst during the financial crisis of the late 1990s. There and elsewhere in Asia, the developmental state seemed in need of fine tuning. Still, for the most part, the region has recovered far more quickly than Latin America did in the 1980s and 1990s, and most East and Southeast Asian economies seem back on track.

The Onset of the Crisis

On July 2, 1997, the Thai government announced that the exchange rate for their national currency, the baht, which had previously been fixed (i.e., the Thai government had guaranteed that its value relative to the dollar remained constant), would henceforth be allowed to float (its value would now fluctuate based on market forces).

> To the casual observer this was . . . hardly worth [much] attention. . . . But to individuals controlling huge pools of investment resources in Southeast Asia [including foreign investors], this was a flashing red light signaling danger for the entire region.[64]

As the value of the baht fell, investments on the Thai stock exchange and bank accounts held in bahts also lost value. For both the Thai government and private companies that had secured extensive loans in dollars from international banks, this meant that the cost in bahts of repaying those loans climbed precipitously.[65] International banks, in turn, curtailed further dollar loans to Thailand, knowing that it would be difficult for debtors to repay. The Thai private sector reduced its demand for foreign loans for the same reason.

> Panic soon set in. Thai and foreign investors began to unload their stocks on the Bangkok stock market and to sell other liquid securities. As confidence in the baht declined, Thais holding baht bank accounts rushed to convert their holdings into dollars or other hard currencies, thereby further undermining the value of the national currency. Rather than basing their decisions on a reasoned analysis of Thailand's economic capabilities, investors increasingly chose "the pure psychology of escape. All controllers of liquid capital . . . began behaving like spooked wildebeests on the Serengeti."[66]

For the many Thai businesses with overextended foreign debts, the costs of repayment were becoming overwhelming. Companies that imported consumer goods or manufacturing inputs (machinery, raw materials, technology licenses) found the price of doing business rising sharply as the value of the baht declined. Before long, many companies were closing down and laying off workers. Had the 1997 economic crisis been limited to Thailand, it would have been tragic for the Thai people but would have had little consequence for the world economy. Not surprisingly, however, foreign and domestic investors in other Southeast and East Asian boom economies began to fear that those countries might also be overheated and plagued by the same fragilities (including excessive external debts) that had undermined Thailand's economy. Indonesia, Malaysia, and later South Korea were all forced to devalue their currencies and were plunged into deep recessions. During the following year, the economic crisis threatened to spread to Hong Kong and sent chills down the spines of the region's two economic giants, Japan and China. At the same time, however, countries with relatively smaller foreign debts (Taiwan, Singapore, the Philippines, Vietnam, and China) were less vulnerable to capital flight and, at least until this point, have survived the crisis relatively well.

Causes of the Asian Crisis

What was perhaps most shocking about Asia's sharp economic plunge was how utterly unexpected it had been. Virtually up to the day that Thailand began the crisis by announcing its intention to float the baht, respected financial analysts had portrayed Southeast and East Asian economies as vibrant and growing. Why were the world's investment specialists so taken by surprise? What caused the initial virus in Thailand, and why did it spread so rapidly and insidiously to neighboring countries?

Several previously unnoticed weaknesses in the region's economies set the stage. Precisely because economic performance had been so spectacular for years, both investors and lending agencies had come to see rapid growth as virtually inevitable. Consequently, they threw caution to the wind. Businesses in Thailand, Indonesia, Malaysia, and South Korea had borrowed and invested excessively. From 1992 to 1997 alone, Asian companies (excluding Japan) had borrowed more than $700 billion from the rest of the world. The result was questionable investments, manufacturing overcapacity, and excess construction of new real estate. The downtown business centers of Bangkok, Jakarta (Indonesia), and Seoul (South Korea) were dotted with new, half-occupied office buildings. Not surprisingly, Southeast and East Asia's external debts eventually exceeded their capacity to repay readily.

In truth, economic growth is invariably cyclical, and no country or region can maintain high growth rates indefinitely. In particular, annual growth of the magnitude of 7 to 12 percent is only possible when economies are first taking off, and such rates usually cannot be sustained once these countries become more developed. Another problem was that credit in some countries was often not directed to firms or industries that could most effectively invest it. In Indonesia, "crony capitalism" saw the Suharto dictatorship steering government aid and bank credits to political insiders, most notably the president's children, who became billionaires. Corruption was not as pervasive in South Korea, but the country's major industrial conglomerates enjoyed a cozy relationship with the government that allowed them ready access to state credit and other forms of government assistance.

These underlying long-term weaknesses were then aggravated by additional short-term problems. For a period of time, several Southeast Asian countries had pegged their currencies to the dollar, meaning that their governments had guaranteed to keep the currencies' values fixed relative to the dollar. The purpose of that arrangement was to assure foreign investors that the value of their investments in the region would not be undermined by devaluation, as it had been in many Latin American countries.[67] But in the mid-1990s, when the dollar strengthened, the region's pegged currencies automatically gained value as well (relative to currencies such as the Japanese yen). As a consequence, the price of Southeast Asia's exports increased while the cost of its imports declined, contributing to a growing trade deficit. This compounded the adverse effects of China's 1994 currency devaluation, which had lowered the price of its exports and enabled it to undersell Southeast Asian products (especially electronics) on the international market. Interestingly, Argentina ran into similar problems when it pegged its currency to the dollar. A four-year recession ended in political and financial meltdown in 2002.

Consequences of the 1997 Crash

While Thailand's decision to devalue the baht was an unavoidable reaction to the country's growing trade deficit, it prompted panic among major portfolio investors elsewhere in Southeast Asia. Before long, as investors pulled out of

Indonesia and unloaded its currency, that government was forced to devalue the rupiah. The crisis next spread to Malaysia and South Korea. Ultimately, its implications were even broader, as international financial institutions watched events in Asia and became increasingly concerned about their investments in other LDCs. Asia's sharp currency and stock market declines spread to Russia and caused steep drops in the Argentine, Brazilian, and Chilean stock markets as well.

As Asia's financial crisis intensified, the region sank into a deep economic recession, inflicting enormous pain on the population. Unable to pay their debts, many companies were forced into bankruptcy, throwing their employees out of work. Inflation heated up dangerously, and domestic banks, faced with extensive defaults on their loans, declared bankruptcy themselves.

> Along the way, billions of dollars in production and hundreds of millions of jobs [were] lost. . . . Since the crisis began [through October 1998], $1 trillion in loans [went] bad, $2 trillion in equity capitalization for the Asian stock markets . . . vaporized, and $3 trillion in GDP growth [was] lost.[68]

Implications for East Asia's Growth Model

What does the economic crisis of the late 1990s imply about the viability of East and Southeast Asia's developmental state and its export-led growth model? Is that model now no longer attractive? Conservative critics argue that the crisis shows the dangers of "too much government control."[69] Because investment decisions in the area were influenced by government planners rather than by market forces, these analysts contend, bank loans and government aid too often went to well-connected industries and industrial sectors, rather than to those who could make best use of the assistance. There is certainly some truth to this charge, particularly where crony capitalism prevailed, as in Indonesia and the Philippines. However, it is unlikely that state intervention per se was the major cause of the crisis. After all, China and Vietnam—market-socialist countries with the highest level of state control in the region—suffered no financial crisis, nor did the developmental states in Singapore and Taiwan. Rather, the key causal factor seems to have been external indebtedness. Countries such as Thailand, Indonesia, and South Korea (or, outside the region, Mexico, Brazil, and, more recently, Argentina), which had borrowed abroad excessively, got into trouble. Those that had either exercised restraint (Taiwan and China) or had been unable to secure extensive foreign credit (the Philippines and Vietnam) were not badly hurt.

The most important elements of East and Southeast Asia's development model—widespread public education aimed at developing a skilled work force, agrarian reform, equitable income distribution, emphasis on manufactured exports—did not contribute to the crisis and remain the region's strengths. The time has probably come to reduce the role of the developmental state, and most countries in the region have already begun to do so. But the model seems to have served its purpose well in getting those economies off the ground and running.

In the future, Asian governments would do well to let their currencies float freely (to continually appreciate or decline in value according to market forces) rather than allow a pegged currency to become seriously overvalued, thereby forcing the government to devaluate it sharply. Borrowers and lenders also need to be more careful about seeking and extending credit. At the same time, the World Bank and the International Monetary Fund (IMF)—both of which failed to anticipate the Asian crisis, as they had failed earlier with the 1994 Mexican peso crisis—must better monitor the financial health of LDCs and must offer the financial community better advance warning about serious imbalances in currency values. So too must private rating services, such as Standard and Poor's and Moody's, which also failed to alert investors of the problem by lowering Asia's credit ratings. Such advance warning regarding Argentina in 2001 prevented that country's crisis from spreading elsewhere.

None of these flaws, however, calls into question Asia's underlying development model.[70] Indeed, experts such as Joseph Stiglitz, chief economist of the World Bank, and Jeffrey Winters argue that bad private-sector decisions, not the developmental state, caused the crisis. Further, they insist that most East and Southeast Asian economies remain fundamentally strong.[71] In fact, by the end of 1998, the financial crisis seemed to be easing, and many countries in the region resumed moderate growth by the year 2000. In the meantime, however, millions of Asians have sunk into poverty, and virtually none of the governments in the region has a social safety net to protect the newly unemployed, homeless, and hungry.

GROWTH WITH EQUITY

Until this point, our discussion of economic development has focused on measurements of production. Indeed, production is often the primary or sole measure of economic development used in popular or scholarly analysis. We read periodically that the economy of, say, Chile, Thailand, or China has been doing well of late, as evidenced by annual GNP growth of 6 or 9 percent. Far less attention has been focused on how that growth is distributed. It is to that important dimension that we now turn.

Early debate on Third World development often pitted conservative social scientists against progressives, with the former primarily interested in the prerequisites of growth and the latter more concerned with problems of equity. For example, while mainstream economists were impressed with Brazil's rapid economic expansion in the late 1960s and early 1970s, progressive critics pointed out that extremely unequal income distribution meant that the benefits of the country's economic miracle failed to reach the poorest half of the population. But while left-leaning economists were favorably impressed by Cuba's far-reaching income redistribution and social welfare programs, conservative critics noted the country's erratic economic growth.

Market-oriented economists generally believed that increased inequality was actually necessary in the early stages of economic development because it concentrated capital in the hands of entrepreneurs who could invest it in productive activities. Critics countered that development of that sort would do little to help the majority of the people in the LDCs. In many developing nations, they argued, the bottom half of the population would benefit more from meaningful redistribution of wealth and income, even with little growth, than from strong economic growth without redistribution.[72]

In time, however, analysts of varying persuasions have concluded that there is no intrinsic contradiction between these two goals. In fact, a proper development strategy entails growth with equity.[73] One study shows that since the 1960s, countries with higher levels of income equality have grown faster than those with highly concentrated patterns. East Asia's economic takeoff since the 1970s and 1980s demonstrates that point. Thus, Taiwan and South Korea have coupled spectacular economic growth rates with some of the world's most equitable income distributions.[74] Indeed, broadly based purchasing power in both those countries has helped stimulate their economic growth. In South Korea, for example, almost all peasant families have acquired television sets over the years (and many are now switching to color), a feat barely conceivable in Africa or Latin America. During the takeoff of the Korean television industry, these domestic purchases supplemented exports in stimulating that industry's growth.

What accounts for the higher level of economic equality in East Asia as compared to Africa or Latin America? One important factor is the pattern of land distribution in the countryside. For a variety of reasons, farm land is generally far more equitably distributed in Asia than in Latin America.[75] While the size of Latin America's largest land holdings has declined in recent decades, estates of several thousand acres were common in the recent past, and today large land owners still dominate the countryside in nations such as Brazil or Colombia. On the other hand, the largest holdings in Asia, where there is much heavier population pressure, are rarely more than one or two hundred acres and are far smaller in countries like South Korea.

Land-holding patterns reflect both historical legacies and contemporary government policies. Spanish colonialism established an agrarian structure in Latin America and the Philippines dominated by large *latifundia*. In contrast, Japanese colonial authorities in Korea and Taiwan encouraged smallholder farming. Although European colonial regimes established large export-oriented plantations in Southeast Asia, land ownership was still never as concentrated in that area as in Latin America. It is surely not coincidental that the nation with one of the most concentrated land and income distributions in East Asia, the Philippines, is also the region's only country that shares Latin America's Spanish colonial heritage. In the postcolonial period, South Korean and Taiwanese agrarian reform led to more egalitarian land distribution in those countries, just as American-imposed reform had done in Japan after the war. By reducing rural poverty, land reform contributed to higher overall levels of income equality in the region.

Another major determinant of national income distribution is the relationship between rural and urban living standards. Although city dwellers enjoy higher incomes and greater social services throughout the Third World, the urban-rural gap is particularly marked in Africa and Latin America. Residents of Mexico City, for example, have incomes averaging four to five times higher than in the countryside. There are many reasons for such discrepancies, but government policy often plays an important role. In Chapter 6 we saw that, until recently, African and Latin American governments kept the price of basic food crops below their market value to satisfy urban political constituencies.[76] By contrast, East Asian farmers generally have received the free-market price for their crops or even subsidized prices above market value.

Industrial policy also affects income distribution. Latin America's ISI strategy encouraged the importation of capital equipment for domestic industries. Such capital-intensive development created a limited number of relatively well-paid, skilled industrial jobs but left behind many poorly paid, unskilled urban workers and rural peasants. Conversely, East Asia's EOI strategy took advantage of that region's large, disciplined, but poorly paid labor force.

Initially employing labor-intensive methods that utilized their pool of cheap labor, both Taiwan and South Korea successfully exported low-tech goods such as textiles and footwear. As increased numbers of workers were employed, two changes took place over time. First, greater demand for labor in export industries caused factory wages to rise; second, rural-to-urban migration due to the lure of factory jobs reduced the supply of rural labor, thereby driving up income levels in the countryside. What had begun as a policy exploiting cheap labor eventually promoted economic growth, higher wages, and greater income equality.[77] As wage levels rose substantially in the four "little tigers," those countries shifted from low-tech products to more sophisticated exports such as electronics, commercial services (most notably Singapore), computer software, computers, and automobiles (South Korea). Production of apparel and other low-wage items was passed on to poorer, low-wage Asian nations such as Malaysia, Thailand, Indonesia, Bangladesh, and Sri Lanka.

A final factor that distinguished East Asia from less developed regions is its relatively high educational level.[78] Table 10.1 offers education data for the United States, four East Asian NICs, four Latin American NICS, and India. The second column presents literacy rates for all adults over the age of 15. The third column indicates the percentage of school-aged youth who are enrolled in school. Finally, the last column (Educational Index) is a composite index of the country's education level. The highest, or best, score that a country can achieve for this index is 1.0, and the lowest possible score is a 0.

Both the East Asian and Latin American NICs presented in this table have literacy rates and education levels that are below the United States (though on some measures the gap is smaller than one might expect) but considerably higher than India, or Africa, the Middle East, and most of South Asia. Not surprisingly, the NICs with the lowest enrollment, literacy rates, and Educational Indices, tend to be those with the highest rates of poverty (Colombia, Mexico,

Thailand). Surprisingly, Singapore, a prosperous country with fairly equitable income distribution, falls below the group's average for the Educational Index and adult literacy. But its extremely high current school enrollment ratio (97 percent compared to 95 percent in the United States and 71 percent in Mexico) suggests that future generations will be far more educated.

While educational attainment generally correlates with economic development and growth, two countries in the table stand out as exceptions: Argentina—a more affluent Third World country with relatively equitable income distribution—ranks second out of the eight NICs for both adult literacy and Educational Index (trailing only South Korea). Yet its economy has stagnated for decades. Meanwhile, Hong Kong, one of the Third World's most phenomenal economic performers for the past 40 to 50 years, has a relatively low Educational Index and a very low enrollment ratio (almost as low as India's). The Argentine anomaly is related to the fact that in the first 30 years of the twentieth century, it used its enormous wheat and beef exports to build an affluent society and a substantial industrial base. In the 1920s, it not only was the richest nation in the Third World, but it had a per-capita income ranked fifth in the entire world, far ahead of Japan and Italy, for example. That early development, combined with a work force largely made up of recent European immigrants, produced high education levels. Since the 1940s, however, despite its strong educational base, Argentina's failure to modernize its agricultural and industrial production has sent it on a downward economic slide. It is also worth noting that its current enrollment ratios, while higher than its Latin American counterparts, are far lower than Singapore or South Korea, indicating that it may be beginning to lose ground. The reasons for Hong Kong's somewhat disappointing educational performance are harder to discern. But it is true that South Korea and the other Asian NICs listed here, with higher educational performances than Hong Kong, also have more equitable distributions of income.

Although Table 10.1 does not indicate *great* differences between the East Asian and Latin American education and literacy rates, earlier data published by the United Nations Development Program do reveal some important differences. Although comparable proportions of the children in both regions attend primary (elementary) school, East Asian students are much more likely to complete their elementary education (97 to 99 percent in Hong Kong, Singapore, and South Korea; 57 to 72 percent in Colombia and Mexico).[79] Another difference concerns how countries allocate their educational resources. The East Asian NICs have concentrated their resources especially on primary and secondary education (K through 12) and, consequently, have higher enrollment ratios than their Latin American counterparts for both those educational levels. On the other hand, Latin American nations are more prone to allocate resources to university and other post-secondary education than their East Asian counterparts. Consequently, they have higher enrollment ratios at that level. Cultural norms limiting women's education have also reduced post-secondary enrollments in East Asia, with the notable exception of South Korea.

TABLE 10.1   Comparative National Educational Levels

Country	Adult Literacy	Primary-Tertiary Enrollment Ratios	Educational Index
United States	99.9%	95%	.98
Hong Kong	93.3	63	.83
Singapore	92.1	97	.87
South Korea	97.6	90	.95
Thailand	95.3	60	.84
Argentina	96.7	83	.92
Chile	95.6	80	.90
Colombia	91.5	73	.85
Mexico	91.1	71	.84
India	56.5	56	.56

Source: United Nations Development Programme, *Human Development Report, 2001* (New York: Oxford University Press, 2001), pp. 141–144. Reprinted by permission.

While all levels of education are important for a country's economic growth, East Asia's education strategy has produced a more widely educated work force at the mass level. Latin America's allocation of more of its educational resources to post-secondary education reflects, in part, the political influence of the middle-class families whose children attend those schools. Because increased education opens up greater opportunities for upward mobility, national educational levels tend to correspond with income equality.[80] Thus, the most educated populations in Latin America (Cuba, Argentina, Uruguay, Costa Rica) generally also have the most equitable income distributions in the region. Conversely, Brazil, with a very poor educational record, has one of the world's poorest income distributions. In general, East Asia's high rate of primary and secondary education has contributed to greater income equity.

ECONOMIC DEVELOPMENT AND THE ENVIRONMENT

Throughout the world, in developing countries as well as developed ones, economic growth inevitably involves a degree of environmental degradation. For example, prior to European settlement, the east coast of the United States was covered with thick forest. Since then, population growth, urban sprawl, and farming have destroyed most of it. Today, industrial pollution, though greatly reduced by environmental regulations, continues to pollute our air and water. Massive dams in China flood valuable farm land and natural habitat. Industrial plants in Germany's Ruhr Valley pollute the rivers and the air. Only in recent decades have environmental groups, organized primarily in industrialized nations, begun to question the tradeoffs between growth and the conservation of our natural resource heritage. Some of the more radical environmentalists in the United States and Europe have proposed zero growth strategies for highly industrialized nations. These proposals include efforts to contain population growth as well as the creation of a less consumer-oriented society.

The Costs of Growth

But the option of zero growth, or even of reduced economic growth, is not really viable in the First World and even less so in the Third World. In countries such as India, Indonesia, Egypt, Nigeria, and Brazil, where substantial portions of the population live in poverty, it would be politically suicidal and ethically questionable for government leaders to propose limiting economic growth. The "green (ecology) movement" arrived much later in the LDCs than in the industrialized West, and its strength and objectives remain more limited. Today, the world's industrialized nations continue to be the major consumers of natural resources, the leading polluters of air and water, and the major contributors to global warming, ozone-layer depletion, and other looming ecological disasters. For example, in recent years, developed nations consumed some 80 percent of the world's paper, 80 percent of its iron and steel, and more than 85 percent of its chemicals. Per-capita use of cars in the developed world is more than 25 times as high as in the LDCs, cement consumption is 3.5 times as high, and iron and steel consumption is 13 times as high.[81]

Yet, ironically, it is those same developed countries that now insist that the LDCs become better environmental citizens. In response, Third World leaders complain that the United States, with only some 4 percent of the world's population, consumes more than 25 percent of the planet's resources.[82] Hence, the LDCs frequently feel put upon when asked by industrialized nations to limit their share of environmental destruction.[83] But because of their more fragile economic and ecological situations, developing nations confront some of the world's most pressing environmental challenges. Peasants hungry for firewood in Rwanda, Nepal, India, and Paraguay deplete nearby forests. In African countries such as Sudan, Nigeria, and Burkina Faso, 75 percent or more of all energy is supplied by burning wood. In Indonesia, wood provides 50 percent of the nation's energy, while in Nepal it contributes 90 percent. Giant cattle ranchers and armies of migrant peasants in Brazil burn vast areas of the Amazonian jungle each year to clear the land for cultivation. In Malaysia and Indonesia, Japanese-owned logging firms cut down large tracts of rain forest to manufacture furniture. Since 1950 alone, more than 20 percent of the earth's tropical rain forests have been destroyed. As a consequence, rains and waterways wash off topsoil, rainfall patterns shift, and both droughts and floods occur more frequently. For example, the devastating hurricane-caused floods that destroyed much of Honduras and Nicaragua along with other parts of Central America in 1998 were exacerbated by deforestation. The same is true of many of Africa's recent droughts. Excessive farming on unforested lands in countries such as Mongolia adds to the problem. In short, in many parts of the Third World, the arable land area is declining and deserts are growing.

Third World cities such as Shanghai, Cairo, New Delhi, Nairobi, and Sao Paulo have grown at alarming rates in recent decades (Chapter 7), producing enormous quantities of raw sewage, auto emissions, and industrial waste. As streets become choked with cars and buses (few of which have proper emission-control devices), air quality rapidly deteriorates. Mexico City, by some estimates the world's largest city, has had some of the world's most polluted air, though it has introduced important environmental protection measures since the 1980s. Elsewhere, operating with few environmental safeguards, many mines, oil fields, chemical plants, and industrial sites pollute their surroundings. In many LDCs, misuse of insecticides and industrial accidents have led to a substantial number of deaths and birth defects. Some of these ecological tragedies have adversely affected only the people living in the developing world. Others have had broader impacts that reached the industrialized world as well, contributing to the concerns of Western environmental activists.

While many environmental problems are unrelated to economic growth or industrialization, and while some of the world's least developed nations face severe ecological difficulties such as deforestation, it remains true that economic growth, urbanization, and industrialization present particular challenges. Population growth—rapid in some parts of the developing world, moderating in others—puts further strain on the world's resources. Some of the environmental damage currently taking place in the LDCs is confined to their own borders, but other problems spill over to their neighbors or have consequences for the entire world.

Environmental Decay as a Third World Problem

Nowhere is the difficult takeoff between economic growth and environmental conservation more starkly illustrated than in China, home to more than one-fifth of the world's population. Since the government introduced free-market economic reforms in the 1980s, the country has enjoyed the world's highest rate of economic growth, averaging about 8 to 10 percent annually. Living standards have tripled, and millions of Chinese citizens have moved out of poverty. The number of people spared from hunger, disease, and early death is undoubtedly staggering. Balanced against those gains, however, is an enormous degree of air and water pollution and extensive destruction of the country's farm land, raising the prospect of future famine just when China has finally managed to feed its population adequately. By 1990, China consumed 10 percent of global energy and was responsible for 11 percent of carbon dioxide emissions, a figure that continues to rise as the economy leaps forward.[84]

Attracted by higher urban living standards, millions of peasants have migrated to the cities, often abandoning farms in productive agricultural regions. In addition, substantial quantities of farm land have been paved over for highways, factories, and urban sprawl. Since the late 1950s, China's total arable land has decreased by somewhere between 15 and 55 percent (depending on what estimate one accepts), while population has grown by some 80 percent. Though China's annual rate of population growth is currently relatively low (1 percent or lower), loss of farm land because of economic development continues to accelerate at an alarming rate. From 1992 to 1993 alone, arable land area fell by 5.5 percent. So far, China has averted hunger by farming the remaining land more intensively, and some recent grain harvests have reached record or near-record levels. But this intensive use of fertilizers and pesticides eventually depletes the soil, and a food crunch likely looms in the coming decades.

Environmental Decay in the LDCs as a Global Problem

The debate over Third World environmental policy is further complicated by the fact that many LDCs are stewards of natural resources that are critical to the entire world. For example, the massive, purposeful burning of the Amazonian rain forest contributes significantly to global warming. Destruction of rain forests there as well as in Africa and Asia deprives the world of many animal species and plant forms that are potentially key ingredients in life-saving medicines of the future.[85] Population growth and the destruction of natural habitat threaten the existence of the world's remaining pandas in China and the lowland gorillas in Rwanda.

Unfortunately, the very economic development to which Third World people rightfully aspire poses potentially disastrous threats to the environment. It would be unthinkable to tell the average Indian or Egyptian that they should not yearn for a significantly higher standard of living. But barring major technological and political breakthroughs, achieving a level of affluence worldwide would overtax the planet's resources. Invariably, economic development includes greatly increased fossil-fuel usage (coal, petroleum, and natural gas) and a corresponding increase in pollution. Brazil, China, and India already rank third through fifth in the world, behind the United States and the former Soviet Union, in greenhouse gas emissions (carbon dioxide and other fossil-fuel emissions that trap the earth's heat and produce global warming). As China's economy continues its rapid growth, and as India further industrializes, these two Asian giants will surely use more fossil fuels for their factories and vehicles, thereby accelerating the greenhouse effect on global warming.

The Search for Sustainable Development

Discussion of the environmental consequences of economic growth often centers on the concept of *sustainable development*, defined as economic development that "consumes resources to meet [this generation's] needs and aspirations in a way that does not compromise the ability of future generations to meet their needs."[86] Whenever feasible, this type of development involves the use of *renewable resources* (such as wind and water power for generating electricity) in place of resources that cannot be replaced (coal and petroleum), or which are currently being consumed at a faster rate than they can be replaced (tropical rain forests, ocean fish such as salmon). It also requires consumption of resources in a way that least pollutes the environment: limiting auto and industrial emissions, finding sustainable substitutes for pesticides and other agricultural chemicals that pollute the soil and water system, reducing the use of chemicals that destroy the world's ozone layer.[87]

In theory these are goals to which all nations, rich and poor alike, can aspire. During the 1990s a number of international conferences (both regional and global) were held and agreements signed designed to protect the world's environment. The most important was the 1992 United Nations Conference on Environment and Development (UNCED, or the Earth Summit as it came to be known) in Rio de Janeiro, Brazil. It produced the Framework Convention on Climate Change—a nonbinding commitment to reduce and limit greenhouse emissions by the year 2000; the Convention on Biological Diversity, designed to protect species and ecosystems; Agenda 21, an action plan for sustainable development into the twenty-first century; and the Rio Declaration, which lists 27 guiding principles on the environment and development, including the LDCs' right to economic development and the alleviation of poverty.

While the Rio Earth Summit and subsequent international conferences, such as the 1995 U.N. Summit on Climate Change in Berlin, have achieved potentially useful accords and have had great symbolic importance, many critics question their actual impact on the environment.[88] Frequently, they produce little more than admirable aspirations and unenforceable regulations. Few would challenge the lofty goal of continued economic growth in the context of environmental conservation. But it is far from clear how those two-pronged objectives can and should be achieved and what trade-offs are appropriate. From the perspective of the developing countries, which most desperately need economic growth, the question is how much of that cost they can and should sustain.

> At the Rio Summit, the conflicts between the rich and poor became evident. The Northern [industrialized] countries, which felt vulnerable to global environment problems such as climate change and biodiversity loss, attempted to extract commitments on environmental conservation from the South. However, the South, which felt more vulnerable to perceived underdevelopment, was concerned with extracting [economic] transfers from the North.[89]

It is well and good, say Third World leaders, for already-industrialized nations to ask China and Mexico to reduce smokestack emissions or to ask Thailand and Brazil to sustain their rain forests, but First World nations, which have historically wreaked the greatest havoc on the environment, have so far been unwilling to defray much of the cost to the Third World. Moreover, the Bush administration recently announced that the United States—the world's greatest producer of greenhouse gases—will not sign the international treaty on global warming.

The difficult trade-off between growth and environmental protection was vividly brought home to this author at a meeting in Jamaica with local social scientists. After one U.S. scholar spoke of the importance of preserving the island's ecology, a Jamaican economist sarcastically replied, "You Americans raped your environment in order to develop your country and raise your standard of living. Now we Jamaicans reserve the right to do the same."[90]

A number of years ago, journalists in northern Brazil interviewed the mayor of a poor fishing village whose local waters had been contaminated by industrial mercury pollution. Knowing that the fish they ate would probably eventually cause them horrible illness or death, the villagers continued to eat it. "For us it is a choice," said the mayor. "We can either starve to death now or face the prospect of mercury poisoning later." Similarly, developing nations face hard choices between short- and long-term consequences. For example, however much Indonesia's political leaders may wish to conserve their country's rain forests, they know that wood-product exports are an important component of the country's industrial development. Furthermore, such exports are also needed to help repay the country's external debt. Similarly, pollution from India's new factories, many of which can't afford adequate emission controls, may eventually contribute to increased cancer rates and pulmonary diseases. For now, however, they create badly needed jobs.

Some Signs of Progress

While environmental problems still loom large, there are some hopeful signs of progress. Both the governments of developing countries and international development agencies have become more conscious of the growth-ecology trade-off. Together they are looking for ways to achieve sustainable development that minimizes harm to the environment. Many LDCs that previously saw the green movement as a Western conspiracy to keep them underdeveloped have come to realize that sustainable growth is in their own interest.

One of the most important means of improving living standards and preserving the environment is population control. Other solutions can also help: the use of renewable fuels such as solar energy and water power (nuclear energy remains far more controversial); organic farming that replenishes, rather than depletes, the soil; government rules and regulations that discourage, rather than encourage, irrational use of rain forest areas (Brazil recently ended tax laws that had encouraged ranchers to clear the Amazonian forest); and stricter antipollution controls. For example, Mexico City has improved its air quality by closing down some local cement plants and oil refineries and moving others out of the city, by requiring private cars to be off the road one day per week, and by replacing city taxis and buses with newer vehicles that have better emission controls.

Ultimately, however, even if all of the most sophisticated environmental measures were to be implemented, they still would not reconcile fully the tension between growth and environmental conservation. Furthermore, most of these measures either require substantial financial outlays or result in foregone income opportunities. If the world's industrial powers want the LDCs to make such sacrifices, they will probably have to underwrite much of the cost. This might involve debt forgiveness, subsidized technology transfers, and even outright grants.[91]

Which of the economic models discussed earlier in this chapter is best equipped to handle the environmental challenge? The answer is not clear. It seems certain that preserving the environment requires active state intervention. Since factory owners cannot be counted on to monitor and limit their own pollution nor citizens to voluntarily limit their use of automobiles, state regulation of some kind is needed. Consequently, the neoclassical model of government noninterference seems inappropriate in this area.

In theory, command economies have substantial capability to defend the environment since the state controls the means of production. In fact, however, communist governments from the Soviet Union and Poland to China and North Korea have had miserable environmental records. On the one hand, directives to managers of state enterprises usually demand that they maximize production, with little thought given to environmental consequences. On the other hand, absent a free society and a free mass media, citizens are unable to organize green pressure groups or even to know the extent of ecological destruction. Thus, it appears that if developing nations are to have any chance at sustainable development, they must combine an honest, effective, and responsible state with a free democratic society where environmental activists can mobilize popular support.

FINDING THE RIGHT MIX

Often it has been easier to recognize what has not worked in the Third World than to identify what has. The dependency theorists' assumption that economic liberation lay in reducing or severing ties to the capitalist core has not held up to the light of careful scrutiny. Similarly, extensive state intervention has failed to provide economic salvation. At the same time, the neoclassical minimal state can hardly address the deep inequities, societal cleavages, and looming ecological nightmares plaguing the LDCs. The challenge for Third World economies is to establish a strong and effective state—one that can promote growth, equitable distribution, and a healthy environment, while avoiding unwarranted interference in the market, crony capitalism, and authoritarianism.

Many Third World countries rushed to embrace East Asia's export-oriented industrial model. Beyond the previously mentioned problem of transferability, however, there are at least two other fundamental concerns about universalizing the East Asian experience. The first concerns the degree to which the world economy can absorb industrial exports. East Asia launched its EOI strategy during a period of unparalleled economic growth in the First World. International trade was expanding rapidly, and the developed world could absorb a rising tide of industrial exports. Since the 1970s, however, First World economic growth has slowed down (with the notable exception of the United States in the 1990s), due first to rising energy costs, more recently to the transfer of industrial jobs to the NICs and, perhaps, most recently due to terrorism. Even should the Japanese and Western European economies recover their former dynamism, some analysts question whether the international market can absorb an ever-enlarging flow of industrial exports, most notably from a looming economic giant, China, or whether protectionist measures in the First World might place a cap on imports.[92] Supporters of EOI counter, however, that there is no sign of a looming cap on industrial imports, particularly since the larger NICs have become major importers themselves.[93]

But if economic growth models were to be successfully applied in Africa, Latin America, and South Asia, a further concern would arise. Rapid economic development has already taken a tremendous ecological toll in Asia and other parts of the Third World. Tropical rain forests in Brazil, Peru, and Indonesia are rapidly being depleted. As we pointed out previously, China's economic expansion has contributed to the removal of up to one-third of the country's farm land from agricultural production, and huge amounts of crop land have been converted to housing (much of it for upwardly mobile peasants), freeways, factories, shopping malls, or the like. Hunger has been averted by increasing crop yields per acre, but such intensive farming further erodes the soil.[94] In addition, ever-growing Chinese energy consumption will likely put a strain on world petroleum supplies in the coming decades and will contribute to global warming. As India begins a more modest but still significant economic takeoff, such problems are certain to be compounded. New models of ecologically sustainable development will have to be formulated. Finally, the recent Asian financial crisis demonstrates that even the most sophisticated and apparently successful development models can run into serious difficulties as new challenges develop and hidden weaknesses surface.

CONCLUSION: DEMOCRACY AND ECONOMIC DEVELOPMENT

Earlier in this chapter, we observed that, in the second half of the twentieth century, the most dynamic Third World economies were often directed by authoritarian regimes. All of Asia's most impressive economic takeoffs—China, Taiwan, South Korea, Singapore, Thailand, Malaysia, and Indonesia—transpired under authoritarian or semi-authoritarian developmental states or (in the case of China) a modified command economy. Chile initiated Latin America's most successful transition from ISI to export-led growth during General Pinochet's military dictatorship. Arguments in favor of authoritarian-led growth focus on its ability to control demands from labor and impose development plans on business.

But for every authoritarian success story, there have been several economic disasters. Corrupt dictatorships throughout Africa, the Middle East, Central America, and the Caribbean have plundered their countrys' limited wealth and used the economy to benefit their political friends. Chile's bureaucratic authoritarian regime performed well economically, but its counterparts in Argentina, Uruguay, and even Brazil were less successful. To be sure, most economic takeoffs begin under authoritarian regimes of some sort. But, in part, that merely reflects the fact that most countries at the early stages of economic development are not democracies. Statistical analyses of Third World economic growth rates in recent decades reveal that authoritarian governments do not perform any better than democratic ones. In fact, one of the most comprehensive and rigorous recent studies shows that dictatorships perform more poorly. Bruce Bueno de Mesquita et al. ranked hundreds of governments worldwide since 1952 and compared the 179 most autocratic governments with the 176 most democratic ones.[95] During that period, democratic rulers achieved an average real annual growth rate (adjusted for inflation) of 3.04 percent, while autocratic governments attained only 1.78 percent, a gap that may appear small but which makes a tremendous difference over time. The authors argue that governments that have to appeal to a broad coalition of many voters (democracies) are more likely to pursue policies that promote general economic growth, while governments that owe their incumbency to a small coalition of strategic allies (dictatorships) are more prone to corruption and to pursue policies designed to keep themselves in power no matter what the cost to the national economy. Of course, the ranks of democratic governments include both strong economic performers and weak ones, as do authoritarian governments. But these findings, along with many others, offer hope that democratic governments and the worldwide movement toward democracy may produce faster economic growth along with greater political justice.

DISCUSSION QUESTIONS

1. What have been the major accomplishments and failures of command economies?
2. Compare the nature of state economic intervention in Latin America to East Asia's developmental state.
3. What are the major arguments presented in the neoclassical development model?
4. What were the major causes of East and Southeast Asia's recent economic crisis? What implications did the crisis have for evaluating the region's economic model?
5. In what ways does economic growth in the Third World contribute to environmental degradation?
6. What evidence is there that authoritarian Third World governments can promote early economic growth better than democracies? What counter-evidence do some scholars bring to suggest that democracies have better economic records? In what ways might each one promote economic growth?

NOTES

1. Of course, we have seen that in the short to medium run, economic growth can be politically destabilizing. But if growth can be combined with equitable distribution, the chances of unrest are greatly diminished. In any event, all other factors being equal, in the long run rising living standards should rebound to the regime's political advantage. The potentially destabilizing effects of unequal economic growth were treated elsewhere in this book and will not be discussed in this chapter.

2. Joan M. Nelson, ed., *Economic Crisis and Policy Choice: The Politics of Adjustment in the Third World* (Princeton, NJ: Princeton University Press, 1990); Dharam Ghai, ed., *The IMF and the South: The Social Impact of Crisis and Adjustment* (London: Zed Books, 1991).

3. Martin Staniland, *What Is Political Economy?* (New Haven, CT: Yale University Press, 1985), p. 6.

4. Ibid., p. 12.

5. In its original meaning, liberalism (as articulated in the eighteenth century) called for limited government. Today, outside of the United States, the terms "neoliberal policies" or "liberalization" refer to policies that reduce the role of government in the economy (contrary to the way the term liberal is used in the United States).

6. Simon Kuznets, *Modern Economic Growth: Rate, Structure and Spread,* 7th ed. (New Haven, CT: Yale University Press, 1976); Hollis Chenery and Moises Syrquin, *Patterns of Development, 1950–1970* (London: Oxford University Press, 1975). Of course, these are general tendencies or trends, not inviolable rules. Thus, East and Southeast Asian countries such as Taiwan, South Korea, and Malaysia have entered or passed through the intermediate stage of development without an appreciable worsening of income distribution.

7. Adapted from Adam Przeworski, *Democracy and the Market* (New York: Cambridge University Press, 1991), p. 105, fn. 10. A number of the insights in this section come from Przeworski.

8. Ed A. Hewett, *Reforming the Soviet Economy: Equality versus Efficiency* (Washington, DC: Brookings Institution, 1988), p. 38.

9. Abraham Bergson, *The Real National Income of Soviet Russia since 1928* (Cambridge, MA: Harvard University Press, 1961), p. 261.

10. Harry Harding, *China's Second Revolution* (Washington, DC: Brookings Institution, 1987), pp. 30–31.

11. Stephen White, John Gardener, and George Schopflin, *Communist and Postcommunist Political Systems* (New York: St. Martin's Press, 1990), p. 322; Harding, *China's Second Revolution*, p. 30.

12. Claes Brundenius, *Revolutionary Cuba: The Challenge of Economic Growth with Equity* (Boulder, CO: Westview Press, 1984); Carmelo Mesa-Lago, *The Economy of Socialist Cuba: A Two-Decade Appraisal* (Albuquerque: University of New Mexico Press, 1981).

13. Erich Wede and Horst Tiefenbach, "Some Recent Explanations of Income Inequality," *International Studies Quarterly* 25 (June 1981): 255–282.

14. An obvious moral and political weakness, not discussed here, is that command economies require government repression. I am taking that very serious flaw as a given and am limiting my discussion in this chapter to the system's economic strengths and weaknesses.

15. Liang Heng and Judith Shapiro, *After the Nightmare* (New York: Collier, 1986).

16. John Sheahan, *Patterns of Development in Latin America* (Princeton, NJ: Princeton University Press, 1987).

17. Ibid., p. 85.

18. Dale Story, *Industry, the State and Public Policy in Mexico* (Austin: University of Texas Press, 1986), p. 68.

19. Both those industries were nationalized in the 1930s. Subsequently, the state also took over electricity and telecommunications.

20. Story, *Industry, the State and Public Policy in Mexico*, p. 21. My statistic is extrapolated from Story's data.

21. Samuel Schmidt, *The Deterioration of the Mexican Presidency: The Years of Luis Echeverría* (Tucson: University of Arizona Press, 1991), pp. 162–164; Elia Marún

Espinosa, "Intervencionismo estatal y transformaciones del sector empresa pública en México," in *El Nuevo Estado Mexicano: Estado y Economía*, ed. Jorge Alonso et al. (Mexico City: Nueva Imagen, 1992), pp. 193–240.

22. For startling data on overstaffing and "ghost workers" in Africa, see Richard Sandbrook, *The Politics of Africa's Economic Recovery* (New York: Cambridge University Press, 1993), pp. 43, 61.

23. *New York Times*, December 7, 1993.

24. *New York Times*, November 2, 1993.

25. Ibid.

26. During Mexico's 1994 presidential campaign, I interviewed a major spokesperson for the PRD, the country's principal left opposition party. Though he had once been a Marxist congressman, he readily conceded that President Salinas's economic liberalization program, involving massive layoffs of state workers, had been necessary. That interview took place a week after the peasant uprising in Chiapas that many analysts believed shifted the Mexican political spectrum to the left.

27. Howard Handelman and Werner Baer, eds., *Paying the Costs of Austerity in Latin America* (Boulder, CO: Westview Press, 1989); Stephan Haggard and Robert R. Kaufman, eds., *The Politics of Economic Adjustment* (Princeton, NJ: Princeton University Press, 1992).

28. Furthermore, even economic growth, though obviously beneficial, does not necessarily translate immediately into higher living standards for much of the population. For example, in 1991 and 1992 Venezuela's economy grew at a rate of some 9 percent, the fastest rise in Latin America. Yet living standards continued to decline for many workers whose wages failed to keep up with steep inflation. As a consequence, during a period of rapid growth Venezuela suffered substantial popular unrest and two failed military coups.

29. Extrapolated from Sinichi Ichimura and James W. Morley, "The Varieties of Asia-Pacific Experience," in *Driven by Growth*, ed. James W. Morley (Armonk, NY: M. E. Sharpe, 1992), p. 6; and Steven Chan, *East Asian Dynamism* (Boulder, CO: Westview Press, 1990), p. 8; UNDP, *Human Development Report, 1997* (New York: Oxford University Press, 1997), pp. 21–22.

30. The World Bank, *Engendering Development* (New York and London: Oxford University Press, 2001), p. 207.

31. Again, China does not fit that model. A large, though rapidly falling, share of its economy continues to be state owned, while another substantial portion is run by cooperatives. State regulation, though reduced, is still formidable. Thus, despite its many changes since the early 1980s, Communist China remains distinct from the other Asian economies described in this section and will be excluded from the discussion that follows.

32. Milton and Rose Friedman, *Freedom to Choose* (New York: Harcourt Brace Jovanovich, 1980), p. 57; David Felix, "Review of Economic Structure and Performance: Essays in Honor of Hollis B. Chenery," *Economic Development and Cultural Change* 36, no. 1 (1987): 188–194; Ian Little, "An Economic Reconnaissance," in *Economic Growth and Structural Change in Taiwan*, ed. Walter Galenson (Ithaca, NY: Cornell University Press).

33. Robert Wade, *Governing the Market: Economic Theory and the Role of Government in East Asian Industrialization* (Princeton, NJ: Princeton University Press, 1990); Gary Gereffi and Donald L. Wyman, eds., *Manufacturing Miracles* (Princeton, NJ: Princeton University Press, 1990); Stephan Haggard, *Pathways from the Periphery* (Ithaca, NY: Cornell University Press, 1990); Chalmers Johnson, "Political Institutions and Economic Performance: The Government-Business Relationship in Japan, South Korea and

Taiwan," in *The Political Economy of the New Asian Industrialism*, ed. Frederic C. Deyo (Ithaca, NY: Cornell University Press, 1987).

34. Chalmers Johnson, *MITI and the Japanese Miracle* (Stanford, CA: Stanford University Press, 1982).

35. Chan, *East Asian Dynamism*, pp. 47–48.

36. Johnson, "Political Institutions and Economic Performance."

37. Chan, *East Asian Dynamism*, p. 49.

38. Johnson, "Political Institutions," p. 159.

39. Haggard, *Pathways from the Periphery*.

40. Robert Wade, "Industrial Policy in Asia: Does It Lead or Follow the Market?" in *Manufacturing Miracles*, pp. 231–266; Wade, *Governing the Market*.

41. Johnson, "Political Institutions."

42. For a criticism of the developmental state concept and its alleged benefits, see Cheng-tian Kuo, *Global Competitiveness and Industrial Growth in Taiwan and the Philippines* (Pittsburgh, PA: University of Pittsburgh Press, 1995).

43. These conglomerates dominate the economy. By the mid-1980s, Korea's ten largest chaebols produced two-thirds of the nation's GNP. See Wade, *Governing the Market*, p. 309.

44. Herman Kahn, "The Confucian Ethic and Economic Growth," in *The Gap between Rich and Poor*, ed. Mitchell A. Seligson (Boulder, CO: Westview Press, 1984).

45. Christopher Ellison and Gary Gereffi, "Explaining Strategies and Patterns of Industrial Development," in *Manufacturing Miracles*, pp. 395–396.

46. Neoclassical economics (or the neoclassical approach) is a revised formulation of Adam Smith's classical economic approach.

47. Wade, *Governing the Market*, p. 11.

48. Alice H. Amsden, *Asia's Next Giant: South Korea and Late Industrialization* (New York: Oxford University Press, 1989); see also the works by Haggard, Wade, and Johnson cited earlier in this chapter.

49. Wade, *Governing the Market*.

50. Richard Albin, "Saving the Environment: The Shrinking Realm of Laissez-Faire," in *International Political Economy*, 2d ed., eds. Jeffrey A. Frieden and David A. Lake (New York: St. Martin's, 1991), p. 454.

51. Bela Balassa, *The Newly Industrializing Countries in the World Economy* (New York: Pergamon Press, 1981).

52. This section draws heavily on Sheahan, *Patterns of Development in Latin America*, pp. 82–98.

53. For example, if a nation's currency was worth 10 pesos to the dollar in the free market, governments might impose official rates of 5 pesos to the dollar for trade purposes. This would artificially double the value of the peso, thereby halving the number of dollars needed to import a forklift or machine lathe. At the same time, consumer goods produced domestically with the imported machinery would still be protected against import competition by tariffs and quotas.

54. Ibid., p. 84; Werner Baer, "Import Substitution and Industrialization in Latin America: Experiences and Interpretations," *Latin American Research Review* 7, no. 1 (1972): 95–122.

55. Helen Shapiro and Lance Taylor, "The State and Industrial Strategy," in *The Political Economy of Development and Underdevelopment*, 5th ed., ed. Charles K. Wilber and Kenneth P. Jameson (New York: McGraw-Hill, 1992).

56. Sheahan, *Patterns of Development*, pp. 86–87.

57. Wade, *Governing the Market*, pp. 34, 36.

58. Barbara Stallings and Robert Kaufman, eds., *Debt and Democracy in Latin America* (Boulder, CO: Westview Press, 1989); Handelman and Baer, *Paying the Costs of Austerity*; Haggard and Kaufman, *The Politics of Economic Adjustment*.

59. Haggard, *Pathways from the Periphery*.

60. Chile has had the most success of any Latin American country in pursuing an EOI strategy since the 1970s. Argentina's efforts, however, were sabotaged by the country pegging its peso to the dollar (one peso is always worth one dollar). Consequently, after a boom in the 1990s, Argentina's economy collapsed in the early years of the twenty-first century as its overvalued peso destroyed its export capability.

61. Gary Gereffi, "Paths of Industrialization: An Overview," in *Manufacturing Miracles*, p. 15. Brazil's proportion grew steadily from 8 percent in 1965 to 45 percent in 1987. Mexico's manufacturing ratio, on the other hand, was quite volatile, falling from 31 percent of exports in 1975 to 15 percent in 1980, only to jump back to 47 percent in 1987. In large part this reflected the shifting price and significance of petroleum exports.

62. Gary Gereffi and Donald Wyman, "Determinants of Development Strategies in Latin America and Asia," in *Pacific Dynamics*, eds. Stephan Haggard and Ching-in Moon (Boulder, CO: Westview Press, 1989), p. 37. Gereffi and Wyman, however, cite Bela Balassa's research warning against overstating the importance of size.

63. Robert Dore, "Reflections on Culture and Social Change," in *Manufacturing Miracles*, pp. 353–367.

64. Jeffrey A. Winters, "Asia and the 'Magic' of the Marketplace," *Current History* 97 (December 1998): 420. Winters offers a clear analysis of the nature and causes of the Asian crisis, and his ideas permeate this section.

65. In other words, if the baht had previously been worth $0.10 then a Thai business borrowing $1 million from a U.S. bank would convert that loan into 10 million bahts. But if the decision to float the value of the baht caused its value to fall to $0.05, then the loan of $1 million would cost 20 million bahts to pay back.

66. Ibid. The Serengeti is the African plain famous for its wild life.

67. In other words, a floating exchange rate presents the possibility that a foreign investor could invest, say, $1 million in the Thai economy (converting it into bahts at, say, 10 bahts per dollar) and then find out the following week that the baht had been devalued to 20 per dollar, thereby reducing the dollar value of the investment by 50 percent.

68. Winters, "Asia and the 'Magic' of the Marketplace," p. 419.

69. Charles Wolf, Jr., "Too Much Government Control," *Wall Street Journal*, February 4, 1998.

70. Meredith Woo-Cumings, "All in the Family: Reforming Corporate Governance in East Asia," *Current History* 97 (December 1998): 426–430.

71. Joseph Stiglitz, "Bad Private-Sector Decisions," *Wall Street Journal* (February 4, 1998).

72. Irma Adelman and Cynthia Taft Morris, *Economic Growth and Social Equity in Developing Countries* (Stanford, CA: Stanford University Press, 1973). A similar argument has been made in research by Keith Griffin.

73. Perhaps the most important seminal work in this area was Hollis Chenery et al., *Redistribution with Growth* (London: Oxford University Press, with World Bank and University of Sussex, 1974). There have been large numbers of World Bank studies supporting this strategy.

74. Richard E. Barrett and Soomi Chin, "Export-Oriented Industrializing States in the Capitalist World System: Similarities and Differences," in *The Political Economy of the New Asian Industrialism*, pp. 28–31; Ward, *Governing the Market*, p. 38.

75. Howard Handelman, ed., *The Politics of Rural Change in Asia and Latin America* (Bloomington: Indiana University Press, 1981).

76. Robert H. Bates, "Governments and Agricultural Markets in Africa," in *Toward a Political Economy of Development*, ed. Robert H. Bates (Berkeley: University of California Press, 1988); see also Michael J. Lofchie, *The Policy Factor: Agricultural Performance in Kenya and Tanzania* (Boulder, CO: Lynne Rienner Publishers, 1989), pp. 57–59; Charles Harvey, ed., *Agricultural Pricing Policy in Africa* (London: Macmillan, 1988), p. 2.

77. Sheahan, *Patterns of Development*; Haggard, *Pathways from the Periphery*, chap. 1.

78. I have previously discussed two other influences on distribution that need not be repeated here. First, as Simon Kuznets has demonstrated, countries in the intermediate stage of economic growth tend to have more unequal income distribution than either poor or developed nations. Second, all other factors being held equal, socialist or Marxist regimes have more equal distribution than capitalist ones.

79. UNDP, *Human Development Report, 1993* (New York: Oxford University Press, 1993), pp. 162–163.

80. Haggard, *Pathways from the Periphery*, pp. 239–240. Haggard notes, however, that some research has challenged the widely assumed correlation between education and income equality. See Frederick Harbison, "The Education-Income Connection," *Income Distribution and Growth in Less-Developed Countries*, eds. Charles R. Frank and Richard C. Webb (Washington, DC: Brookings Institution, 1977).

81. Gareth Porter and Janet Welsh Brown, *Global Environmental Politics* (Boulder, Co: Westview Press, 1996), p. 113.

82. Bhaskar Nath and Ilkden Talay, "Man, Science, Technology and Sustainable Development," in *Sustainable Development*, ed. Bhaskar Nath, Luc Hens, Dimitri Devuyst (Brussels, Belgium: VUB University Press, 1996), p. 37.

83. For a general discussion of international environmental debates, see Jacqueline Vaughn Switzer and Gary Bryner, *Environmental Politics: Domestic and Global Dimensions* (New York: St. Martin's Press, 1998), pp. 200–234.

84. Marian A. L. Miller, *The Third World in Global Environmental Politics* (Boulder, CO: Lynne Rienner Publishers, 1995), pp. 43–44.

85. A surprisingly high proportion of advanced, modern medications use ingredients drawn from tropical rain forests.

86. Nath and Talay, "Man, Science," p. 36.

87. For information on the debate over sustainable development, see Ken Conca, Michael Alberty, and Geoffrey D. Dabelko, eds., *Green Planet Blues: Environmental Politics from Stockholm to Rio* (Boulder, CO: Westview Press, 1995), pp. 205–238.

88. Colin Sage, "The Scope for North-South Cooperation," in *Environmental Policy in an International Context: Prospects*, ed. Andrew Blowers and Pieter Glasbergen (New York: John Wiley & Sons, 1996), pp. 188–189. For strong criticism of what the Rio Earth Summit failed to accomplish, see p. 190 of that chapter.

89. Andrew Blowers and Pieter Leroy, "Environment and Society: Shaping the Future," in *Environmental Policy*, p. 262.

90. Meeting of Oxfam Study-Tour participants with an economist at the University of the West Indies, Kingston, Jamaica.

91. Some environmental experts believe that it will be impossible to maintain sustainable development and that the world faces certain ecological disaster. See Joseph Wayne

Smith, Graham Lyons, and Gary Sauer-Thompson, *Healing a Wounded World* (Westport, CT: Praeger Publishers, 1997).

92. Robin Broad and John Cavanagh, "No More NICs," *Foreign Policy* 72 (Fall 1988): 81–103.

93. Communication with Stephan Haggard, April 6, 1994.

94. *New York Times*, March 27, 1994.

95. Bruce Bueno de Mesquita et al., "Political Competition and Economic Growth," *Journal of Democracy* 12, no. 1 (2001): 58–72. See also their forthcoming book, *Staying Alive: Political Institutions and Leadership Incentives* (working title). Note that they were analyzing the performances of individual governments, not of countries. Hence, over a period of nearly 50 years, during which most countries had multiple governments, there were many hundreds of cases from which they selected their sample of about 355.

Glossary

Agrarian reform Distribution of farm land to needy peasants along with the government support programs such as roads, technical assistance, and lines of credit needed to make beneficiaries economically viable.

Ancien régime The old political order. The term is often used to describe a decaying regime threatened or ousted by a revolutionary movement.

Apparatchik A career bureaucrat in the Soviet government. Often used more broadly to refer to a bureaucrat whose primary interest is in protecting his or her authority and perquisites.

Authoritarian system A political system that limits or prohibits opposition groups and otherwise restricts political activity and expression.

Autonomy A substantial amount of self-rule for an ethnic group or region that falls short of full independence.

Baht The Thai national currency.

Barrio A poor urban neighborhood in Latin America or the Philippines.

Bourgeoisie A Marxist term (also used by non-Marxist scholars) for those who own society's productive resources, most notably businesspeople.

Bureaucratic-authoritarian regimes Military dictatorships, found most often in Latin America's more developed countries, that were based on an alliance between the military, government bureaucrats, local business elites, and multinational corporations.

Capital goods (or equipment) Goods such as machinery that are used for production of other goods rather than for consumption.

Capital-intensive production Industrial or agricultural production that relies more heavily on machinery and technology than on human labor.

Caretaker government An interim government (sometimes military) that steps in to restore order but plans to retire relatively quickly.

Caste system A rigid social hierarchy in which individuals are born with a status that they retain regardless of their education or achievement.

Chaebols Powerful industrial conglomerates that dominate the South Korean economy.

Christian (or Ecclesial) Base Communities (CEBs) Small Catholic neighborhood groups in Latin America that discuss religious questions and community problems. Commonly located in poor neighborhoods, many CEBs were politicized or radicalized in the 1960s and 1970s.

Civic action programs Development programs such as road or school construction carried out by the military.

Civil society The network of politically relevant groups that are relatively independent of state control.

Class consciousness A measure of how much a social class (workers, peasants, or the middle class) view themselves as having common goals that are distinct from, and often opposed to, the needs of other classes.

Clientelism The dispensing of public resources by political power holders or seekers who offer them as favors in exchange for votes or other forms of public support.

Collective farming (collectivization) Joint farming activity by a peasant community, state farm, or cooperative of some sort. In communist countries, the government often collectivized farming against the wishes of the rural population.

Colonization Asserting control over a previously independent region. Also used to describe the settlement of tropical forests or other previously uninhabited areas by migrating farmers or large agricultural operations.

Coloreds: A South African term coined during the period of white rule to describe people of mixed racial background.

Command economy An economy in which most of the means of production are owned and managed by the state and in which prices and production decisions are determined by state planners.

Commercialization of agriculture The process whereby subsistence farmers (i.e., those raising crops largely for their own family consumption) convert, sometimes unwillingly, to farming for the commercial market.

Communal politics (communalism) Politics that have a strong ethnic base and often involve conflict between ethnicities.

Comparative advantage A country's capacity to engage in economic activity efficiently and cheaply relative to other nations.

Consociationalism A division of political power between formerly antagonistic groups (such as ethnicities) based on power sharing, limited autonomy, and mutual vetoes.

Consumer subsidies: Payments made by the state that allow consumers to purchase goods at prices below their free-market value.

Core nations The richer, industrial nations of the world.

Correlation A tendency of two or more factors (variables) to change in the same direction (e.g., higher income correlates with greater education). Negative correlations move in opposite directions (e.g., alcoholism and education).

Coup d'état (coup) A seizure of political power by the military.

Crony capitalism A corrupt form of capitalist development in which powerful, well-connected businessmen use their government ties to accumulate vast wealth.

Cultural pluralism A diversity of ethnic groups.

Culture of poverty A sense of powerlessness and fatalism allegedly commonly found among the urban poor.

Currency exchange rates The value of a nation's currency relative to major currencies such as the dollar or Euro.

Democratic consolidation The process through which democratic norms (democratic "rules of the game") become accepted by all powerful groups in society, including labor, business, rural landlords, the church, and the military.

Democratic transition the process of moving from an authoritarian regime to a democratic one.

Devaluation (of a nation's currency) Allowing a currency that was previously overvalued relative to the dollar and other "hard" (stable) currencies to decline in value. This is normally done to correct a negative trade balance in which the value of imports exceeds exports.

Developmental state A state that intervenes actively in the economy in order to guide or promote particular economic development goals such as full employment.

Dirty war The military's mass violation of human rights during their fight against subversive groups in countries such as Argentina and Peru.

Double day The burden facing working women, who continue to perform most of the family's domestic responsibilities (such as cooking and child care) while also working outside the home.

Economic disincentives Economic policies or practices that discourage desired outcomes, such as government-enforced low food prices that discourage agricultural production.

Economies of scale Economic efficiencies achieved through large-scale operations.

Ejido Communal farms in Mexico that were given special status under the country's agrarian reform programs.

Employer of last resort An employer (normally the state) that hires people who can find no other employment.

EOI See Export-oriented industrialization.

Ethnicity or ethnic group A group that feels it has common traditions, beliefs, values, and history that unite it and distinguish it from other cultures.

Export-oriented industrialization (EOI) An industrialization model heavily tied to exporting manufactured goods.

Federalism A government form that divides power between the national government and smaller governing units.

Fundamentalism A theological doctrine that seeks to preserve a religion's traditional worldview and to resist any efforts by religious liberals to reform it. It also frequently seeks to revive the role of religion in private and public life, including dress, lifestyle, and politics. Used interchangeably with "revivalism."

GDP See Gross Domestic Product.

Gender development index (GDI) An index measuring a country's key social indicators (literacy, income, life expectancy) for women as compared to men.

Gender Empowerment Measure (GEM) An index of women's political empowerment based on the proportion of women holding major business positions and national political offices.

Gender gap A systematic difference in social status or achievement between men and women (e.g., income).

GNP See Gross National Product.

Great Leap Forward China's effort (1958–1961) to accelerate economic development rapidly by extracting tremendous sacrifices from the population.

Green movement The political movement seeking to preserve the environment.

Green revolution Dramatic increases in grain production due to improved seeds and other technological breakthroughs in the Third World (most notably in Asia).

Greenhouse effect (greenhouse gases) Carbon gasses produced by burning fossil fuels that threaten to warm the world's climate dangerously by limiting the dispersion of heat from the atmosphere.

Gross Domestic Product (GDP) A measure of a nation's production that excludes certain financial transfers normally included in GNP.

Gross National Product (GNP) A measure of a nation's total production (see Gross Domestic Product).

Gross Real Domestic Product Gross Domestic Product as measured by purchasing power rather than currency exchange.

Gulags Internment camps for political prisoners. Originating in the Soviet Union, the term is also used to describe other repressive systems.

Hacienda A Latin American agricultural estate that, until recently, often included pre-capitalist labor relations.

HDI See Human development index.

Historical dialectic A Marxist term used to describe the ongoing tension between particular forces in history.

Human Development Index (HDI) A composite measure of educational level, life expectancy, per-capita GDP, and income distribution.

Import-substituting industrialization (ISI) A policy of industrial development based on manufacturing goods domestically that were previously imported.

Informal sector The part of the economy that is unregulated by the government while similar activities are regulated and taxed.

Infrastructure The underlying structures (including transportation, communication, agricultural irrigation) that are needed for effective production.

Internal warfare Military action aimed at controlling guerrilla unrest or other domestic civil insurrection.

Invisible hand The capitalist notion that the good of society is advanced most effectively when individual actors (businesspeople, workers) seek to maximize their own economic advantage.

Iron rice bowl The Chinese government's policy of guaranteeing employment and a basic living standard to its population.

ISI See Import-substituting industrialization.

Islamism Islamic fundamentalism or revivalism. A movement designed to bring the Islamic faith to its fundamental, strictly interpreted beliefs and traditions.

Jihad An Islamic holy war.

Khamer Rouge The communist revolutionary movement in Kampuchea (Cambodia).

Kulaks Wealthier peasants. Originally a term used in Russia but later applied more broadly.

Labor-intensive industry Industries that make more extensive use of human labor, as opposed to machinery and technology.

Laissez faire A policy of minimal state intervention in the economy.

Latifundia Large agricultural estates.

LDCs (Less developed countries) The term is used synonymously with Third World and developing countries.

Liberal democracy A democracy that respects civil liberties and upholds basic freedoms.

Liberalization of the economy Reducing the degree of state intervention in the economy (referring to the eighteenth-century classical liberalism of Adam Smith).

Liberated zones Areas (most notably in the countryside) controlled by the revolutionary army. Used in China and Vietnam.

Liberation theology A reformist interpretation of Catholic doctrine that stresses the emancipation of the poor.

Lost decade The decade of the 1980s during which Africa and Latin America suffered severe economic declines.

Machismo Male chauvinism (used particularly in Latin America).

Macro-economic policy Economic policies that affect society as a whole.

Maquiladoras Mexican assembly plants that import parts from the United States and re-export assembled goods.

Marginal population People excluded from the mainstream of the nation's political and economic life.

Market socialism A hybrid of Marxist economics and free enterprise that has been adopted by countries such as China.

Mass mobilization The process whereby large segments of the population are activated politically. Governments or revolutionary movements may choose to mobilize the population.

Mestizos Persons of mixed Indian and European cultural heritage (Latin America).

MNC See Multinational corporations.

Moral economy The web of economic and moral obligations that bind a social unit together. Often used in reference to peasant-landlord relations in the countryside.

Mujahadeen Islamic "freedom fighters" or guerrillas.

Mullah A Muslim cleric.

Multinational corporations Corporations with holdings and operations in a number of countries. Overwhelmingly based in the developed world, many of them exercise considerable economic power in the Third World.

Nationality A population with its own language, cultural traditions, and historical aspirations that frequently claims sovereignty over a particular territory.

Neoclassical economics Economic theory that supports a free market and very little state economic intervention.

Neocolonialism Economic and cultural dominance of one sovereign nation over another.

New social movements Grass-roots reformist movements that are free of traditional political party ties or class-based ideologies.

New world order A vision of a more peaceful world order under U.S. leadership that many had expected to follow the collapse of the Soviet bloc and the end of the Cold War.

NIC (Newly industrialized country) Countries in East Asia and Latin America (Taiwan, Mexico) that have developed a substantial industrial base in recent decades.

Nurturing professions Occupations such as teaching and nursing that are commonly filled by women and that involve roles commonly associated with motherhood.

Parastatals Semi-autonomous, state-run enterprises.

Patron-client relations Relations between more powerful figures (patrons) and less powerful ones (clients) involving a series of reciprocal obligations that benefit both sides but are more advantageous to the patron.

People's war The term used by Chinese leader Mao Zedong and others to describe mass-based guerrilla struggles.

Perestroika The restructuring of Soviet society (most notably its economy) by President Mikhail Gorbachev.

Periphery Third World countries, commonly seen by dependency theorists as occupying a lesser rank in the international economy.

Pirate settlement Low-income urban settlements whose members have purchased their lots but lack legal title.

Pluralist democracy: A form of government that allows a wide variety of groups and viewpoints to flourish and to engage in political activity independent of government control.

Political culture The set of political beliefs and values that underlie a society's political system.

Populism A multi-class, reformist political movement that promises increased welfare programs for the poor and middle class but rejects a basic restructuring of the economic order. Third World populist movements are often led by a charismatic (and sometimes demagogic) political leader.

Praetorian politics Politics lacking in legitimate authority, leaving competing groups in society to use whatever resources they have at their disposal (including violence, bribery).

Private sector The sector of the economy that is owned by individuals or private companies.

Privatization The process of transferring to the private sector portions of the economy formerly owned by the state.

Procedural democracy Standards of democracy based on political procedures (such as free elections) rather than outcomes (such as social justice).

Professionalized military A military whose officers receive a great degree of professional training.

Progressive church The reformist and radical wings of the Catholic church (primarily in Latin America).

Proletariat The working class (blue-collar workers).

Public sector The sector of the economy belonging to the state.

Real wages (income) The true purchasing power of one's wage or income when the effects of inflation are factored in.

Reconciliation approach A more contemporary perspective of modernization theory that holds that it is possible for LDCs to simultaneously attain some development goals that were previously considered contradictory, at least in the short run (such as early economic growth and equitable income distribution).

Relative deprivation The gap between an individual or group's expectations or desires and their actual achievement.

Responsibility system China's policy of transferring collective farm land to peasant owners.

Revivalism Attempts to revive traditional religious practices and, sometimes, to revive the role of religion in politics. See also Fundamentalism.

Rupiah: The Indonesian national currency.

Secularization The separation of church and state and, more generally, the removal of religion from politics.

Shantytown A community of poor homes or shacks built by the inhabitants. Unlike slums, they are generally in outlying urban areas rather than the central city.

Sites and services Housing arrangements in which the state sells or gives each inhabitant a legal title to a plot with basic services such as electricity and water, leaving the recipient to build his or her own home.

Smallholder Peasants owning small plots of land.

Social mobility The ability to move from one rank or social class in society to another.

Spontaneous shelter Urban housing built by the occupant.

Squatter settlement Communities built by the poor who illegally or semilegally occupy unused land.

Stabilization programs Government programs, often imposed by the International Monetary Fund (IMF), to cut budget and trade deficits. The purpose is to reduce inflation and stabilize the currency.

Sub-Saharan Africa Countries in Africa below the northern tier of Arab nations. Also called Black Africa.

Subsidized housing Housing provided by the state at prices below their market value.

Substantive democracy Standards of democracy that measure government policy outcomes, such as literacy and health levels or socioeconomic equality, not just democratic procedures (as distinguished from procedural democracy).

Sustainable development Economic development that "consumes resources to meet [this generation's] needs and aspirations in a way that does not compromise the ability of future generations to meet their needs."

Technocrat A government bureaucrat with a substantial degree of technical training.

Theocracy (theocratic state) A state run by religious clergy or their allies. Church and state are joined tightly.

Third wave The widespread transition from authoritarian to democratic government that has taken place in the Third World and Eastern Europe since the mid-1970s.

Third World countries Less developed countries in Africa, Asia, Latin America, and the Middle East.

Traditional society Societies that adhere to long-standing values and customs that have not been extensively transformed by modernization.

Tribe Subnational groups who share a collective identity and language and who believe themselves to hold a common lineage.

Wars of national liberation Wars of independence fought against colonial powers.

Index

religion and politics, 57
revolutionary movement, 150, 159, 220
Roman Catholicism, 50, 57
rural population, 147, 149, 150, 153, 159, 169
urban population, 190
women's status, 119, 133
Pinochet, August, 25, 31, 238, 248, 252, 267, 291
Pirate settlements, 184
Poland, 34, 42
Political culture, 38–39
Political economy, 259–292
democracy and, 292
East and Southeast Asia's economic crisis, 276–280
environmental problems and, 284–290
growth with equity, 280–284
industrialization strategies, 272–276
role of the state, 260–272
Political leaders, women as, 70, 131–134
Political stability
agrarian reform and, 154–155
democratic government and, 11
military regimes and, 246–247
Political underdevelopment, 10–13
Politics
of agrarian reform (*see* Agrarian reform)
economy and (*see* Political economy)
peasant, 149–152
religion and (*see* Religion, and politics)
of urban poor, 185–193
women and, 70, 116–119, 126–136
Polonordeste (Brazil), 166
Pope, 56
Port-au-Prince, Haiti, 178
Portugal, 25
Poverty, 3–6, 8, 10, 19, 124, 146, 259, 260. *See also* Rural change; Urbanization
Powell, G. Bingham, 15
Power-sharing arrangements, 100–102
Premadasa, Ranasinghe, 85
Premdas, Ralph, 103
Price controls, 167–168
PRI (Mexico), 33
Procedural democracy, 27, 28
Proletarianization, 168
Prostitution, 124
Protestantism, 41, 50, 71, 72
Przeworski, Adam, 42–43, 262
Public housing, 182–183
Puerto Rico, 187
Punto Fijo, Pact of (Venezuela), 234
Putin, Vladimir, 29
Pye, Lucian W., 14, 234

Q

Qadhafi, Muammar, 236, 238, 244
Quebec, 96, 101
Quran, 55

R

Race, 88–94
Radical fundamentalism, 60–66
Ramos, Fidel, 26, 229
Rawlings, Jerry, 237
Ray, Talton, 193
Reagan administration, 35
Reconciliation approach, 16–17
Redfield, Robert, 149
Refah (Welfare) Party (Turkey), 55
Regime decay, 204–206
Reinhardt, Nora, 167
Relative ethnic harmony, 95–96
Religion
conflict between religious groups, 91–94
and politics, 48–72
cultural values and church-state relationship, 71–72
democratic transition, 40–42
Hindu fundamentalism, 53, 61, 64–66
Hinduism, 50, 52–53, 57–58
Islam, 41, 50–52, 54–56, 58, 59, 70–72
Islamic fundamentalism, 17, 31, 49, 58–64, 70
meeting of church and state, 49–50
modernization, 51–54
religious fundamentalism, 58–66
resurgence of fundamentalism, 69–70
Roman Catholicism, 41, 42, 48–52, 54, 56–57, 66–72
separation of church-state issue, 71
structural and theological bases of church-state relations, 54–58
third world religions, 50–51
women's status and, 137
Religion and Democracy (Marquand and Nettler), 71
Remmer, Karen, 246, 249
Renewable resources, 287
Revivalism, religious. *See* Fundamentalism
Revolution, 12, 30, 199–222
causes of, 202–210
defined, 200–202
democratic government and, 220–222
goals of regimes, 242–243
leadership, 215–217
levels of popular support, 210–213
peasants and, 150–152, 159–161, 165, 206, 213–215, 217
revolutionary regime policies, 217–220
urban poor and, 186, 192–193
women and, 134–136
Revolutionary Armed Forces (FARC) (Colombia), 215
Reza Khan, Shah, 61–62
Reza Pahlavi, Shah Mohammad, 61–63, 106, 209, 210
Rhee, Syngman, 240
Rio Declaration, 288